Nuremberg

The Blackest Night In RAF History, 30/31 March 1944

Martin W. Bowman

Pen & Sword
AVIATION

First Published in Great Britain in 2016 by
Pen & Sword Aviation
an imprint of
Pen & Sword Books Ltd
47 Church Street, Barnsley, South Yorkshire S70 2AS

The right of Martin W Bowman to be identified as author of this work
has been asserted by him in accordance with the
Copyright, Designs and Patents Act 1988.

A CIP catalogue record for this book is
available from the British Library.

Typeset in 10/12pt Palatino
by GMS Enterprises PE3 8QQ

Printed and bound in England by
CPI Group (UK) Ltd, Croydon, CR0 4YY

Pen & Sword Books Ltd incorporates the Imprints of Pen & Sword
Aviation, Pen & Sword Family History, Pen & Sword Maritime, Pen & Sword
Military, Pen & Sword Discovery, Wharncliffe Local History, Wharncliffe
True Crime, Wharncliffe Transport, Pen & Sword Select, Pen & Sword
Military Classics, Leo Cooper, The Praetorian Press, Remember When,
Seaforth Publishing and Frontline Publishing.

For a complete list of Pen & Sword titles please contact
PEN & SWORD BOOKS LIMITED

47 Church Street, Barnsley, South Yorkshire, S70 2AS, England
E-mail: enquiries@pen-and-sword.co.uk
Website: www.pen-and-sword.co.uk

Contents

'To the Lancaster crews of 166 Squadron at Kirmington a broadcast of 'Grand National' echoing in mess halls, hangars, crew-rooms and even in latrines, was a warning that the station had been alerted by 1 Group for a 'maximum effort' operation that night. For Flight Sergeant Whitlock RAAF, a Londoner born in Constantinople [now Istanbul], the code words booming out that morning on the Tannoy public address system were to trigger a sequence of events and procedures which, though initially familiar, were to culminate in a night that Sidney Nicholas Whitlock would never forget.

The Nuremberg Massacre by Flight Sergeant Geoff Taylor RAAF a Lancaster pilot on 207 Squadron which was shot down on 18 October 1943 on Hanover. All seven crew survived their crash landing and became PoWs. Taylor ended up at Stalag 4B which he wrote about in _Piece of Cake_.

Chapter 1

Flashes of yellow flame pierced the darkness as Merlin XX engines were run up and eased back. Flight Lieutenant Brian B. Mill taxied Halifax LL287 'S-Sugar' on to the runway at Tempsford just to the north of Sandy in Bedfordshire and cleared his engines. The noise from its four airscrews, running at full throttle shattered the stillness of the night. A green Aldis lamp flickered to the left of the runway from the control wagon parked on the grass triangle. Flight Lieutenant Dennis R. Beale sitting in his second pilot's collapsible seat tightened his safety belt and slammed shut the side window. It was quieter in the cockpit now. The roar from the clandestine bomber's engines increased to a thunderous snarl, slowly, picking up speed with each second as the 138 'Special Duties' Squadron Halifax rolled smoothly down the runway, lifted and climbed steadily into the night, the navigational lights twinkling. The blue lights marking the edge of the runway whipped towards them at a fantastic speed as Mill hauled back on the control column and the Halifax yawed over the boundary markers. In the rear turret Flight Sergeant G. W. Kimpton saw the lights pass under him and he knew that they had left the runway. A chimney of a farmhouse flashed beneath his feet. Seconds later Kimpton looked down at the Great North Road, deserted now.

In the fuselage of the Halifax the rest of the crew and two Belgian Lieutenants, 27-year old Albert Giroulle ('Troilus') and 23-year old Robert Deprez ('Lucullus') were braced against the main wing spar. They had spent the day nervously waiting to board the Halifax at Gibraltar Farm to be parachuted into occupied Europe to assist the secret armies engaged in covert warfare against the Nazis. The Special Duty Squadrons had amassed a wealth of experience on varied 'cloak-and-dagger' missions in the Low Countries and France and as far afield as Austria, Norway, Poland and Czechoslovakia. 'Osric 27' had been laid on by the Special Operations Executive using the maximum effort raid on Nuremberg on Thursday 30 March 1944 as cover. SOE used several lovely country mansions deep in woods and thickets in remote parts of Britain as club houses and dormitories for secret agents.[1] Apart from carrying out acts of sabotage, the resistance movement in Belgium had a very efficient escape line for downed Allied airmen. Capture however, spelled almost certain death and there were many traitors - male and female who were prepared to betray these brave operatives and their contacts. The Belgians saw nothing and knew nothing until the rear gunner's voice came over the intercom.

Warrant Officer2 Frederick Anderson RCAF the 21-year old Canadian bomb aimer from Winnipeg pulled off his leather gauntlets and dragged a pair of newly washed white silk gloves from his pocket and thrust his hands into them. He screwed and twisted the silk until his fingers fitted smoothly into the sockets. The heavy flying gloves were too bulky for him to feel sensitively in the blacked-out nose for the delicate switches on the bomb panel. Flying Officer Eric Francis DFC the navigator who was from Hessle in Yorkshire laid down his dividers, swallowed his two Wakey-Wakey pills and debated whether he should slip into the nose when they sighted the drop zone just to the south of Antwerp. Like *Troilus and Cressida,* a tragedy by William Shakespeare, 'Osric 27' too would end in disaster. Five of the crew were the first of fifteen men shot down that night.

Shortly after midday amid intense activity at Bomber Command's underground headquarters housed in a country mansion, screened by dense wood, on the outskirts of High Wycombe in Buckinghamshire the master teleprinter had begun clacking out the first alert signal to the six Bomber Groups and Group commanders who were given the code name of the target, which in turn was sent to stations and squadron commanders. The code names were chosen from the 'Fish Code' devised by the 47-year old deputy Commander-in-Chief Sir Robert Henry Magnus Spencer Saundby, a keen fly fisherman who had gained five victories in the Royal Flying Corps during World War I. Berlin for instance was 'Whitebait'. 'Grayling' was Nuremberg. Security was immediately put into force. All out-going telephone calls were blocked and those incoming were intercepted, cutting stations off from the outside world as preparations for the raid began. Only those with the special but little known buff coloured passes were allowed in and then they were thoroughly checked before being escorted down a long dimly-lit passage, down dark stone steps, which led deeper and deeper into the earth. A massive steel door flanked by two tough-looking armed sentries of the RAF's Special Police blocked the entrance to the Command's Operations and Planning Room. As the bulky figure of a stern faced man in the uniform of an Air Chief Marshal strode briskly towards the door the two sentries snapped rigidly to attention, their steel heeled boots ringing on the cold stone.[2]

Sir Arthur Travers Harris, a compact, silent, bull-terrier of a man with one outstanding characteristic, a bitter hatred of the Hun and all that he stood for, was 51 years old, born in Cheltenham, Gloucestershire on 13 April 1892, the son of a member of the Public Works Department of the Indian Civil Service. At the outbreak of war in 1914 he had joined the Rhodesia Regiment as a boy bugler. After taking part in the German South-West African campaign in 1915 he left for England and enlisted in the RFC and was posted to France. He ended the war as a major with an AFC. In the next twenty years Harris commanded bomber squadrons and from 1933 to 1937 he served in staff positions at the Air Ministry. He took command of 4 Group in 1937 and was Head of the RAF Purchasing Mission in America in 1938 before taking command of 5 Group in 1939, a position he held until 1940 before acting as Deputy Chief of Air Staff at the Air Ministry. On 22 February 1942, having been recalled from the USA where he was head of the RAF Delegation, Air Chief Marshal Arthur Harris CB OBE arrived at High Wycombe to take over as commander-in-Chief of RAF Bomber Command.

Throughout the Battle of Berlin 'Bomber' Harris believed in 'a state of devastation in which surrender is inevitable'. Perhaps a raid on the birthplace of Nazism would go some way to proving it even though, since the end of November 1943 Harris had despatched thirty-four major assaults on Germany's sixteen of them against the 'Big City' and still no German surrender was in sight. Thirty-five major attacks were made on the 'Big City' and other German towns between mid-1943 and 24/25 March 1944; 20,224 sorties, 9,111 of which were to Berlin. From these sorties, 1,047 aircraft failed to return and 1,682 received varying degrees of damage. At the start of battle Harris had predicted that Berlin would 'cost between 400-500 aircraft' but that it would 'cost Germany the war.' He was proved wrong on both counts. The Battle of Berlin had proved not so much a gallant failure, but rather, a defeat. But very shortly Bomber Command would be called upon to support the invasion of Europe and Sir Arthur Harris was anxious to strike at one last major target before this happened.

Nuremberg was a target he knew was very dear to Winston Churchill the British Prime Minister's heart.

To Winston Churchill the Bavarian city was the living symbol of Nazism, more closely associated with Adolf Hitler's notorious regime than any other city in the Reich. A Bomber Command document agreed, describing it as 'one of the Holy Cities of the Nazi creed and a political target of the first importance'. The Führer called Nuremberg the 'most German of German cities'. Because of its relevance to the Holy Roman Empire and its position in the centre of Germany - on the Pegnitz river and the Rhine-Main-Danube Canal, about 110 miles north of Munich - the Nazi Party chose Nuremberg to be the site of huge rallies in 1927 and 1929 and annually after Hitler's rise to power in 1933. These Nazi propaganda events became a centre of Nazi ideals. The 1934 rally was filmed by Leni Riefenstahl and made into a propaganda film called *Triumph des Willens (Triumph of the Will).* At the 1935 rally Hitler specifically ordered the Reichstag to convene at Nuremberg to pass the infamous Nuremberg Laws, the series of anti-Semitic edicts which revoked German citizenship for all Jews and other non-Aryans. A number of premises were constructed solely for these assemblies, some of which were not finished. The city was also the home of the Nazi propagandist Julius Streicher, the publisher of *Der Stürmer.*

But Nuremberg was more than just an important political target. By March 1944, with an estimated population of 426,000 of whom 220,000 were potential war workers, it was high on the list of the British Cabinet's Combined Strategic Targets Committee and several raids had been planned and then postponed. Nuremberg with Fürth was an important centre of general and electrical engineering with fifty factories and 46 other commercial plants. The famous Maschinenfabrik Augsburg-Nürnberg Aktiengesellschaft heavy engineering works produced land armaments of all kinds, from heavy tanks and armoured cars to diesel engines for tanks and U-boats. This factory became doubly important since many of the Berlin tank works had been destroyed in earlier raids and the huge diesel engine manufacturing workshop at the M.A.N. factory at Augsburg had also been all but destroyed. The G. Müller works manufactured special ball-bearings for magnetos and the Siemens Schuckertwerke made electric motors, searchlights and firing devices for mines. The Siemens factory in Berlin had been damaged during recent air attacks and the Nuremberg plant had therefore assumed a vital role in the German war effort, turning out electrical equipment for the Kriegsmarine. The Zundapp motor works built vehicles for the Wehrmacht. Nuremberg was the headquarters of Wehrkreis (military district) XIII and a sub-camp of Flossenbürg concentration camp was located here so that extensive use could be made of slave labour in the factories in and around Nuremberg.

Early in the day Station Commanding Officers waited in the Operations Rooms for a teleprinter message from Group headquarters containing orders for the next bombing operation to be carried out by the squadrons on his bomber station. With him would probably had been the Wing Commander and Intelligence Officer. Aircrew checked the notice boards in their Mess or Squadron office to see if their name was on the Battle Order for that night. Orderlies would also awaken aircrew asleep in their billets if they have been called upon to do consecutive night operations. Weather forecasts had to be prepared by the Meteorological Officer and the Signals and Medical Officers were also notified about the impending operation.

Upon receipt of the Operation Orders the airfield became a hive of activity as the ground staff trades set about their tasks to bring the Squadron aircraft to a state of readiness for the night's operation. Scores of airmen and WAAFs took a hand in getting every aircraft on the Squadron ready for the appointed take-off time. Operational aircraft stood up to severe punishment during the course of a bombing operation. Not only from normal wear and tear, but all too often aircraft returned with flak or night fighter cannon shell damage. Consequently its serviceability depended upon the work carried out by the Squadron ground staff. Each bomber aircraft had its own ground crew made up of men who were skilled in a particular job and headed by a corporal. He usually possessed the trade qualifications of Fitter One; the highest grade of any trade in the Royal Air Force. Under his supervision were a crew of eight aircraft hands (ACII) consisting of two flight mechanics (engines) and two flight mechanics (airframe) plus a wireless mechanic, electrician, instrument repairer and fitter armourer.

During the day the Intelligence Officer gathered together all the information on file about the target for that night. Target information had been painstakingly collected over a long period in readiness for such an operation. At the briefing he would highlight enemy ground and night fighter defences and distinctive landmarks which would help pilots and navigators check their position en-route and over the target. To supplement all this information the Intelligence Officer contacted the Group Intelligence Officer to see if he had any fresh information about the target and enemy defences. The Met Officer awaited a report from the latest Met Flight over enemy territory before putting together his weather forecast covering take-off, en-route, target area and return to base.

The bulk of the work in preparing the aircraft was carried out by the ground staff, but the aircrew nevertheless kept a sharp eye on the various tasks to see that nothing was left undone. If necessary an air test was carried out by the aircrew in order to check out the engines and various electrical and mechanical systems. The air gunners would also test their guns by firing hundreds of rounds at flame floats dropped into the sea. These flights were also part of the endless training an operational crew undertook to improve their chances of survival. Because of operational losses and tour expired crews, the Squadrons were made up of aircrews with varying degrees of operational experience. The successful aircrews, the 'Gen Men' of the Squadron, were the ones who had flown together many thousands of miles and had achieved a high level of understanding and trust in each other's ability. This team spirit plus a lot of luck was essential if they were to survive a thirty operation tour.

Nuremberg was to be a 'Maximum effort' - ten squadrons in 1 Group, eight squadrons from 3 Group, seven squadrons from 4 Group, twelve from 5 Group, nine from 6 Group RCAF and twelve squadrons from 8 Group (Path Finder Force). Security was immediately put into force. All outgoing phone calls were blocked and those incoming were intercepted, cutting stations off from the outside world as preparations for the raid began. This time it was definitely 'on' - unless there was a significant change in the weather forecasts. The weather did seem to be worsening, with a threat of snow and sleet that strengthened the feeling that the raid would eventually be scrubbed. Some thought that it might even be cancelled before the navigation briefing, which always preceded the main crew briefing but there was no such doubt in 'Bomber' Harris' mind. At the pre-planning conference at High Wycombe the Commander-in-Chief announced that 795 RAF heavy bomber and 38 Mosquito crews were to be employed on the raid. On a huge wall map a line of red tape wheeling around marking pins traced the route that the bombers were to follow to and from their target. From a dead-reckoning position off the Naze where the force was to rendezvous, the tape streaked in a south-easterly direction to cross the Belgian coast near Bruges. With no change of course, it then went on to just short of Charleroi in Belgium; dangerously close to three known radio beacons - Funk Feuers' - 'Ida' just south of Aachen and 'Otto' and 'Heinz' close to the Ruhr, which were used as gathering and waiting points for the night-fighters; and from there it stretched in a straight line that represented nearly 265 miles to the final turning point at Fulda, north-east of Frankfurt. At Fulda the force would swing on to a south-easterly heading for the bomb-run on Nuremberg. But for two slight changes the return route the bombers were to follow after the raid was just about as direct as the outward course.

This planned route flew in the face of everything that had gone before. In the month leading up to Nuremberg, Harris had decided that because of mounting casualties he must, whenever possible, avoid sending single streams of bombers on deep-penetration raids since such streams could be easily plotted by the Germans and intercepted before reaching their target. The alternative was to divide the striking force and send the two parts to different targets or send both to the same target but by different routes, thus confusing the enemy's air defences and making it more difficult for the German controllers to plot the raid. Yet the plan was to send a large force on a long flight in what was virtually a straight line that was ideally suited to 'Tame Boar' interception.

Low lying Fenland and dykes were no barrier to chill winds and rain that came sweeping in from the North Sea to make life on the far flung airfields in Lincolnshire quite unbearable for the men of all nations who had come to fight in Bomber Command. Primitive wartime facilities cloaked in wintertime fog threatened to dampen the resolve of resolute Aussies and Kiwis who had left their antipodean sunshine and equally, those from Canada's prairies and occupied Poland and the cities, towns and villages all over Britain. At the beginning of 1944 the ramshackle base at Skellingthorpe two miles to the south-west of Lincoln in 5 Group was shared between 50 Squadron and 61 Squadron. But as both were building up their operational strength, it was not long before an acute accommodation problem arose and the 'Lincoln Imps' had forsaken 'Skelly' to move to Coningsby on a three month detachment. It meant sharing the base with 619 Squadron though Coningsby at least offered more in the way of home comforts. But for young 'green' aircrew arrivals like Norfolk-born Sergeant 'Pat' Patfield and others, most of whom were in their late 'teens or early twenties, it was still a shock to the system after their training in Canada.

The young bomb aimer had learned Bombing and Gunnery instruction at Lethbridge, Alberta'. And he had attended Air Observation classes at Malton, Ontario, before returning to England with ice skates bought in Moncton, a petrol cigarette lighter given as a Christmas present by a family in New Brunswick and many photos including the snows near Niagara Falls. Further training had continued at places from Newquay in Cornwall to near the Welsh border at Hereford and quite a number of airfields around the Midlands and Lincolnshire before the seven crew members concluded their training at the Lancaster Finishing School at Syerston near Nottingham. Like debutantes they 'came out' to join the ranks of the Lincoln Imps.

With the exception of Tommy Thomas, the navigator from 'somewhere in London', who had crewed up with them only a week or so before, they had trained together for a number of months previously. Two of the crew really were returning home after their travails. Pilot Officer Desmond 'Denny' Freeman their 21-year old RAFVR pilot was from Gainsborough. On 29 December 1940 Denny Freeman's father, Luther Henry Freeman, had died on service with the 11th Lindsey (Gainsborough) Battalion, Home Guard aged 42. Sergeant Leslie 'Jimmy' Chapman, the wireless operator hailed from Melton Washway near Spalding. Eva and Ernest Chapman's only son had gone to the Saracen's Head School in Whaplode before going to work on the land and there he could have stayed because his work in food production was so important that he was not conscripted. But the 20-year-old had insisted on joining up. Frank Devonshire the flight engineer was a Brummie from Birmingham. Bill Smith the rear gunner was from somewhere near St. Helens, Lancashire. On ops Bill would talk about women until they got to the enemy coast and then even he shut up. 'Old Bill' was a real 'rough diamond'. His only interest in life was meeting girls and going out with them. He always said he had a hell of a job to convince girls he was christened Bill Smith! After the war he said he was going to be a gigolo and get paid to keep women happy! As 'Pat' Patfield said, 'He was just the bloke for a rear gunner'. Arthur 'Dep' Sherriff was the mid-upper gunner and oldest member of the crew at thirty-four years of age.

The crew had flown their first op to Frankfurt on 18/19 March and the second had followed on 26/27, to Essen. 'The experience of being told that 'There's a war on tonight' and 'you're on the list', recalled Sergeant 'Pat' Patfield 'was received with a certain amount of foreboding, in spite of the fact that during training we had been anxious to get on with the real thing. Word would go round operations were on. The standard phrasing was, 'There's a war on tonight.' You went into the Ops Room and there'd be a list of the crews on the big Ops board, but it wouldn't say the target. That was usually about lunchtime. Just after lunch you went out to the aircraft and checked all the equipment - which you did everyday even if you weren't on ops. The ground crews would be working on them anyway and we'd just take it up for a short air test.'

Though short in stature Derek Patfield had a lot of nerve and courage. During his boyhood he had dived from the rigging of a moored sailing vessel into a river, which was quite a feat for a boy of his age. He always had an eye for a pretty girl. Though Lincoln had a castle and a cathedral, he and his friends were not interested in them. They were only interested in meeting the girls at the *'Saracen's Head'*. Since enlisting in the RAF in 1942 Derek's mischievous sense of fun, which he had demonstrated during civilian air raid duty, had not deserted him either. The Norfolk 'dumpling' was now the perfect little Lincolnshire 'imp'.

'Usually two crews shared a Nissen hut. We've been there and seen the adjutant come along and collect all the stuff out of their lockers and you knew that crew hadn't made it. Within a day or so, a new crew came in and they'd ask, 'What's it like?' 'We'd say, 'Oh, bloody awful. It's terrible.' You put the fear of god into them. We were a rotten lot in that respect. It was just devil may care. On low flying exercises if we saw people on farms working on a haystack we made a point of just shooting over the top and pulling the nose up quickly so that the slipstream from the four fans blew the straw all over the poor buggers! The times we were reported for this! The CO just told us not to blow anymore haystacks down. May as well talk to a brick wall.

'When operations were on, pilots, navigators and bomb aimers reported to the various sections for the individual briefings. We'd be told the bomb load, but not what the target was. We always had a flying meal of eggs and bacon. The flight engineer told you the fuel load and by that you'd pretty well know if it was going to be a long trip. If you had a heavy bomb load and medium fuel load, chances were it was going to be a short trip. Then we went in for the main briefing all together. We'd be briefed on the different coloured Target Indicators and bombs and which ones to bomb. The actual bomb load was explained, what we were carrying and the terminal velocity of the bombs (the speed of the bombs going down). Terminal velocity, height of the target from sea level, forecast wind speed and direction and the speed of the aircraft all had to be set on the bombsight. Then we would be told the target and issued with our target maps before going over any salient points, landmarks en route and what to look for on the target. Then it was a question of going back to the crew room to check personal equipment. If you were lucky you got an Irvin jacket but it was mainly a canvas-type flying-suit with two or three jumpers underneath. Our girlfriends gave us all a lucky charm. I had a tin badge and a stocking, which I would wrap around the bombsight. I didn't go bananas if I hadn't got it with me. We wore a Mae West and a parachute harness but the parachute was stowed in a little cubbyhole in the side of the fuselage. In an emergency you had to clamber out of position and hook the parachute on to the harness before you dived out. The advantage of my position was that I actually knelt on the escape hatch so I could pull the rubber pads back and get out - hopefully. You'd be lucky if you had time to do that.

'When you drew your parachute from the parachute section you also drew your escape kit with little silk maps of the area you were operating, Wakey-Wakey tablets, fishing line, unnamed packets of cigarettes and currency. If you came down over Europe and fell into the hands of the escape committees they could forge all the documents for you, but they couldn't get photographs. We had photographs taken on the squadron and sewn into our flying suit, so we already had the pictures for them. Flying rations consisted of a packet of boiled sweets and a flask of coffee or tea. My biggest faux pas was when I was throwing 'Window' out of the chute. I'd go to get my sweets and find that I'd thrown them down the hatch as well! Some rotten Jerry had my sweets.

'We'd all come together and wait for the crew buses to take us out to the aircraft about an hour before take-off. Most crews peed on the tail wheel for good luck. Damn silly things we did! Then we piled into the aircraft and made ourselves comfortable. On some of the daylights in the summertime it was terribly hot in the aircraft, which had been sitting out in the sun. We had no fans and all this flying gear on, which we needed because we'd freeze up higher. We sat there swearing our eyeballs out, waiting to take off. Then the Green flare would go up and No.1 aircraft would taxi out and the others all followed. It was an Air Ministry directive that bomb aimers should not be in the nose on take-off or landing but I'm afraid I disobeyed this order. I could hardly move for bundles of 'Window' stacked in the nose. By the time you got all your maps sorted out you didn't want to move just for a few minutes and then fight your way back down again. You knew damn well that if you didn't take off and it crashed you were going to be killed anyway. Whether you were a few yards back didn't make any difference. The take off was the worst part. On board were 2,000 gallons of high-octane petrol, eight tons of high explosive bombs, one and a half million candlepower magnesium flares and high-pressure oxygen bottles. If the aircraft didn't get off the ground there'd be quite a big bang, so you always breathed a sigh of relief once you got in the air!

'We didn't take the Wakey-Wakey pills until we were on the way. It was the sensible thing to do. Some blokes took them as soon as they got in the aircraft at the dispersal but you might be on the dispersal for half an hour or more before you took off. Sometimes, especially if the weather clamped in, the op was scrubbed. Some crews had already taken the Wakey-Wakey pills, so they couldn't sleep when we went back to the billet. The pills would give you a bit of a headache but we put that down to tiredness and stress.

'When we left the English coast, it was the bomb aimer's job to select and fuse all the bombs on the panel. It usually brought a corny remark from someone, as I passed my message, 'All bombs fused and selected' to the navigator to enter in his log.

'What do you mean, 'foosed'?'

Apparently my Norfolk dialect didn't lend itself kindly to the word 'fused' and it sounded like 'foosed'. I was usually referred to as a 'Swede' or a 'Dumplin'.

'Getting back to base it was often misty. The 'dromes were so close together there was the risk of collision, in the circuit, with other aircraft. We were all circling and fatigued and it might be ten minutes before we landed. If you were firing off reds because you'd got injured on board, or damage to the aircraft, you got priority. As soon as we landed we had to open the bomb doors. At dispersal the bomb aimer would look in the bomb bay to make sure you'd got the fuse links hanging down from each lug. That meant the bombs had gone down live. If you didn't fuse the bomb, or the solenoid froze up, the arming links wouldn't be caught by the solenoid and held in the aircraft pulling away from the fuse of the bomb. If the arming links weren't in the bomb bay they'd gone down attached to the fuse and that bomb went down safe. The arming links prevented the detonator going down to detonate the bomb. The chances were, even though you were dropping from thousands of feet, that the bomb wouldn't explode but just make a dirty great hole in the ground.

'The squadron buses would come out to pick us up. First we'd hand in our parachutes and parachute harness, our escape kit and any special maps we had. Then we went to de-briefing and had a cup of tea and a cigarette. 'What was it like? What was the opposition like? What was the condition of the target?' The morning after the operation the bombing photographs were on the board in the Ops Room. Everybody ploughed in to see how they'd got on.

'You hoped you'd finish the tour, but basically all the time nobody really thought that they would. You'd wake some mornings and see empty beds of crews that had gone and then you saw them scrubbed off the operations board. It was peculiar really. You just accepted the fact you'd be bloody lucky if you got through and the chances were you wouldn't. It was a peculiar world. At night all the might of the Luftwaffe and Wehrmacht was against you, trying to kill you. Then, a few hours later - perhaps that evening if you weren't on ops - you'd be in Lincoln going out with the girls, or in the pub among normal people. You jumped from war to peace, peace to war, within a few hours and so it went on week after week.'

At Coningsby the crew on Lancaster LL777 *Royal Pontoon* would be flying as one of the 'wind-finders' as usual. This aircraft's nose art showed a hand containing three cards with the number 7 and was skippered by Flying Officer Bernard Charles Fitch. On one occasion when an engine caught fire he had dumped his crew out of the aircraft in their parachutes all over Lincolnshire and he struggled on with it alone, but eventually landed it safely, minus crew. He was commended by the ground staff but sworn at by the crew who ended up all over the place, in fields, trees and in brambles etc! Born 13 May 1920 and educated at Stationers School, Hornsey, London Fitch was a keen sportsman, receiving his colours at cricket and football. He had met Sheila his future wife, a WAAF, at a tennis club in Felixstowe and they had married at the St. Andrew's Church in Bedford on 20 November 1943 the day after he had returned from a perilous operation over Germany. The crew had already taken part in the Leipzig raid, 19 February with a loss of 79 and Sergeant Leslie Cromarty DFM the rear gunner recalls: 'We were on the Berlin raid on 24 March when Bomber Command lost over seventy aircraft and so we only had fourteen crews left. We had an outstanding navigator, Sid Jennings and also the best aircraft in the squadron. *Royal Pontoon* was a Canadian built Lanc with Rolls-Royce Packard engines with paddle-bladed props. It could climb much higher than most other Lancasters could. We never did find out just how high it could go because at 30,000 feet the contrails would begin and we would drop below that height for obvious reasons. We were the most experienced crew. Next came Squadron Leader Moss.'

The 'Gen Men' or 'Old Sweats' on Lancaster 'P-Peter' flown by 32-year old Squadron Leader Edward Henry Moss DFC were on their twentieth operation. Moss, a tall, fresh-faced man who was from Sevenoaks in Kent, had been a house master at Radley College, Oxford. He had survived Dunkirk with the Territorial Army before transferring to the RAF for a quiet life! Popular with his crews, he was well liked and respected by all who knew him. His own crew consisted of Flying Officer Arthur David Bull the navigator, who was from Reigate, Surrey; Flight Sergeant Thomas Duff the wireless operator came from Salford, Lancashire; Flying Officer Harry Drinen Glover the bomb aimer was from West Brompton, London; Sergeant Lindsay Snowdon Suddick the flight engineer came from Hylton, County Durham; Flight Sergeant William Enos Blake the mid-upper gunner was from Hounsdown, Southampton and Sergeant Reginald Thomas Wevill the rear gunner was from Torpoint, Cornwall.

Twenty-two-year old Flight Sergeant Donald George Gray's Lancaster crew on 'T-Tare' on 50 Squadron at Skellingthorpe had not had leave for three months or been allowed to leave camp for fourteen days after their arrival at Skelly in case they were sent on a cross-country flying exercise. Gray, who was from Ilford, Essex had been bored with his job as an RAF Training Command staff pilot and then a classroom instructor in navigation. He had wanted 'action' but his natural aptitude as a navigator had kept him off operational flying, until that is, he made himself enough of a nuisance by indulging in some unauthorized low flying, which resulted in a reprimand and a posting to a Conversion Unit. He had been promoted to Warrant Officer but the notification had not yet come through and leave still beckoned. The favourite inn with the NCOs was the 'Crown', whilst the officers usually repaired to the 'Saracen's Head', more commonly known amongst the crews as the 'Snake Pit'. Both were recognised as the most favoured pubs in 5 Group. It was said that if you wanted to find where the target was for the night go along to the Saracen's Head about lunch time, ask the barmaid and she would tell you. Careless talk was not encouraged! The most popular topic of conversation was how many ops various people had done, who had 'got the chop' on the last raid and who, if anyone, had amassed the seemingly impossible total of thirty trips and become 'tour expired'. At this stage of the bomber war, very few did. The 'White Hart Hotel' near the cathedral was the discreet rendezvous where the single officers could wine, dine and romance their current 'popsies' when they weren't scheduled to fly next day. Some liked to go pub-crawling before taking in a dance, while others preferred to see the latest Judy Garland movie or the show at the Theatre Royal where vaudeville artistes performed twice nightly. After the second show there was always time for baked beans on toast or fish and chips before catching the station transport back to base.

On Wednesday evening, 29 March, some members of Donald Gray's crew decided it was time to visit Lincoln. Sergeant Herbert Arthur 'Bert' Wright the wireless operator was a Londoner from Bellingham. Sergeant Douglas Maughan, the rear gunner was from Craghead, County Durham. Sergeant Joseph Grant the flight engineer was from Edinburgh. Sergeant Frank Benjamin Patey the mid-upper gunner was from Bromley in Kent. Flight Sergeant Alan Argyle Campbell the navigator was one of two Australians on the crew. The other was the bomb aimer, Flight Sergeant George Wallis. The pubs shut at ten and the last bus went at ten, so there was always an element of uncertainty about getting home but they need not have worried for their impromptu leave was nipped in the bud when their skipper was ordered to get the crew back as Wing Commander Anthony W. Heward wanted them for flying duties. Heward was a stickler for discipline and in June would be ordered to take command of 97 Squadron and 'shake them up'. Gray had not gone on the pub crawl; it so happened that a friend of his from Civvy Street, now a staff pilot at Cranwell, had turned up at Skellingthorpe to see him that night so he and Gray had a good time and he was able to remain in the Nissen hut. Early on the morning of Thursday 30 March, Gray escorted his wayward crewmembers to the Orderly Room to see Heward only to be told that he was too busy to see them. That same evening Gray was sitting in the Sergeant's Mess having tea when a young WAAF reputed to be a 'chop-girl' began chatting to him. From that moment on he regarded the coming 'op' with trepidation.

On the 30th Pilot Officer A. E. 'Ted' Stone on 61 Squadron at Coningsby drew his pay, travel vouchers and the Nuffield bounty for Pilot Officers and senior NCOs on operational leave and was about to go back to his home in Bridgewater, Somerset but just before he left camp he was called into the CO's office. Wing Commander Reginald Melville Stidolph DFC the 28-year old Rhodesian had been in the RAF since November 1935 and had a distinguished career in the Middle East and the Far East. He asked Stone to delay crew leave for 24 hours and fly a maximum effort operation later that night. In return Stidolph promised that upon their return to Coningsby the following morning, he would have a 'Sprog' crew fly Ted to the nearest airfield to his home. Stone agreed though he and everyone else at aircrew level for that matter did not know what the maximum effort was. He would fly ED860 'N-Nan' which he had first flown at the end of January and then regularly from 1/2 March onwards and it now had ninety plus trips to its name. 'Nan' had been transferred to 61 Squadron in early August 1943 after surviving 25 hazardous Path Finder operations on 156 Squadron which started to receive aircraft fitted with the new blind bombing equipment H_2S. Little did the crews know that she was a lucky aircraft and would go on to complete a further 105 ops over the following year. Nuremberg would be Ted Stone's eighth trip on the veteran aircraft.[3]

The deadline that Thursday, for announcing whether the operation was 'on' or 'off' was four o'clock in the afternoon. The first of two Mosquitoes on 'Pampa' weather observation flights returned to Wyton at about 1235 hours after flying a weather check over the North Sea and inspecting the route of a mining operation scheduled for later in the evening. Their report stated that the operation could proceed, providing that the bombers took off early. It also urged the force return before a mass of cumulonimbus, which could cause severe icing, came too far south over the North Sea. Before the first 'Pampa' flight returned, a second Mosquito crew took off to look in more detail at the outward route to Nuremberg. In just over three hours they covered almost 1,000 miles, flying within 100 miles of Nuremberg, Flying Officer T. Oakes and his Canadian navigator, Flight Lieutenant Robert G. 'Bob' Dale DSO DFC of Toronto, Ontario before returning to Wyton at 1525 hours. Immediately upon landing, Dale rushed to the telephone at Flying Control and made his report simultaneously to Bomber Command and to the various Group Headquarters. In his report, the Canadian navigator confirmed that the outward flight in the bright moonlight had little chance of cloud cover and if the cloud seen over Nuremberg persisted it would rob the Path Finders of the ability to mark visually by moonlight. A further forecast was handed to Sir Robert Saundby at 1640. It read: 'Large amount of stratocumulus with tops to about 8,000 feet and risk of some thin patchy cloud at about 15 to 16,000 feet.' Many years after the war, Sir Robert recalled:

'I can say that, in view of the met report and other conditions, everyone, including myself, expected the C-in-C to cancel the raid. We were most surprised when he did not. I thought perhaps there was some top-secret political reason for the raid, something too top-secret for even me to know. The conditions reported by the Mosquito were not passed down to the stations. Every effort was made to keep from crews the unpleasant fact that they were to fly a constant course through a well-defended part of Germany for 265 miles in bright moonlight with little chance of cloud cover. At a dozen stations Met officers forecast that there would be cloud cover at operational height. No one, not even the Path Finder squadrons, was told of the 'large amounts of stratocumulus' now forecast for Nuremberg.'

The attack was in fact planned for what would normally have been the middle of the stand down period for the Main Force, when a near full moon would be visible. And their lords and masters had opted for a 'straight in, straight out' route, with none of the jinks and deviations that might cause the night fighter controllers to make the wrong decisions about their destination. An indirect route with four shorter legs was suggested by Air Vice Marshal Donald Clifford Tyndall Bennett DSO but the forthright Australian AOC of 8 (PFF) Group was the single dissenting voice. In 1943 Bennett had been promoted with the upgrading of PFF to Group status to Air Commodore, then in December to Acting Air Vice Marshal - the youngest officer to ever hold that rank - giving him a rank similar to those of the other commanders of Groups. The creation of the Path Finder Force was a source of a bitter argument. Initially the brainchild of Group Captain (later Air Vice Marshal CB DFC) Sidney Osborne Bufton (Deputy Director of Bombing Operations for whom 'Bomber' Harris had special contempt), Harris and many of his Group Commanders thought an elite force would breed rivalry and jealousy and have an adverse effect on morale. Sir Henry Tizard, advisor and one of the chief scientists supporting the war effort, said however, 'I do not think the formation of a first XV at rugby makes little boys play any less enthusiastically.'

Bennett, who saw his own appointment as a victory for the 'players' over the 'gentlemen' was a personally difficult and naturally aloof man who nevertheless earned a great deal of respect from his crews but little affection. As Harris wrote, 'he could not suffer fools gladly and by his own high standards there were many fools'. Nor did Bennett get on well with the other RAF Group Commanders: not only was he twenty years younger, he was an Australian.

'Normally', recalled Group Captain Hamish Mahaddie DSO DFC AFC, 8 Group Training Inspector responsible for the selection, recruitment and training of the Path Finder Force, 'the PFF planned the route, which took account of many factors such as the avoidance of heavily-defended areas and the upper winds. The usual dog-legs associated with a bomber raid were inserted into the route to give a false impression of the ultimate destination and the Mosquito Light Night Striking Force carried out 'spoof' attacks on either side of the main track with 'Window' attacks and actually dropping TIs on probable targets along the route.'[4]

At Path Finder Headquarters at Castle Hill House Huntingdon the Path Finder chief drew up, on a huge glass-covered table, a detailed flight plan for the bombers to follow. The finalised result would then be transferred to another great map which took up an entire wall. Much of the plan was based on the meteorological findings brought back earlier by the two 1409 Met Flight Mosquitoes at Wyton. As was Path Finder plotting custom, Bennett formulated the route backwards from the target and was influenced by his preference for down-wind attack rather than into wind to avoid 'creep back' from the aiming point (or drop bomb-loads short of the target). Because of the uncertainty of the weather and the likelihood of thick cloud over the city the Path Finder chief advocated using 'Newhaven' and 'Parramatta' markers and 'Wanganui' flares floating in the sky. This, he was aware, was the least accurate of methods but the only possible one if a target was covered by cloud.[5]

'The route' wrote James Campbell[6] 'was sent to High Wycombe and to the utter astonishment of the Path Finders was rejected by Bomber Command Headquarters. The route that had been decided on, they were told, would be a straight run-in with no 'zigzags', feints or minor raids on diversionary targets. But in what the Path Finders took to be a half-hearted bid to fox the German controllers, a small force of Halifaxes were to lay mines off Texel and in the Heligoland Bight. In addition, they were informed, a fifty strong force of Mosquitoes of 8 (PFF) Group were to attack ten other targets, mostly in the Ruhr, some of them with orders to shoot-up night-fighter airfields in the area. Detailed orders of the attack tactics were transmitted to the Groups. They were informed that the duration of the raid would be from 0105 hours to 0122 hours, during which time Nuremberg was to be saturated with high explosives and incendiaries. The weather forecast given to them warned Groups 4 and 6 to expect valley fog when they returned.'

The plan was countenanced by the AOCs of the three Lancaster Groups - Air Marshal Sir Ralph A. Cochrane KBE CB AFC commanding 5 Group, by Air Vice Marshal Edward Arthur Becton Rice the South-African commander of 1 Group and Air Vice Marshal Richard Harrison of 3 Group, a Yorkshireman. Then, under protest, approval was finally given by New Zealander, Air Vice Marshal C. Roderick Carr of 4 Group and Air Vice Marshal Clifford Mackay McEwen of 6 Group RCAF. Popularly known as 'Black Mike' because of his dark complexion, a native of Griswold, Manitoba, he had volunteered for the RFC in 1917 and shot down 28 aircraft flying from Italy. McEwen and Roddy Carr knew that their Halifaxes were more vulnerable than the faster and more reliable Lancs.[7] A strong tail wind was expected, which would speed the bombers along the 'long leg' in just sixty-two minutes' flying time. Reports were that there would be high cloud on the outward route and that the target area would be clear for ground-marked bombing.

Saundby was obliged to draw up a detailed flight plan for the operation in accordance with Harris's instructions but before doing so he contacted Path Finder Headquarters at Huntingdon on his 'scrambler' telephone and informed Air Vice-Marshal Don Bennett DSO of the proposed route. Save for Roddy Carr, Bennett's proposed Path Finder route found no favour with the Main Force commanders, who believed that the long outward leg would fool the JLOs into thinking that the bomber stream would suddenly veer off to attack some other objective than the one for which it seemed to be heading. 'Air Vice Marshal Sir Ralph Cochrane,' Saundby told Bennett, 'did not favour a dog-leg route because he believed it would only lengthen the flying time to the target and in turn greatly increase the risk of night-fighter interception.' Such 'tactical trickery', he said, would only increase the time required to '...get in and get out, as quickly as possible...' The 'austere and humourless' baronet and the straight-talking Australian could not have been more different. Bennett once described Ralph Cochrane 'an energetic and conscientious man. Seldom have I known any Air Force officer who had more ardour and more zeal than he. In my opinion, however, Cochrane's decisions were most unfortunate. He was mentally restless and had to be doing something all the time. I believe that if Ralph Cochrane had been given the opportunity to operate as a captain of a heavy bomber for fifteen or twenty raids before being given a Group, he would have been a wonderful Group Commander. He had a magnificent brain and had he had the experience behind it, the results would have been wholly exceptional.'[8]

Endnotes Chapter 1

1   See *The Bedford Triangle* by Martin W. Bowman (PSL 1988, Sutton Publishing Ltd 1996; The History Press, 2001 and Pen & Sword, 2015).

2   Bomber Stream Unbroken by James Campbell (Cressrelles Publishing Co Ltd 1976, Futura 1977).

3   ED860 swung off the runway on take-off at Skellingthorpe on 28/29 October 1944. It dug in and the undercarriage collapsed. The starboard outer engine was ripped off, all the noise and lower part of the fuselage, including the bomb bay, were crushed. Fortunately the bomb load did not explode but the aircraft was a write-off.

4   *Hamish; The Memoirs of Group Captain T. G. Mahaddie; The Story of a Pathfinder* (Ian Allan 1989).

5   These code names were so-named by Donald C. T. Bennett, the founder of the Pathfinder Force. 'Newhaven' was for ground target indicators on the ground; 'Parramatta' was when the target was ground marked using H_2S only, owing to bad visibility or broken cloud; and finally 'Wanganui,' which was pure sky-marking, when Main Force crews were required to bomb through these sky-markers on a required course detailed by 8 Group..

6   *Bomber Stream Unbroken* by James Campbell (Cressrelles Publishing Co Ltd 1976, Futura 1977).

7   See *The Nuremberg Raid* by Martin Middlebrook (Penguin 1973).

8   *Pathfinder* by AVM D. C. T. Bennett CB CBE DSO (Frederick Muller Ltd 1958).

Chapter 2

Lissett, 'a rural hamlet of cobble-stoned cottages' straggling both sides of the secondary road which five miles to the North intersected the main Bridlington to Hull road near the Yorkshire coast, was home to 158 Squadron in 4 Group. At one end of the village was the 'Ostler' public house; at the other the 'Swan'. In between was a general store which also housed a sub-post office. Behind the 'Swan' on a grassy hillock 200 yards from the main street stands St. James, perhaps of 14th-century origin, rebuilt with rough hewn sandstone in 1876 and housing the oldest bell in England, dated 1254. Two miles to the east lay the aerodrome with its high wide hangars carefully camouflaged by splotches of dark-brown and green paint, built in 1942. The main runway ran directly towards the shore line and the grey waters of the North Sea where a low thick fog would crawl in, roll up the cliff face 'and sprawl over the dispersals draping the black shapes of the Halifaxes in a mantle of murky yellow.' James Campbell, a Scot born in Inverness, who flew thirty-eight operations on Halifax bombers on 158 Squadron, which flew the most Halifax sorties in Bomber Command - 5,161 sorties - and lost a total of 145 Halifaxes in air combat plus a further twelve destroyed in crashes, described the scene at briefing time[9] when sixteen crews gathered in the briefing hut: 'The huge Nissen hut was filled with a sea of blue splashed with the heavy white woollen polo neck sweaters the crews wore under their battle-dress tunics. Eye catching Air Ministry contents bills with bold headlines screaming, 'Have You Done This?' 'This is Important'. 'Remember That?' plastered the green painted walls of the main briefing room. Aircrews sprawled over the rough wooden forms and leaned inertly across the ink-stained tables. Others, who could not find seats, lounged along the walls in attitudes of complete and utter boredom. Through the blue-white haze of tobacco smoke, a hundred-and-sixty voices rose in a noisy babble. The older crews made pungent remarks, bitterly resenting that the early transport into town had been cancelled until the briefing was over. The veterans had long since trained themselves to show the minimum of emotion. Others on the new crews were so boyish looking that they must have come straight from school. Replacements were getting younger but their faces were prematurely old. Many looked lost and utterly bewildered.' As H. E. Bates had once observed on a visit to an RAF station he was 'assailed by the impression that he had somehow strayed into a gathering of Sixth Form school boys grown prematurely old. 'I think it true to say that of all the officers assembled there that evening scarcely more than a dozen were over 25... (However) it was the eyes of these young but prematurely aged officers that made a powerful and everlasting impact on me.'[10]

   A shuffling of massed feet, punctuated by a few wooden forms crashing to the floor, greeted the Wing Commander as he entered. Charles Cranston 'Jock' Calder, a farmer's son, born on 12 July 1920 at Edin Killie, Morayshire, leapt lightly on the raised dais in front of the huge wall map constructed from sections of Mercator charts. He had become the youngest squadron commander in Bomber Command at the age of 23. A highly distinguished career on Whitley, Halifax and Lancaster bombers saw him receive the DSO, the DFC and Bar and the American DFC. 'Jock' searched the rows of white faces in front of him, contemplating for a full half minute the assortment of brevets and uniforms. 'Sit down, gentlemen! Smoke, if you wish,' he said crisply. The clamour of conversation had died down and the aircrews were seated quietly on the wooden forms in front of the plain tables. The Wing Commander toyed with a bright red pin. Attached to the pin was a long narrow red cord. He surveyed the room for a few moments... 'Tonight it's Nuremberg!' He waited until the low murmur of whispered comments died. Calder then handed the red cord to the Squadron navigation officer and watched him plunge the pin into the black square that was Lissett. Deftly the navigation officer placed another pin in a minute triangle over a Dead Reckoning position in the North Sea. Swiftly, from there he laid off the legs to the enemy coast and then across Germany to the target.

'I don't put a great deal on what they think about you at Group. If you have had higher losses than other squadrons, then you're obviously not as efficient as they are... And if you go out thinking you won't come back' thundered the Wing Commander, 'you give the Hun that psychological advantage which comes from your own inferiority'. A cathedral silence stifled the room. Someone at the back coughed. The sound reverberated sharply. 'For the benefit of the new crews, I must remind you that you do not divulge the target or anything which may identify it - not even to the rest of your crew. They will know soon enough at the main briefing.'

One of the assembled pilots, Flight Sergeant Joe Hitchman, who was from Derby, did not particularly want to go on the operation as he and his crew had been looking forward to a well-earned leave. Hitchman had arrived at Lissett on 10 December right in the middle of the Battle of Berlin and he flew his first op, as 'second dickey' with his flight commander Squadron Leader Samuel Davis Jones DFC to the 'Big City' on 20 January. Hitchman and his crew had actually got to the main gate at Lissett when they were recalled. He shared HX349, better known as 'G-George', with his flight commander. When he got to briefing, Hitchman discovered that Jones was taking 'G-George' and he had been assigned LV907 'F-Fox' a new Halifax III, which had arrived on the station on 10 March. The story goes that 158 Squadron had lost seven Halifax aircraft coded 'F-Fox' in succession, within a year!

When 'Jock' Calder completed his briefing of the pilots, the Navigation Leader took over. Slowly and clearly he gave instructions, repeating some points, stressing others.

'Navigators have already been briefed and have prepared their charts and their captains' maps. 'To minimize enemy radar detection, the main force will maintain a height of no more than 2,000 feet across country and the coast, with navigation lights on to the first turning point at 51° 50' North 2° 30' East approximately halfway between Great Yarmouth on the Norfolk coast and Bruges in Belgium. Please keep a very sharp lookout at this point, captains and gunners. At this point you will start a steady climb, switching off all lights when the turn is completed on to your south-easterly course of 130°. The Belgian Coast will be crossed at 8,000 feet just to the east of Binges to the next turning point at 50° 30' North 4°36' East, just short of Charleroi; there you will alter course to port, gradually climb to your bombing height and reach your last turning point before the target, at Fulda 50° 32' North 10° 36' East and then on to the target. After leaving the target continue for a short distance to 49° North 11° 5' East; then to 48° 30' North 9° 20' East and on to 50° North 3° East to cross the French coast at 50° 40' North 2° East, at a height of 4,000 feet.

'Indicated air speeds will be 172 mph to the first turning point. Then climbing at 150 across the coast to the next turning point where airspeed will be increased to 162 mph and held to the target. If it is necessary to make a second run on the target, orbit left to avoid others in the main force coming up behind you. On leaving the target, increase speed to 182 and hold this, gradually losing height to cross the coast at 4,000 feet. Corrected winds will be broadcast to the main force every half hour between 2340 and 0340.'

Two hours later, the main briefing hall was packed. This time the gunners, wireless operators and flight engineers were in the big room. They were promised heavy cloud cover and were relieved to hear it. If the conditions were clear they would have to shoot their way through to the target. Not even the foolhardiest of gunners reckoned much for their chances in a duel with a night-fighter which with its heavier calibre machine-guns and cannon could stay well out of range of their puny .303s and pump shells at them at will.[11] Such were the thoughts of Sergeant Reginald Cripps who was the rear-gunner on 'L-Love' skippered by 26-year old Flight Sergeant Stan Windmill, six feet tall and an ex-policeman from London. The bomb aimer was 35-year-old James Cooper from Glasgow; the wireless-operator 28-year-old Richard Avery from Bristol; and the flight engineer 23-year-old Peter McKenzie from Islay in the Western Isles. Manning the mid-upper turret was another Glaswegian, 35-year-old Sergeant Matt Wyllie, who was a good fifteen years older than the average bomber gunner.

Sergeant Kenneth Dobbs, one of the wireless operators on 158, had flown a recent raid on Berlin when his 78 Squadron aircraft had returned to Breighton badly shot up over the 'Big City'. His pilot never flew again, the crew was disbanded and Dobbs found himself transferred to 158 Squadron. He had hoped to get crewed up because as he said, 'a crew is a crew, you live and eat together', but he was just a 'spare bod'. 'Twice I was called in as a spare wireless operator to fly with the squadron commander.' Dobbs discovered that he was on the battle order at the last minute. 'I hadn't been detailed to fly and was going home. I went up to the flight office just to see what was going on and Flying Officer R. G. A. Harvey DFM the deputy signals leader came up to me and said, 'We're a wireless op' short for Flight Sergeant Albert Brice's crew; his WOp's gone sick.' 'I said 'I'll go' because I had thirty trips to do for a tour and I wasn't getting them done very quickly.'

The Officer i/c Flying said his piece: 'As a military target, Nuremberg is an important industrial city and a centre for general and electrical engineering. You've already disproved, on many occasions, Goering's earlier boast that no bombs would ever fall on the Fatherland. Now you'll have an opportunity to dissuade the Nazis from holding further mass rallies in the city most favoured for these. Nuremberg deserves a maximum effort and that is what it will now get. Ten squadrons in 1 Group, eight squadrons from 3 Group, seven squadrons from No. 4, twelve from No. 5, nine from No. 6 and twelve squadrons from 8 Group Path Finder Force will participate - altogether 820 Lancasters and Halifaxes. In addition fifteen Mosquitoes will adopt an 'Intruder' role to seek out night fighters and destroy them. So you'll have plenty of company and it behoves every one to keep a good look-out at the turning points to avoid collisions.

'H-hour is 0105 to 0122 (seventeen minutes). After the PFF have marked the target, the main force will bomb from H-hour +5 for the remaining twelve minutes. Our time on target is set for H-hour +9 between the band of 20,000 to 20,500 feet. Take-off time is 2200 hours. Good luck; have a good trip!'

'Met will tell you that a fairly stiff crosswind can be expected on target, so bomb aimers will need to be pretty snappy with their bombing. On the other hand, they must be careful to avoid the tendency to 'creep-back' with their bombs and miss the vital areas. Make a good job of it, chaps. We don't want to go back again.

'Window': one parcel a minute over the coast and up to the first turning point, over Charleroi in Belgium. At your next turning-point (Fulda) release 'window' at the rate of two parcels a minute for five minutes and at the rate of one a minute at subsequent points after leaving the target, as specified.'

The Intelligence Officer weighed in: 'The very direct nature of the route to the target tonight has been the subject of great discussion between Bomber Command and Group Commanders. In particular Air Vice-Marshal Bennett strongly advocated a far more indirect approach. His views, however, were opposed by other Air Officers commanding, including Air Vice Marshal Cochrane. They supported the Commander-in-Chief's plan on these grounds that the distance involved precludes wasting time and fuel on too many doglegs, that the present route suggests a number of perhaps more vulnerable targets to the German defences, thus persuading them to disperse and thin-out fighter concentrations, that the sheer simplicity of this route will surprise the Germans and keep them off-balance sufficiently long for you to complete the operation without too much trouble. I think you deserve this explanation and it may help to dispel any misgivings you have about the direct route as laid down.'

The wing commander, a light cane in his right hand, walked over to the wall map and traced the course and heights they were to fly at, the estimated time of arrival at their turning points. With the aid of a weather chart Calder explained why the diversions they had come to expect could not be laid on. Tapping his thigh with his light cane he told them: 'However, a force of fifty Halifaxes will start dropping mines in the Heligoland Bight as a diversionary move to keep German ground controllers confused. That we hope will help to fox them. Met reports are fairly encouraging. They anticipate cloud cover to Nuremberg, with probably a fair amount of it on the way back. But the gunners had better keep a sharp look-out; there will be a half moon...' He broke off and smiled sympathetically as he heard them groan.

'Additional to this and a while before the main force reaches the target, 34 Mosquitoes will make dummy feints a hundred miles from their landfall towards Aachen, Cologne and Kassel between 2355 and seven minutes after midnight. A further force of twenty Mosquitoes will also drop fighter flares, markers and 'Window' on Kassel between 26 and 28 minutes after midnight in an attempt to 'spoof' the German controllers into believing the main attack is to be the Ruhr and thus lead them to send the bulk of the fighters there. So far as ground defences are concerned, we've tried to route you over the coast both going and coming back where flak and searchlights are believed to be thin and the use of 'Window' here will help to blur the picture from the ground. Again, the route takes you across the southerly end of the heavy Ruhr defensive area. Obviously much depends on the accuracy of your course-keeping and your ability to maintain a well bunched-together pattern and no straying away from the main stream.

'Night-fighters can as usual be expected, but with cloud-cover and the Mosquito attacks to keep them grounded, the danger from these, we believe, will be minimized. Keep a sharp lookout for them however and, wireless operators, make sure your 'Fishpond' is working at all times.'

'The Bombing Leader, thankful he himself was not going out, said: 'Your all-up weight tonight is just short of 65,000lbs. Bomb load is just over 7,000lbs with 4 x 1,000lb HEs and 3,000lb of incendiaries. You have six tanks of petrol - altogether 2,200 gallons - more than sufficient for the trip tonight.

'Including this squadron's contribution, altogether 3,000 tons of bombs will fall on the target tonight. There are three main concentrations for your attack - here and here - (pointing on map) and depending on what cloud cover there may be, Path Finder Force will employ either 'Wanganui' sky flares if the target is completely obscured by cloud, 'Parramatta' markers, dropped on H_2S, if there is broken cloud partially obscuring the target, or 'Newhaven' ground markers dropped on visual identification, aided by H_2S.

'Night maps should be marked accordingly.

'Initially red markers and incendiaries will be dropped; then green markers turning yellow; then these will be further fed by red markers, with target illuminators, from 0109 to 0122.' The backers-up would aim at the reds with green markers in as tight a circle as the Mark 14 bombsight would allow. Using the Mark 14 sight enabled bomb aimers to bomb fairly accurately without the pilot having to fly dead straight and level. Even so its capabilities were limited. Exceed a climb of five degrees, a dive of twenty degrees, a bank of ten degrees and the gyro toppled. Then it was useless for twenty-five minutes; the time it took the gyro to recover.

'So your primary aiming points are the reds. If they are bombed out or otherwise obscured, bomb the greens.' He moved over to allow the Met Officer to be seen. Suddenly he hesitated; Remember,' he added sternly. 'Check your bombing stations for hang-ups.'

'The Met Officer, a mild soft-spoken man with large horn-rimmed glasses, nervously unrolled his chart. He might as well keep it rolled, he thought. It was always the sign for a ripple of laughter to go round the room. He resented deeply this enforced role of briefing jester, for there were only two questions they ever wanted to know. The rest were phrased either to raise a laugh or make him look foolish. Pointing out on his chart he said: 'At the line 'LW' warm air is overtaking the cold air forming a warm front which is moving northward over North East Yorkshire and South West Scotland. The line 'LC' marks a cold front now over Ireland and approaching the western side of England. It may lead to cu-nim cloud, although we do not expect this to be continuous.

'What is forecast is broken but fairly good cloud cover for you all the way to the target and back, with some low cloud and precipitation in coastal areas. Winds over the Continent moderate 40/50 mph at 18,000 feet and generally blowing from southwest or west. There may be some low cloud and poor visibility down to 2,000 yards at base on return.'

Glancing apprehensively at his weather chart, he was about to amplify a point he was making when a long-haired bomb aimer with a Cockney accent rose to his feet. 'Say, what's it like over the target? Is it likely to be clear?'

He waited for a moment. He half turned to the Wing Commander and the Group Captain. They were smiling faintly but still, they were smiling. The Met Officer spun round quickly, flushed and icily retorted; 'I was coming to that. Obviously, since you are to bomb visually, we expect fairly clear conditions.' A loud cheer burst from the centre of the hall as they applauded his retort.

Confidence restored, he concluded: 'To sum up then: for the outward flight, broken cloud can be expected everywhere except Southern Germany where it is expected to be layered. Winds, West-Southwest 40/50, veering West-Northwest 50/60 mph over target. Local industrial smog in Groups 4 and 6 areas, with valley fog towards dawn.'

Finally, the wing commander stepped briskly forward. 'You have now been briefed on one of the thirty operational flights you will have to survive to complete your first heavy bomber tour. Some of you will be flying on ops for the very first time, others have only one trip to go; a few of you will be on your second tour of twenty trips. Several crews are due for a week's leave as from tomorrow.

'That's all then, except - Good Luck Gentlemen and Good Bombing.'

Following this main briefing, crews more than likely went to their messes for a meal, including bacon and egg and then a stroll across to the crew rooms to put on flying kit, gather up 'chutes and bits and pieces and climb aboard one of the crew buses for their particular flight at dispersal. The captains would issue the flying rations/escape kits to their crews, run up the engines for a final check and sign the Forms 700. Then they would all have to wait around for a Very light from the control tower, most inwardly hoping that it would be a red one indicating a last-minute cancellation! On this occasion, though, it would be 'green' at all stations. The raid was on!

The crews still had a couple of hours before take-off. Some went to their billets to try and relax while others went to the mess for their pre-ops meal of bacon and eggs just in case they didn't get back in the morning. Meanwhile the navigators still had to work out their courses based upon take-off times and target estimated time of arrival (ETA). Aircraft captains also had a number of last-minute jobs to do that could not be done until after briefing. Next they would meet in the aircrew locker room, change into their flying kit and collect their parachutes and safety equipment. Outside the lorries and buses lined up to take them out to their aircraft's dispersal.

When dusk approached ground crews would see various types of vehicles travelling hither and thither to distant dispersals, dropping the crews off by their aircraft. On the dispersal nearest to us, the aircrew would be seen sitting around on the grass smoking and chatting. As take-off time approached, they stubbed out their cigarettes, picked up their parachutes and threw them inside the aircraft. The crews made final checks around the kite, after which they carried out their individual rituals, a last minute cigarette or wetting the rear wheel for good luck. One by one they climbed aboard through the rear starboard doorway and would be lost from sight as each took up his crew position inside the aircraft. Even then there could be a last minute scrub of the operation due to bad weather en-route or in the target area. A Very light would be fired from the control tower signifying engine start-up time had arrived for the waiting bomber crews. The pilot, sliding back the cockpit window on the port side, would give instructions to the ground crew to proceed with engine start up. An electrical starter trolley was wheeled out, rations were put aboard and emergency rations were stowed near the collapsible dinghy in case the aircraft had to be abandoned over water. Meanwhile the armourer gave a final check to bomb load and machine guns. With bomb doors closed and engines started each pilot tested his aircraft's controls and then applied the brakes, revved and cleared all four engines and then throttled down again to a tick-over to assure himself that everything was in order before leaving the dispersal.

With all four engines performing correctly, chocks would be waved away followed by a hiss of escaping air as the brakes were released and the aircraft slowly moved out from the dispersal to join others of the Squadron on the perimeter track and then forward in single file towards the main runway.

When his turn came, each pilot would turn his aircraft onto the perimeter track and join other aircraft weaving their way to the holding point at the end of the runway, awaiting a green light from the Flying Control caravan. The Air Traffic controller in the caravan at the end of the runway allowed aircraft to take-off alternately from each Squadron. On a maximum effort raid this could mean controlling thirty Lancasters over a 25-minute period. Once the runway was clear, the controller's green Aldis lamp would flash at the waiting aircraft and each aircraft taxied onto the end of the main runway. This was always greeted by a loud cheer from a large group of off-duty personnel that had assembled nearby to wave good luck to each aircraft. The pilot applied the brakes, revved the engines and closed the throttles again before slowly revving the engines up again into a mighty roar. As throttles were advanced, the ensuing power generated by the four Merlins produced a sound that drowned all conversation and once the brakes had been released the aircraft slowly rolled forward down the runway before gaining speed in a series of gentle bounces on the undercarriage hydraulics under the weight of a full bomb and fuel load. This was a most critical time as the pilot concentrated to control the aircraft's tendency to swing to port due to the massive torque created by four Merlin engines at full power. The loss of power from one of the engines or a burst tyre could spell instant disaster for the crew.

Three quarters of the way down the runway the aircraft slowly rose into the air and, with undercarriage retracted, quickly disappeared into the failing light on the first leg of its nocturnal operation. This may be a non-stop run of over a thousand miles before returning. Once in the air, nothing more would be heard from the aircraft until the captain sent a coded message telling base that the mission had been completed. Only in an emergency would he break radio silence while over enemy territory.'

The ground staff had not yet finished. Even though the 'blokes' out on the open dispersals were tired after working long hours, in all kind of weather, they still hung around until take-off time just in case their kite developed a fault. This was a rare occurrence compared with the number of sorties flown. Only after their aircraft's navigation lights disappeared into the night sky would they slowly wander back to their billets in small groups chatting as they went about the day's events and the job the aircrew were doing that night.

After the last aircraft had clawed its way into the air and departed with the sound of its laboured engines fading away, the airfield fell strangely silent. Rural tranquillity descended once again on the surrounding woods and fields and, as the group of WAAFs and airmen strolled back to their billets, rabbits came out of hiding and scurried across the main runway before disappearing once again into the long grass that edged this great expanse of concrete. While in the distance, ground crews could be seen tidying the dispersals in readiness for their aircraft's return or cycling around the perimeter track to the cookhouse for their evening meal. Some of the aircraft would not return from the night's operation, but of those that did, it was inevitable that one or two would suffer severe airframe damage and would become patients the next morning.[12]

At Kirmington, eleven miles northwest of Grimsby, Flight Sergeant Sidney Nicholas Whitlock the WOp/AG on Flight Lieutenant Frederick Taylor's crew on 'B-Baker' on 166 Squadron reported to the signals section. His pilot made his way to the office of his 'A' Flight commander where he was informed that Sergeant Allen Wakley Hughes, from Teignmouth in Devon, a pilot instructing at an OTU who had never been on operations, was given a seat in the front turret. At the same time Flight Sergeant L. F. McCarney, the Irish navigator; Flight Sergeant W. Watson, bomb aimer; Sergeant Eric Norman Whitfield, flight engineer who was from Wallasey, Cheshire; Pilot Officer H. A. Standen, mid-upper gunner and Sergeant F. A. Thrower, rear gunner were also reporting to their respective sections. Nuremberg would be the crew's eighteenth operation. With the primary specialist briefings completed, Taylor and his crew cycled thoughtfully out to their dispersal where their ground crew, similarly alerted by the Tannoy's broadcast of 'Grand National', were completing inspection and maintenance of the engines, systems and armament of Lancaster I ME638 'B-Baker'. Since night-flying tests prior to operations were not carried out on 166 Squadron unless some previously reported defect had been rectified and had to be tested in flight, there was no need for Taylor and his crew to check-fly the Lancaster that morning as 'B-Baker' had a clean sheet. The ops meal when it came was a quickening of relief after the hours of waiting for dull time to pass. Crowded four to a table, the crews ate in an atmosphere alive with young voices raised in animated, nervous chatter and frank, extroverted speculation about the target and their prospects for the night. Like the other crews on 166 Squadron at the main briefing they were consoled, if not cheered, by the meteorologists who promised them cloud cover so there would be no great need to worry about the rising moon. Ironically, Whitlock was to recall that shortly after 'B-Baker' had completed the North Sea crossing and was over Belgium, he heard his pilot and the gunners reporting that the little cloud that had been around was rapidly breaking up.[13]

Sergeant Sidney Lipman, a flight engineer on 'B' Flight had also heard the 'Grand National' alert on the Tannoy. He and the others on New Zealander Alan Gibson's crew had joined 166 Squadron on 8 March from No. 3 Lancaster Finishing School at Feltwell where they had undergone a week's conversion course on Lancasters having originally trained on Stirlings. In September 1939 Stanley Lipman had been contacted by the District Surveyor's office in Stepney where he lived. 'They were in the process of setting up a Heavy Rescue Party, as war was imminent and I was asked if I was willing to join them. This would mean that if we had any bombing I would be in a group of men whose job would be to shore up dangerous structures, cut off main water and gas supplies in buildings and of course rescue people who were trapped. I was suited to this work as I was working for my father in the building trade. I willingly accepted the task and also took a course and passed out as a PT instructor, to keep the men fit and active for their arduous tasks. It wasn't a pleasant experience in the Heavy Rescue Party and we were on duty 24 hours on, 24 hours off. Many of my colleagues were lost on those long and dangerous nights when we had to pull people out of the wreckage. We thanked God if they were alive and unhurt, but all too often it was too late to save them. On one occasion my own house was bombed to the ground and another night I was called upon to rescue relatives of mine out of a bombed building.

'After 2½ years there was a lull in the bombing and four of us from the Heavy Rescue Party volunteered for the RAF as aircrew. I was accepted, got through three days of rigorous mental and physical examinations and was given an RAFVR badge and told that they would call for me. I didn't have long to wait! The training was an exciting and mind-broadening time for me. I had the opportunity to test my physical strength and abilities to the limit and was very proud of studying at Clare College, Cambridge for a few months for Initial Training Wing. At this period Lancasters had just come out and flight engineers were being trained for them. It sounded an exciting challenge and I volunteered to go for training, which was at St. Athan, South Wales. We started on our training on the Stirling four-engine bomber and after passing out we were transferred onto Lancasters. After a nine day conversion course we were sent to 166 Squadron at Kirmington.'

Kirmington airfield had opened in October 1942 on the Grimsby to Scunthorpe road. Crews could go to the pub without leaving the station, as the 'Marrowbone & Cleaver' or the 'Chopper' as it was known to all bomber crews, was across the road from the sick quarters but it was not used often. Brigg was just down the road. Then there was the Café Dansant on the seafront at Cleethorpes, where there were ATS and WAAF girls to dance with, but very few of the much-prized Wrens from the naval station in Grimsby. The delights of Grimsby, a popular haunt for half a dozen 1 Group stations in the area, included a studio in Abbey Road where Sid Burton took crew's portraits and many a good night was spent at the 'Mucky Duck' and the old Black Swan.[14] Luscious Lil', a full-bosomed woman in Grimsby, who had a penchant for revealing outfits, was available for any who wished to lose their virginity while there was still time.[15] 'Screwed, blued and tattooed' Canadians especially could not wait to tell of their adventures. The bus queues to Grimsby were always an indication of whether the squadron was on ops. A lot of men in the queue for Grimsby meant a quiet night at the 'Marquis of Granby' in Binbrook village where Rene Trevor sang for the 'Wild Colonial' boys and played the piano. An empty queue meant another raid on Germany. At Scunthorpe there was the 'Oswald', the 'Bluebell' and the 'Crosby' or one could see a floor show and get drunk at the 'Berkley' on the outskirts of the blacked out town. It was generally accepted that aircrew NCOs used the 'Bluebell'. It would not have been out of place in a Western. It had a large, open saloon bar with a sawdust-covered floor and a raised wooden platform in the corner on which a man in bowler hat played non-stop. It only needed busty, silk-stockinged girls to complete the illusion but the ladies provided did their best and this made up in humour what it lacked in propriety.

Returning to Kirmington from leave on 26 March, Sidney Lipman agreed to go on operations that evening to Essen with Flight Sergeant Fransden's crew as they were short of a flight engineer. 166 Squadron lost two Lancasters that night. A few days later, on the afternoon of 30 March, Lipman was again called to the 'B' Flight commander's office and asked if he would fly another trip with 'V-Victor's crew whose flight engineer was ill. Sidney Lipman recalled that 'I felt that it was extremely nice of them to think of me and said I would be pleased to go.' He was told that he would fly with Flight Lieutenant Gordon Arbuthnot Procter from Clapham Common, London.

'He introduced himself to me and was a very affable type of person. I inspected and checked over the aircraft and found everything perfect. Later on we went to the briefing room where we were given all the gen about the raid and what to expect in the way of enemy resistance and were wished the best of luck by 'Pop,' the briefing officer. As we were leaving the briefing room a chap came over to Procter and spoke to him and then they both came over to me. Procter said that the fellow [Sergeant Henry Longton, who was from Lancaster, Lancashire] was his flight engineer who had been given an all-clear by the MO and would like to fly on this trip [their second operation] if I had no objection. I said that as long as the CO did not mind I would be quite willing to forgo the trip. After putting it to the CO it was agreed that he would take my place. I wished them luck.'

From out by the rain-swept runway Sidney Lipman watched Procter's eight man crew on 'V-Victor' and eighteen other Lancasters taking off into the darkness when he felt a firm but friendly hand on his shoulder. It was Wing Commander Don Garner DSO DFC the commanding officer of 166 Squadron. 'You're just the chap I wanted to see,' Garner said. 'One of the flight engineers is not well. Unless his crew can get another engineer they will be unable to go on this op. Can you help us out? Of course, you have the right to refuse.' By now Lipman no longer fancied the trip but although his heart said no, he agreed to go. Garner, naturally enough, was delighted. 'He whipped me off to the parachute section in his car,' Lipman recalled, 'ran me back to the runway where a kite was revving-up and helped me into the open door of the aircraft. I then met my pilot, Pilot Officer Bridges, took my place alongside him on 'Z-Zebra' and off we went.'

Pilot Officer D. M. Bridges' Lancaster was one of the last of twenty aircraft to take off from Kirmington. At dispersal, Sheffield-born pilot Flight Sergeant Jack Gagg had warmed up the engines on ED905[16] just as he had done on his previous four operations and ran each one up to full power but he had a magneto drop on one and it was spitting and spluttering. The ground crew came out and changed all the plugs but that did not fix the problem, so they changed the magneto but it still gave problems. The wing commander arrived and told Gagg to take DV367 'T-Tommy' the spare aircraft but by the time they were ready to take off the rest of the squadron had been in the air for 45 minutes. As Gagg taxied out, the Wingco called up and said they were too late; he would never catch up with Main Force and asked what Gagg wanted to do. He asked the crew what they thought and to a man they all wanted to go so Gagg went.

'Nobody liked to scrub after getting so far' said Gagg.

Endnotes Chapter 2

9   *Maximum Effort* (Futura 1957).

10   *The World in Ripeness* (Michael Joseph, 1972).

11   *The Bombing of Nuremberg* by James Campbell (Futura 1973). Campbell himself was probably the rear gunner on his crew on 158 Squadron. A Scot, he was born in Inverness. The fictional rear gunner in one of his RAF novels was 'Jock, a Glaswegian'.

12   *Adapted from Aircraft Maintenance* by Ray Meredith and *Ops Are On Again Tonight in Thundering Through The Clear Air; No. 61 (Lincoln Imp) Squadron at War* by Derek Brammer (Toucann Books 1997).

13   See *The Nuremberg Massacre* by Geoff Taylor.

14   *Maximum Effort: The Story of the North Lincolnshire Bombers* by Patrick Otter.

15   *The Red Line* by John Nichol.

16   Lancaster III ED905 Ad Extremum! went on to fly over 100 sorties on 103, 166 and 550 Squadrons before going to 1LFS and 1656 CU where this Lancaster crashed and was written off on 20 August 1945. As BQ-F 'F-Fox' on 550 Squadron it set off from North Killingholme, Lincolnshire on its 100th operation - to Düsseldorf - on the evening of 2 November 1944. Two other Lancasters on 550 Squadron also completed over 100 operational sorties.

Chapter 3

Eighteen Lancaster crews on 57 Squadron's Battle Order entered the briefing room at East Kirkby on the gentle southern edge of the Lincolnshire Wolds between Spilsby and Coningsby to find out what the fates had in store for them. Pilot Officer J. 'Cas' Castagnola DSO DFC, who had begun his operational tour in January, piloting his Lancaster on three Berlin raids in four nights, had a strong feeling at this time and he was not a suspicious type, that several operations were known to the Germans in advance. 'A number of times, when we were at full stretch and most vulnerable we would find the German fighters already there above us, waiting. Specialist raids were never talked about but the Main Force mass raids were different. It could happen quite simply. Maybe a crew would be stood down from a raid for some reason and they would naturally head for the 'local' to celebrate. Someone would say, 'You not going today?' And they would answer, unthinking, 'No thank God. It's Nuremberg via Fulda and they're welcome to it'. No leak was intended but we were only kids. You could certainly hear such a conversation about 5 Group too often for comfort in any one of the three pubs we used in Boston. There was the 'Red Cow' in Market Square; the 'White Hart' in the town centre; and in another pub known as 'Rose and Twink' the landlord had two lovely daughters.'

Thirty-one-year old Flying Officer John C. 'Jock' Langlands crew was one of sixteen Lancasters on 630 Squadron which shared East Kirkby with 57 Squadron that were dispatched. They had flown just the one operation, to Essen on Sunday 26 March. 'Sprogs' they might be but they were well-disciplined like their skipper. Tall and slim, Langlands, who had been an Edinburgh policeman once landed an ailing Stirling and had also made an emergency landing in a Wimpy at Operational Training Unit where the small airfield normally only handled Tiger Moth training aircraft. Pilot Officer H. B. 'Benny' Bryans his bomb aimer was from Leicester. Twenty-three-year old Sergeant Norman 'Hermann' Goring the flight engineer was a motor mechanic from Hull. Flying Officer Bob Guthrie the navigator was from Reading. A keen long-distance cyclist, Guthrie had been a GPO telephones clerk for two years before joining up. He had met Miss Sybil Lewington at a dance in Reading after returning from training in Canada and they married on 18 November 1943. He had turned 21 the day before the Essen operation. Soon after arriving at East Kirkby from 1661 HCU Winthorpe, where the crew had flown the disliked and 'dodgy' Stirling, Guthrie had scraped together £25 to buy a Singer saloon to run the crew around the area. Sergeant Geoff Jeffery, the 22-year old wireless operator was from Sevenoaks in Kent. The rear gunner, Flight Sergeant Alan Drake, a married man from Wigan in Lancashire was a veteran of ten years' service and had been an armourer before becoming an aerial gunner. Sergeant Harry Morley 'Bud' Coffey the boisterous and wisecracking 21-year old Canadian mid-upper gunner was from Saint John, New Brunswick. Langlands had been allocated ME664 'T-Tommy', the Squadron Commander's Lancaster, which had only arrived at East Kirkby on 24 February and had only 67 hours' flying time. Wing Commander William Inglis Deas DSO DFC* was a 29-year old South African from Piet Retief, Transvaal. When a heavy snowfall brought airfields to a standstill late that week everyone from the wing commander downwards was given a shovel and they set about clearing the runway of snow so that on the morning of the 30th crews could perform their air test.

Sergeant Ronald E. Walker's crew on 'N-Nan' on 'B' Flight, who had completed two ops after arriving on 14 March, had crewed up at 16 OTU Upper Heyford where, at the satellite airfield at Barford St. John Sergeant Ronald Alfred 'Ginger' Hammersley the 5-feet 4½-inch wireless air gunner (his missing half-inch was overlooked when he was recruited into the RAFVR) met Leading Aircraftwoman 'Nan' Webber, who became his future wife. Hammersley was one of five children, born on 21 July 1922, who having left school in the summer of 1939 at age 14 trained as a barber. His father was a carpenter and joiner by trade. He had served in France with the Royal Field Artillery in WWI. His mother had worked for Ovaltine at Kings Langley and when war broke out, joined John Dickenson's at the Apsley End factory. They all lived in a three-bed roomed council house in Hertfordshire with a fair sized garden. Ron Walker his pilot was physically a well-built strong man, a natural pilot and a quick learner. Flying Officer Harry Bertram MacKinnon RAFVR the London-born navigator had some time earlier completed a tour of operations on 226 Squadron, flying 'daylights' on Boston aircraft. Tom Quayle, mid-upper gunner, whose home was in the Isle of Man had been in the RAF Regiment before re-mustering for flying duties. Ken E. Bly the air bomber was Canadian. The two other members of the crew were Sergeant Esmond 'Essie' Chung, flight engineer and Sergeant Bill Carver, rear gunner.

On Friday 24 March, Ron Walker's crew had found themselves on the Battle Order for Berlin. Then came two raids on Essen on the 26th and 29th. 'On the 30th' recalls Hammersley, the same aircraft (ND560/N) had been allocated to our crew for the night's operation. The bomb load was ten 500 pounders together with a full load of fuel. Like the flight to Berlin, it looked as if we were set for a long trip and this proved correct. We were issued with amphetamine tablets. These were taken just prior to take-off and would keep the crews wide awake and on a 'high' for the duration of the flight. If the operation was cancelled, it meant a sleepless night which, for most of the crews, meant that a wild night of drinking would take place in both the Officers' and Sergeants' mess until the effects of the drug wore off and sleep could take over. It was customary for a meal to be prepared for the crews before we flew. We were then issued with a flask of tea or coffee, with chocolate, sandwiches and an apple; armed with a 0.38-revolver and parachute. Codes and Very pistol with cartridges which when fired, would give the coded colours of the day. We were even given what were understood to be those in use by the German forces that day. After emptying my pockets and locking my personal items into my cage type locker, I joined the crew in the crew bus with WAAF Connie Mills at the wheel. The bus that collected the crews from near the Control Tower was often driven by Connie. We were then taken out to 'N-Nan'. We had another look around the aircraft with the ground crew and about an hour before we were due to take-off we settled into our places to await the take-off order.

'When the first part of the take-off procedure commenced, we were lined up on the airfield perimeter with seventeen other Lancasters on the squadron. All crews would by now have taken their amphetamines and would be wide awake. The first Lancaster was given the 'Green Light' from the Mobile Watch Tower and we watched as it slowly climbed away. The remainder all slowly moved around the perimeter track towards the runway and then it was their turn for destination Nuremberg! The smoke from the engines and the smell of burning high octane fuel eddied across the airfield. Sixty tons of explosives and incendiaries were to be dropped by 57 Squadron that night and the sight of eighteen Lancasters each under full throttles roaring away into the evening sky was an awesome spectacle. Sergeants Frank Beasley and Leslie Wakerell with their ground crews and a number of other well wishers watched us away before retiring to while away the long hours before our return. The smoke and smell slowly thinned and drifted away over the silent airfield and we were on our way. We were airborne at 2211 hours. As the weather reports came in and I decoded them it became apparent from 'Mack' MacKinnon s findings that they were not as he expected.'[17]

Having just had a very welcome seven days leave, Flight Sergeant C. R. 'Tubby' Holley had to get up at 0530 on 30th March to catch a train from his home in Southall, which would get him to Kings Cross in time for the early train back to Huntingdon. Holley was rear gunner on Lancaster 'D-Dog', a primary blind-marker Lancaster on 156 Squadron in 8 (Path Finder) Group at Upwood south west of the market town of Ramsey, Huntingdonshire. Most of the crew were on their second tour of operations. Holley, Flying Officer 'Blackie' Blackadder the tall, well-built bomb aimer and radar operator from Birmingham and Flight Lieutenant 'Robbie' Bagg the wireless operator arrived at Upwood just after ten that morning to find to their intense disgust that they and their pilot, Squadron Leader Walter Thomas Brooks were down for 'ops' that night. On 20 January 1944 the 27-year old pilot had been posted to 156 from PFFNTU for flying duties. Born at Hampstead on 8 January 1917 Brooks had been educated at Reading School and had a home in Ramsey. A RAF pupil pilot in 1937 he had been commissioned that same year and flew Spitfires on 72 Squadron.

'Having just spent a hectic week on leave we were all feeling dead-beat and in need of a few days' rest' recalled Holley. 'We cursed the clot who put off-leave crews on the 'blood-list'. 'We were not altogether happy either when we saw we were being routed on a few miles south of the Ruhr.'

Upwood was a former RFC airfield, which overlooked the Bronte villages of Haworth and Oxenhope just over a mile away, one of many that had benefited from the major expansion of the Royal Air Force announced in 1934 was home not just to Lancasters on 156 Squadron but also to Mosquito bomber crews on 139 Squadron that were putting up eleven Mossies. Early in the war a Jamaican newspaper had started a fund to buy bombers for Britain and in recognition of money raised to buy Blenheims it was decided to link Jamaica with a squadron of the Royal Air Force. Now 139 was part of 8 Group, having become part of the Path Finder force in July 1943. The squadron was briefed to drop 500lb general-purpose bombs on TIs dropped by other PFF Mosquitoes ahead of the Main Force stream of Lancasters and Halifaxes. After bombing, they were to orbit the target and assess results.

At least one of the officers at Upwood was surprised that, although a raid had been announced, people were still allowed to leave the station and outside telephone calls had not been cut off. He and many others expected to hear at any time that the operation had been cancelled.[18]

Flight Sergeant Jack Cuthill's crew had arrived at Upwood after flying four operations on 626 Squadron at Wickenby followed by seven days' leave. Sergeant

Ron Smith, the rear gunner had wondered how they could have been accepted for Path Finder Force; that is until Dougie Aspinall, the mid-upper who was from Doncaster, enjoying the consternation on Smith's face, told him 'The skipper volunteered a few weeks ago, Smithy. He didn't let on, as he thought we wouldn't be accepted, especially after that balls-up on Berlin when we aborted.'

'They must be pushed for crews', interjected another gunner smugly. 'They must be getting the chop right and left.'[19]

Cuthill was a Canadian, from Richmond, British Columbia - later to become a Squadron Leader with the DSO and DFC. The navigator was Geoff Thorneycroft, 'a cheerful individual', from Manchester. The observer/bomb aimer was Bob Trotter, 'a warm, kind individual' from Durban. The wireless operator, Ross 'Toby' Tobin was an Australian from Melbourne, who unlike many of his countrymen was rather shy and introverted. Tony Britton, the engineer, was a bright, engaging personality and the crew comedian, whose occasional impressions of 'Popeye the Sailor man' over the intercom lightened many a 'hairy' situation. By 30 March Ron Smith had completed sixteen operations; three in the preceding ten days and the Squadron's catastrophic losses had been made up again by replacement crews like Walter Brooks' from the PFF Training Unit 'down the road' at Warboys. 'None was without experience and quite a number were on second tours.'

'There was little out of the ordinary about this particular day of squadron routine, although there had been the usual 'flap on' as ops were announced for that evening and some comment at briefing when the route to the target revealed an unusually long leg, without any deviation, direct to Nuremberg from a point near the Belgian-German frontier. 'True, we had not operated to Nuremberg before, but a number of ops in that direction to Schweinfurt and Augsburg had been our lot and although our target that night was some distance further south, no particular alarm, other than the usual pre-op nerves [his diary at the time contains the details of the mental struggle he underwent], troubled my mind as we dressed before being driven out to our aircraft. Yet this raid and its disastrous consequences will remain in the annals of Bomber Command as the cross-roads at which a complete reappraisal of the whole strategy of our offensive was to be undertaken.[20]

The bright moonlight had called forth from Australian Wing Commander Walter Winston Gilronan Scott, the new 'B' Flight commander who had been posted to 156 Squadron at Upwood on 24 February, the remark at briefing to the gunners to keep their eyes peeled, as it would be a night fighter night. This was good advice and all the more pertinent because it came from the mouth of a former Mosquito night fighter pilot.[21]

Twenty-nine year old Flying Officer Sydney Harley Johnson, one of two specialist navigators on Lancaster 'X-X-ray' on 156 Squadron skippered by Squadron Leader 'Dickie' Walbourn DSO DFC had joined the RAAF the day after the bombing of Pearl Harbor. Syd had graduated in law from the University of Western Australia in 1937 and was admitted to the bar in 1940. He tried to enlist as a pilot but was forced to become a navigator. But he argued his case and was one of only a few commissioned as a pilot officer. After initial training in Western Australia and then schools in Mount Gambier, Port Pirie and Nhill he left Melbourne on the *Queen Elizabeth* in 1943. He soon qualified for the rare distinction of being both Primary Visual Marker and Primary Blind Marker. Johnson noted only the customary crew reaction to the briefing when, as usual, the gloomy mid-upper gunner Arthur Irwin, from Birmingham, shook his head at the night sky and said glumly to William Johnson Harrigan Love, the tough, hard-bitten little Australian rear-gunner, 'There's blood on the moon tonight, Bill.' Love, better known as 'Billie' or the 'Dook of Sydney', agreed. Then, again as usual, Irwin began eating the flying rations he was supposed to keep for the return flight from the target. Love, who wore the ribbons of both the DFC and the DFM, was not only the rear turret gunner on 'X-X-ray but also virtually the crew mascot and a popular squadron character. Short, square-shouldered, plain-spoken and aggressive, he was also intensely loyal and a natural imitator and comic and was regarded as 'terrific' by the English airmen whom he lampooned and entertained. To anyone of his own stature his invariable greeting was: 'The trouble with all you little blokes is that you have the same aggressive inferiority complex.' Painted around his four-gun rear turret was the declaration 'Love will find a way'. Legend had it that on one memorable night the intercom warning he gave 'Dickie' Walbourn when the Lancaster was about to be attacked by a night fighter was: 'Love's last word is spoken - dive port!'

'Wally' Walker DFC the wireless air gunner from Sydney rounded off the Aussie contingent on the crew. Walbourn's navigator-plotter was Squadron Leader Les Glasspool DFC born in Stepney, London in 1919 and Sergeant N. R. Truman DFC was the English flight engineer. Another Aussie, Harold Wright, was navigator2. When Harold had applied to join the air force he was considered underweight for his height but after much pestering was finally marked B1 by the doctor who said 'And don't blame me if anything happens!' It took two or three months before his Mr. Wright finally signed his papers - because his son was under 21 - and as he did so the tears were rolling down his cheeks - he honestly believed he had signed Harold's death warrant. In England his son certainly came close on occasion. Wright was on leave when he met Flight Lieutenant George Bruce Loder DFC RAAF who had finished his tour of 45 operations on 156 Squadron but was going to fly a few more trips so that his crew could complete their tour together. As his navigator had fallen off a bus and broken his wrist, Loder asked Wright to fly as a replacement. Wright had agreed but the CO blocked him. Loder was killed over Germany on 20 December 1943, on what would have been his second-last trip. Wright became a 'spare bod' and flew occasional operations. Later, when 'Dickie' Walbourn asked him to join his crew as a permanent member he was not keen. Pestered by Walbourn, Wright tossed a coin and its fall determined that he went with Walbourn to 582 Squadron which formed as a Path Finder Squadron in 8 Group the day after the Nuremburg raid. Wright's replacement on 156 Squadron died on his first operation after he left.[22]

On 83 Squadron at another Path Finder base at Wyton in Huntingdonshire, Australian mid-upper gunner Warrant Officer Alan Geoffrey Strickland from Dromana, a seaside town on Port Phillip Bay near Melbourne sat and listened attentively to the briefing. He was the only Aussie on an otherwise all-English crew on Lancaster 'R-Roger' on 'B' Flight who would act as one of the blind markers. Strickland's pilot was Flight Lieutenant Roy Arthur Charles Hellier DFC*. Flying Officer G. Baxter was the navigator; Pilot Officer R. Haynes, the bomb aimer; Flight Sergeant Frank Wildman DFM, the flight engineer; Flight Sergeant G. Cassey, the wireless operator-air gunner and Flight Sergeant G. Harrison, was the rear gunner.

Strickland noted mainly that the weather forecast indicated the crews could expect cloud cover over most of the route and over the target area.

The briefing would always remain in the mind of Warrant Officer Ken Lane the skipper on Lancaster III ND333 OL-F who felt 'privileged' to be a Path Finder on 83 Squadron. 'Some people are able to remember incidents or dates without difficulty, but with me it has to be something really outstanding to maintain a lasting impression in my mind. The night of 30 March 1944 is a night I cannot forget because my memory is reinforced by three basic points. First, this was the night of the big wind. Second, it was the night when the Lancaster showed qualities which endeared her to all who flew in her. Third, the question is posed 'was this the biggest air defeat of the war'? When Nuremberg was discussed at briefing, there were no exclamations or subdued murmurs such as usually arose when Berlin was mentioned. Not that any target was easy, but Nuremberg did not appear to be worthy of undue comment and naturally no one could be aware of events to follow. Wind speed and direction at a given height was of paramount navigational importance to aircraft of the main force, but perhaps for the Path Finders it was of lesser importance, as special equipment was carried which made it reasonably easy for navigators to find new winds. Using these new winds, appropriate corrections were made and the result was amazing accuracy in navigation which enabled aircraft to be over a given spot at the exact time planned. At take-off, conditions could be perfect, yet only a few hours later the bombers could run into vicious storms, with towering cumulo-nimbus clouds tossing them around like straws in the wind. A cold front could cause ice to build up, often freezing control surfaces, while gale force winds could drive the stream many miles off track.[23]

Richard F. 'Dick' Raymond, his 19-year old flight engineer who had been brought up in North Devon where his father ran a small bakery business founded by his grandfather, had seen more than most men see in a lifetime. On joining 83 Squadron in September he and the rest of Flying Officer Horace Hyde's crew were shown into Wing Commander John Searby's office by the Adjutant. Searby saw all new crews on arrival. He looked at Raymond and said: 'How old are you Sergeant?'

Raymond replied: 'Nineteen Sir.'

'Good God' said Searby.

What Searby did not know was that his flying experience including the training unit was 35 hours and that his first operation would double his night-flying hours.'[24]

On the afternoon of 26 November Raymond survived the ground explosion of Lancaster III JA686 'K-King' which had been bombed up, in this case with one 4,000lb 'Cookie' and six 1,000lb TIs as well as about 1,600 gallons of fuel, just after the crew was dropped off at dispersal for pre-flight checks before the raid on Berlin. Raymond had been in and completed his checks leaving the navigator and the wireless operator still in the aircraft with an electrician who made final adjustments to the flare chute mechanism which contained a live and highly sensitive magnesium flare - commonly referred to as the photo-flash, which was released with the bomb load to record the point of impact of the bombs. While Raymond was having a cup of tea with the ground staff in their Nissen hut 100 yards away, there was a sensation as if someone had hit him in the left ear and he found that he was lying under a piece of corrugated iron and the aircraft had disappeared with its full bomb load, in this case. It was said afterwards that the photo flash slipped from the launching tube and exploded immediately, setting off the 4,000lb bomb which atomised everything within range. Nothing was found of the navigator and wireless operator. Raymond, who had only minor injuries with bits of rubbish in his head and a leg was one of four injured in the explosion, which left three aircrew dead. Five of the ground crew including Warrant Officer Maurice Murphy and Marion White McDowell, a popular WAAF corporal who drove the tractor which pulled the bomb trolleys also perished in the explosion. Raymond's leg turned septic and he was admitted to the RAF General Hospital in Ely. He was still in hospital when, on the night of 28/29 January Flight Lieutenant Horace Hyde's crew were killed when their Lancaster was involved in a collision with a 463 Squadron Lancaster on the trip to Berlin [25].

'Dick' Raymond next flew operationally on 15 February with a new crew on another raid on Berlin. He returned to the squadron without any survivor's leave and sat in the mess until Ken Lane said 'You're flying with me.' After what had happened the smell of an aircraft almost made the young flight engineer vomit. Raymond found it 'shocking' to re-enter a Lancaster. It was almost a death sentence. 'Once you saw your name on the battle order and went to briefing and saw the target and had time to think, that was the worst time. When you were on your way it was better.'

At Wickenby in 1 Group five miles south-west from the town of Market Rasen, Sergeant Ted Shaw, a Canadian rear gunner on Pilot Officer Alfred William Moore's Lancaster crew on 'B' Flight on 12 Squadron attended the briefing with his pilot, who was born in Kintbury, Berkshire. Shaw was a stockbrokers' salesman from Moncton, New Brunswick. The navigator was Warrant Officer J. T. Goodrick, an Australian; Flight Sergeant P. Hocking, the wireless air gunner was a Devon man; Flight Sergeant R. Robinson, bomb aimer, a Welshman from Colwyn Bay; Flight Sergeant V. Peters, mid-upper gunner from Doncaster in Yorkshire and Flight Sergeant T. Ferguson, flight engineer, another Welshman. Shaw reacted cheerfully enough to the explanation that there would be several diversionary raids and this would appear to be another attack on Berlin. 'It was felt that fighter opposition would be concentrated around Berlin and that this could be a rather easy trip,' he recalled.

The need for diversionary ploys had been made uncomfortably clear only a month earlier, when the attack on Leipzig on 19/20 February had cost 82 bombers; Bomber Command's highest loss rate to date. Forty-nine Halifaxes were to sow mines in the Heligoland area and 34 Mosquitoes of 8 Group would be employed on diversionary 'spoofs' to Aachen, Cologne, Kassel and other cities. Thirteen more Mosquitoes would strafe night-fighter airfields at Twente, Volkel, Deelen, Juvincourt and Juliandorf and five aircraft would fly RCM patrols and nineteen Mosquitoes in 100 Group would carry out 'Serrate' patrols.[26] Before the main force reached Nuremberg, nine Mosquitoes were to make a feint attack on Cologne between 2355 hours and 0007 hours. And a second force of twenty Mosquitoes would drop 'spoof' fighter flares, 'Window' and TIs on Kassel between 0026 hours and 0028 hours in the hope that it would fool the JLOs into thinking that the main attack would be somewhere in the Ruhr.[27]

During navigation briefing 19-year old Sergeant W. J. Blackburn and his navigator on 12 Squadron would study intensely the faces of the other navigators and bomb aimers in the room and predict which crews would 'get the chop' that night.

'Sadly, our predictions were astonishingly accurate' recalled Blackburn, who with his crew had by now flown four trips - to Frankfurt twice, Berlin and Essen - all within eight days. The raids had left them, to say the least 'edgy'. Number five would be no different. 'Uncertainty and plain simple terror permeated the stuffy briefing room at that time. Those long, long legs into the heartland of Germany just begged for fighter activity. We finally decided that two of our relatively senior crews appeared to be showing the greatest amount of strain and would likely 'buy it' that night.'

'Foreigners,' wrote Cecil Beaton,[28] only one of many artists who visited RAF stations during the war 'often say that we British do not feel anything deeply. A casual visitor to a RAF station would certainly get this impression from the light-hearted way in which unpleasantness, danger and the war itself are banished from talk. Death is mentioned flippantly, if at all. Someone has 'gone for a Burton' [a beer] or had 'got the chop'; or 'bought it'...But the feeling is there, controlled and smothered by a self-preservation instinct. The realisation of their proximity to danger is never far removed from the minds of the men, in spite of their easy grace of heart.' Very seldom did crews, amongst themselves, say they were on 'operations'. It was either 'dicing with death', 'juggling with Jesus' or 'gambling with God', reduced in most cases to 'dicing', 'juggling' or 'gambling'. Such possibilities could only be accepted by crews with a philosophical shrug of the shoulders. It came with a host of other things but even so most crews were optimistic and they set their sights on completing the mandatory, magical number of thirty operations before being taken off for a rest at some training squadron. In comparison to the numbers involved, very few managed to achieve this; the average could have been as low as five operations before the Grim Reaper called the tune.[29]

Ted Shaw remembered too that the most memorable part of the briefing was the met officer's forecast of five- to seven-tenths cloud 'which proved to be completely wrong.' In the final analysis the Met men preferred their original forecast of wind speeds of up to 50 mph and the flight plan was therefore tailored to complement this assumption. By the 4 o'clock deadline the afternoon, the weather report showed no appreciable change. The only additional information was that on take-off visibility would be poor at most bases but not bad enough to prevent the Lancaster and Halifax bombers from getting airborne. Nos. 4 and 6 Groups were warned to expect valley fog on return and its expectation of a heavy, overcast sky over Germany with thick layers of cloud near to the target. Group commanders were also told that they could expect large amounts of strata cumulus to 8,000 feet with a risk of patchy medium cloud at 15,000 to 16,000 feet. Bomb aimers were warned that with a forecast wind speed of 60 mph at 21,000 feet over Nuremberg in direction 280° they would have to be quick with their bombing. And pilots were told that the wind speed was expected to increase to 70 mph over the French coast on the way home. At 0059 hours two Mosquitoes were to mark with green target illuminators and eight other Mosquitoes would bomb the city one minute later. These aircraft were to release four bundles of 'Window' per minute. The main force was also to use 'Window', dropping it at the rate of one bundle a minute and increasing it to two per minute when the planes were within thirty miles of the target. The duration of the attack would be from 0105 hours to 0122 hours, during which time Nuremberg was to be saturated with 3,000 tons of high explosives and incendiaries.

Twelve Squadron shared Wickenby airfield with 626 Squadron, which had been formed with some crews who had already completed some bombing raids on 12 Squadron. Nineteen-year old Flight Sergeant Brian Soper, flight engineer on Warrant Officer Arthur Rew's crew thought that Nuremberg was probably the 'most frightening of all his raids on Germany. Soper had decided to join the RAF as aircrew following the death of his brother. 'Naturally I was hoping to be a pilot. Unfortunately so was everyone else. I enlisted for aircrew in January 1942 and went for the aircrew medical and a variety of exams and other tests. Rejected as a pilot I was offered 'aircrew' to train as wireless operator-air gunner, which I accepted. Arthur, who was a rather pleasant pilot, already had a navigator, Flight Sergeant 'Butch' Lynn and a wireless operator, Warrant Officer Don Sinnot from Newfoundland. The bomb aimer and front turret gunner, Warrant Officer George Annersly was from Edmonton, Alberta. We had about the oldest man on the squadron; 'Wild Bill' Redding the mid-upper gunner ('who wasn't at all wild') was in his thirties and like me, a sergeant. Bill had a 500cc Norton motor bike on which he used to take part in trials before the war. Any weekend or during standard leave periods he used to take me pillion down to London from whence I got the tube while he went on to Chesham where he lived. This was always quite a lively ride. Finally Sergeant Frank Boyd, rear gunner. No nicer group of guys you could ever wish to meet.'

Soper and his fiancée Mary had agreed to get married if the young flight engineer got through his tour of 'ops'. She was working in a factory in Battersea during the bombing raids, machining uniforms by day and doing part time duties with the London Fire Service so many nights a week.

'It was a clear moonlit night as we were climbing to bombing height. We realised that we were all showing heavy vapour trails. Most of the weather forecast, including wind-speed, was apparently wrong. There were many night fighters about and we saw several aircraft blow up. Because it was so light we also saw aircraft where the crews were bailing out. We had seen Lancs blow up before, but never in so much detail. The pilots changed height several times to try to lose the vapour trails because the night fighters were just sitting above and picking them off from the vapour trails. We also saw what we had been told were 'scarecrows', a device which exploded between 18,000 and 20,000 feet with a lot of smoke and flame but were otherwise harmless. We found out a year or two later that, as we suspected, they were just other exploding bombers. There was so much going on during that first leg of the route, that it was difficult to tell whether aircraft were mostly lost to flak or to night fighters. Some of those shot down must have been Path Finders since some burning on the ground contained ground TI colours. We suspected that the early part of the route may have been known to the Germans. As we continued to gain height up to 22,000 feet - flying at approximately 155mph we lost some of the vapour trails and felt a little safer although it was still very clear. Most of the losses were around the Ruhr area on the first long leg out; Frankfurt, Cologne etc. There was a lot of flak, but I think that the losses were mostly due to the night fighters.'

On 625 Squadron in 1 Group at Kelstern, eighteen miles inland from the seaside resort of Mablethorpe, on the East coast off the Louth to Market Rasen road, thirteen Lancaster crews waited anxiously to see what the fuel load would be that night. For Pilot Officer John Edward Goldsmith, navigator; a Nova Scotian from Halifax, the briefing was bad news. Goldsmith had been a student before joining the RCAF. When the target was announced he and his crew were 'a little shaken up' because this would be the deepest penetration they had so far made into Germany. During the month of March they had already flown on six major operations over Germany in their Lancaster III CF-S, ND407 - Stuttgart on 1 March when four aircraft were lost; Stuttgart again on 15 March, with 40 aircraft lost; Frankfurt, on 18 March with 22 aircraft lost; Frankfurt, again, on 22 March, with 33 aircraft lost; Berlin on 24 March with 73 aircraft lost; and Essen on 26 March with nine aircraft lost. Goldsmith's main reaction to the deep-penetration briefing was a feeling of tiredness and nervousness. Coincidentally, it was the crew's thirteenth operation.

Although crews only discovered at briefing what the 'target for tonight' was, airmen like Russell Margerison, the Lancastrian mid-upper gunner on Lancaster ED940 'P-Peter' could at least make an informed guess. 'Should each Lanc take a bowser and a 'bit' of petrol (2,100 gallons)' he explains, 'the flight would be a long one. Alternatively, should the bowser move on to another aircraft to empty the remainder of its contents - the flight would be of shorter duration. The bomb loads could also be watched as they were winched in. Full bomb loads meant a comparatively short flight, a smaller bomb load a long one. The rest was a guessing game most of the time and whistles of derision went up when the huge wall map was uncovered showing the ribbons leading to Nuremberg. In view of the fact that this was our longest trip to date - we would be airborne for eight hours - this route was not to our liking. But worst of all a bright moonlight was forecast.'

As a youngster brought up in Blackburn in one of the thousands of rented 'two-up' and 'two-down' houses, which all looked alike from within and without, Russell Margerison would run and play in the cobbled streets and run errands to the little corner shop to buy groceries on 'tick'. Young Russ thoroughly enjoyed 'a happy, but uninspired childhood' despite an often strict upbringing. His father, who on seeing him preparing one evening to tackle some homework, carefully picked it up, studiously screwed it into a ball and, with perfect aim neatly threw it into the glowing fire. 'You're at school from 9 o'clock until 4 o'clock, after that the time's your own. Don't ever bring any more homework here.' And so saying he thus guaranteed that his son would never become a bank manager - 'thank God!' 'I did however possess a very strong urge to fly and the outbreak of war ensured that later, I would get the chance I dreamed of and I volunteered for air crew on my eighteenth birthday in November 1942. Much, I may say, to the understandable consternation of my father, who had not only lost his wife but also six of his seven children, I being the only remaining child. He, quite correctly, was far more interested in me making a success of the apprentice compositor's job I had fortunately managed to get on the local newspaper.'

At Operational Training Unit Whitchurch,[30] an attractive village lying amidst the cultivated flats of Shropshire, where training was carried out in old, slow but strong and stable twin-engined Whitleys, Sergeant Sawyer, a pilot, had approached Margerison a number of times. But for some inexplicable reason he always put him off with some lame excuse, finally giving him an outright 'No.' 'It was as well I did for within two weeks he and his new-found crew crashed whilst taking part in a cross-country flight, all six being killed.'

'One afternoon at 1656 HCU Lindholme, a very busy conversion unit near Doncaster, a Lanc taxied into the back of another, slicing through the rear turret and stopping a few feet short of the mid-upper turret. The 19-year old mid-upper gunner, whom I knew well, sat there petrified, staring speechless at this huge monster, so close to his face, which had just gobbled up his best pal. He eventually climbed out, walked slowly over to the flights section, ignoring everyone else around, threw his helmet on the gunnery leader's table and said simply: 'I shall never climb into an aircraft again.' The boy was immediately posted LMF. The initials 'LMF' were well known in aircrew circles and periodically cropped up in conversation. It was a distasteful subject for it stood for 'lack of moral fibre'. As will always happen in wartime, some men (or should I say boys, for that is what we were) crack and can go on no farther. When this happened the boy in question was sent to the Isle of Sheppey, reduced to the rank of AC2 and treated shabbily by men who had never set foot in an aircraft. This never ceased to annoy us and at no time did I ever hear one word of reproach against the 'guilty' person for we were only too well aware that it could happen to any of us. It lies purely in the mental make-up of an individual and one never knows how he will react to a given set of circumstances until tested. Flying was a peculiar job, as indeed were many jobs in the forces. One day a flight would be so thoroughly enjoyable one wanted to do it forever; the next could be so frightening you never wanted to see another plane.'

'During training Taffy, the bomb aimer, who apart from being a bit of a loner, could be rather argumentative and as a consequence caused crew rumblings, was replaced by Arthur 'Brick' Brickenden who, before joining up, was at medical school in Toronto. The Canadian navigator who was prone to air sickness was replaced also, as was Fred Wade their original pilot after crashing while on 1662 HCU in 1 Group at Blyton, a few miles north east of Gainsborough, Lincolnshire. Margerison found out later that from September 1943 to September 1944 there had been no fewer than 120 crashes from Blyton, many of them fatal. 'It was with some trepidation on the part of the remaining four of us who had been involved in the crash that we once again climbed into a Lancaster. Four long months had passed since those eventful seven days.'

Frank Moody, from Huddersfield, a tall, slim, sharp-featured lad of nineteen joined the crew as flight engineer. He proved easy-going and fitted in well with the rest in spite of the disadvantage of being a latecomer to the crew, which finally consisted of one American, three Canadians and three English 'lads'. And then, in January 1944 at Lindholme where numerous trips were made into Doncaster, mainly to Silvio's Cafe followed by the 'Green Dragon', a lively pub in the High Street, a pilot and navigator were found by pure accident. They chattered at length with 1st Lieutenant Max Dowden of the USAAF as he lay sprawled on his bunk eyeing the five of them, a cigarette dangling from his long fingers. 'So us guys are going to crack it together, eh? Dowden announced. 'Welcome aboard' he added.

'We were immediately impressed with this 'Yank; even if he was an 'old man' of twenty-eight years' recalled Margerison. Not only was Margerison and this tall, rangy and craggy-faced American skipper worlds apart; they were quite different in mind and body. Max Dowden was from Santa Cruz, California, where, following a broken engagement, he had joined the RCAF before Pearl Harbor when the US was still neutral. Dowden brought with him his room-mate 'Handsome Dave' Weepers. The navigator's brevet and the word 'Canada' on his shoulder had told its own story.

'Oh no. Bloody hell. Don't tell me we're going to have another Canadian with us,' Dick Reeves the wireless operator said delicately.

'We've enough with this mad bugger,' nodding at Gilbert 'Gib' McElroy the smaller Canadian gunner, who was built and looked incredibly like Edward G. Robinson. 'He was, as Margerison first suspected, a no-nonsense Canadian. If you were his friend, fine; if not then watch out'.

'Handsome Dave' smiled slowly, lifted his hand which was holding his officer's hat and waved it at Dick.

'You don't deserve me you big bastard' 'Handsome Dave' said good-humouredly as he addressed Dick Reeves, six foot two, broad-shouldered and big-nosed, 'but they've sent me over here to show you Limeys the way around.' Dick, who hailed from Tilbury, was a constant source of amusement. He and Margerison were destined to get to know each other like the best of brothers. We were a crew once more.'[31]

Whistles of derision had gone up at briefing at Kelstern when the huge wall map had been uncovered showing the ribbons leading to Nuremberg. 'From the Luftwaffe's point of view' continues Russell Margerison, 'this period of night bombing belonged to them. They had undoubtedly got the upper hand, mainly due to three things. Firstly, the Me 110, whilst not a fast machine, had proved itself to be a very capable night fighter, its twin engines giving it a good operational range - vital for the territory which had to be covered. The machine had recently been fitted with the new secret SN-2 radar, which rendered our 'Window' dropping virtually useless and picking up the bombers had consequently become a far easier task for the German pilots.

'Secondly, the 110 had been fitted with two upward-firing 30 centimetre cannons mounted in the roof, set to fire almost vertically upwards and slightly forwards. The orthodox night fighter attack came from behind, but the fitting of 'Schräge Musik' ('slanting music') as the Germans coded it, enabled the fighter to stealthily climb and fly directly underneath the bomber without being spotted. So successful had this method of attack proved for the Luftwaffe that a number of their pilots had been lost due to the resultant explosion of the target when hit and as a consequence, due to the Me 110 being a very stable gun platform, the pilots actually began aiming at a particular spot - the engines - leaving the bomb bays well alone. A few explosive shells in these were all that was needed. Little wonder the Luftwaffe had nicknamed the 110 the 'Destroyer'.

'And thirdly, they had developed an uncanny knack of ascertaining where a particular raid would be. On this they had a few pointers. The German listening posts situated on the enemy coastline were capable of detecting the switching on of radios and the navigational equipment on the British airfields during the morning tests taking part on each squadron on operation days. They therefore knew a raid would take place that night - but where? It required only the odd agent in England to watch an airfield through field glasses to decide whether a raid would be of deep penetration or otherwise. The rest was a guessing game most of the time, but this knowledge did enable the Luftwaffe to switch their night-fighter force around long before a raid took place. Such was the scene as we raced down the runway in faithful ED940 on our way to bomb Nuremberg, blissfully unaware, as indeed was the whole of Bomber Command, of these recent innovations - and the impending disaster.'[32]

At 1830 at RAF Snaith, Yorkshire in 4 Group seventeen Halifax crews on 51 Squadron entered the briefing room with armed SPs standing guard at the entrance doors and took their seats like expectant patrons at a cinema who had queued waiting to see the 'big picture'. At least two new crews were going to fly their first operation. Flight Sergeant Geoffrey Graham Brougham the 21-year old pilot of LW544 MH-QZ was from Marouba, a beachside suburb east of Sydney. Flight Sergeant Lloyd Francis Peel the 22-year old mid-upper gunner was from Laurel Hill in the south east part of the Riverina near Wagga Wagga straddling the Murrumbidgee River in New South Wales. Flight Sergeant Arthur Henry Williams the 21-year rear gunner was from Pingelly from the wheat-belt region in Western Australia; Flight Sergeant Kenneth McDonald Radley the wireless operator from Dunkeld in the Southern Grampians of Victoria and Flight Sergeant J. H. Gowland the bomb aimer was from Pennant Hills, NSW. There were two Englishmen on the crew: Sergeant H. Williams the flight engineer and Flying Officer Harold Bowling the 32-year old navigator, who was from Whitby in Yorkshire.

The other neophyte crew, on Halifax MH-L on 'B' Flight was skippered by 29-year old Flight Lieutenant Joe Pawell, a cigar-chewing American from Philadelphia who had joined the RCAF with the intention of becoming a 'Yank' in Canadian clothing in Bomber Command. Surrey-born Flight Sergeant William Albert Stenning the married wireless operator on the otherwise all-British crew was a former motorcycle salesman. Flight Sergeants R. F. 'Nobby' Clark, navigator; Robert Burgett, bomb aimer; Alf Barnard, flight engineer and Sergeants Wilf Matthews, mid-upper gunner and 'Jock' Baxter, rear gunner made up the rest of the crew. They had arrived at Snaith on 27 March from forty-eight hours leave after having completed a conversion course from Whitleys to Halifaxes at 1652 Heavy Conversion Unit, Marston Moor, where Group Captain Leonard Cheshire VC had instilled crew discipline in the air and on the ground. Bill Stenning, 'Nobby' Clarke and Alf Barnard reported to the Snaith guard-room on arrival from London and after signing in they were driven in a crew transport by a WAAF driver to their billet about a mile away, almost in the village of Pollington. The Nissen hut was deserted. Unknown to the new arrivals the other occupants had gone to Berlin that night. 'About four in the morning I heard them come in and remember listening to three of them discussing what must have been their worst-ever trip,' said Bill Stenning. 'Apparently the squadron lost two crews that night.' Shaken awake by a corporal next morning, Stenning, Clarke and Barnard were told to report to their pilot, Flight Lieutenant 'Joe' Pawell.

'We were straight away on a familiarization flight,' Stenning recalls. 'We were also detailed for ops that night but the squadron was stood down due to bad weather. Next day the weather was again dicey but we were given a five-hour cross country and then, hardly having had time to think much or look around, 30 March was with us and ops were on again. About 150 of us were present and the big map board was covered. We know overload tanks had been fitted but this, at that stage, didn't mean much to me. Group Captain Noel Holroyde Fresson DFC the station commander entered and our commanding officer Wing Commander Ling opened the proceedings.'

Thirty-two year old Wing Commander Christopher William Mitchell Ling, who was born in Kashmir, India had only just succeeded Wing Commander Richard Cecil Ayling and Squadron Leader Frederick Peter Hill DFC of Bognor Regis, Sussex took the briefing. Hill would fly the operation with a crew consisting of Warrant Officer Reginald Hartley Adams the 24-year old navigator from Wolstanton, Staffordshire; Flight Sergeant Eric Montague Buckingham the bomb aimer from Felixstowe, Suffolk; Flying Officer Albert Peter Cummins the 21-year old wireless operator who hailed from Crewkerne, Somerset; Pilot Officer Frank Leonard Newstead the flight engineer from Balham, London and the two gunners - both 21 - Flight Sergeant Kenneth Dadds was from Twickenham, Middlesex and Sergeant Frank Hobbs came from Swindon, Wiltshire. Most were on their thirteenth operation.

'I remember the cover coming off the briefing map' says Bill Stenning 'and looking at this long, long red tape which seemed to stretch a hell of a long way into Germany. It must have also impressed the others judging by the remarks I overheard. The wing commander informed us that we would be that second wave of a heavy attack on Nuremberg and warned new crews, including us, about keeping in the Main Force bomber stream. Weather seemed good and apart from a long trip carrying mainly 500lb HE bombs and incendiaries it all sounded fairly straightforward. We were to go out over the east coast and cross the enemy coast somewhere below the Frisian Islands. There was to be a feint attack on Berlin while we maintained a course to Nuremberg. Intelligence spoke of expected night-fighter opposition, flak areas on the way back and the fact that Nuremberg was a city with many old timbered buildings. There was a separate signals briefing which I attended and, as a newcomer, was duly detailed to go around the dispersals and check huge quantities of 'Window' parcels for each of the aircraft.

'We met in the sergeants' mess for the ops meal at about 2000. Take-off was scheduled for 2130. By 2100 we were on the crew bus and soon out at the aircraft, checking and re-checking. Wilf Matthews looked like a commando with his two knives, a Colt .45 and a police truncheon.'

At Fiskerton five miles east of Lincoln, Flight Sergeant Walter Frank Morrisby RAAF a 'spare bod' attended main briefing for the crews on 49 Squadron. He was down as rear gunner on Pilot Officer Frank Clark's crew on Lancaster JB178 'Bandlaw V-Victor' on 'B' Flight. He did not know the crew very well, nor was he even sure of their names. After the main briefing he noticed only that, like himself, many crewmembers commented critically on the long, direct, undeviating section of the route from south of Aachen to the turning-point north-west of Nuremberg. The planning also seemed unusual because in contrast to previous operations against heavily defended German cities, this attack was being carried out during a moon period. There was some consolation that 49 Squadron's Lancasters would be flying in the first wave of the bomber stream and might therefore arrive over the target before the night fighters had been directed into action by their controllers.

Earlier in the day, at 1100 hours at Leconfield, north of the windy Humber with the balloon-barrages that guarded the busy port of Hull, Flight Sergeant Harry 'Spider' Webb, from Sketchley Hall, Hinckley, Leicestershire saw Flight Sergeant D. Johnson's crew names listed on the 640 Squadron readiness board. As well as his own and his pilot, they were Flight Sergeant D. J. Hancock, navigator; Flying Officer R. F. Lane RCAF, bomb aimer; Sergeant R. Mitchell, flight engineer; Sergeant J. B. Smith, wireless air gunner and Flight Sergeant C. W. Ellis RCAF, rear gunner. They would be flying Halifax III LW654 C8-D better known as 'D-Dog' on 'A' Flight. Later, Harry checked over his mid-upper turret guns, the gun sight and the hydraulic system. He was not to know how much he would need his guns that night - or the knuckle-bruising trouble he would experience with them. At 1500 sixteen Halifax crews on 640 Squadron and sixteen on 466 Squadron RAAF attended the main briefing. Wing Commander Dudley Thomas Forsyth DFC the 28-year old Commanding Officer of 466 Squadron from South Yarra in Melbourne was on the Battle Order on 'J-Jig'. His DFC Citation said that he 'always displayed the greatest determination to make every sortie a success'. One night in January Forsyth piloted a Halifax detailed to attack Berlin. Early on the outward flight the air-speed indicator became unserviceable. A little later his navigator became deprived of the use of some of his instruments. These difficulties in no way deterred Forsyth, who flew on to the 'Big City' and pressed home his attack. Forsyth's crew consisted of Englishmen Warrant Officer F. Wooton, the navigator from West Bromwich; Flight Lieutenant Nicholson, flight engineer; Flight Sergeant Bennett, WOP/AG and Sergeant E. Dent, rear gunner, Newbiggen, Northumberland and Rhodesian bomb aimer Pilot Officer S. R. Jeffrey and an Australian mid-upper gunner, Pilot Officer J. R. Downton of Sydney. Crews learned that they would be attacking Nuremberg with the second wave of the main bomber stream, assembling for rendezvous over the Wash before setting course for the enemy coast. Forsyth thought that this was the first Bomber Command operation of any size and depth of penetration carried out in the 'moon periods'.

At least one man on the Battle Order had been to the city before, on a school trip. Born André Wejcman in Berlin on 20 January 1923 to Polish Jewish parents (his father was Polish, his mother was American), 'Andy' Wiseman had changed his name on the advice of the Squadron Adjutant. His early childhood was defined by the rise of the Nazis. He was educated at the famous Werner Siemens Real Gymnasium in Schöneberg, saw the rise of Hitler and experienced his first anti-Semitism. In 1934 the Wejcmans fled to their native Warsaw and in August 1939 his father decided to send his son to England to escape the gathering clouds of war and possible German invasion. Upon arrival, Andy attended school in the south of England and then avoided being called up into the Polish army in exile thanks to the timely intervention of General Władysław Eugeniusz Sikorski, to enlist in the RAF to train initially as a pilot and then as an air bomber in South Africa. After finishing training Sergeant 'Andy' Wiseman joined 24-year old Flight Sergeant Barry William Casey's crew on 466 Squadron. He always took a lucky doll knitted by his girlfriend Jean on operations and he would hang it from one of his Australian pilot's instruments in the cockpit of the Halifax.

After the briefing Casey's crew and the others got kitted up and after 'the last supper' went out to their Halifaxes. At 1830 hours, Flight Sergeant Johnson lifted 'D-Dog' and a bomb-load of eighteen 1,000lb bombs plus incendiaries off from Leconfield.[33]

Flight Sergeant Donald Brinkhurst DFM the mid-upper gunner on Lancaster 'L-Love' on 101 Squadron at Ludford Magna was at a friend's house in Lincoln when he was told to report back to camp and also collect any of the crew skippered by Flight Lieutenant William Ian Adamson DFC from Bathgate, West Lothian that he could find. Donald Brinkhurst was born in June 1921 at Wandsworth. He and his brother John Derrick Brinkhurst shared the same parents, Howard Marchant Brinkhurst and Cicely Cox, who married in June 1919 and lived in Slough. John Brinkhurst became a Sergeant pilot on 106 Squadron at Syerston and was killed in action on the night of 21/22 December 1942 when he was the skipper on Lancaster R5914 which was attacked by a night-fighter on the raid on Munich. Two others of his crew were also killed, but Flight Sergeant J. A. Shepherd RNZAF, one of the four survivors (all of whom were taken prisoner of war), reported on the outstanding courage of his pilot. According to Shepherd, when John Brinkhurst was told that the forward escape had jammed he left the aircraft's controls and went into the Lancaster's nose, where the hatch was located and released it. Returning to the cockpit he held the Lancaster steady to enable those who could to escape. John Derrick Brinkhurst was awarded the DFM on 17 April 1945 with effect from 20 December 1942.

It was February 1939 when Don Brinkhurst first made up his mind to join up. On 13 June the eighteen year old was sworn into the RAF and posted to Scampton in Lincolnshire. When training finally started in full swing he was given a rifle and did seven hours drill each day. Pay was two shillings (10p) per day, but after deductions he ended up with only about ten bob (50p) a week. Mostly he walked to Lincoln 4½ miles away. Training lasted about three months, during which he had four days 'Grant', so when he was posted he felt 'pretty smart and thought he knew all the tricks'. After ground crew postings overseas, he re-mustered as an air gunner and finally, on 24 August 1943 a whole crew of sergeants arrived at Ludford Magna to find they had joined a Lancaster squadron in 1 Group.

The Scottish skipper did his 'second dickey' trip to Mannheim on 5/6 September and Brinkhurst and the rest of the Glaswegian's crew flew their first op the following night when the target was Munich. 'We were in the last wave and the kite would not climb too well being a very old kite, but the engineer said the engines were good and that sounded good to me. We soon found ourselves over Augsburg with too much flak for comfort and also not enough of our boys around. But we passed over and made Munich and dropped our bombs before Jerry paid us a visit by giving us a burst which passed under our port wing after the pilot had started a turn to starboard. He started doing a corkscrew and after about five minutes there was no further sign of the Jerry night-fighter. Soon after some flak came up very close on our starboard which made the old kite rock about like a leaf. So we went port and then got another lot under our starboard wing which had us right at nerves end.' They finally landed at Ford and then the engines spluttered one by one having been airborne for nine hours ten minutes on a trip which was to have taken seven and three-quarter hours and for which they had petrol for eight and a half hours!

'We were then given a new 'kite' of our own - 'L-Love' DV264 - and she was the tops. There was never any trouble with her and she was always on the list for flying. The crew was a little different now from when we started ops and Sergeant Murray Cohen RCAF, a Jew and 'a Yank' was the Special Operator.' He did two ops before we went on leave, but would not come with us, so went with another crew and was shot down on Lancaster LM371 on the Berlin raid on the night of 29/30 December

1943.[34] We came back from that leave and met Warrant Officer Fred Honey our new Special Operator who had ten more to do for his second tour. This chap was with me at Kabrit in North Africa and we got on together, so on our crew he was well liked. He flew on eight consecutive operations with us, from 14 January to 24 February 1944 and we managed to finish Fred off with 57 ops under his belt.' Flying Officer Norman Marrian (24) of Chorlton-cum-Hardy, Lancashire took over from him on 25/26 February when the target was Augsburg. Brinkhurst, who was approaching double figures, adds: 'On 15/16 March when we had done twenty trips he had 49 ops to his credit.

The bomb aimer on the crew was Warrant Officer2 Allan G. Hall RCAF of Kingston, Canada; flight engineer was Flight Sergeant Norman Hugh Bowyer DFM of Croydon; the navigator, was Pilot Officer Ernest McClure Kippen DFC of Edinburgh; the wireless operator was Flying Officer Leonard Ryland 'Luff' Luffman DFM of Bournemouth; the rear gunner was Flight Sergeant James Alexander Goodall DFM of Banff, Scotland. All the DFM recipients had gained their awards for an operation one night in December 1943.[35] Luffman's DFM was announced in The London Gazette of 25 January 1944 with the following citation: 'This airman was the wireless operator of an aircraft detailed for a sortie over enemy territory. Before the target was reached the aircraft was hit by shrapnel and the mid-upper gunner was wounded. Sergeant Luffman immediately went to his comrade's assistance, helping him to a rest position and then rendering first aid. Afterwards, he manned the wounded gunner's turret. Soon after leaving the target the aircraft was attacked by four fighters. Sergeant Luffman soon proved his skill by shooting down one of the enemy aircraft whilst his excellent evading directions enabled his pilot to out-manoeuvre the remainder of the attackers. During another sortie, some nights later, his aircraft was attacked by a Junkers 88. Once again Luffman co-operated well with his pilot who successfully evaded the enemy aircraft. This airman has displayed great skill and his courage and resource have been of a high order.'

Now, seven months and several operations later, at about 11.30 on Thursday 30 March, Brinkhurst went out to old 'L-Love' and did his D.I [Daily Inspection]. 'She looked like a million dollars with 33 bombs painted on her side, and fifteen of them were Berlin trips. Also she showed a couple of fighters shot down and at that time two DFMs, which is not a bad record for any aeroplane even as it was she was the oldest kite on the Squadron and we were the oldest crew and so we more or less matched up very well.'

When the crew of 'L-Love' went to the Operations Room and found that the target was Nuremberg, Bill Adamson the Glaswegian skipper who was on his last but one trip, looked worried. 'Normally he would have cracked a joke, as he hardly ever spoke without one; recalled Don Brinkhurst. 'That's what made him the pilot who I would have flown through hell with and known if there was one chance in a million of getting through we would be through.

'We were due to take off first so we would have to be ready before the other crews. I rushed up to my billet as we were going to have an Air Test in the afternoon. So in my hurry I only changed my shirt and slacks. I carried my identity discs and my lucky button. So that was one thing that was off the record for us. Next was the fact that the crew's mascot had left Ludford and gone to Leeds to his father. His name was 'Bill' and he was the funniest little boy I had ever seen and the crew thought the world of him.

'At about 2200 hours the CO came round and said take off was put forward fifteen minutes, so that meant we had to get in straight away and taxi out. Well, in this hurry we nearly all forgot the rear turret duty and so that made things look really blacker for me as I had just remembered that I had my best slacks on and nothing to show for identity if we were shot down. When we went along the runway I felt lost and was glad when we were on our way across the Channel three quarters of an hour later and my mind was on my job and not on fate.'

'Another thing. Mrs. Robinson, where I had breakfast, was talking about people owing her money and how much she would be worth if she could only collect it all. So I said 'Well, I owe you 55/-' and she said 'I am sure of getting yours as you get paid tomorrow.'

'But a bird said to me 'That is a debt you will not pay off Mr. Brinkhurst.'

Endnotes Chapter 3

17 *Into Battle With 57 Squadron* by Roland A. Hammersley DFM (Privately Published, 1992).

18 *The Nuremberg Raid* by Martin Middlebrook.

19 *Rear Gunner Pathfinders* by Ron Smith DFM (Goodhall 1987).

20 *Rear Gunner Pathfinders* by Ron Smith DFM (Goodhall 1987).

21 *They Led The Way; The Story of Pathfinder Squadron 156* by Michael P. Wadsworth (Highgate Publications (Beverley) Ltd 1992).

22 Suffering from sinus trouble one night, Wright was sent to hospital and while there his crew picked up a spare navigator and on 4 October 1944 their aircraft was shot down on a raid on Frankfurt. Wright flew 71 night operations and six day operations, from Düsseldorf in September 1942 to Stuttgart in July 1944. *Chased By The Sun.*

23 Quoted in *The Lancaster at War* by Mike Garbett and Brian Goulding (Ian Allan Ltd, 1971 & 1973).

24 Quoted in *The Lancaster at War* by Mike Garbett and Brian Goulding (Ian Allan Ltd, 1971 & 1973).

25 Quoted in *The Bomber Battle For Berlin* by Air Commodore John Searby (Guild Publishing 1991).

26 'Serrate' was designed to home in on Lichtenstein radar. See *Confounding The Reich* by Martin W Bowman. (Pen & Sword 2004).

27 Additionally, three 'Oboe' Mosquitoes to Oberhausen and one Mosquito to Dortmund and six Stirlings would lay mines off Texel and Le Havre.

28 *In Winged Squadrons* (Hutchinson & Co, 1942).

29 Quoted in *The Nuremberg Raid* by Martin Middlebrook. (Allen Lane 1973).

30 This airfield had opened in 1942 as Whitchurch Heath. Units based here were 81 OTU and 1665 Heavy Conversion Unit for the training of pilots and crews in the operation of Whitley, Stirling and Halifax heavy bombers. In June 1943 Whitchurch Heath was renamed RAF Tilstock.

31 *Boys At War* by Russell Margerison.

32 *Boys At War* by Russell Margerison.

33 *The Nuremberg Massacre* by Geoff Taylor.

34 Seven of the eight crew, including Cohen, survived; the only man to lose his life was the rear gunner, Sergeant John Morton. Cohen was sent to Stalag IVB (Mühlberg).

35 The DFM recipients had their awards Gazetted on 21 December 1945, 25 January 1944 and 21 December 1945 respectively.

Chapter 4

Although built 400 feet above sea level on the southern end of the Lincolnshire Wolds in the space of only ninety days by navvies employed by George Wimpey, Ludford Magna was known as 'Mudford Magma' because it was still marshy. Situated between Louth and east of Market Rasen the airfield was as bleak as the countryside around so locals were few and far between. Just as well. At the bomb dump off the airfield men carefully loaded the 4,000lb high explosive cookies, TIs and incendiaries and tens of thousands of shells on tractor-drawn bomb trolleys and WAAF drivers towed them to the aircraft. Fuel and oil drawn from huge tanks buried remotely filled the great 2,500 gallon capacity petrol bowsers and the oil bowsers, each of which held 450 gallons. All of the 26 'ABC' or 'Airborne Cigar' Lancasters on 101 Squadron could take up to 2,154 gallons in their six wing tanks. When the flight engineer learned the fuel load he would know if it was going to be a long trip. A heavy bomb load and medium fuel load meant it was going to be a short trip. It was no surprise therefore, to one skipper on 'A' Flight, when briefing revealed a red route-tape stretching deep into Germany to Nuremberg, a target that was further even than Leipzig but there was nothing which seemed to indicate to Pilot Officer Robert McHattie that this operation, his fourth, would be any different from the others. Born on 1 March 1916 in Glenrinnes (Dufftown), 'Bob' attended school in Aberdeen and then University where he achieved his MA. In 1939, at 22 years old, he joined Aberdeen City Police before being granted leave to join the RAF in support of the war effort. Like all the secret 'Airborne Cigar' aircraft, McHattie's would be carrying a crew of eight, not seven for its specialized role in the operation. Six of the crew were British by birth - Flight Sergeant Steven Wall, navigator; Flying Officer John Sutherland, bomb aimer; Flight Sergeant John Maxwell, flight engineer and a fellow Scot; Sergeant John Allison, wireless air gunner; Sergeant Colin Bleach, mid-upper gunner and Sergeant Kenneth Exelby, rear gunner. Flight Sergeant Montague Barss RAFVR, son of Daniel and Lily of Ruislip, Middlesex the Jewish special operator was British by naturalization having volunteered on 10 December 1941. Those of the special operators like Monty Barss who were sufficiently fluent in German would also transmit false instructions to the Nachtjagd crews on R/T, diverting them from the bomber stream.

Alone and in the dark half way down the fuselage between the main spar and the mid-upper turret 'Monty's job was to monitor the range of VHF voice radio transmissions between the Jägerleitoffizier (JLO or GCI-controller) and his fighters on a massive piece of equipment consisting of three enormous VHF powerful transmitters covering the radio voice bands used by the Luftwaffe. To help identify the place to jam there was a panoramic receiver covering the same bands. The receiver scanned up and down the bands at high speed and the result of its travel was shown on a time-base calibrated across a cathode ray tube in front of the operator. If there was any traffic on the band it showed as a blip at the appropriate frequency along the line of light that was the time-base. When a 'blip' appeared, one could immediately spot tune the receiver to it and listen to the transmission. If the language was German then it only took a moment to swing the first of the transmitters to the same frequency, press a switch and leave a powerful jamming warble there to prevent the underlying voice being heard. The other two transmitters could then be brought in on other 'blips'. If twenty-four aircraft were flying, spread through the Bomber stream and then there were a potential seventy-two loud jamming transmissions blotting out the night fighters' directions. Jammed off the air the JLO would return on other frequencies but each time Barss and other special operators like 22-year old Pilot Officer Adrian Montague Marks RAAF would patiently hunt down the transmissions until they jammed these too. 'Monty' Marks was born on 12 June 1921 at Potts Point in Sydney. Perhaps he was named Montague because his parents thought he should be in the diplomatic corps and be an ambassador. His pilot was Ken Fillingham, who had been a test pilot for over twelve months. 'This impressed me' 'Monty' recalled 'and Denis Goodlet the flight engineer looked a likely lad, as they say in Yorkshire. Stan Licorice the navigator was the father of our crew. He'd been a school teacher in Canada. At briefing we were advised by the met officer we would have some cloud cover to and from the target. But it was a bright full moon with little cloud cover. Our usual aircraft, 'G-George', was not serviceable at the time, so we were allocated 'J for Joy', whose crew were on leave.'

Flying Officer Edward 'Wally' Wallis RAFVR and crew had arrived at Ludford in early January and had flown seventeen operations. They normally flew 'T-Tare' but were also allocated a replacement aircraft. In their case it was DV407; SR-V Squared'. Flight Sergeant Leslie Francis 'Dig' Condon the crew's Australian wireless operator had a carton of cigarettes stashed away in 'T-Tare'. Although he was just about 'out' he did not want to touch them because they might be a 'good omen'. He hoped he would never need them urgently.

'We were on the Battle Order again and the usual chores were carried out during the day. Briefing was at seven pm and the usual supper at six.'

'Bloody cheese and Goddam Jap tucker again!' said 'Canada' otherwise Flight Sergeant Harvey Elliot Cuthbert RCAF the crew's air bomber. 'Well' I said, 'at least we've got a bloody egg with it this time.'

'Yeah' he said, 'I guess a man should be thankful for small mercies!'

In between chores 'Dig' had sent his fiancée Dianne a telegram and a letter on her twenty-sixth birthday. He did not send her a present as he could not find anything suitable in 'this neck of the woods'. He would have to go to London for cigarettes and he could get her a present there. Also he had something else on his mind. 'Hell, a guy in Boston had wanted to sell me an engagement ring on the way over. Ten bloody dollars he wanted and he reckoned it was worth seventy. I happened to be with a little guy who was a jeweller in Melbourne. He tried it on a plate-glass shop window and reckoned it was the real McCoy. What the bloody hell did I want with an engagement ring at that time though? It sure would have come in handy now.

'We finished our supper and went to Briefing. The target was a place called Nuremberg, to become famous in later years, but not for bombing raids. 'Never bloody heard of it', I told Wally. He had, he assured me. 'Should be better than bloody Berlin', 'Ginger' remarked. 'Ginge' was the nickname given to Sergeant John Wilson Dunbar RAFVR the mid-upper gunner. The rest of Wallis' crew consisted of Flight Sergeant Philip Langley Walker Cairns RAFVR, navigator, who went by the name 'Len'; Sergeant Patrick 'Paddy' Morrisey RAFVR was the flight engineer; rear gunner was Sergeant John 'Jock' Edwin Powney RAFVR and Flying Officer Clyde Frank Adams Clothier RAFVR who was nicknamed 'Eddie' was the Special Operator.

SOs worked concentratedly on the journeys out and home for several hours, but over the target they could only wait. Once the bombers were near the target it was obvious to the enemy where they were going, so jamming was superfluous. The jamming and transmitting of false instructions by transmitters carried by the bombers and high-powered transmitters in England were very effective. The Luftwaffe night fighter force war diarist noted: 'Korps VHF radio jammed by bell sounds; R/T traffic hardly possible; jamming of Korps HF by quotations from Führer's speeches. Korps alternative frequency strongly jammed.'[37] In an effort to break through the jamming, German controllers tried to use slow Morse, which was then countered by installing false slow Morse transmitters in the 101 Squadron Lancasters. German conversations and call signs were logged and passed to RAF Intelligence, before being countered. The frustration among the Nachtjagd controllers at times came to the surface when 'ABC' operators suddenly heard 'Get off the air you English Swine!' The Germans tried all manner of devices to overcome the jamming, including having their instructions sung by Wagnerian sopranos. This was to fool the operators into thinking it was just a civilian channel and not worth jamming.

101 was a three flight squadron, flying up to 24 Lancasters in the bomber stream. Because of the weight of the radio equipment and extra crew member the aircraft had a reduced bomb load. On 'B' Flight, Flight Lieutenant Robin Herbert Knights DFC captain of Lancaster LL773 SR-D, was carrying a 4,000lb 'cookie' or high-blast 'blockbuster' bomb and fourteen containers of clustered thermite incendiary bombs for fire-raising. He too had not thought there was anything especially significant about the briefing - 101 Squadron would as usual be flying its Lancasters spaced out at intervals of one minute along the bomber stream - but there was, as Knights recalls it, the usual 'sinking feeling' when the target location was revealed as being so deep inside enemy territory. Knights had been a farm worker and a regular soldier before transferring to the RAF in June 1941. Bomb aimer Sergeant Morgan and the mid-upper gunner, Sergeant Hart were second-tour veterans who had replaced Knights' original two gunners, killed over Berlin on 20 January 1944. That same night Flying Officer Ferguson George Donaldson Smith DFC* the special operator sustained severe injuries, being wounded in the back, the chest and the leg, but refrained from reporting his injuries, instead working heroically to rescue the two gunners who were trapped in their turrets. Not until it was apparent that both men were beyond assistance did Smith relax his efforts. Meanwhile the pilot pressed on to the target which the crew bombed successfully before making the long and hazardous return trip. Despite his wounds, Smith remained at his post and skillfully navigated the defenceless Lancaster back to base where the pilot made an emergency landing. Both men were awarded an immediate DFC, the citation for Smith concluding that 'his courage, fortitude and determination were worthy of the highest praise'.

Smith spent several months recovering before returning to 101, where he flew on operations for another year. Known as 'Ferg' or 'Fergie', Smith was born in Aberdeen on 5 October 1914 into a family of wholesale grocers who claimed to have introduced Robertson's marmalade to the breakfast tables of northern Scotland. He was an outstanding sportsman at Aberdeen grammar school, where he was head of school and captain of rugby and cricket. With the Cairngorms just a long bike ride away, he developed a lifelong love of mountains. Apart from eighteen months as a constable on the beat and his wartime service, he spent his whole working life in Special Branch, which he joined in 1936. His mother disapproved of his career choice, regarding it as 'a thorough waste of a good education'. He enlisted into the RAF volunteer reserve in July 1941 and trained as a navigator in Canada, where he was commissioned. A man with a rigorous attention to detail, quiet manner and dry sense of humour, on his return to Britain and after further training, in August 1943 he joined 101 Squadron where his ability to speak fluent German, French and Russian was invaluable. After Berlin his place in the crew was taken by Flying Officer Crosette. The others in the crew were Sergeants Pinner, navigator, Ferry, flight engineer, Bromeley the wireless air gunner and Sergeant Murphy, rear gunner.

For Smith, Crosette and 'Monty' Barss and the other special operators the nightly game of electronic cat-and-mouse were as demanding as it was frustrating, if not disastrous for the Luftwaffe controllers and their impatient pilots. It was also dangerous. 'Monty' Barss was killed in action on the night of 12/13 August on Lancaster III LM598 SR-M2 over Brunswick.

'The trip would take seven-odd hours' recalls 'Dig' Condon 'and all the rest of the gen was passed on to us by the various group leaders. In the crew room there was laughter and swearing as usual. Over in one corner of the room, quietly gathered together, was Pilot Officer Donald James Irving's crew.' Irving was twenty-six and came from Bondi, New South Wales. He was one of six Australians on the crew of Lancaster I LL861 'H-Harry'. 'They'd only been here a couple of weeks. I hadn't had a chance to have a good yarn to them, as I never saw them in the ante-room at the Mess or in the pub. They were a pretty 'churchy' mob, which was uncommon. Maybe I should have gone and met them there. They didn't appear to drink at all and definitely weren't the rowdy types. They were gathered around one of the crew at the moment. I sauntered over and 'Wally' followed me. It was the wireless operator they were apparently worried about. He was really in a bad way. He was scared and reckoned he had a premonition that they weren't coming back. Wally and I both tried to console him with a few chosen words. He was as white as a sheet. He said he'd probably be OK once they got into the air. I sincerely hoped so as a guy in that frame of mind wouldn't be much good on ops. That scary feeling can be contagious and spread to the rest of the crew. We wished them the best of luck and left them, as it was time to go. There were only two crews in front of us now as far as ops went, except of course for the three Fight Commanders. Neither of those two crews made the elusive bloody thirty.'

Climbing into flying gear, collecting flight rations and stowing escape kits in their battledress jacket pockets, 'Bob' McHattie and his crew were out at their waiting aircraft, Lancaster III DV298 SR-E, an hour before take-off. After checking all their equipment for serviceability they spent the last, long half-hour chatting with their ground crew and the crews of Lancasters at neighbouring dispersal points. At 2135 hours ME565 SR-W *Wing and a Prayer,* captained by Pilot Officer Russell 'Rusty' Waughman was the first of 26 Lancasters on 101 Squadron to take off. The 20-year old son of a Durham colliery worker had already won a personal battle, triumphing over adversity; as a child he had suffered bouts of diphtheria and tuberculosis but had sailed through the aircrew medical.

'You were not just one sitting at the front; we had seven others at the back doing a job: John 'Curly' Ormerod, flight engineer; Alec 'Jumbo' Cowan, navigator; Idris 'Taffy' Arndell, wireless operator; Tommy Dewsbury, mid-upper gunner; Harry 'Tiger' Nunn, rear gunner; Norman 'Babe' Westby, bomb aimer and Edward 'Ted' Manners the special operator. We trusted each other and relied on each other. If the rear gunner said 'dive starboard go!' you didn't say 'why?' It was too late if we did.'

One by one the heavily laden bombers followed at ninety-second intervals to allow the 'ABC' jammers to spread throughout the bomber stream. All were airborne by 2215 and they were soon over the North Sea where they rendezvoused with the Lancasters and Halifaxes of 3, 4, 5, 6 and 8 Groups that would make up the main bomber stream which, when complete, would stretch for sixty-eight miles. At Ludford the service personnel on the station went about their duties and waited for the bombers which were expected return in eight hours' time.

On Lancaster III DV276 Pilot Officer John 'Jimmy' Batten-Smith DFC the 22 year old skipper and Pilot Officer Howard Ernest Beer, the 21-year old flight engineer of Mutley, Plymouth in Devon started 'R-Robert's engines, ran them up and went through their check lists. Flight Sergeant Allan Henry Ross the 22-year old wireless operator who was from Edinburgh, sat at his station and checked his radio equipment and other systems. In the nose of the aircraft Pilot Officer Graham Harries Williams the bomb aimer of Millom, Cumberland checked his bombing panel, bomb sight and front turret. Sergeant Robert Armstrong the 20-year old navigator of Auldgirth, Dumfriesshire checked his instruments and radar aids. The rear gunner, 21-year old Flight Sergeant Arthur Haynes of Foxton, Cambridgeshire, checked his turret to make sure that everything was as it should be. The rear gunners on 'ABC' Lancasters had heavier machine guns than usual, because the aircraft were especially vulnerable transmitting over enemy territory. Sergeant Robert Russell Roberts the 23-year old Scottish specialist operator from Stenhousemuir in Stirlingshire took his seat aft of the main spar on the port side of the aircraft immediately above the bomb bay at a desk with three transmitters and a cathode-ray screen. His nearest human contact were the boots of the 19-year old mid-upper gunner, Sergeant Hugh Fleming McClenaghan from High Blantyre, Lanarkshire, four feet away. Since there was no room for the SO in the heated forward section of the Lancaster he and Haynes and McClenaghan had to wear bulky electric suits, slippers and gloves, dangerous if a rushed exit were required. At 20,000 feet over Europe in winter, temperatures often fell to minus 50C, so the SO would have to wear gloves even though these made it difficult to operate switches. He would lose the skin of his fingers if he attempted to touch metal without them. It was common to have to pull off chunks of frozen condensation from oxygen masks during the flight. The concentrated work of jamming kept the SO's minds off minor discomforts for most of the flight.

'Jimmy' Batten-Smith took 'R-Robert' off at 2205 watched by his girlfriend, WAAF Section Officer Patricia Bourne and others on the flight line. 'Jimmy' had left her a letter written to his parents John and Kathleen Beulah who lived at Fernhill, Nilgiris in India. It was something he had done on each of his 21 operations but this time he also gave her his writing case and asked her to say a silent prayer for his safety at one o'clock that night before she went back to sleep. Patricia, who serviced the aircrews' flying equipment, agreed to his request and set her alarm clock accordingly.

'Taxiing out and take-off were normal' says Robert McHattie. 'It was a very cold, frosty evening and there was a cloudless sky with a very bright moon already high in the sky. We climbed to 6,000 feet over base before setting course for rendezvous with the bomber stream at the enemy coast at the appointed time. I was detailed to a position near the front of the stream. A friendly aircraft passed overhead and on looking up, I could see the aircraft's contrail clearly in the moonlight although I could not see the aircraft. This was a bad sign to me because I estimated the height of the contrail at about 15,000 feet and I turned to my crew and said that this indicated a record 'chop'. 'Soon our troubles started. During initial climb the navigation lights refused to go out when switched off. This was easily remedied by removing the fuses. Before we reached the enemy coast the mid-upper gunner reported electrical failure. This would mean that he would have no suit-heating. It was a bitterly cold night: -45° centigrade at 21,000 feet and I felt sure he could not survive long as a useful crew member in these conditions. I ordered him to stay in his turret as long as he could but to vacate it before he lost consciousness and to go to the astro position and keep a fighter watch from there. About half an hour later he reported he was leaving his turret. By this time we were above 16,000 feet and making contrails. Enemy activity in the form of night fighters had begun and contrailing was consequently very dangerous. The enemy fighters merely had to fly along the contrails until they came to their quarry and then shoot it down.' The main impression that Knights had of the events after take-off was of 'a long drag on a very dark night'.

Pilot Officer 'Monty' Marks the Australian Special Operator on 'J for Joy' recalled that once airborne the crew had a real problem. 'The aircraft could not gain altitude at the speed of the bomber stream, so we had a choice: to keep up with the others and be well below their height, or to climb to the height of the others, but fall well behind and risk arriving over the target alone. The crew discussed the options over the intercom and agreed to gain the operational altitude of the stream rather than have bombs from our own aircraft falling around us and possibly on us and to accept the risk of being alone to and from the target. Twenty-five or so minutes prior to the time the raid was scheduled to begin, I picked up on my 'ABC' receiver the message, 'Achtung Nürnburg'; the target having been identified. I warned my crew that we could expect more night-fighters than normal. As usual it was a zigzag course to and from the target and I often wondered if someone back home had been careless in their conversation and that it had been picked up by an unfriendly person and made known to the Germans. We arrived over Nuremberg 20-25 minutes late, all by ourselves, but at the correct altitude. The city appeared to be on fire in several areas, as I could see the target once the bomb doors were open.' As we approached the target Ken Connell our bomb aimer was directing the pilot and he suddenly burst into song:

The game was played on Sunday
It was played in Christ's back yard
Jesus was playing left forward
And Moses playing left guard.

'We dropped our bombs and got the hell out of the area and headed for home. At no stage did we encounter any enemy aircraft.'

'We took off and climbed for height, again through cloud' recalls 'Dig' Condon. 'I had 'Monica' switched on and it worked well under these conditions. Not a plane came close enough to worry us before we broke the tops of that cloud. Besides, this climbing through cloud wasn't as hairy now. We didn't just circle around base anymore, but flew three sides or courses, predetermined by the navigational wizards, of an equilateral triangle, measured in such a manner to have us track back over base at the correct time and height to set course out over the Wash. Each squadron had, in theory, its own piece of sky. It was supposed to be almost impossible to be on a collision course with other aircraft. How well it worked I don't know, but at least it made our minds a bit easier. We broke cloud at fourteen thousand and as predicted the further we flew in an easterly direction the thinner the cloud became. There was none at all up to our north. Our route took us in just south of or skirting the Ruhr Valley, where the Dam Busters had caused such havoc. We were to learn later it hadn't affected those bloody searchlights to any degree. We crossed the enemy coast at 22,000 feet. As we approached the Ruhr, every searchlight in the south of the Valley was switched on. They weren't searching and wavering in the usual manner; they weren't close enough for that, but they certainly lit up the night sky. They just pointed in our direction, or along our route. Then the fighter flares appeared along our course as well. That was bloody unusual this far away from the target. Something bloody very funny going on here. 'Hey, Len' Wally said, 'How would it affect you if I veered seven or eight degrees to the south?' 'Wait a minute' Len said. I moved so he could have a look at the situation. 'A good idea by the look of things', Len reported when he got back to his table. Wally started to slowly edge to the south. 'Keep your eyes open for other kites' Wally said.'We did, but the only other aircraft we saw were Lancs and they were below us. There were plenty where we'd just left though, to our port, easily seen against those stinking searchlights and fighter flares. We turned back on our original course and Len gave a slight change in that. 'That's the best bloody idea he's had for a month Len', I said. 'Yes', he said, 'I think so too!'

'How are you gunners going down there? We may need you shortly by the bloody look of things', I said. They were both OK. All hell had broken loose to the north. Tracer bullets were whizzing across the night sky in all directions. I saw a couple of Lancs go up already. They disappeared down into the cloud like flaming meteors. Eddie, the special, reported the biggest babble of words on German radio he had ever heard. Within the space of five minutes I must have seen another ten Lancs go up like those first two to go the same way. The bloody fighters were well and truly into the stream of bombers. Twice we were attacked, but as they came in from our starboard to catch us against the light, we corkscrewed in that direction. The fighters kept bearing towards those lights, looking for easier prey. Ginge and Jack helped speed them on their way with heavy bursts from their guns. One was a Focke Wulf 190; the other a Me 109. Those corkscrews had been pretty violent and my gear was scattered all over - but bugger it. I was too busy watching what was going on. Eddie reported again: 'They know our course and everything, Wally.' 'Oh well', Wally said, 'Can't be helped now. We're doing alright so far.' Paddy then piped in: 'That must be those new rockets the gunners are using.' 'What do you mean, Paddy?' I asked him. 'Those meteor-like lights you see going along and down into the cloud.'

'Use your bloody noggin, Paddy; they're burning bloody Lancs or Hallies. That's what that is! Rockets, my aching arse!'

'Yes I think you are right 'Dig' looking again', he said.

'Course he's bloody right', interrupted Ginge. 'OK, you chaps', from Wally, 'Less yapping and more looking for bloody fighters. Concentrate on our starboard, you gunners. You, Dig, will have to look into those lights. Have you tried that visual 'Monica' Dig?' 'A couple of times Wally' I told him. 'Not worth a bellyful of piss!'

'OK 'Dig' he said. We all kept quiet now. Hell, they were sure getting the shit kicked out of them to our north. Some bastard had dropped his guts, or German Intelligence had found out something they shouldn't have. It was a bloody trap if ever there was one, or a bloody sell-out. Every fighter Hitler had at his disposal for bloody miles around was up here. They were shutting that trap and how. That change of course was paying off dividends for us. But, we weren't half way to the target yet! If they know our course, the German bastards may even know our target. I asked Eddie, but he hadn't heard it mentioned. They knew we had these specials up here with us, though, so if they did know the target they weren't about to let us know they did. It would be bloody lovely if they met us over the target as well! Gradually we left the carnage behind us and droned on into the welcome darkness. Len gave us the thumb when it was twenty minutes to ETA target. Not a light or a flare in front of us. Hope he hadn't made a blue in his navigation. However, we were now - thank Christ - right at the head of the main force on ops. Zero hour minus two minutes. That was our time for bombing now that we had the experience. Hope those Path Finder boys had got through back there.

‘With only a couple of minutes to go, Canada yelled: 'I see the markers, Wally. Five degrees to starboard.' 'Yes, I see them now, ‘Canada', Wally said. 'Bloody hell, they're scattered. I'll aim for the thickest clump I can see.'

'OK', Wally said. 'Talk me in ‘Canada'.

'OK, Wally' from ‘Canada'. 'Two degrees to port. Bomb bay doors open.' Then a few searchlights, but scattered also. I couldn't see another bloody plane. Canada said: 'I can see a couple more Lancs below us. This must be the bloody joint'.

‘Canada' gave a few more small corrections of course. I was down over the Cookie. Then 'bombs gone' from ‘Canada'. I waited for the photoflash to go off. I got an instant glimpse of built-up area, I think, before the bomb-bays closed. Shit - where was every other bastard? They may be late owing to that shemozzle back there. Jesus, this was the most sporadic attack we'd ever seen, we all reckoned. ‘Piss-poor' ‘Canada' described it. There were no fighters. The bastards were all back at the Ruhr. They wouldn't have the range to follow us without refuelling and rearming; also, by the amount of tracer they had let loose near the Ruhr. By the look of things, though, those bloody fighters had done a good job for the Fatherland. They had broken up the Bomber Command attack. Bugger their luck. We changed course south, then westwards and headed home. We'd miss that Ruhr Valley on the way home, but as Eddie pointed out; if they knew our way in, they may know our way out. By the time we reached the enemy coast, they would have had time to land, refuel, rearm and be waiting for us again. Couldn't be as bad though. They'd be without those searchlights to see us against. They still had their fighter planes, but we could dodge them; put our nose down and get out of Germany like a bat out of hell, now we'd got rid of the bombs. We'd be a bit more bloody versatile on the way out and that was for sure.'

‘The trip back, as it turned out, was long, dark and uneventful' recalled ‘Dig' Condon. ‘Ten minutes from base, Wally called ‘Millpond'. The husky female voice answered and sounded relieved. She even asked if we needed any aid on landing and Wally assured her we did not. Something was wrong for sure. There wasn't another Lanc in the circuit and the airwaves were conspicuously quiet. We got our landing instructions. The runway was No. 1, north to south. Winds were gusting up to forty miles an hour and would cause a drift to port. That wouldn't worry us - we were home. Then, as we were on the downwind leg, we heard a male voice and it sounded very bloody worried. He requested emergency landing procedure and also an ambulance.

We were told to go round again. We did just that and Wally said, 'That's bloody old 'Screwy'[36]. He told me he was taking a sprog crew on 'S-Sugar'. He must have troubles to request an ambulance.' We caught sight of his navigation lights as he made his final approach. We weren't a minute behind him and taxied round to our dispersal. He was in the next bay. We got quickly out of the aircraft and there were bods running everywhere. We scrambled straight across to their dispersal and wished we hadn't been so bloody inquisitive. Lights were now focused on the back of the plane. The tail plane and the turret were a tangled mass of bloody scrap metal. Half the rear turret was missing, as was the rear gunner. 'Oh Jesus', I thought and could have easily spewed. My guts heaved. We all moved away, except 'Wally'. There was absolutely nothing we could do. Wally rescued 'Screwy' from the mob around the plane. He took him aside. Another vehicle pulled up near the rear of the plane. We knew what that would be. After about five minutes, Wally left 'Screwy' and came across to us. They took Screwy to the ambulance and the rest of the crew also.

'Anyone else hurt?' we all asked Wally at the same time.

'No', said Wally. 'They are all shook up a bit, that's all. They're taking them to Sick bay. Probably give them a sedative or something. The wireless operator may need more. By what Screwy was able to tell me, they had a pretty rough bloody trip. They got off course approaching the Ruhr and it had to be north of track. The navigator blames himself for the lot. Screwy can't recall as yet how many times they were attacked by fighters. He tried to scramble out of it to the south. The rear gunner claimed he blew a Me 109 to pieces, verified by the mid-upper gunner and the wireless operator. They were almost out of strife when the last attack caught them unawares. The rear gunner, as you saw, was killed instantly by a cannon shell. The wireless operator went back to assess the damage. When he saw the mess the gunner was in, he just spewed into his oxygen mask. He chewed it up and swallowed it, he told Screwy. No one else got a scratch and as the kite was handling alright, they decided to press on. Nothing they could do for the rear gunner anyhow.'

'We were all silent for a minute and then Canada said: 'Fancy swallowing your own Goddam spew.' He spat on the ground.

'Aw shut up, Canada' said 'Ginge'- 'You big, gruesome Canadian bastard!'

'Bloody hell', I said; 'I nearly threw up myself, Ginger. Let's shut up about it.'

'Come on', Wally said, 'The crew truck's waiting for us.'

'We went back to our own dispersal, climbed aboard the truck and it took us round to the Flights. Everyone around here seemed to be in a helluva flap. We got out of our flying gear in a hurry and two Flight Commanders were waiting for us. They ushered us into the big interrogation room with its separate cubicles. We wouldn't have had to worry about getting a cubicle tonight, as no other bastard was in the place except us and the interrogation officers. There were the Flight Commanders and a couple of other officers as well. We had a good audience. One of them asked: 'What's been going on over there? You're only the tenth to land. Six of them didn't reach the target. Four more don't know if they did or not. That's fourteen out of a total of twenty-eight.

'Where's the rest of them?'

Endnotes Chapter 4

36 Pilot Officer Harold Davies RAFVR pilotting DV245; SR-S *The Saint* to Nuremberg that night.

37 Quoted in *Sky Battles! Dramatic Air Warfare Actions* by Alfred Price (Arms & Armour Press 1993).

Chapter 5

Sergeant Donald Stewart RAFVR, a 20-year old wireless operator from Finsbury Park, Middlesex on 424 'Tiger' Squadron RCAF at Skipton-on-Swale had an extra special reason for wanting to return from the raid on Nuremberg. Two weeks' earlier he had married his fiancée Joan and had been promised leave for a honeymoon if he volunteered as a replacement wireless operator and air gunner on Halifax III LV879 'A-Apple' skippered by 31-year old Flying Officer John Doig who was from Winnipeg, Manitoba. The rest of Doig's crew consisted of Sergeant John Stanley Bolton RAFVR, the flight engineer from Birmingham, Flying Officer John R. Marsh RCAF the navigator; 22-year old Flight Sergeant Alfred Hirst Crosland RCAF the air bomber of Pickering, Ontario who would be flying only his second operation and the two gunners, 27-year old Sergeant Robert James Atkins RCAF of Petrolia, Ontario and Sergeant Thomas James Rogers RAFVR who was from Kidwell, Carmarthenshire. The crew was on its second operation.

In all, twelve Halifax crews on 433 'Porcupine' Squadron and another dozen on 424 'Tiger' Squadron in 6 Group RCAF attended the briefing at Skipton-on-Swale, which was about four miles west of Thirsk on the east bank of the River Swale north of the small village in the Hambleton district of North Yorkshire. A squally March wind spattered the windows and rattled the roof as the Met man took the stage. The briefing was remarkable only in that the met officer was 'a bit vague' about what the weather would be like over the target. That was according to Sergeant George Dykes, the rear gunner on Pilot Officer Ronald Reinelt's crew on 'Q-Queenie' on 'B' Flight on 433 'Porcupine' Squadron. Dykes, who was born in Troon, Scotland in 1906, had moved to Canada where he enlisted on 9 November 1939 in Saskatoon, Saskatchewan. After having flown four ops on 429 'Bison' Squadron, Reinelt's crew had been posted to Skipton as part of the nucleus of five crews to start 433 Squadron, which had been adopted by the Porcupine District of Northern Ontario. Its motto was *Qui s'y frotte s'y pique* ('Who opposes it gets hurt') or 'whoever rubs himself there will be pricked there'. Sergeant Doug Carruthers was the crew's Canadian mid-upper gunner; Sergeant A. R. W. 'Johnny' Hardes, navigator; Sergeant J. E. Peppercorn, flight engineer; Sergeant D. H. 'Taffy' Williams the Welsh wireless operator-air gunner and 21-year old Pilot Officer George 'Geordie' Wade, bomb aimer, who recalled: 'At Skipton we flew Halifax Mk III's under the leadership of Wing Commander Clive Sinton, a superb CO and the aircraft were totally trustworthy and good performers. In a tragic accident in late December 1943 an aircraft piloted by Flying Officer Peter Rowland Humphries was taking off at Skipton and crashed into our aircraft which was parked at dispersal. The five crew members and two ground crew members were all killed and both planes were destroyed in the resulting blaze. Since I was the only officer in our crew at the time, I was appointed officer in charge of the escort party at the funeral of these seven men. The funeral took place in Harrogate on Christmas Eve which was a very frosty day. It was a truly miserable occasion. I cannot imagine what was put in the coffins since both planes were reduced to ashes. Normally each carried 1,800 gallons of petrol plus ammunition for the guns and some flares.'

'Geordie' had trained on H_2S and 'Gee' while the Squadron was expanding and his task apart from bombing was to take and log fixes every two minutes when possible, sitting alongside the navigator. He assisted the pilot with engine controls on take-off and landing and took over from him occasionally especially on training flights and returns from operations. He was also expected to be emergency pilot as well as deputising for other crew members, should the need arise.

Pilot Officer Jens Paul Christian Nielsen RCAF and crew on HX272 *Nielson's Nuthouse* on 'B' Flight on 433 'Porcupine' Squadron had 27 operations on 419 'Moose' Squadron and before that on 405 'Vancouver' Squadron in the Path Finder Force. Just one more trip and the crew could say goodbye to the 'Porcupine' Squadron. Screened from operations after surviving a full tour, they would be sent home as instructors. Warrant Officer2 John Gilchrist 'Moe' McLauchlan the rear gunner who had been educated at Fort Garry schools and was a member of the Wildwood Badminton club, had trained at Saskatoon and graduated as an air-gunner from Macdonald, proceeding overseas in February 1943. He now had a total of 26 bombing trips over enemy territory and had already chosen the RCAF station in Canada where he would be posted. Yet, uneasily, he could not really believe that their luck would last. Observing ground crews fitting overload fuel tanks to the Halifaxes, he hoped that the long-distance target was not Nuremberg. The crew had been there twice before; a long, dreary, eight-hour trip. The last time McLauchlan had shot down a Dornier 217 night fighter which had attacked and damaged *Nielsen's Nuthouse*. Nielsen, or the 'Mad Dane' as he was known, was born in Denmark on 1 November 1922 and arrived in Montreal, Quebec on 5 September 1929. He enlisted in Toronto in August 1942. He and Pilot Officer Don McLean Awrey RCAF the navigator had both been awarded the DFC for this action.

As the day wore on McLauchlan could not suppress the feeling that the crew would not be coming back. So much so that, after a briefing at which the aircrews were assured of cloud cover all the way into the target and most of the way back again, he gave away all his shirts and a new uniform to another crew not on operations that night. Then, having checked and cleaned the guns in his turret, he settled down to an unusually hearty ops tea of four poached eggs. 'Somehow I knew it was to be my last meal in England,' he recalled.

Chris Nielsen would have with him Canadian Flight Sergeant William Francis Rost from Montreal, a new pilot on the squadron who was making his 'second dickey' trip to gain operational experience before taking his own crew on their first operation. The others on the crew were Warrant Officer Leo Victor Milward, bomb aimer from Moosomin, Saskatchewan; Sergeant Christopher Witton 'Chris' Panton the 19-year old flight engineer from Old Bolingbroke in Lincolnshire, who wanted one day to become a pilot; Warrant Officer Harry Cooper, wireless air gunner and Sergeant James Sturgeon Thompson, mid-upper gunner from Belfast. After chuckling over a bawdy story told them by the padre who had come out to wish them luck and farewell at their darkened Halifax, they climbed into *Nielsen's Nuthouse* and once more went through the familiar drills and rituals which had brought them safely home on all their other trips before. Take-off was 2149 hours, four minutes after 'Q-Queenie', whose crew got away without incident, but George Dykes heard Reinelt and his flight engineer on intercom discussing the sluggish performance of the Halifax III. It was noticeable that climbing to the prescribed height of 20,000 feet before crossing the Dutch coast was not easily achieved. 'Flak was light along our track on the way in and we did not see any enemy aircraft. Nor did we see too many of our own aircraft despite the fact that there were about 800 bombers taking part.'

Skellingthorpe, within the boundary of the City of Lincoln was in 5 Group. At 1930 hours, 23-year old Pilot Officer David Austin Jennings RAAF, a Tasmainian from Hobart, and his crew sat down to a comparatively relaxed pre-operations meal with eighteen other Lancaster crews. His crew, on VN-N in 'B' Flight on 50 Squadron were the usual mix of nationalities. The skipper and Warrant Officer W. C. Hughes, wireless air gunner and Flight Sergeant Brian John Francis Xavier Hayes, mid-upper gunner were Aussies; Pilot Officer T. Carroll, navigator; and Flight Sergeant's H. Turton, bomb aimer and A. C. Matthews, rear gunner were Englishmen. A lone Scotsman, Flight Sergeant 'Jock' Stevens, was the flight engineer. The crew had volunteered for the Path Finder Force so this was to be their last trip on 50 Squadron. Hayes had noticed nothing significant about the reaction of 50 Squadron's crews to the briefing. If anything there was a noticeable lack of the muttering and uneasy stirring, which customarily greeted briefings for the traditionally tougher targets of the 'Big City' or 'Happy Valley'. Even the weather forecast for clear skies and moonlight did not unduly disturb them.

At another table sat Pilot Officer R. H. 'Rusty' Lloyd DFC and crew on Lancaster LL842 VN-F. Lloyd, a Londoner, received the immediate award of the DFC for getting his badly damaged Lancaster back to base from Berlin on 15 February after they were shot up by a Me 210 over Denmark, 250 miles from the target. All turrets, hydraulics and Air Speed Indicators on DV363 were put out of action in the fighter attack and the intercom and oxygen systems were damaged. The bomb bay doors were left flapping and the tail wheel was punctured. Even so, Lloyd carried on to the target and bombed the 'Big City' before returning and landing safely at Wittering. They had been airborne for seven hours fifty minutes. Lloyd's navigator was Pilot Officer (later Squadron Leader) Donald Samuel Richardson, who attributed more and more his survival to good luck - similar to winning a lottery. 'Like many others I said my prayers - of five crews that started war operations at the same time we were the only crew to finish our tour of operations.' The rest of Lloyd's crew consisted of Flight Sergeant L. T. 'Pat' Dewhirst, bomb aimer; Sergeant 'Monty' Avenell, flight engineer; Flight Sergeant 'Paddy' Hewson, wireless air gunner; Sergeant Alan 'Mac' McCarthy, mid-upper gunner and Sergeant N. F. 'Maxi' Bacon, rear gunner.

Meal over, main briefing was at 2030. Don Richardson's responsibility to his skipper was to have 'F-Freddie' over the target during the 180 seconds which would elapse between 0110 and 0113. The last 'time over target' report was at 0122. Bombing would be from 23,000 feet. Path Finders would drop red target-indicator flares as a route marker at 50° 46' North; 06° 06' East. The target would be marked by the Path Finder Force with 'Newhaven' illuminating flares and green target-indicators with salvoes of red and green followed by reds. 'Wanganui' marking would consist of red flares with yellow stars. Path Finders would also carry out 'spoofs' with green TIs on Cologne and red target- indicators on Kassel. For the guidance of the outward-bound bomber stream, the beams of two searchlights would be crossed at 10,000 feet over Lowestoft on the Norfolk coast between 2300 and 2330. On their return, a single searchlight would be shining at Selsey Bill, elevated to 70° on a heading of 350°, between 0410 and 0530.

Flight Sergeant Garth Alec 'Jimmy' Waugh's crew on EE174 'A-Apple' had joined 50 Squadron in late January 1944. Sergeant R. J. 'Jack' Dunn the WOp/AG from Truro in Cornwall recalls; 'We were unaware of the history of the squadron or of the famous personalities who had been and were to become fellow members. At this time the squadron was commanded by Wing Commander A. W. Howard DFC AFC (later Air Chief Marshal Sir Anthony Howard, KCB OBE DFC AFC). We were later to learn that among the squadron's previous commanders was the much respected Sir Arthur 'Bomber' Harris, commanding the whole of Bomber Command; and the respected 'Gus' Walker (later Air Chief Marshal Sir Augustus Walker GCB CBE DSO DFC AFC MA). Also that Flying Officer Leslie Manser had been flying with the squadron when he was posthumously awarded the Victoria Cross. There were many more but we were yet to learn these details.

'Our crew was placed in 'A' (Dingo) Flight, the deputy flight commander being Flight Lieutenant 'Mike' Beetham (later to become Marshal of the RAF Sir Michael Beetham GCB CBE DFC AFC). 'Jimmy' Waugh was from New Zealand: Sergeant Dennis Alfred 'Chas' Chaston the navigator came from Coventry; Sergeant Denis C. 'Jerry' Lynch from Buckinghamshire was the bomb aimer; Sergeant George Prince, flight engineer grew up in New Malden in Surrey; Sergeant Donald Leslie Sehlin the 20-year old mid-upper gunner came from Millet, Alberta and Sergeant Roy Frederick Thibedeau the 23-year old rear gunner was from Echo Bay, Ontario. The period in which we were operating was fairly intense and losses were generally high. On our first operation to Leipzig on the night of 19/20 February there were 79 aircraft lost (8.6%) and on our ninth operation to Berlin (the Big City) on the night of 24/25 March the loss was 73 aircraft (7.1%). We had trips to 'Happy Valley'. Essen, Frankfurt, Augsburg, Stuttgart and Schweinfurt; some more than once, in between time and were soon aware of our chances of surviving a tour. Training was also very intensive over this period and 50 Squadron losses were not heavy when compared to other squadrons. According to the CO this was due to the training programme. On the night of 30/31March we were briefed for what was our thirteenth operation. Take off was at 2115 hours and we were a little surprised at the fact that a moon was a possibility, being a change in the normal moonless raids.'[38]

22-year old Sergeant Ernest D. Rowlinson of Northenden was the wireless-operator on 'H-Harry' on 50 Squadron flown by Flight Lieutenant George Charles 'Chas' Startin, a Queenslander. Rowlinson recalls: 'There was the usual back-chat among the crews but at the same time there was a feeling of tiredness amongst us. My crew had been on 50 Squadron only a fortnight yet this was to be our seventh night on flying duties and our fifth operation - one of which was on Berlin a few nights earlier.' At the briefing he remembered that there was surprise expressed by many when the curtain concealing the route was drawn aside to reveal that they would be flying just south of the Ruhr. But anxieties had been allayed to some extent when they were told that thick cloud cover was forecast for most of the way.

Flight Sergeant Les Bartlett DFM, bomb aimer-front gunner on VN-B LL744 on 50 Squadron skippered by Flight Lieutenant Michael Beetham DFC flew as his rear gunner. On his twelfth operation to Leipzig, Les used the nose guns to destroy a Ju 88 night fighter, for which he was awarded the DFM. 'At 2200 we taxied out and were first airborne. Everything was quiet during the climb to 20,000 feet over the

Channel. We crossed the enemy coast and it was eyes wide open.'

'We had done 25 ops by then' recalled Mike Beetham 'and we were expecting the Nuremberg raid to be cancelled because it was a full moon and we didn't usually fly during the full moon period because it was too easy for the German fighters to spot us.' He loved the Lancaster; 'it felt right, it handled beautifully and was a delight to fly. If it was heavier on the controls than we now consider proper, back then this weight gave a young pilot confidence and you got used to it.[39] His father, who had been awarded the Military Cross in the Great War as an Army major in the trenches, wanted his son to go into the Army but when the Battle of Britain began in the summer of 1940 Mike was a schoolboy staying for the summer in Hilsea, just outside Portsmouth, where his father was running an Army training battalion. He saw the German aircraft coming in to bomb the harbour and the Hurricanes and Spitfires cutting into them. It was spectacular and Mike said to my father: 'That's for me.' Mike, who was educated at St. Marylebone's Grammar School, went to the RAF recruiting office when he turned 18 in 1941 and was 'lucky enough' to be selected for pilot training and sent to America to be taught to fly.

'In common with almost all of the other pilots, I was in the slightly peculiar position of being able to fly a four-engined heavy bomber without being able to drive a car. Few people had cars in those days and petrol was rationed so there wasn't the opportunity to learn. After being commissioned in December 1942 I trained on Wellingtons and then converted to Lancasters at an Operational Training Unit, joining 50 Squadron at Skellingthorpe in October 1943. I was twenty years old and was responsible for a Lancaster and a crew of seven. It was a pretty intense period for Bomber Command and when the crew lists were put up on the board for what should have been our first operation, we weren't on it. I was pretty disappointed, because I was keen to get going, but the Squadron Commander came to see me and said: 'The target is Berlin and I think that's a rather tough one so we've left you off this one.'

The following night we did make it onto the crew list, so we went to the briefing room, where we were to be told the target and the planned route. When the map was unveiled I was surprised to see that, lo and behold, the target was Berlin. The Squadron Commander shrugged and said: 'It looks like it's going to be all Berlin from now on, so you might as well get on with it.' My first three trips were to Berlin, the most heavily defended city in Germany, but we didn't get into any trouble until our fourth trip, which was to Leipzig and in theory a much less dangerous sortie. We dropped our bombs and turned for home when suddenly a fighter came up behind us and started firing. I couldn't see the fighter but I could see the tracer going into the wing. I was aware that my own gunners were firing back and then the rear gunner shouted 'corkscrew port!' which was the evasive manoeuvre we all practiced in training and involved banking violently down and to one side to shake off the fighter. The more violent you could make it, the better chance you had of getting out alive. We managed to shake off the fighter but one of our fuel tanks was holed and we were losing fuel rapidly. I knew we weren't going to make it back to base but we pressed on and I managed to get as far as Wittering. We all knew the dangers we faced, but that brought it home to us. People sometimes ask how we managed to stir ourselves for each operation knowing it was going to be dangerous and I think the key was that everyone was behind you. When you taxied out onto the runway to go on ops the entire base would turn out to wave you on your way. What could you do but press on? I would have been more frightened of chickening out than I was of carrying on; particularly knowing I had six other members of my crew depending on me. At that young age, you also tend to think it will always happen to the other chap and not to you.'

The Path Finder Force heading to Nuremberg was led by 23-year old Wing Commander Sidney Patrick 'Pat' Daniels DFC* RAFVR , Commanding Officer of 35 PFF Squadron at Graveley, in 'S-Sugar'. Fresh crews would be shown into his office where an axe was suspended above his desk. Daniels would point to it and tell them: 'That's what you'll get here - the big chop' followed by an explosive laugh so infectious that the assembled 'sprogs' immediately relaxed![40] Daniels had joined the RAF at the age of eighteen and in September 1940 had started his first tour of ops on 58 Squadron, flying Whitley Vs at Linton-on-Ouse. In June 1941, as a flight lieutenant, he was awarded a DFC and was then rested at the end of his tour. In 1942 Pat Daniels, now a squadron leader, joined 83 Squadron to start his second tour. In December he undertook the role of Master Bomber for an intended raid on Munich, but the raid was cancelled due to severe weather conditions and it fell to Guy Gibson VC and then later, John Searby, formally to introduce the 'Master Bomber' role on operations.[41] Nuremberg was his sixty-sixth op. 'For once,' Daniels recalls, 'I was not 'Master Bomber'. Instead, he and Squadron Leader Edmund Keith Cresswell DSO DFC, who flew 'B-Beer', were the primary visual markers, responsible for finding the target and marking it for their supporters in the Path Finder Force. On hearing about the planned straight route, Daniels warned Donald Bennett that the force might well suffer 'the highest chop rate ever'. Patiently the Path Finder chief took his Wing Commander aside and explained that he had already protested to Bomber Command HQ but had been over-ruled by a vote of the Group Commanders who wanted to test their theory that the German controllers would be unlikely to believe that the bombers were in fact flying straight and true to their target. There was nothing else to do but follow the route they had been given. Bennett went on to explain that the reason for the long straight leg across the Rhine east to the target was because of the distance to be covered. Intelligence, furthermore, had claimed that southern Germany was not as heavily defended as the more frequently attacked targets areas of central and northern Germany.

'There is no reference in my log book to having carried out a night-flying test' recalled Daniels. 'Presumably I made someone else do this for me. As CO there was a lot of work to do: preparing the briefing that I would give the squadron, studying weather reports and talking of tactics with the AOC and Group on the scrambler telephone link-up, checking maximum number of squadron aircraft and crews available, checking correct loading of bombs and fuel, checking the route with the navigation officer, signals arrangements with the signals leader and giving a separate briefing to whatever crew I was taking with me. As CO, I was not allowed my own crew and usually took one where the captain was sick or on leave or else I just made up a crew of odd bods from around the place or sometimes I took a new crew. This system was unpopular with all but a necessary evil.'

Daniels crew included Pilot Officer Copp, Flight Lieutenant Wilkinson, Flight Sergeant Moffat, Warrant Officer Campbell and Second Lieutenant Wang, a Free

Norwegian Air Force officer who had escaped to England in 1940.

Shortly after 1800 hours - three hours before 35 Squadron was due to taxi out at Graveley, 'Pat' Daniels briefed the crews he was going to lead. He opened with a general pep-talk in which he emphasised the importance of the target they were going to attack and then he gave details of the types of flares and illuminators the Lancasters would carry and the precise times at which they would mark Nuremberg. With a billiard cue in his hand he went over the route, tapping the wall-map to indicate places along the course, which were dangerously close to heavily defended areas and he ended with a brief warning.

'Eight hundred aircraft are going to Nuremberg tonight and if we are to avoid collisions it's important that you keep to your heights. Be particularly alert and weave your aircraft into gentle banks so that the gunners can get a better chance of seeing any night-fighters that may be around. Good luck and a good trip.'

'I probably took off first with the rest of the squadron behind me at thirty-second intervals, about five to ten minutes ahead of Main Force.'

The briefing for sixteen Lancaster skippers and their crews on 44 'Rhodesia' Squadron at Dunholme Lodge about four miles north of Lincoln began at 2000. John Chadderton DFC had a feeling of unease, not helped by the fact that he was flying the squadron's spare Lancaster, 'E-Easy', instead of his beloved 'Y-Yorker', which was having an engine change after 'collecting some heavy metal' over Berlin six nights previously. Nuremberg would be the crew's 23rd op.

'After some early mistakes and a great deal of luck we had developed into a competent crew, able to rely totally on each other. Some time ago with our accumulated experience and Jack's navigational skill, we had been made the squadron's 'wind-finder' and PFF supporter. I relished this job of wind-finder. It meant that we took off alone about half an hour before the rest of the squadron came queuing up along the perimeter track with radiators and tempers overheating and we then flew along in a relatively uncluttered sky to join the first wave of the Path Finders in order to give them support against the searching German radar by thickening the shower of metal foil called 'Window'. For the last five months we had spent night after night clawing our way through varying densities of cloud to attack the major cities of Germany, including eight to the 'Big City' itself. Despite the constant anxiety of icing and flak, this damp cloak of darkness was just what we burglars needed to enable us to creep in and creep out again, without being apprehended by the vigilant night fighters. But tonight it would be different. We were promised cloud on the outward route.'

Twenty-seven year old Wing Commander Francis William Thompson DFC AFC from Blackpool, veteran of more than fifty operations over Germany, skippered 'Z-Zebra'. He had already done a tour on 10 Squadron on Whitley bombers in 1941 and came from 1658 HCU to command 44 Squadron. His flight-engineer Flight Lieutenant Stephen Burrows DFC of Evesham, Flight Sergeant Middleham the 23-year old mid-upper gunner who was a factory hand from Leeds and Flight Sergeant J. Hall the rear-gunner, a mill hand from Yorkshire were on their second tour of operations too. Flight Sergeant Tony Stancer the 22-year old navigator had been a London office worker. Flying Officer William Clegg the 25-year old bomb aimer was a bank clerk from Manchester. Another ex-clerk and fellow Mancunian, 23-year old

Pilot Officer Peter Roberts was the wireless-operator. 'To some the Wing Commander's briefing seemed routine' recalled Stephen Burrows. 'On a large map of Germany was displayed the defended areas marked according to their strength and nature - flak in red, searchlights in blue and fighter areas indicated by small aircraft symbols. We were told it was to be a 'maximum effort' deep into enemy territory and this shook us a bit since the Leipzig raid was still fresh in our minds. As various crews entered and glanced at the map, the usual 'Cor! Bloody hell!' remarks filled the air, especially as the target was shown deep in enemy territory. My own reaction to all this was the usual butterfly tummy, especially due to the fact that we, being the most experienced crew, had been detailed to take photographs and assess bombing after doing our own bombing run. This operation obviously meant hanging around the target far too long for comfort, having to run backwards and forwards and being bombed from above by our own aircraft (which incidentally had happened before, having had incendiary bombs in the wing) and the usual flak and night fighters being assisted by the bright lights.'

After the briefing, the crews were unusually quiet this particular night. There was much yawning and stretching as the men picked up helmets, Mae West life-jackets, gloves, parachute harnesses and packs, navigation satchels, charts, logs, coffee flasks, computers, dropped pencils and clip-boards of classified signals and navigation information. There was, at this point, a tendency to move and walk in a slowed down, slightly disorientated kind of way like mourners after a burial.[42] Each crew were taken by crew bus out to their aircraft dispersals with a 'Good luck! Have a good trip.' from the WAAF driver. Burrows' crew being what their driver called her 'ace' crew were delivered last so that she could stay around while they carried out their ground checks and smoked their last cigarettes. Despite a standing Bomber Command order forbidding it, Burrows 'spent' his usual superstitious nervous 'penny' by the port wheel of Lancaster ND515 KM-Z; after that they were ready to go. 'Z-Zebra' was loaded with approximately 10,000lbs of bombs including one 4,000lb high-explosive 'cookie' and approximately 6,000lbs of incendiaries.

At Metheringham, a wartime aerodrome on the edge of the Fens twelve miles south-east of Lincoln where in winter it could be foggy and cold, seventeen Lancaster crews on 106 Squadron sat through the briefing. One of the pilots present was 21-year-old Pilot Officer 'Dick' Starkey who skippered 'Q-Queenie' whose crew had flown 21 operations. At the end of January 1944 Starkey had made three raids on the Reich capital in four nights. 'I did nine Berlin trips' he recalled. 'At the end of the Battle of Berlin our crew had flown on nine operations to the city; three of them out of four nights at the end of January when we were in the air for twenty four hours out of ninety six. It was also a period of changing situations; you could be watching *Alexander's Ragtime Band* featuring Tyrone Power, Don Ameche and Alice Fay in a cinema in Lincoln at eight o'clock one night and the next night at eight o'clock be over Berlin.

'Our ground crew who looked after 'Q-Queenie' were of the best. They did their job magnificently and nothing was too much trouble. I remember asking them if they could find a leather cushion for the pilot's position and the next time I flew it was in place; I think they took it from the flight commander's aircraft. They also named the aircraft *Queen Of Sheba* and painted a picture of a nude lady just under the pilot's window. When we returned from an operation the crew shot a line to them saying the flak over the target was so hot she came back tanned. We had a drink with them once a week at the local village pub when operations permitted.'

Starkey's crew had been scheduled to take part in a raid on Brunswick on the night of 29 March. However, four crews were on the last ten trips of their tours and it looked as though they would complete their tour at about the same time, so it was decided to stagger the remaining trips. They were therefore told to stand down for the Brunswick raid but this operation was then cancelled because the Met forecast was not good. On 30 March Starkey's Flight Commander told him that 'Q-Queenie's crew would be stood down. 'I informed the lads of the order' Starkey recalls 'but as one man they said that as we had been a stand down crew for a cancelled operation one of the other crews should do so for the raid and they asked me to see the Flight Commander again. Although I had to decide whether or not to let the order stand, I agreed that we should be put on the Battle Order and gave my views to the Flight Commander. At first he said the order would not be reversed but after some thought he changed his decision.'

Many, not least among the 'old sweats' and 'Gen Men' like Starkey's crew, with only three weeks to go to the end of their tour, began to have reservations. He and his crew got a couple of hours rest after being briefed. The crew lay on their beds wide-awake and not a word was spoken. They had 'Wakey-Wakey' tablets which some people used to take before they got to the flights but they would start to wear off when they needed them so Starkey would wait until they were in the air before swallowing his. When the time came they were like men going to the gallows. In the locker room there might be 100 aircrew men putting on their kit and it was as quiet as anything.

The sense of foreboding was not just confined to the veteran crews. It was the same for the 'sprog' crews. Even though they had completed just two operations thus far, 23-year old Flight Sergeant Thomas William John Hall DFM and crew on Lancaster JB586 'C-Charlie' had seen all they needed to see six nights' earlier when they had flown to Berlin on the first operation of their tour. Hall, from Wraysbury on the Thames in Buckinghamshire was cheerful and positive. The night of 24/25 March was when unexpectedly violent winds had caused Bomber Command much trouble and seventy three bombers had been lost. Hall, like many others, had arrived at Berlin too early, but while others bombed and made for home, he did a complete orbit over the city before bombing. On the return flight the winds took them, again like many others, over the Ruhr where his Lancaster was hit by flak and two engines caught fire.

Thirty-three-year-old Sergeant Robert D. Dack was the wireless operator. One of his duties was to listen out for the wind speeds and wind directions which the Path Finder wireless operators were sending back to base on their T114 transmitters with the red, yellow and blue dials. Once received, the base then analysed them and the mean average was re-broadcast to all bombers ensuring that all would navigate to the same wind and so keep the concentration of the stream intact. The Main Force bombers' calculations had to be based on the known wind speed to get them to the target at a certain time as timing was crucial. But when the relay came through on the R1155 receiver set with its half moon dial in the centre they were informed that the winds at 20,000 feet were 60 mph when in fact they were nearer 160 mph.

One of seven children, Bob Dack had lived at the family farm in the Lincolnshire village of Barholm. His father also owned four blacksmith's shops. He was a hard man, who made his children leave school at fourteen to start earning a wage. Bob, who could have gone to grammar school, worked on the farm and gained experience in a smithy. He saved hard from his low wages for flying lessons at Peterborough Flying Club because, more than anything, he wanted to fly. He was married, to Anne. The couple had two daughters, six year old Sheelagh and Valerie a baby. Unsurprisingly Dack was known as the 'Granddad' on the crew. The two gunners were however, at eighteen, little more than schoolboys. The mid-upper, Sergeant G. A. 'Tony' Poole, came from Sleaford, Lincolnshire, where he had worked in a bank. Sergeant G. S. 'Jock' Robertson, a sturdy well-educated youngster from Carlisle, Cumberland was the tail gunner. Navigator, Flight Sergeant R. H. G. 'Ronnie' Parker, a shy quiet Australian, was from Naremburn on the lower North Shore of Sydney in New South Wales. Flight Sergeant J. T. 'Tom' Gill the 32-year old bomb aimer who was from Sandgate, a coastal suburb in Brisbane, Queensland where he had been a range boss, was blunt and outspoken. Sergeant Cyril Beston the 29-year old flight engineer from Nuneaton was short, energetic and quick thinking.

'Tommy' Hall brought his crew home from Berlin after a desperate flight, although EB593 'Y-Yorker' had to be written off. On their next trip, on 26 March they took JB566 'C-Charlie' to Essen. They had a problem with the boosters and the 4,000lb 'Cookie' had to be jettisoned over the North Sea. They carried on and dropped four 500lb armour-piercing bombs and canisters of incendiaries through 10/10th cloud at the target. On 30 March the flight commander told the crew that they could take a week's leave after Nuremberg and Bob Dack had written to his wife telling her to expect him. Desperate to see his wife and daughters Dack was looking forward to that leave, especially since his younger brother, Eddie, a soldier, was killed at the Anzio beachhead in Italy. But though the moon period was too far advanced, no one thought that they would go and they waited for the telephone call to tell them it had been scrubbed but the call never came.

Flying Officer Fredrick Robert Stuart, an Australian Halifax gunner on 'M-Mike' on 10 Squadron at Melbourne, Yorkshire attended his squadron's briefing but there was actually no need for him to be there as his crew had already completed its tour of operations on 10 Squadron and had been 'screened' from operational flying. But Stuart did not relish the prospect of returning to a training unit to fly as a tour-expired gunnery instructor so he had elected to remain on operational flying on 10 Squadron. Stuart's night over Nuremberg began after returning from leave in London. From early in 1942 the 'Boomerang Club' - motto: 'I go out to return' was a favourite haunt of Aussie airmen, just north of the Strand on the Aldwych curve leading into Kingsway. The Club took up two floors of Australia House and served all Australian services and ranks. Men registered at the reception centre (entrance off Melbourne Place), scanned the Club for friends and consulted the notice boards - one for the men to attach notes for mates and the other listing entertainment. The Club helped men find accommodation, sold drinks, snacks and meals and provided a place to write letters, read Australian newspapers, gather around the piano, have a haircut and play billiards and yarn. The 'Boomerang Club' attracted and disturbed aircrew; they wanted to catch up with news and comrades but so often they learnt of the deaths of another three or four of their old course from Narrandera or Parkes or Calgary. The Strand was central to many of the places the Australians had to or wanted to visit. In December 1941 the Overseas Headquarters of the RAAF opened in Kodak House at 63 Kingsway just off the Strand, which the Australians made their own.[43]

Fred Stuart reported to the squadron's gunnery leader, Squadron Leader George Lowe DFC - better known to the air gunners on 10 Squadron as 'Jarge' - who had already completed one tour of operations. A cheerfully cynical type he had grinned when Stuart asked him if there was anything doing because if there wasn't Stuart intended dodging off to his quarters for a recuperative sleep after his London leave and the long trip in the slow, crowded train back to Yorkshire. Squadron Leader Lowe had sat back in his chair, closed one eye in a conspiratorial wink and said, 'I think you'd like to be on this one. It's a DP'. Stuart found that he was on the squadron battle-order to fly this deep-penetration attack with a new, all-RAF crew. In view of his operational experience he would be flying in the mid-upper turret as fire controller.

After checking with the station intelligence section to see if the Luftwaffe had introduced new fighting tactics, or any other tricks, Stuart went out to 'M-Mike' and began checking and harmonizing the two Browning .303 machine-guns in the mid-upper turret while the rest of the crew busied themselves with their own checks of equipment and armament. Stuart had often flown on 'M-Mike' and liked the aircraft. He was reassured but not surprised when the battle-tried Halifax responded to all the demands put upon her by their keen young pilot during the course of a routine night-flying test in the squadron's local flying area. After they had landed, taxied back to dispersal and left the aircraft for the ground staff to re-fuel and bomb up Stuart settled into the usual routine with which he had become so familiar and which had so sustained him during his tour of operations - the hasty meal, the checking of oxygen masks and intercom and, in the case of the gunners, the bright yellow, electrically heated Taylor suits. These were designed to keep them warm and therefore alert in their draughty, unpressurised turrets, far from the heating system which served the cockpit and navigation stations in the aircraft. Sometimes, of course, the electric flying suits did not work and the result was a night of seemingly endless misery. Then there was the quick nap, if possible. For Stuart, there was his own private ritual which he always observed before going out on an operation. The shower and the shave and then for warmth during the forthcoming night's work, silk underwear next to his skin, the RAF-issue lambs-wool underwear topped by a clean shirt and his battledress. Last came a pair of silk stockings which he wore as an inner flying scarf. The stockings were valued more for the luck they had brought during a tour of operations than the charms of their original wearer, a London actress.

Flying Officer Denis Eyre Girardau, rear gunner who was from East Malvern, Victoria was the only Australian on Warrant Officer 'Paddy' Clarke's typically mixed Halifax crew on 'B' Flight on 10 Squadron. The pilot was from Northern Ireland. The mid-upper gunner was a Canadian, Pilot Officer D. Johnson; the wireless air gunner was a Londoner, Pilot Officer Frank Harvey; the flight engineer was a Welshman, Flying Officer Geoff Fenton from Manchester; the navigator was a New Zealander, Pilot Officer J. Whiteman. For Girardau the Nuremberg operation had begun with reporting to the gunnery section where he was told that the squadron was on call for operations that night. Cycling around the perimeter track to 'B' Flight dispersal he located ZA-L the new Halifax Mark III which had been allocated to his crew. Since it was a new aircraft, Girardau decided to carry out a more than usually thorough inspection of his rear turret and its four .303 Browning machine guns.

At 1900 the twelve Halifax crews on the battle-order for that night, with one other crew on stand-by gathered in the main briefing room at Melbourne. There was the usual air of tense expectancy until the squadron commander, Wing Commander Dudley Spencer Radford DFC AFC uncovered the big wall map to reveal the big, blood-red button - Nuremberg - was in position. 'Paddy' Clarke's experienced Halifax crew looked at each other. They had mixed feelings. The last time they had attacked the city on the night of 27/28 August 1943 they had been caught in the cold blue glare of a radar-controlled master searchlight on the way past Frankfurt-am-Main and had been coned by a concentration of 'slave' searchlights for seventeen minutes while their skipper had taken violent and seemingly endless evasive action. They had escaped without being shot down but had lost their bomb aimer, a victim of the ferocity of the Frankfurt defences and Clarke had had to belly-land the Halifax at Manston in Kent where the North Foreland stands guard over the confluence of the Straits of Dover and the wide and windy approaches to the Thames Estuary. Now they were going to Nuremberg again. Admittedly there would be a night fighter's moon but there would also be nine-tenths cloud cover for most of the eight-hour flight. Girardau was glad to hear it. This attack would be the last of their tour of operations.

After the customary warnings about searchlights, flak and fighters, according to the RAF's current intelligence summaries of the German defences, the crews drew their parachutes and cracked the usual jokes with the parachute section WAAFs. Then they climbed aboard the crew buses driven by more WAAFs. By 1915 hours the squadron's crews were out at their dispersals. There was the usual cynical chaffing and ribaldry as they climbed out of the buses and dumped their miscellany of gear by their aircraft. After final checks Warrant Officer Clarke's crew was ready and at 2000 he was taxiing out onto the perimeter track. By 2005 ZA-L was rumbling down the flare-path on take-off from Melbourne with the navigator, Pilot Officer Whiteman RNZAF, still mindful of the earnestness with which his crew had admonished him to 'keep his finger out'. The weather was 'very fine' with what seemed to Denis Girardau to be almost a full moon. Crossing the French coast at 22,000 feet he could see no sign of the cloud cover that the meteorologists had promised: there was no cloud in sight at all.

The weather over Belgium and eastern France was 0/10ths to 4/10ths thin cloud while Holland and the Ruhr were cloudless. At Nuremberg there was 10/10ths cloud at 1,600 to 12,000 feet but the cloud veiled at 16,000 feet with generally good altitude visibility.

For Wing Commander Thompson's crew on 'Z-Zebra' on 44 Squadron, the trip out over the English coast and the North Sea from Dunholme Lodge was without incident. Being heavily laden with maximum fuel as well as the bombs, 'Zebra' climbed slowly to an operational height of about 18,000 feet. Weather conditions improved gradually and on crossing the enemy coast there was good visibility with patchy cloud. They would soon be out of range from the UK based 'Gee' navigation beacons and rely on dead reckoning from the forecast winds. Selected crews were tasked to radio back their estimate of the actual winds, which would be averaged at Group HQ and rebroadcast. Navigators would then use this revised wind estimate to adjust their heading and regain track. The system depended on many accurate calculations by navigators in the cold and cramped bombers and should have kept the concentrated on the planned route and allow crews to bomb the target at their allocated times. Tony Stancer, Thompson's navigator in the nose of 'Z-Zebra', studied his navigational charts, frowned and leaned across his plotting-desk to take another reading from the green metal 'Gee' box in front of him. Lines of minute dog-teeth danced across the screen. The former London office clerk quickly aligned the jagged points of light and plotted the latitude and longitude fixes on his Mercator chart. Then he flicked the switch on his oxygen mask that activated his intercom system and said, 'Navigator to Skipper. The Met forecast winds are all bull. Heavy tail winds have given us an incredible groundspeed. Unless we're to be well ahead of our ETA on the next turning point, we'll have to dog-leg. First dog-leg course coming up.'

Thompson asked if Stancer was quite sure of his calculations.

'Absolutely' replied Stancer.

Thompson then asked him whether the 'Gee' set could be on the blink but Stancer assured his Skipper that he had checked and re-checked the set and that it was 'working perfectly'. Thompson knew he would now have to alter course 60° port for one minute and then swing 120° back; flying two sides of an equilateral triangle. It would lengthen their time to the first turning point, giving them two minutes to fly to a point they would otherwise have reached in half the time but other aircraft would be doing the same thing and the collision risk would be high. The wing commander set the new course on his compass and swung the Lancaster in a gentle bank on to the first dog-leg. No sooner had he done so than Flight Sergeant Hall the rear-gunner reported on intercom. 'Unidentified aircraft coming towards us; port quarter.'

Thompson was just about to throw 'Z-Zebra' into a violent corkscrew when he saw the massive shape of a Halifax also dog-legging to lose time so as to stay with the flight-plan, as it zoomed about twenty-five feet over the top of them, too close for comfort. Someone gasped over the intercom: Jeeze, that was close!

'The incident passed and everything appeared to be quiet again,' said Burrows. 'However, after travelling approximately twenty miles inland things really began to happen. There appeared to be combats going on all around us with the consequent explosions of raiding aircraft receiving direct hits. Some blew up so close to us that the whole of our aircraft shuddered alarmingly, as if every rivet would pop out of its socket. It was our duty to report each combat to the navigator who logged same, viz. height, time, speed, position, etc. After approximately ten aircraft had thus been reported the skipper told the crew to disregard this order. The atmosphere was rather tense. I however continued to do so and was frightened out of my wits when the skipper dug me in the ribs and shouted 'I said enough!'

Under conditions which seemed ideal for the defences, with little or no cloud protection, it seemed to Burrows that the way in to the target seemed to last for 'ages' with the British force obviously suffering alarming casualties. Near Frankfurt, 'Z-Zebra' was coned and held by searchlights for 'some considerable time' with Wing

Commander Thompson taking violent evasive action. During this time the crew noticed that no flak came up, thus indicating that German fighters were operating in the area. 'Our first combat happened after approximately one hour but, most fortunately, the rear gunner saw this FW 190 trying to get into position and directed us clear, losing him fairly easily. This was most remarkable as the conditions were ideal. This happened two or three times. We saw fighters going towards other aircraft and exchanging shots but were left alone most of the time ourselves. The final number of attackers sighted, going towards the target, were too numerous to mention.'

As the newest crew in 'B' Flight on 78 Squadron at Breighton in 4 Group Flight Sergeant Paul Eric Christiansen RCAF and his crew still did not have their own aircraft. They were allocated 'A-Able', an old Halifax Mark III for the crew's second operational flight. By 1030 Sergeant David George Davidson the Scottish flight engineer from Inverness and former taxi driver was out at the dispersals checking over 'A-Able' and cleaning the perspex panels of the cockpit. The ground crew succeeded in convincing him that although 'Able' was old she had no 'snags'. It was then that Davidson noticed the ground staff installing overload fuel tanks in the belly of the aircraft. Immediately there was much joking about the prospects of spending the night over Berlin. By 1500, bombing-up had begun at Breighton with tractors and low-slung bomb trolleys rolling around the perimeter track to the dispersals where the empty bomb-bays were waiting. Davidson cycled back out to 'Able' to see that incendiaries only were being winched up to the racks so that an overload fuel tank could be fitted in the belly compartment. There was no doubt now that it was going to be a long trip.

At 1930 Davidson sat down to flying supper with his crew. There was not much talk in the mess that evening but everybody looked washed, shaved and very neat. 'There was an atmosphere like you get before a big show begins' recollected Davidson. Briefing for 78 Squadron was at 2030. The scene at briefing was a familiar one. David Davidson remembered that 'Dozens of crews could be seen cycling from the perimeter track towards the briefing hut.'

Before cycling over to the briefing hut, Warrant Officer2 Frederick Wills Topping RCAF and his crew sat down to their bacon and eggs ops supper. Because it was to be a major raid, almost everyone was shaved and neat, as if going to an off-base dance. Somewhere in the background, a radio was playing Anne Shelton singing *You'll Never Know Just How Much I Love You*.[44] The crew, the usual mix of RAF and Dominion airmen, were on their third operation: Topping was from Prince Albert, Saskatchewan. Sergeant William Joseph Batchouski the wireless operator was from Bethnal Green, London; Flying Officer William Lorne Cruse the navigator was from Winnipeg; Sergeant Walter Acklam Littlewood the flight engineer came from Nosterfield, Yorkshire; the two gunners, 21-year old Sergeant John Gilmore Vaughan RCAF, hailed from Windsor Junction, Nova Scotia and Sergeant Leo Lanaghan was from Felling, County Durham. Flight Sergeant George Dudgeon Torbet the bomb aimer, who was born in Glasgow on 31 March 1922 before his family emigrated to Oshawa, Ontario in 1926 hoped he would be observing his birthday shortly before 'Bombs Away'.

'Inside the briefing hut the wall map stood out as we entered' wrote David

Davidson. 'All eyes followed the route ribbon. Long, very long, it was. As we got near the front Sergeant King our navigator mumbled 'Nuremberg'. Groans were heard from crews entering and seeing the route.' For the rest of the briefing Davidson was preoccupied with fuel tank drills and engine-handling techniques for conservation of fuel. The trip, he sensed, would mean that he would have to watch over every drop of petrol in 'Able's tanks.

Twenty-six year old Flight Lieutenant Harry McCormick Hudson RCAF, an American from Largo, Florida and his crew had been posted to 78 Squadron on 22 October 1943. They would fly Halifax HX241 EX-P. Hudson's rear gunner, Flying Officer J. D. Lane was replaced by Sergeant John William Morris of Hexham, Northumberland because the Wing Commander had asked Lane to fly with a 'sprog' crew. Hudson's navigator, Flight Lieutenant Wilbert James Robertson, from Saskatoon was ill and could not fly. He was always air-sick, but flew though it was something more serious this time and his place had been taken by 23-year old Flight Lieutenant Alan George Taylor DFC who was from Beckenham, Kent. Robertson was eventually lost on 21 November 1944. Twenty-six year old Flying Officer William 'Bill' Uyen RCAF, bomb aimer was from Hamilton, Ontario; Sergeant John Hillis the 26-year old flight engineer came from Inver, County Antrim; Sergeant Harold 'Harry' Monks the 23-year old wireless operator was from Hyde, Cheshire. Flight Sergeant Leslie 'Scouse' Nugent, the 23-year old mid-upper gunner on the crew recalled: 'There we were, 112 of us each with our own private thoughts but all thinking along similar lines, such as; 'Will our crew be one of the lucky ones?; 'Is this it?'; 'Will I ever see the wife again?' and so on but all around the same theme being 'Will I live or will I die?' It was obvious that we were of the same mind because a noisy and jocular dispersal was the norm after briefing but on this occasion we just sat and looked at each other - no words passed but the message was clearly conveyed through an atmosphere that was electric.'[45] Nuremberg was Hudson's crew's 27th operation.

'At 2115' continues David Davidson on Flight Sergeant Christiansen's crew, 'briefing over, everybody walked down to the parachute section to collect their gear. Hanging about now, smoking and nattering and waiting for the crew buses to arrive, I got into conversation with Sergeant F. R. Wilson, the rear gunner on 'Z-Zebra'. His captain was Sergeant Ron Horton from Leicester. The crew had just returned from leave and this was their first operational flight. We exchanged take-off times. They were taking off two minutes ahead of us. 'See you later' I said but it was to be two years later at Catterick camp before I was to see him again.

'The crew buses arrived. There were three crews in ours: [Sergeant Horton whose crew were on their first operation] for 'Z-Zebra'; an Australian - Constable, I think his name was [sic] and his crew for 'H-How'[46] and ourselves for 'A-Able'. Horton and his crew got out first. Then it was our turn. As the bus pulled away I walked towards the Halifax. My God, it looked so large in the dark. A good-look round and then everybody was aboard. The ground staff corporal got Christiansen to sign the Form 700. He wished me good luck on the way out. I got down the fuselage with him to check 'Door shut' at 2150.

'2152: Start-up. 2159: Chocks away. Moving out of dispersal and waving to ground crew we joined the queue for the runway with our brakes squealing as we slew round to catch some wind in the engine cowlings to keep our cylinder-head temperatures down. A green from the ACP to turn onto the runway. 2209: Throttles opening up power with brakes on. Brakes off and we were away. We were swinging. Straight again, on and on with the nose down. Then we lifted and climbed away slowly. 2210: Time to set course. We kept climbing on course at 2,400 rpm and +2 boost but this kite was slow. 2300: Out over the English Channel now. The French coast was coming up. It looked big and dark against the sea. 2325: We crossed north of Cape Gris Nez. 2326: Sergeant A. Fleet RCAF the rear gunner reported flak off port quarter but quite some distance away. 2334: Fighter flares were dropped close to starboard. 2335: Combat reported to starboard and below us. A Halifax was on fire. We could see the square fins. 2336: The fire in the other Halifax went out. There was no explosion. 2338: Three combats were reported to port and ahead of us. 2340: Two explosions were seen on the ground ahead of us and to starboard of track. Quite a lot was going on and so soon. We were still climbing on course. The moon had come up. It shook us a bit because it came out of the cloud looking like a Jerry fighter flare and Sergeant Fleet the rear gunner and Sergeant H. Darani the mid-upper gunner started firing at it. When we realized it was really the moon it was a relief to be able to laugh. We are now making vapour trails. Quite a few of our kites are above us and in front of us but not many behind. 0045: King reported to the skipper that we were ten minutes late and suggested we return to base as we would be too late to bomb with the main stream. Christiansen said, 'No, we go. We're too far in now to start arsing about.' The crew agreed. The navigator said 'OK. I told you.'

At 0018, Davidson could see the target coming up.

Of the sixteen Halifaxes dispatched from Breighton, four aborted on the outward journey. East of Thetford, LV916 returned early when the wireless operator's parachute opened accidentally. Another returned early when the port outer engine went unserviceable and its bombs were jettisoned safe in the sea. 'W-William' also suffered an engine failure and aborted the raid after bombing a position on the German border. A fourth Halifax returned while in mid-Channel where the bombs were jettisoned safe in the sea.

Twenty-seven year old Squadron Leader Arthur Doubleday DFC RAAF the 'B' Flight Commander on 467 Squadron RAAF at Waddington in 5 Group never felt any different before an operation 'other than for 'waiting to go into bat [when] the fast bowler looked a lot faster from the fence but when you get there it's not so bad'. In February 1933 Arthur had gone to Sydney where he watched the fifth test in the 'bodyline' series. While in Sydney he went out to Mascot aerodrome, paid his ten shillings and took a flight over the city. His second flight, seven years later was in the RAAF.[47] After first flying 31 ops and completing his tour he married Miss Phyllis Buckle at Beckenham, Kent on 14 August 1943. Doubleday's great friend, 27-year old Squadron Leader William Lloyd Brill DFC, 'B' Flight commander, 463 Squadron RAAF, which shared Waddington airfield with 467 Squadron RAAF and who was also on his second tour, had been his best man. The Doubledays had enjoyed four months of marriage before Arthur flew to Berlin on the first operation of his second tour. Doubleday and Brill were farmers in the peaceful eastern Riverina district near Wagga Wagga in New South Wales, who after volunteering for the RAAF were called up together in 1940 and thereafter their promotions were simultaneous. Both were original members of 460 Squadron RAAF. Nuremberg would be Bill Brill's forty-second operational flight as a pilot and crew captain.[48]

Right from the moment that Bill Brill and his crew had walked into the briefing room that evening he sensed that there was something amiss with the planning for the night's operations. They would be flying deep into the heart of Germany in the light of a half moon. Secondly, over potentially the most dangerous leg of the planned route near Charleroi in Belgium to southern Germany north of Nuremberg, the heavies would be flying a long, straight, undeviating course for two hours. Brill was so concerned about the long leg that he drew big meat choppers on this Section of the route as plotted on the chart of his navigator, Flying Officer Edward R. 'Blue' Freeman RAAF. Jokingly but emphatically, Brill warned his crew that they would have to be alert to slip past underneath the German 'choppers' which would be held in readiness that night. Brill did not like the diversionary ploy of three 'spoof raids on Aachen, Cologne and Kassel, which were on a tangent to the long eastward track of the Main Force bomber stream across the Rhine before the final run-in to the target. The moon would be well down in the west and therefore behind the bombers on their long eastward run to Nuremberg past the threat of the German night fighters. This would at least give Flying Officer Ron 'Tubby' Fuller RAAF the mid-upper and Bill McDonald the rear-gunner a chance to see the night fighters as they approached and attacked from astern which was their usual tactic. 'Nice', Brill thought cynically, to be able to see who was shooting you down. He was at least thankful that the meteorologists had forecast cloud cover all the way across Belgium, France and Germany to Nuremberg with clear bombing weather over the target itself. However, as Brill later recalled, the forecasting data was 'painfully meagre and in the event we had a cloudless run to within twenty miles of the target and then encountered cloud at up to 15,000-20,000 feet over the target.'

During the briefing, all crews on 463 and 467 Squadrons had been promised leave on return to Waddington. Bomber Command had been flying a number of maximum efforts with the result that many crews were long overdue for leave. Pilot Officer Ernest Andrew Mustard, pilot of 'C-Charlie' on 463 Squadron RAAF felt that the crews' thoughts of going on leave might be a contributory factor in the events of the night. 'If the situation was the same on other Bomber Command stations then there were a lot of tired men flying on the night of 30 March' said Mustard. Nuremberg would be 'Ern' Mustard's seventh trip over Germany, including two as a 'second dickey' on joining the squadron's 'A' Flight and the fifth with his own crew, which consisted of Sergeant W. H. Goodwin, navigator; Flight Sergeant A. P. Mustard RCAF, bomb aimer; Sergeant S. B. Maltman, flight engineer; Sergeant H. McClelland, wireless air gunner; Sergeant D. A. L. Herbert, mid-upper gunner and Flight Sergeant T. K. Wills RAAF, rear gunner. Nuremberg would prove to be what Mustard later described as, 'A long, deadly haul through a reception committee'.

Fellow 'A' Flight crew on Lancaster 'J-Jig' skippered by Pilot Officer Arthur Rhodes Sydney Bowman RAAF from Singleton, a town on the banks of the Hunter River in New South Wales, were no more worried about this trip than about the eighteen others which they had already completed, including ten to Berlin. Five of the crew were English: Sergeant R. E. Clarke, flight engineer; Sergeant L. F. Westgate, wireless air gunner; Sergeant A. C. Wilson, mid-upper gunner; Sergeant M. C. J. Barber DFM, bomb aimer and Sergeant F. Dobson, rear gunner. The navigator,

Sergeant R. L. Seton RAAF, was the only other Australian member on the crew. To Bowman it seemed that the meteorological forecast at briefing was satisfactory from an operational point of view even if it meant a considerable amount of instrument flying with so much cloud expected along the route to Nuremberg, clearing to seven-tenths over the target area. Their bomb-load that night was 10,796lbs and the all-up weight for take-off was 65,400lbs.

Acting Flight Lieutenant Daniel Thomas Conway DFC RAAF from Cottesloe, Perth, Western Australia, the pilot of Lancaster LM450 'K-Kitty' on 'A' Flight on 467 Squadron RAAF, noted that the briefing was 'routine except that there was some talk among the crews about this being the first major attack for a long time to penetrate so deeply into Germany so late in the moon period'. Conway's mother was Irish and he dutifully crossed the Irish Sea - in borrowed civilian clothes as the Irish Free State was neutral - and headed for Killarney, County Kerry. There he watched Gaelic football, went to dances and was surrounded by people 'all of whom seemed to be my cousins'. Conway 'crewed-up' at 29 OTU Bruntingthorpe, ten miles south of Leicester in mid-1943. Pilots, navigators, gunners, et al, were assembled in a hanger and told to sort themselves out. Conway, an officer, hung around shyly, 'not wanting to inflict myself on anybody', when he was approached by Joe Wesley, an English navigator, one of five RAF Sergeants on the crew. Conway, according to Wesley, a draughtsman from Watford, Hertfordshire was 'a big fellow, six feet three, thirteen stone; a real solid Australian'. Wesley knew a wireless operator, who knew a gunner and so on. Ray Tanfield was the flight engineer; Redman, the wireless air gunner; Stone, the mid-upper gunner and Day, rear gunner. One other Australian - Sergeant McDade - was the bomb aimer. Conway described it as marriage without the courtship and wondered, now that they were stuck with one another, how they were going to make the relationship work: 'The problem was quickly solved as everyone except Ron Day enjoyed a beer and so we began a series of visits to the local pubs. It was good fun and the Mess saw little of me as my social life outside blossomed - as did our comradeship.'[49] This crew had flown on nineteen operations together, including six on Berlin. Conway had also flown a 'second dickey' trip to Berlin on 16 December 1943 and four days later to Frankfurt. He had been introduced to weaving on his two trips as 'second dickey' and would be forever grateful to those two experienced pilots. Conway flew his first bombing raid with his own crew on 14 January 1944. Later his brother John also volunteered for bombers although he could have gone to Coastal Command.

It was a maximum effort at Waddington with 35 aircraft dispatched, the most out of any one station. It could have been even more but one pilot, Pilot Officer Anthony Bowen Loftus Tottenham, from Eire, was ill just before take-off so he and his crew missed out. (Flight Lieutenant Tottenham DFC was killed on 13 June). One by one eighteen Lancasters on 463 Squadron and seventeen on 467 got the green 'go' flashed by Aldis lamp from the plastic bowl in the roof of the black-and-yellow-striped 'pie-cart' near the threshold of the Waddington runway and took off. Pilot Officer 'Ern' Mustard lifted 'C-Charlie' off at 2215, which came as some relief as L7539 was an old veteran from a Lancaster finishing school with thousands of circuits and bumps to its name and was powered by Merlin XXs with no boost override for take-off. 'This reduced the all-up weight for take-off by about one ton' recalled Mustard 'and while it wasn't very satisfying to hear the reduced bomb-load being read out at briefing it was very useful to be able to bomb from the top of the stack and still have no petrol worries on the way home.'

There were two early returns to Waddington: Flying Officer Bruce Buckham on 463 Squadron returned just after midnight after the rear turret failed on ME701 '*Whoa Bessie!*'. An hour later, Pilot Officer Noel McDonald on 467 Squadron came back in LL792 when the electrically heated suits of the bomb aimer and both gunners failed.

Squadron Leader Arthur Doubleday gathered his crew together before they boarded LL843 'X-X-ray'. With the exception of the flight engineer, Sergeant J. Slome, his crew were all commissioned: Flight Lieutenant G. G. Abbott, navigator; Flying Officer F. J. Nugent, bomb aimer; Flying Officer B. Sinnamon, wireless operator air gunner; Flying Officer Sydney Bruce Gray-Buchanan DFM of Brisbane, the 27-year old mid-upper gunner and Flying Officer A. A. Taylor, rear gunner. Most of them had flown with Doubleday on 'Dog's first operation on 9/10 March when Group Captain Sam Elworthy DSO DFC AFC the Waddington Station Commander, flew as the eighth man.

'Look boys', Doubleday said: 'It's on for young and old tonight. Just keep your eyes on the sky.'

Brill likewise warned his mainly Australian second tour crew, who had flown their first operation together when they went to Berlin on 20 January that they could expect to have 'a rough night'. 'Tubby' Fuller the mid-upper gunner hailed from Booleroo Centre in the southern Flinders Ranges region of South Australia. Ted 'Bluey' Freeman the navigator was from Melbourne, Bill McMahon, bomb aimer was from Taree in New South Wales and Bob Curtis, wireless operator and air gunner came from Sydney. Bill McDonald the rear gunner was also Australian, he was picked up at Waddington. Len Smith the flight engineer from London was English. Curtis had flown a first tour in North Africa and only Brill and 'Bluey' Freeman had previously flown a full tour in Bomber Command. Len Smith, Bill McDonald and Bill McMahon were three months into their first tour. In volunteering for a second tour Brill and Doubleday had committed themselves to another twenty raids. All would see out the war. McMahon was fortunate. On 1/2 February 1945 on a flight with another crew on Siegen, his pilot was killed and he was one of seven men who bailed out. He landed on the roof of a German farmhouse and was taken prisoner.[50]

Apart from the DR compass going unserviceable before take-off which meant he would have to fly all night by careful monitoring of the P6 compass, it seemed to Doubleday that this operation had forebodings similar to Leipzig on the night of 19/20 February when seventy-eight aircraft failed to return. As he taxied 'X-X-ray' out at Waddington and his friend Squadron Leader Brill took off in his Lancaster JO-K there was a small amount of cloud overhead in Lincolnshire but this soon cleared as they flew south to the Channel coast. By the time they had reached 'Position B' near Charleroi, the weather was, as Brill sardonically put it, 'delightfully clear'. 'There was a three-quarter moon,' said Doubleday. 'Condensation trails were present for the major part of the period over the Continent. I believe this was above 16,000 feet. The winds from the north were not as strong as forecast.'

At another dispersal point that evening Bill Brill's brother Vale Vic Brill, the navigator on Pilot Officer Charlie Cassell's crew clambered aboard JO-B. At 22 he was five years younger than Bill. He had trained as a school teacher before beginning aircrew training in 1941. He was also a passionate trade unionist, environmentalist and advocate for the rights and needs of Aboriginal people. The flight engineer, Sergeant Eric Morrey from Cheshire was the only Englishman on a crew of Australians: Flight Sergeant Tom Morris, bomb aimer; Flight Sergeant Max Merry, wireless air gunner; Pilot Officer Ian Paul, mid-upper gunner and Flight Sergeant Max Milner, rear gunner made up the rest of the crew. Morrey was too busy to worry overmuch about the far distant target for that night. After checking that the pitot head cover was off and that all engine cowlings and inspection panels were secure he climbed into the aircraft and made his way forward to his jump-seat alongside Charlie Cassell, checking that first-aid kits, hand fire-extinguishers and portable oxygen sets were in position, that emergency escape hatches were secure and that all pyrotechnics were safely stowed. Fuel booster pumps were then tested, carburettors primed and fuel tank contents noted. With Cassell he then carried out engine controls check, cockpit check and pre-flight drill. One by one the four engines were then started and when they were warmed up and running satisfactorily, the hydraulic system was tested to operate flaps, bomb-doors and turrets. Oxygen and intercom systems were also tested with the rest of their crew at their stations. On arrival at the runway holding-point, Morrey and Cassell made a final check of engine temperatures and pressures. All engines were then run-up for the last time. Leaning forward, Cassell set the directional gyro on his instrument panel to a zero heading for take-off. They were ready to go.

Finally, at 2220, an Aldis lamp flashed green in the darkness and JO-B rolled out onto the runway and lined up for takeoff. The take-off was routine with Cassell opening up all four throttles to full power but leading slightly with the port outer throttle to counteract the Lancaster's tendency to swing to port. At 800 feet over the darkened Lincolnshire countryside, Morrey returned the flaps to normal - 25° of flap was the recommended setting for take-off and JO-B, a Lancaster Mark I with Rolls-Royce Merlin XXII engines, settled down to a steady climb at 145 mph with a maximum fuel load and the usual bomb-load of a 4,000lb blockbuster and containers of clustered 4lb incendiaries.

'Strict silence was observed now,' Morrey recalls, 'unless to indicate any incident which required attention and this was only broken at regular intervals with Charlie Cassell checking with each member of the crew.'

Dan Conway, the pilot of Lancaster 'K-Kitty' on 467 Squadron, likened the four or five minutes of take off and holding the Lancaster close to the ground to build up air speed as equal in tension to the bombing run over the target. Some crews ignored the flight plan requiring them to keep to a delaying route before setting course at a specific time. They immediately left for the first marker, but at a slower speed to save fuel.[51]

'After the two previous trips - Berlin and Essen - it was a nice change to have a southerly trip to what for us was a new target' says Joe Wesley. 'After a satisfactory ground check we got airborne at approximately 2145 with our bomb load of 12,000lbs on the first leg out across the east coast to a point in the North Sea where we were to change course slightly about 10° starboard to cross the enemy coast near Zeebrugge, flying in a south-easterly direction to a point about thirty miles south of Brussels. The Met was fairly favourable as it indicated some cloud cover but this eventually proved to be far from accurate and there was bright moonlight with almost complete lack of cloud. Also, we were told about the special marker flares to be used by PFF. These were to be positioned on the way out, off the actual route and were to be falsely indicated turning-points.'

The *Sydney Morning Herald* had sent their London correspondent to Waddington around the time of the Nuremberg raid. Betty Wilson spent three days on the station and the article she wrote about the visit, eventually published on 20 May 1944, captures something of the atmosphere of a bomber station at war:

'At the moment, *Salome* is the Australians' favourite gramophone record, probably because they have their own words which they sing when the WAAF officers have gone home. Anyhow, they put it on at least fifty times a day.

'These men are living an unnatural life and, at the same time, a completely absorbing one. There are long periods when they have little or nothing to do. There are equally long periods of concentrated activity when all the sickness of waiting and anticipation is crystallised into Lancasters crawling up runways like great earth-bound insects; when the day's work comes to a climax in the planes' lovely, inimitable lift as they become airborne and ends, for some men, with a burst of bullets from a fighter's machine-guns, for others, with breakfast and the 'operational egg.'

'There is always a knot of people waiting to see them take off, standing there with thumbs jerked up as the Lancasters taxi up to the runway, accelerating with brakes on until the aircraft get off on a sort of a catapult release which will lift them and their bomb-load. The rear-gunner waggles his guns in farewell and all Lancasters - from 'A-Apple' to 'Z-Zero' - waddle forward to become airborne like great swans and circle the airfield until the sky seems full of planes against the gathering dusk. The Lancasters get off to their rendezvous. The watchers go back to the crew rooms to tidy up and get ready for the crews' return. In the mess the gramophone, rewound by WAAF stewards, still grinds out *Salome* in a horrid - but temporary - emptiness.'

Endnotes Chapter 5

38 *A Lucky Break* by Sergeant R. J. 'Jack' Dunn.
39 *Lancaster; The Biography* by S/L Tony Iveson DFC and Brian Milton (André Deutsch, 2009).
40 *Bomber Barons* by Chaz Bowyer (William Kimber 1983).
41 *Bomber Barons* by Chaz Bowyer (William Kimber 1983).
42 *The Nuremberg Massacre* by Geoff Taylor.
43 *Chased By The Sun; The Australians in Bomber Command in WWII* by Hank Nelson (ABC Books 2002).
44 *Through Footless Halls of Air: The Stories of Men Who Failed* by Floyd Williston. (General Store Publishing House 1996).
45 Quoted in *The Nuremberg Raid* by Martin Middlebrook. (Allen Lane 1973).
46 Flight Lieutenant Donald Frank Constable DFC RAAF and crew on Halifax III LV903 EY-H were shot down on the night of 24/25 March. Constable and five of his crew were killed. The two others were taken prisoner.
47 *Chased By The Sun; The Australians in Bomber Command in WWII* by Hank Nelson (Allen & Unwin 2002).
48 When they became wing commanders, Brill commanded 463 Squadron RAAF and Doubleday 61 Squadron. Each was awarded the DFC and DSO. Brill added a bar to his DFC later.
49 Dan Conway, *The trenches in the sky,* Hesperian Press, Victoria Park, 1995.
50 See *Chased By The Sun; The Australians in Bomber Command in WWII* by Hank Nelson (Allen & Unwin 2002).
51 See *Chased By The Sun; The Australians in Bomber Command in WWII* by Hank Nelson (Allen & Unwin 2002).

Chapter 6

On the morning of 30th March when he found out that he and his crew were 'on' that night Flight Sergeant Donald Gray on 50 Squadron at Skellingthorpe thought that 'at least it wasn't Berlin' and that this operation 'might be an easy one'. Though the weather had seemed to be worsening, the threat of snow and sleet had not materialised and with it the chance that the raid would eventually be scrubbed had evaporated. With everyone keyed up for the off a 'scrub' or cancellation went down like a lead balloon. It meant that the whole procedure would have to be gone through the next night and maybe the next night and for the crews, no trips being deducted from tour requirements. The only thing that had disturbed the 22-year old pilot at briefing was when Wing Commander Anthony Heward, who liked to close his briefings by selecting a gunner from one of the crews to come to the front and repeat the main points of the briefing, had chosen his mid-upper gunner, Sergeant Frank Patey, but he had promptly 'made a hash of it' much to the dismay of his pilot and the annoyance of the wing commander.[52] They left the Briefing Room to while away the hours until take off time. During this time no-one was allowed off the station.

As take-off time drew near the WAAF crew bus driver drove Gray's crew out to 'T-Tare's dispersal where their faithful ground crew flagged them in after each op. Gray walked round the aircraft carrying out the laid down external check. Sergeant Joe Grant, his Scottish flight engineer chatted to the ground crew to ensure everything was OK from his angle and then the crew prepared to board. Entering the Lancaster, Douglas Maughan turned left towards the rear gun turret housing four Browning machine guns and Frank Patey only had a few steps to reach his two gun turret but the rest of the crew had to clamber over the notorious centre spar. Donald Gray and Joe Grant started the four Merlins, intercom was checked with each member of the crew and all the necessary routine checks made, many of these with Grant who would be at his pilot's right hand side at all times. Finally, a signal to the waiting ground crew to pull away the wheel chocks; a last thumbs-up to them and the first of nineteen Lancasters started to roll - slowly at first, because the perimeter tracks were narrow and the undercarriage wide. One Lanc dropping a wheel into the soft earth at the side of the track could abort the trip for everyone behind. At this time, loaded with maximum petrol and bomb load each bomber weighed over thirty tons. At take-off time the nineteen Lancaster crews on 50 Squadron soon became eighteen when Australian Flight Sergeant Geoff Bucknell crashed after a tyre burst and W4933 skidded out of control. None of the crew was injured but this Lancaster, in part funded by Andover's magnificent total of £232,787 raised in a *'Wings for Victory'* campaign and which had completed forty-seven operational sorties, was subsequently struck off charge.[53]

'T-Tare's turn for take-off eventually arrived by way of a green Aldis lamp flashed from the small black and white chequered hut at the end of the runway and Gray slowly moved out onto the 2,000 yard runway lowering 20° of flap to give added lift to the wings for take-off. With the pitch of the propellers in fully fine he lined up the Lancaster on the runway, applied the brakes, came to a stop and revved up the engines to screaming point. The Rolls-Royce Merlins developed 1,500 horsepower each, so they had 6,000 horsepower roaring. He must not hesitate too long; the

Lancasters behind would all be anxiously awaiting their turn. He therefore eased the four throttles slowly forward, to waves from the small knot of station personnel who always turned up for ops take-offs. The friendly WAAF sergeant reputed to be a 'chop girl' who had shared a cup of tea with Gray in the Mess was at the forefront of well-wishers vigorously waving 'T-Tare' off. The Lancaster started to swing; it always did and Gray checked it by correction on the throttles. As the tail came off the ground and he had rudder control he moved all the throttles to fully open. Then he left the throttles to Joe Grant whose hand had been following closely behind his and he concentrated on the take off. The throttles fully open gave 18lbs boost; which was in excess of the recommended setting for the Merlin engines. Pilots could only hold this throttle setting for three minutes. Joe Grant shouted out the airspeed. Gray had no time to look at his instruments; 60, 70, 80 and at about 110 mph he felt the heavy Lancaster wanting to leave the 'deck', the end of the runway looming ever nearer until suddenly they were airborne. Gray reached down and selected the undercarriage lever to the 'up' position and immediately he gained a few more miles per hour. The speed was now 145 mph and if an engine failed at this time they might just make it. The three minutes were up and Gray throttled back to a powered climb at 2,850 revs and +9lbs boost. At about 300 feet he started to ease off that 20° of flap. If he did it too quickly he would sink back into the ground. So slowly, very slowly, he climbed away until he reached a safe height where he could throttle back to a normal climb at 7lbs boost and 2,650 revs per minute.

One by one the remaining Lancasters routinely took off without further incident; the vibration from their Merlins running at climbing power making the glasses dance on the bars of Lincolnshire's pubs, much to the wonder of the locals who could only watch and wait their return. Pilot Officer David Jennings and his crew had clambered out of the dark, crowded confusion of the crew truck with no great feeling of strain and certainly no presentiment of trouble. If anything, they were elated at having almost completed their tour on 50 Squadron, pleased with the prospect of leave and eager to join the elite ranks of the Path Finder Force. Jennings and his flight engineer, 'Jock' Stevens started the Merlins on VN-N and taxied out. Mainly, it looked like being a long trip, a typical deep penetration attack; at least eight hours according to Pilot Officer Carroll, the navigator. In all that time a lot could happen before they tumbled thankfully back into bed again at Skellingthorpe.

At 2207 Flight Sergeant 'Jimmy' Waugh took EE174 'A-Apple' off and on past the 800 years' old Norman cathedral in Lincoln. Once airborne each of the bombers' engines beat steadily and monotonously through the night sky with only the occasional pitch of the aircraft when they hit the slipstream of some aircraft ahead upsetting the smoothness of their flight. Take-off and the flight out were routine on VN-N also but Flight Sergeant Hayes in the mid-upper turret had never before been able to see so many of their aircraft so clearly at night. 'Crossing the enemy coast was uneventful and we had penetrated deep into enemy territory before the first alarms began. These were in the form of large red splashes on the ground caused by falling aircraft and tracers in the sky. By this time we were about thirty minutes away from the target and first enemy aircraft sighting occurred about this time.'

At Snaith where press correspondents and photographers watched seventeen Halifaxes on 51 Squadron take off, 'Joe' Pawell in a Halifax about half-way in the line-up was chewing his usual Phillies cigar which he never lit but always rolled around until it was oxygen time. During engine run-up he and Alf Barnard the flight engineer had some trouble on the port inner motor with some unexpected magneto drop which had not been there during the morning's run-up. The ground crew gave the all-clear after some minutes and all seemed OK on re-starting the motor. Back in the rest position the crew prepared for take-off as they saw the green from the ACP.

'Airborne, we circled base keeping a look out for Halifax aircraft coming up from Burn only a few miles away' recalled Bill Stenning the crew's wireless operator. 'I could see the lights at Selby and Goole and didn't think much of the black-out. We climbed to about 5,000 feet and then set course for The Wash where we were to cross the coast. We climbed to about 12,000 feet over the North Sea and after what seemed a short time Alf Barnard kicked me on the shoulder to come and have a look from the astrodome. (In a Halifax the wireless air gunner's station was down in the nose-section, with the navigator and bomb aimer forward of the cockpit.) There were flares ahead and it looked like a never-ending line ahead with flares making a sort of avenue for us to fly down. Wilf Matthews in the mid-upper turret was giving us a running commentary and occasional warnings of other aircraft to port and starboard.'

A total of eleven Halifaxes on 578 Squadron had taken off from Burn. One of them was Halifax LK-E in 'A' Flight skippered by 22-year old Pilot Officer Cyril Joe Barton who had lifted off at about 2200 hours. Cyril Barton was born at Elveden, Suffolk on 5 June 1921 and was brought up in New Malden, Surrey, where he had attended Beverley Boys School and Kingston College. He volunteered for aircrew duties and joined the RAFVR on 16 April 1941. He entered pilot training in the USA under the Arnold Scheme in late 1941 having set sail from Gourock, Scotland to Halifax, Canada aboard the transport ship Pasteur. After acclimatization at Maxwell Field, Montgomery, Alabama he received his Primary Training at Darr Aero Tech, Albany, Georgia and was one of a relative minority who were allowed to complete their training, having been 'held back' by illness or accidents, finally qualifying as a sergeant pilot on 10 November 1942. He then trained at 1663 Heavy Conversion Unit at Rufforth, Yorkshire. On 5 September 1943 Barton and his crew joined 78 Squadron and Barton was commissioned as a Pilot Officer three weeks later. Undertaking their first operational sortie against Montluçon, Barton completed nine sorties on 78 Squadron until 15 January 1944 and was then posted to 578 Squadron. The crew's second sortie on the new squadron was to Stuttgart in Halifax LK797. Barton was promoted to Flying Officer on 26 March. By 30 March, he had completed four attacks on Berlin and fourteen other operations including six sorties in LK797 - which the crew had named Excalibur. On one of these, two members of his crew were wounded during a determined effort to locate the target despite appalling weather conditions. The crew consisted of Pilot Officer Wally Crate RCAF, bomb aimer; Sergeant Maurice E. Trousdale, flight engineer; Sergeant Jack Kay, wireless air gunner; Sergeant Harry 'Timber' Woods, mid-upper gunner, Sergeant Fred Brice, rear gunner and Sergeant John Leonard Lambert from Newcastle on Tyne, navigator, who was unaware that he had been commissioned since 21 March, just nine days earlier. The crew's principal worry was the bright moonlight although, as usual, Lambert saw little from his navigation position of what was happening outside. Busy as he was with head down over his charts and log, Lambert was nevertheless concerned at the number of crew intercom reports about aircraft being shot down.

'We were equipped with tail-warning radar,' Lambert recalls, 'but this became unserviceable early in the night.'

At Spilsby near the railway linking Boston and Louth, inland from Skegness on the Wash, eighteen Lancaster crews on 207 Squadron took off early because they were to fly with the Path Finder Force. The first to take off was Lancaster 'V-Victor' which Pilot Officer Frank Collis in 'B' Flight lifted off at 2200. Born at Megantic, Quebec Province, Canada he had been a police constable in the London metropolitan force before enlistment. His crew were: Sergeant Griffiths, his Welsh navigator; Flying Officer Essery, a Canadian from Toronto, bomb aimer; Sergeant Atkins, a local from Lincolnshire and the crew's flight engineer; Sergeant Fox, from Tunbridge, wireless air gunner; Sergeant Topple, from Welwyn Garden City, mid-upper gunner; Sergeant Skinner, a Kentishman, rear gunner. Climbing and circling over Spilsby Collis set course thirty-eight minutes after take-off on a heading of 141° Magnetic. 'At 2304 the bombs were fused and navigation lights turned off. 'At 2315, over the North Sea, we commenced 'Windowing', Collis recalled. 'At 2327 we crossed the enemy coast at 20,000 feet. At 2346 we passed to the west of Brussels and had by then climbed to 21,000 feet, our height for bombing. Prior to bombing I can recall much more enemy activity behind us along our track than was usual but we were, ourselves, having it very easy. We had a detailed view of the whole affair with no possible chance of harm coming to us but it was obviously coming to others. In the distance, too, we could see PFF dropping the target-indicator markers for the diversionary spoofs, as briefed, on Cologne and Kassel.'

At Bourn a few miles west of Cambridge fourteen Lancasters on 97 Squadron PFF were dispatched. Pilot Officer Sidney Albert Edwards took 'Q-Queenie' off at 2210. Ten minutes later Flight Lieutenant Cliff S. Chatten, a confirmed teetotaller, took 'H-Harry' off. The previous August he had been shot down over Norfolk by Oberleutnant Wilhelm Schmitter, Staffelkapitän of 15/KG2 flying a Me 410A-1 on return from Berlin. Chatten was wounded in his legs and chest. He ordered the rest of the crew to bail out and left it late to get out. As he came down in his parachute he was injured when the Lancaster exploded below him. After this experience three of the crew refused to fly again.[54] Twenty-two year old Flying Officer Ross Orval Ellesmere RCAF from Powassan, Ontario took ND706 'A-Apple' into the sky over Bourn at 2230 hours.

'O-Oboe', skippered by a tough 31-year old Australian by the name of Flight Lieutenant Henry Stewart van Raalte, took off at just about the same time as Chatten. Flight Sergeant Maurice Durn, his 24-year old flight engineer, had been injured by flak on 2/3 December 1943 and had lost his entire crew the following night while recovering from his injuries. He had then joined another crew just in time for the trip to Berlin on Thursday 16/17 December, which has gone down in folklore as 'Black Thursday'. Twenty-five Lancasters were shot down and 29 more plus two Stirlings returning from mine-laying operations either crashed or were abandoned when their crews bailed out. In the vicinity of Ely, Durn's life and that of his fellow crewmembers was almost certainly saved by the decision of his skipper, Pilot Officer F. Smith, to abandon the aircraft, which went on to crash four miles northwest of Orford Ness, Suffolk and not far from the village of Sudbourne. Parachuting out into the darkness and fog, Durn was badly shaken by this sequence of events and he vanished off the station for some while before re-joining 97 Squadron. On the maximum effort on Berlin by 677 bombers on the night of 28/29 January, having failed to find the 'Big City' Van Raalte had bombed Kiel instead. Flight Sergeant Lionel George Laurie, his Australian rear gunner was decapitated by flak.

On the night of 30 March two 'B-Baker's - ND501 skippered by Pilot Officer Edward Leslie John Perkins and ND415 by Flying Officer Peter James Drane RAFVR, took off fifteen minutes apart. The 21 year old skipper, son of Albert Edward and Florence K. Drane of North Harrow and husband of Barbara M. Drane, had, in July 1943 been posted operational with his crew to 207 Squadron then based at Langar, Nottinghamshire, moving in September 1943 to Spilsby, Lincolnshire. Peter Drane and his crew completed 18 operational trips on 207, all of them German cities during what has been called the 'Battle of Berlin'. At the end of January 1944 the crew had transferred to 97 Squadron.

'The whole aircraft vibrated as the four Merlins savagely roared into life, injecting confidence into the crew for the mission ahead' said Flight Sergeant Ron Buck, Drane's 22-year old experienced rear gunner. 'Suddenly, the green Aldis flashed and the four-engined monster thundered down the runway on its mission of death and slowly but sedately, the heavily loaded Lancaster climbed into the night sky. For the rear gunner it was a great relief to look down and see the flare path going away and away. The rear gunner was far from the rest of the crew, shut off behind the revolving turret's door.'

A quiet, stocky fellow and a boxer up to international standard by the time he enlisted on 17 December 1940, Ronald Edgar Charles Buck was turned down for aircrew, but in 1941 he was sent to Calgary in Canada to open up the Empire Training Scheme and it was there that he re-mustered as U/T (Under Training) air gunner and completed the training. He married Betty Marsh, his childhood sweetheart at Trinity Church, West Ham on 15 May 1943.

'Wheels up, flaps up, OK lads - 1,000 feet, settle down' said Peter Drane on intercom. Ron Buck centralised the rear turret and looked down at the dark countryside and then switched on the gun sight and put the safety catches on the four Browning machine-guns to fire before settling down to the task ahead. The four Merlins beat out a rhythmic drone as he scanned the night sky. Buck was another on the squadron who had been thankful for his skipper's actions on 'Black Thursday'.

'I saw the glow of fires beneath the fog and knew that aircraft were going into the deck. We were tired and tensed up. It had been a long trip and we were keen to land and get to bed. A discussion broke among the crew concerning whether to attempt to land or abandon the aircraft. Pete Drane cut the discussion short.

'I'll take her up to five thousand and anyone who wants to bail out has my permission to do so'.

'There were no takers and we all decided to stay and take out chances. It was our eighteenth op and I'm sure we all felt a little ashamed of ourselves.

'At last came the order 'A-Able you may pancake'.

'Drane said 'Right, everyone, I'll put this cow down if it's the last thing I do'.

'I settled down as best I could and concentrated all my attention on the blackness below. We banked and straightened up. Suddenly I saw the ground and I screamed over the intercom 'Pull up!' There was no hesitation. The nose lifted and we climbed into the night sky to overshoot. Pete Drane came on the intercom and told me we couldn't have been on the deck; he had 300 feet on the clock when I shouted. It turned out that we had the wrong QFE and I believe that many others did the same that night, but they never lived to find out. Pete called up the control tower; they gave him a new QFE and we started our approach all over again. We were lucky the second time. The wind exposed part of the flare path and Pete was able to line the aircraft up. As I felt the wheels touch the runway, I turned the rear turret on the beam, sat back and watched the runway lights flashing by. We seemed to run down the runway for a long time and then, to my horror, there were no more lights. We began to bump and bounce about and I knew we were on the grass. After what seemed an eternity we came to a halt. It was an experience I shall never forget...'[55]

'Enemy coast two minutes, skipper', came the voice of Flight Sergeant Charles Trotman, Peter Drane's navigator. Born on 18 April 1921 and hailing originally from Woking, Trotman worked for the Post Office before joining the RAF. He wanted to get in early because he thought he would have more choice than if he was drafted and initially signed up to be a wireless operator. He went on to do pilot training in America. 'The instructor was rather a strange chap,' says Trotman. 'He didn't say a lot. He could speak to me in the aircraft but I couldn't speak back to ask a question. He said: 'Tomorrow we will perhaps do some stalls.' The following day I had no instructions. I thought I couldn't do stalls at just 2,000 feet and better get higher. He still didn't say anything. In the end he said: 'Brother, are you meeting some friend up here?' I shook my head. He said: 'In that case get down to goddamn 2,000 feet!' And that was the end of pilot training.' Failed as a pilot, Trotman re-trained as a navigator.

On reaching 21,000 feet, Sergeant George Prince, 'A-Apple's' flight engineer on 50 Squadron found the starboard outer engine to be overheating. The son of a garage owner, he had left school at fourteen to work for his father as a mechanic, a job in which he learned many skills that would prove useful when he became a flight engineer.[56] 'Jimmy' Waugh's crew had experienced similar trouble on two previous trips but had completed each operation successfully. They did not want to blot their copybook with a 'boomerang' so they agreed with their skipper's decision to press on. Their route was via the North Sea, crossing the enemy coast near Antwerp and then Brussels and Namur, keeping south of Aachen to Bonn and direct to Fulda where they would change course, heading south towards Nuremberg, with approximately 75 miles to the target area.

The chain of giant 'Freya' radars, their huge bowls constantly scanning the eastern coast of England from the Wash to Harwich, were first to pick up masses of blips on their cathode ray screens which emanated from the Norwich area and converged over the Northern part of the English Channel to take a south-easterly course. At the same time blips from a smaller bomber formation appeared in the southern sector of the North Sea. The shorter range Würzburgs with their thinner but more accurate beams, detected the air activity some time later. They were used to direct night-fighters near enough to the bombers until the bordfunker could pick up the Viermot or four-motor bomber and vector his pilot to administer the coup-de-grace.

When the bomber stream crossed the Belgian coast at Zeist Generalleutnant Josef

'Beppo' Schmid's Headquarters at Treuenbrietzen was immediately alerted and the codeword 'Fasen' ('Pheasant') was flashed to all night-fighter units to warn them that raids were imminent. Schmid, a Bavarian, born on 24 September 1901, was a close friend of Hermann Göring and had commanded Abteilung 5, the Luftwaffe's Military Intelligence Branch from 1 January 1938 to 9 November 1942. Adolf Galland later criticized Schmid for doing nothing to upgrade the low quality of the intelligence service. In late 1942 Schmid was put in charge of Division 'General Göring' in Tunisia, known as 'Kampfgruppe Schmid'. On personal orders from Göring, he was flown out of the Tunisian pocket. Promoted to Generalmajor on 1 February 1943 and Generalleutnant on 1 July 1944 he was given command of I Jagdkorps.

Schmid had studied the British radio reports that had been intercepted by his listening stations and handed to him in a teleprinter flash by one of the Luftwaffenhelferingen auxiliaries. It said, 'Mosquitoes making low level attacks on night-fighter airfields in Holland'. Radar blips confirmed that a raid in some strength could be expected with the Ruhr the likely target. The smaller stream approaching the Heligoland Bight must, deduced Schmid, be minelayers.

Among Schmid's night-fighter divisional commanders was Oberst im Generalstab Johannes Janke, Chief of Staff of 7 Jagddivision with headquarters at Schleissheim. Janke was responsible for the night and day air defence of southern Germany and he and his equally skilful staff had made JD 7 the foremost Jagddivision in the Nachtjagd. Over the next hour a total of 246 single and twin-engined aircraft were concentrated in waiting areas, predominantly near Bonn (radio and light beacons 'Ida') and Frankfurt (radio and light beacons 'Otto').

All approaches to occupied Europe and Germany were divided into circular and partly overlapping areas, which took full advantage of Bomber Command's tactic in sending bombers singly and on a broad front and not in concentrated streams. Each Himmelbett Räume ('four poster bed boxes') about twenty miles square with names like 'Hamster', 'Eisbär' ('Polar Bear') and 'Tiger', was a theoretical spot in the sky, in which one to three fighters orbited a radio beacon waiting for bombers to appear. Each box was a killing-zone in the path of hundreds of incoming prey. The first fighters of NJG1 and NJG4 were sent up from their bases in the Low Countries over radio-beacon 'Ida' south of Aachen on the orders of 3 Jagddivision commanded by 38-year old ex-Battle of Britain and Spanish Civil War pilot, Generalmajor Walther Grabmann at his HQ at Deelen. Grabmann, a former policeman in the Luftpolizei (Air Police) before the war, had been credited with seven aerial victories during the Spanish Civil War, claimed in 137 combat sorties. Units of 1st Jagddivision at Döberitz under the command of Oberst 'Hajo' Herrmann were in orbit around radio-beacon 'Otto' east of Frankfurt. Also above 'Otto' were the gruppes of 47-year old Generalmajor Max Ibel who commanded 2nd Jagddivision at Stade. Victories were mainly achieved on the return journey when the bomber stream had been more dispersed than on the way in. It was easier too for the Jägerleitoffiziers (JLOs or GCI-controllers) in their 'Battle Opera Houses' to orchestrate Nachtjäger movements and pinpoint individual target aircraft in the Himmelbett Räume. Though the JLOs were far removed from the actual battles, high tiered rows of Leuchtspukers or 'Light Spitter girls' wearing headphones and laryngophones with trays containing thick black crayons within easy reach received curt, precise orders which came through their headphones and using bold arrow symbols, copied the information onto a huge transparent glass screen for them while operators moved the plots on the Seeburg plotting tables. These women were highly-trained and they made up about 75 per cent of the personnel of the aircraft-reporting service.

'A few minutes after listening to the Group broadcast at midnight,' said Flight Sergeant Sid Whitlock on 'B-Baker' on 166 Squadron 'a fighter put a burst into the belly of the aircraft, having come up from the pitch black below.'

Their attacker was 40-year old Hauptmann Berthold 'Petz' 'Sneak' Ney of Stab III./NJG2 flying a Ju 88C-6 who claimed the 'Lanki' at Westerburg west of Becken at 0039 hours for his sixth Abschüsse.[57]

Flight Lieutenant Fred Taylor, Whitlock's pilot had never been a religious man but that night he recited the 23rd Psalm for hours on end. His recital however was in vain. With smoke and flames rising from the bomb inspection panels on the floor he knew that 'B-Baker' was doomed. He gave the order to bail out. 'The aircraft rocked' continues Whitlock, 'my set started smoking and the aircraft started filling with smoke. The R/T was dead, transmitter and receiver out of action and not a sound on the intercom. Flight Sergeant McCarney, the navigator and Flight Sergeant Watson, bomb aimer came back to me and pointed to the rear of the aircraft, indicating it was time to leave. By this time flame was spouting through the inspection panels and acrid smoke had filled the aircraft. Getting Pilot Officer Standen down from his mid-upper gunner turret, we made for the rear entrance door of the aircraft, on the starboard side, where we found that Sergeant Thrower the rear gunner had already jettisoned the door. On our approach he left the aircraft followed by the mid-upper gunner. I was next and on looking around was aghast to see McCarney with his parachute canopy opened and spilled out, having caught his rip-cord handle on part of the mid-upper turret mounting. I then left the aircraft and as I floated down flames were streaming from the bomb-bay of the aircraft. Landing with a breathtaking jolt I found the ground covered in light snow.'

Sidney Whitlock found the frozen earth too hard to dig a hole in which to bury his parachute. He carried the tangled canopy in his arms until he came to a ditch where he dumped it hoping that it would not be noticed for some time because of falling snow. 'I had left the fields where I had landed, to try and get my bearings as the navigator had had no time to carry out our long-prepared plan of letting us know where we were in case of having to bail out. Before I had gone more than a short distance I was surrounded by armed German civilians with snarling dogs on leashes.'[58]

Whitlock was taken to a police station where he was joined by Watson, Standen and Thrower. After hours of standing at the police station, with most of the local village population coming along to inspect them, the four crewmen were taken to a country railway station nearby. In a buffet there they encountered their Irish navigator and their pilot. McCarney had broken his leg when he dropped from a tree where he had been hung up by his parachute canopy. Taylor had waited until the last possible moment for the slap on his thigh from the last member of the crew to leave the aircraft, which was his own signal to bail out. Too late to get to the escape hatch in the nose Taylor had gone out through the emergency escape hatch in the cockpit canopy above his head and had broken his thigh when he hit the tail-plane of the aircraft. Standen and Thrower carried their pilot on a stretcher to a waiting goods train. Cradling arms with the bomb aimer, Whitlock carried the navigator 'who involuntarily screamed at every step, not having had his broken leg attended to'.

By nightfall on the day after Nuremberg, the airmen had arrived by freight train at a larger town where Taylor and McCarney were taken away to hospital and Sid Whitlock, the two gunners and the bomb aimer were each put into separate cells. At first light the following day they were taken by train to a French PoW camp where they were thoroughly searched to the extent of bending over with backsides bared. This was the first time they had been searched apart from an initial frisking of their flying gear. Just forty-eight hours after being shot down they arrived at the Luftwaffe interrogation and transit camp, Dulag Luft at Oberursel near Frankfurt-am-Main where civilians spat on them. After that came documentation and solitary confinement in an overheated cell with barred, closed windows. During interrogation it was made clear to Whitlock that many crews had been shot down. It was also made clear by the interrogating officers that they knew far more about the operation than Whitlock did. While at Dulag Luft the crew learned that their flight engineer, Sergeant Eric Norman Whitfield of Wallasey, Cheshire and 29-year old Sergeant Allen Wakley Hughes had both been killed. Before Whitlock left Dulag Luft, interrogation officers told him that 132 British aircraft had been shot down on the attack. 'The transit camp was so full it could quite easily have been true,' he commented.[59]

Flight Sergeant Roger Bouldin Callaway RCAF on 'B' Flight on 426 'Thunderbird' Squadron RCAF at Linton-on-Ouse, had volunteered to fly as the rear turret gunner on Lancaster OW-N piloted by 32-year old Flight Lieutenant Frederick Randolph Shedd of Toronto. Callaway recalled:

'We were told at briefing that the diversions towards Berlin would draw any fighters away from us. However, it sure seemed that Jerry had all our turning-points marked well in advance. My buddy [Sergeant Hubert Eric Sjöquist who was the mid-upper gunner on Lancaster II DS852 'Q-Queenie'] had walked out to the dispersal area where he said goodbye and added that he wouldn't be seeing me again. North of Nuremberg I spotted a Ju 88 firing at a Lancaster on our port beam and shooting it down. This was about 0100. The Ju 88 then hauled around to starboard and was coming at us when we let go a burst at him. He veered off and tackled another Lancaster on our starboard beam which blew up. This was Sjöquist's aircraft.'

'Q-Queenie', piloted by Warrant Officer2 R. G. S. Douglas RCAF was claimed shot down north of Schmalkalden, 150 kilometres east of 'Ida' by Leutnant Paul Fehre of 5./NJG3 for his fifth victory. Sjöquist, who suffered minor injuries, walked for several days until he reached the outskirts of a large town during a snowstorm and, lonely and exhausted, he finally gave himself up to a wounded soldier on leave. Douglas, Sergeant H. J. V. Vincent, the flight engineer, Pilot Officer Edward George Wey RCAF the 29-year old navigator who was from Vancouver and Flying Officer D. T. Stewart RCAF were also taken prisoner. Wey died of natural causes on 3 March 1945, while a prisoner of war. He left a widow, Agnes. Pilot Officers Harold Alexander Clark RCAF the 21-year old rear gunner, from Marville, Ontario and Sidney Herman Cullen RCAF the 24-year old wireless operator of Port Arthur, Ontario were killed.

According to Ted Shaw's log book, take-off was at 2159 hours. 'The bomb-load consisted of a 4,000lb blockbuster and incendiaries. On crossing the Channel I watched the explosion of the bomb load of an aborted aircraft from about 7,000 feet. I had never seen a big one blow up so close and was amazed at the power and the pink and orange fire which seemed to last for about twenty or thirty seconds.

'Upon reaching the enemy coast the usual flak and lights were encountered but we had no trouble until we were approaching the target. For the first time on our tour we sighted flaming objects, resembling burning aircraft, floating in the sky and which, I believe, were called scarecrows. After we had crossed the enemy coast it was a brilliant moonlit night with practically no cloud. It was so clear that we could easily make out other aircraft in the bomber stream.'

Any lingering hopes that Flight Sergeant Walter Morrisby had of arriving at the target before the night fighters had been stirred seemed to hold true. After crossing the Belgian coast there was some sporadic but accurate flak that necessitated evasive action but no fighter flares, dropped to illuminate the bomber stream, were observed, nor any attacks. But from about half way along the leg from Aachen to the turning-point for the target run-in, the position changed radically. 'German fighters had marked the route very efficiently with flares and this, coupled with the half-moon and cloud below our height of 21,000 feet, tended to silhouette aircraft flying at a lower altitude to a very marked degree. At this stage I observed many combats in the waves following behind us and aircraft falling.'

Bill Stenning on 51 Squadron saw a huge burst in the sky ahead over the enemy coast and on the intercom someone said, 'They've had it'. 'I went back down into the nose and spoke to Bob Clarke the navigator who had been very quiet and matter-of-fact. He wasn't at all surprised that we were well and truly in the bomber stream.'

After they crossed the enemy coast of occupied Belgium, Fred Stuart in the mid-upper turret of 'M-Mike' on 10 Squadron saw the first British aircraft going down. 'Hell, the fighters are up already,' the skipper's voice rasped over the intercom. 'It looks as if they're waiting for us. Gunners, test your guns and everyone keep a sharp lookout.' By this time Stuart and the rear gunner needed no reminding. 'We had barely finished testing our guns,' said Stuart, 'when a Ju 88 fired at us from the beam at about a hundred yards range. A quick burst from our guns in reply seemed to deter him and he presumably went off in search of easier prey. I remember saying to the skipper that I didn't like the look of things and that it could be a really sticky night. This proved to be somewhat of an understatement as we had more combats before we reached the target area. Both of these attacks were pressed home with vigour, courage, skill and determination and I can assure you that we were glad when they broke off their attacks. Heavily laden though she was, 'M-Mike' had behaved like a thoroughbred.'

After a steady climb out over eastern England, Pilot Officer Charlie Cassell, piloting JO-B, levelled out at 19,500 feet at a speed of 165 mph which was maintained during the outward flight. Sergeant Eric Morrey his flight engineer could tell when they reached the enemy coast: 'There was the usual moderate flak coming up with tracer in front of the aircraft and fading away again in the darkness. Searchlights were occasionally picking out aircraft but we were fortunate and not troubled. Tom Morris, the bomb aimer and I were now putting bundles of 'Window' down the chute to upset the enemy radar system. It was very cold now inside the aircraft and the hot-air system seemed to have no effect at this height.'

'Soon after we flew over the coast,' Pilot Officer Arthur Rhodes Sydney Bowman on 463 Squadron RAAF, a 24-year old grazier from Singleton, New South Wales, flying Lancaster 'J-Jig', recalled, 'we could see fires on the ground and plenty of enemy night fighters and we soon realized that the fires were our own aircraft that were being shot down one after another. The night turned out to be not only very clear with hardly a cloud but there was almost a full moon and they were waiting for us. I remember saying to my navigator that we did not need his skill that night as one only had to follow the fires (of shot-down aircraft burning on the ground) to keep on track. From this moment on we really had to keep on our toes. It was so clear and it was so easy to see where our other bombers were that I decided that I would alter course as much as possible so as not to be such a sitting duck. Many fighters flew over and under us and we would no sooner get one alert and there would be another, only minutes after. Our gunners had plenty of practice this night and I think that they shot up two.'

As the blips on German radar headed over the Scheldt estuary to the Liège-Florennes line, Generalleutnant 'Beppo' Schmidt's staff decided, correctly, that a smaller RAF formation in the southern sector of the North Sea approaching the Heligoland Bight must consist of mine laying aircraft. Jamming was carried out on a large scale but Mosquito 'spoof' attacks on Cologne, Frankfurt and Kassel were also identified for what they were because to the German defences they were apparently flying without H_2S. Thanks to the 'Naxburg' and 'Korfu' ground receiving stations, the defenders had no difficulty in distinguishing the RAF feint attack forces from the main body of raiders. The German war diarist noted: Assembly, leaving England and approach could be followed correctly by 'Rotterdam' bearings ['Rotterdam' was the German code-name for H_2S]. Feint attacks on Cologne, Frankfurt and Kassel by Mosquitoes appeared quite clearly, as the Mosquitoes were flying without 'Rotterdam'.[60]

The heavies on the other hand could quite clearly be followed on radar by their H_2S bearings. As the bomber stream was clearly recognized from the start, it was attempted to switch in night fighters as far west as possible.

The weather over Belgium and eastern France was 0/10ths to 4/10ths thin cloud while Holland and the Ruhr were cloudless. At Nuremberg there was 10/10ths cloud at 1,600 to 12,000 feet but the cloud veiled at 16,000 feet with generally good altitude visibility.

High over Holland an orange glow splashed the darkness below and signalled that the first combats were 'on'. The fiery outline of a Lancaster plunged earthwards, tracer screaming from the rear turret. A searchlight flashed on, dead straight and blinding. As rapidly as it appeared it went out. Suddenly it was there again, slowly toppling backwards as if pointing their course to the fighters hurtling through the night towards Belgium. 'S-Sugar' skippered by Flight Lieutenant Brian Mill heading for the drop zone at Antwerp had evaded the fighters but it could not outrun the enemy flak. Mill was probably grateful that he could not hear the mass thunder of the barrage below, above the roar of the bomber's four Merlins, but the spine-tingling crump of the shells as they burst uncomfortably close, spewing out their shrapnel jarred the tensed nerves of the eight man crew. Finally, over the Westerschelde 'Sugar' was hit. Mill could not prevent the bomber crashing into the River Scheldt (Schelde) two kilometres west of Hansweert (Zeeland). The two Belgian agents, 'Troilus' and 'Lucullus', died quickly as a result of a rapid in-surge of water into the fuselage. Three of the Halifax crew also failed to survive, but the rest were able to paddle ashore in the aircraft's dinghy. Flying Officer Eric Francis DFC the navigator, Warrant Officer2 Frederick Anderson RCAF the bomb aimer and Flight Sergeant Edwin Bates the 30-year old wireless operator who was from Ashton-under-Lyne in Lancashire were killed and are commemorated on the Runnymede Memorial.

Splitting into two groups the survivors set off in different directions. The Canadian flight engineer, Warrant Officer2 S. E. Godfrey RCAF, Warrant Officer J. Weir RAAF the Australian mid-upper gunner and Flight Sergeant G. W. Kimpton the rear gunner were taken prisoner at s'Gravenpolder, Zuid Beveland, Holland. Flight Lieutenants Brian Mill and Dennis R. Beale enjoyed better fortune, at least at first. They met members of the Dutch Resistance at a farm near Biezelinge and in due course were taken across the Scheldt Estuary to Breskens, twelve kilometres north of the Belgian border. Early in May 1944 they were taken to the Belgian town of Zelzate where they were put with the Pierets and De Colvenaer families who were already hiding forty-seven other Allied airmen. Some while later they were joined by a Dutch lieutenant, Gilbert Beleir and by an American airman, H. Lang. Finally, on 7 September 1944 the alarm was raised when a German patrol was identified heading to raid the house of Albert de Colvenaer in which the four evaders were living. Mill, Lang and Beleir managed to get out over the roof and disappeared into the woods. Beale hid in a bedroom, but was discovered. He and Albert De Colvenaer, his seventeen-year-old son Yvan and Andre Pierets were taken to the German Feldgendarmerie at Zelzate, where they were interrogated by a Leutnant Hoffmann. De Colvenaer and his son were taken to Vlissingen (Flushing) and after trial by a German military tribunal under Oberst Reinhardt, were condemned to death. At 8 o'clock on the morning of 11 September 1944, together with two other so-called 'convicts', M. Dieleman and Wim Niesthoven, they were taken to the dunes of Koudekerke and shot. Beale saw out the rest of the war in Stalag Luft I at Barth in Pomerania.[61]

Flight Sergeant Thomas Noel Heyward 'Tom' Fogaty DFM, Skipper of a 115 Squadron Lancaster crew - average age 23 - operating from Witchford near Ely, recalled.

'Frankly, we were shaken when we saw that we were going straight to Nuremberg without any of the usual diversions; even though we were assured that there would be ten-tenths cloud cover for most of the way.'

Fogaty, who has been described by another man on his crew as 'a brave man but in a sense a very ordinary one, just a level-headed man from Devon' had flown thirteen operations. He had been awarded the DFM for bringing back a crippled Lancaster (DS629 KO-H) on the night of the 14 January 1944 after it had been attacked by a night-fighter while bombing Brunswick. The target was identified by means of red and green markers and Fogaty dropped his bombs from 22,000 feet. After leaving, the aircraft was attacked from below by a Ju 88. The enemy aircraft not being seen until it broke away. The starboard inner was hit by cannon shells and caused violent shuddering of the aircraft. Sergeant Stephen Richard Life, Fogaty's 19-year old flight engineer, was hit in the hand and leg and the mid-upper and front turrets were put out of action. Hydraulic oil and smoke filled the aircraft. In a second attack the starboard wing was hit again. A third attack was made by the Ju 88 but was unsuccessful. The Lancaster by this time was down to 12,000 feet and it was observed that the starboard inner engine had been shot away. Fogaty remained calm throughout the attacks and encouraged his crew. A course was set for home, with the aircraft now down to 5,000 feet. Fogaty was determined to bring his aircraft and crew home or ditch rather than fall into enemy hands. Skilfully, he flew his damaged aircraft back to the emergency landing airfield at Woodbridge, executing a successful landing with a burst tyre, without further damage to aircraft or crew. This was Fogaty's fourth operation as captain and only his first on Lancasters. He was recommended for an immediate award of the DFM.[62]

In the first three months that 115 Squadron had operated Lancasters nearly thirty were missing or written off in accidents in one of the highest casualty rates in Bomber Command.

Endnotes Chapter 6

52 *The Nuremberg Raid* by Martin Middlebrook.

53 Bucknell and his crew later went to the Path Finders. All were killed on a daylight raid on Bois de Cassan on 6 August 1944 when they were shot down by flak near Paris.

54 *Intruders over Britain: The Luftwaffe Night Fighter Offensive 1940 to 1945* by Simon W. Parry (ARP 2003). On 8 November 1943 Schmitter and his bordfunker Unteroffizier Felix Hainzinger were killed when their Me 410 was shot down near Eastbourne by Squadron Leader W. H. Maguire DFC and Flying Officer W. D. Jones on 85 Squadron flying a Mosquito XII. Schmitter was posthumously promoted to Major and awarded the Oak leaves to his Ritterkreuz.

55 Quoted in *The Berlin Raids* by Martin Middlebrook (Viking 1988).

56 *The Red Line* by John Nichol.

57 Major Ney was forced to bail out on the way back from Unnternehmen (Operation) 'Gisela' on 3/4 March 1945 as he could not find an airfield to land in the atrocious weather and he was badly injured in the process. The result was a paralysis from the waist down. Ney remained bed-ridden for the next 55 years, finally passing away in February 1996. See *Nachtjagd: The Night Fighter versus Bomber War over the Third Reich 1939-45* by Theo Boiten (The Crowood Press, 1997).

58 Quoted in *The Nuremberg Massacre* by Geoff Taylor (Sidgwick & Jackson 1980).

59 Recounted in *The Nuremberg Massacre* by Geoff Taylor.

60 Quoted in *Sky Battles! Dramatic Air Warfare Actions* by Alfred Price (Arms & Armour Press 1993).

61 See *RAF Evaders: The Comprehensive Story of Thousands of Escapers and their Escape Lines, Western Europe, 1940-1945* by Oliver Clutton-Brock (Grub Street 2009).

62 Flight Sergeant Harold Edward George Pugh, who flew as a spare bomb aimer on this trip with Fogaty, would lose his life on the night of the 18/19 April when his aircraft was shot down over Witchford during the Intruder incident. Sergeant Life was admitted to East Suffolk and Ipswich Hospital with machine gun wounds. Tragically, after recovering from his injuries he drowned at Denver Sluice near Kings Lynn during dinghy drill on 11 July 1944. See *Memories of RAF Witchford* by Barry & Sue Aldridge (Milton Contact Ltd 2013).

Chapter 7

Near the picturesque little town of Mildenhall, nineteen miles north-east of Cambridge, sixteen Lancaster crews on 622 Squadron and eleven on XV Squadron assembled for briefing at the airfield in 3 Group in Suffolk. On XV Squadron 21-year old Pilot Officer Oliver Villiers Brooks and his crew waited for the off. Brooks, who was from Hampshire where he was raised and educated, had left school at the age of seventeen and worked for a short time as a temporary civil servant at the Royal Naval Armament Depot at Corsham near Bath in Wiltshire. A keen amateur boxer, he did not think his eyesight was good enough for pilot training and he considered becoming a RAF physical training instructor but he was accepted and in 1942 he honed his flying skills in the USA and Canada. In April 1943 Brooks formed his first crew at 12 OTU at Edgehill, a satellite to Chipping Warden, when their mount was the old Wimpy. Unfortunately, their time together was brief because Brooks had fractured his hand in a *'Wings For Victory'* boxing tournament. The injury, which put him back two months, most likely saved his life. Crews were being fed into 3 Group, which at that time was operating Stirlings and the 'chop' rate was very high. He had no idea what happened to his original crew and could only assume that they found another pilot.[63] Brooks took a new crew with him when he resumed flying Wellingtons in July; Flight Sergeant Ken Pincott, was navigator, Robert Allan Gerrard the 23-year old Canadian bomb aimer was engaged to be married, Harry 'Whacker' Marr, air gunner and Les Pollard, wireless operator. Later, at 1651 HCU at Waterbeach, Ron Wilson the mid-upper gunner and Sergeant Cecil Harry 'Chick' Chandler the flight engineer joined the crew. Before joining up 'Chick' had been in reserved occupation, manufacturing parts for anti aircraft guns. Like many, Chandler was superstitious and would always carry a grey silk scarf with black markings which his mother had given him. Though he was the 'baby' on the crew, he knew just what the dangers were after flying thirteen operations and how easy it was to be shot down and killed. In February Sergeant Robert Edward Barnes replaced Pollard as wireless operator. Brooks' first operation on the Lancaster was on the night of 20/21 January when he took 'O-Orange' to Berlin and back. This would be the aircraft they would fly on the Nuremberg operation.

While Pilot Officer Raymond Curling RAAF and Sergeant J. K. Humphries the flight engineer on 'A-Able' on 'A' Flight on 622 Squadron started the Lancaster's four Merlins, ran them up, checked flight and engine instruments, the hydraulic, pneumatic and electrical systems, the oxygen system and flight controls, the rest of the crew carried out their own ground tests. In the nose Flight Sergeant J. R. Short RNZAF checked his bombing panel, bomb sight and front turret. Barely five feet tall, fellow New Zealander, Flight Sergeant Featherstonehaugh at his navigation table behind the black-out curtain in the fuselage tunnel aft of the cockpit checked repeater compass, altimeter, airspeed indicator, radar aids, red plotting light and the sharpness of his plotting pencils. Sergeant H. Harris and Sergeant H. P. R. Russell checked the rotation of their mid-upper and rear gun turrets, elevation, depression and cocking of their guns and illumination of their gun-sights. Harris, who earlier in the war had shot down an enemy aircraft while serving with an ack-ack unit, had re-mustered to aircrew to avenge the death of his twin brother who was killed on ops. Aft of the navigator, Flight Sergeant R. I. Smith RAAF the wireless air gunner at his radio station ran through the R/T and W/T equipment, crew intercom system plugs and microphones, flares, Very pistol and signal cartridges. Seated before the bright red, green, blue and yellow knurled knobs of his bank of radio equipment, Smith carried out no actual test broadcast for, as usual radio silence had been imposed lest German signals monitors Channel, drew obvious conclusions from any sudden and significant increase in radio traffic. The five trips the crew had already flown together had not been uneventful. In 42½ hours' operational hours they had experienced flak damage, fighter attack and a mid-air collision.

'On this occasion' recalled Curling 'Butch' Harris decided to take a risk on the moon which was almost full and ideal for enemy fighters. By 2200 we were well on the way. As soon as we reached the enemy coast the enemy defences went in to attack. We were equipped with an instrument called 'Boozer'. This was a warning device in the form of two lights in the pilot's cockpit. One, a yellow light, would blink on if an enemy aircraft picked the aircraft up on his radar beam and the other light, a red one, would warn of anti-aircraft ground defences. In the event of either coming on we would immediately go into evasive action. The instrument had a reputation of going haywire. As soon as we reached enemy territory I thought my 'Boozer' had gone berserk but the convincing puffs of black smoke behind us confirmed that the ack-ack indicator was working OK. From that point to the target, enemy fighters seemed to be on us in swarms and the sky was continually criss-crossed with tracers. It was truly grim and we were extremely tensed. Every second I was waiting for the word from my gunners to weave. We were not attacked. All we could see was my little light blinking from time to time, streams of tracer and the all-too-frequent sight of a dead aircraft diving to earth in flames.'

The first Nachtjäger reported making contact close to Liège, which was the start of a running battle that lasted ninety minutes until 0130 hours. The bombers would pass any point on the route at an average of 46 per minute. That was sufficient to saturate the defending gun and searchlight defences and present far more targets than they could possibly engage.[64] Even so, on the long 400 kilometre leg from Namur to the target, the Nachtjagd would shoot down 79 bombers. Nuremberg, as far as the Nachtjagd was concerned, was the 'night of the big kill'. Despite the British jamming the first interception of the bomber stream in the area south of Bonn was successful. From there on in the bomber stream was hit repeatedly and the majority of the losses occurred in the Giessen-Fulda-Bamberg area.

As Squadron Leader Bill Brill was later to recall, 'All went well until we had settled down on the long leg but before we were abeam of Aachen the rot had really begun to set in. For the next ninety minutes the bomber stream was continuously under pressure from fighters. It seemed to me that during this entire period I could, at any one time, see three of our aircraft falling in flames. Cannon tracer could be seen in almost every direction - and if it were cannon it was certainly not ours because we did not carry such armament. In practically every instance, following a burst of cannon-fire, one of our bombers exploded or began to burn. Some aircraft blew up within fairly close range whilst one or two flew past in flames from stem to stern. The incendiaries from the many doomed aircraft spread over a large area of the ground below and almost the entire track on this leg was traced out in a carpet of burning white incendiaries. The cannon-fire being thrown around seemed to be in three colours

- white, red and green - and these apparently slowly floating balls of light formed what, under other circumstances, would have been pretty patterns. However, there was one thing about the tracer which did puzzle me. Although I saw dozens of our aircraft being shot down, on only one occasion did I see any bombers return tracer fire. This was hard to understand as we were flying down moon. I decided then and there that the night fighters were using upward firing cannon. This was later confirmed when the RAF captured a night fighter and found that it was equipped with two 30-millimetre cannon fixed at an angle from the vertical. It was merely a matter of: find the quarry, close in from underneath which was in the bomber's blind area, press the trigger and roll clear.[65]

'The forecast winds were a little astray. The force, or what was left of it, ended up north of track at turning point 'C'. The tendency was for all crews to turn near Fulda, north of and short of 'C' and this had some dire results. The searchlights and flak of Schweinfurt came into operation and to many crews it seemed to lie where Nuremberg ought to have been. The moment one anxious crew loosed its load on Schweinfurt dozens followed suit. The previous hour-and-a-half had been enough inducement for anyone to want to unburden his aircraft of the bomb-load as soon as possible and it could well have been that many crews knew they were not over Nuremberg. About twenty miles from Nuremberg we ran into heavy cloud, some of which appeared to tower over 20,000 feet. However, through a small break we could see incendiaries burning where some crews had attacked a town fifteen miles up the river. Two or three minutes from the target we came out of the cloud at our level although there was still complete cloud below us. Just as we came out of the cloud there was a violent explosion immediately ahead of us. The ball of flame accompanying the explosion was quite intense and in its light a pall of black could be seen just for an instant. Almost coincidental with the explosion our aircraft bucked and vibrated. The Path Finder 'Wanganui' flares could be seen directly ahead so we began our bombing run. However just as we lined up, the rear gunner reported the rear turret out of action and then, as the bombs fell away, the port outer engine lost all power. I directed the flight engineer to feather the airscrew on this motor.

'The light from the 'Wanganui' flares above the cloud was being reflected and the whole upper sky was illuminated. It was no surprise therefore when 'Tubby' Fuller reported an enemy fighter lining up astern to make an attack on us. He gave me a good running commentary and when we considered that the fighter was about to fire I turned towards his line of attack and his cannon-fire passed harmlessly astern. We threw a little tracer his way and he went off to find someone he could surprise.

'As we set course for the long run home the second motor on the port side lost all power and the prop began wind-milling in the slipstream. The thought of a five-hour or more run home on two motors hardly raised a cheer from the crew. However, I ordered everyone to check parachutes and keep them handy and then checked to see if any engine fault could be located. Nothing amiss was evident so I told the flight engineer to feather this motor also. Before he could press the feathering button there was a cough, a shower of sparks and a sheet of flame from the second sick engine and it burst into life.'

Sergeant Ron Walker's crew on 57 Squadron, which was in the first wave after the Path Finders had been briefed to expect 'Wanganui' coloured sky markers positioned over the target by 'Oboe'-equipped blind-marking Mosquitoes.

'As we were turning to go south to the target' his navigator, 'Mack' MacKinnon recalls, 'Ken Bly reported that he could see TI flares going down. As I estimated we were more than sixty miles from the target I said that he must have darned good eyesight. He insisted they were there, pretty well on our starboard bow and we were going past them. Ron Walker then plaintively asked me where we were to go. H_2S was behaving well and I insisted that we go straight on. Nevertheless, I was relieved when the bomb aimer duly reported further TI flares straight ahead, where they were supposed to be. Later we learned that, in error, PFF had marked Schweinfurt.'

Sergeant 'Ginger' Hammersley, the crew's wireless operator adds: 'PFF crews were on special squadrons that marked the target with various coloured flares to control where our bombing would take place. On this occasion these were hardly required as the moon was brilliant and other aircraft were plainly visible in the air nearby. This was also a bonus for the German night fighters and they were soon into action. Although our wave received little attention during the attacks, we could see the battles taking place around us and there were a considerable number of aircraft being shot down as we flew on deeper into Germany. The Path Finder aircraft were about five minutes late on target and their marking was rather scattered. However, my crew bombed from 21,000 feet and 'Mack' informed me later that we had hit our target.'[66]

On the long leg, 'C-Charlie' on 106 Squadron was hit in the bomb-bay and petrol tanks. Sergeant 'Bob' Dack describes what happened:

'The Skipper said, 'It's time to get out. Get out everyone.' I was a careful sort of bloke and I always kept my parachute underneath my seat. I put it on but then she went down with all four engines flat out. It went through my mind that it was just like a scene from one of those American films with the aircraft screaming downwards out of control. Once that started I knew we couldn't get out. I was thrown on top of the navigator [Flight Sergeant Ronald Henry George Parker RAAF, who was from Naremburn] and we were rolling about together. I remember my face being pressed against two dials which I remembered were in the roof so I knew we were upside down. I tried to prod the navigator up towards the front to get out of the front hatch. An added nightmare was the knowledge that we had a blockbuster on board which went off on impact. I forgot that we wouldn't survive the impact ourselves. Then there was an almighty explosion and I was sent spinning. I thought we had hit the ground but it eventually dawned on me that I was in the air. Then something whizzed past my face and I was sitting nice and peacefully up in the sky under my parachute. I remember shouting for my wife - I was apologising because I had promised to be home on Saturday.'

'We crossed Belgium and into Germany. There was flak here and there, not giving us much trouble, then the gunners started reporting a lot of bombers going down. They got the skipper a bit edgy and he told them to shut up. Then he started weaving because night fighters were in the stream. We were on a long leg which was taking us across central Germany and directly between two of Germany's biggest night fighter stations. I can't imagine which clots put us there. Shortly after the rear gunner reported we were leaving vapour trails from all four engines I heard an enormous thump. It was a Me 110 with 'Schräge Musik', attacking from the rear. Our gunners hadn't seen it. Just one burst: 'Brrrrh!' and it was gone. I felt the whole aircraft shiver as if a giant had hit us with a club.

The Nazi Party chose Nuremberg to be the site of huge rallies in 1927 and 1929 and annually after Hitler's rise to power in 1933.

Below: Air Marshal A. T. Harris (later Air Chief Marshal Sir Arthur), Air Officer Commanding-in-Chief, Bomber Command, at work in his office at Command Headquarters at Naphill, near High Wycombe. With him are his senior officers, Air Vice-Marshals Ronald Graham (left) and Robert Saundby, Bomber Command SASO (Senior Air Staff Officer) and Deputy AOC-in-C.

Left: Air Marshal Sir Ralph A. Cochrane KBE CB AFC commanding 5 Group who favoured the long straight route to Nuremberg.

Right: Air Vice Marshal Donald Clifford Tyndall Bennett DSO the forthright Australian AOC of 8 (PFF) Group who argued in vain for a change of route.

Below: Squadron Leader Frederick Peter Hill DFC briefs 51 Squadron crews at Snaith for the Nuremburg raid, 30/31 March 1944. Group Captain Noel Holroyde Fresson DFC, the station commander, sits in the front row. That night the squadron lost the highest proportion of aircraft dispatched on the raid. Twelve hours after this photograph was taken 35 of these men were dead and seven were prisoners of war.

Above: Squadron Leader P. Jousse DFC of Rhodesia, the Snaith station navigation officer, goes over a point with Yorkshireman Flying Officer Harry Bowling (32) on 21-year old Flight Sergeant Geoff Brougham RAAF's crew on Halifax LW544 on 51 Squadron prior to the crew's first operational flight on 30/31 March 1944. Brougham and Bowling and three others were killed. Two men survived and were taken prisoner.

Below: Crews check their equipment.

Top: Crew of JR-G on 61 Squadron: Sergeant Whitehead, mid-upper gunner; Flight Sergeant John Taylor, flight engineer; Flight Sergeant John Kershaw, wireless operator; Flight Sergeant Les Cromarty DFM, rear gunner; Flight Lieutenant Bernard Fitch Pilot. Flying Officer Sidney Jennings, navigator; Flying Officer Alfie Lyons, bomb aimer.

Right: Flight Lieutenant Bernard Charles Fitch DFC.

Below: Lancaster LL777 *Royal Pontoon* skippered by Flying Officer Bernard Charles Fitch on 61 Squadron at RAF Coningsby.

Left: Six of the crew of Lancaster GT-X on 156 PFF Squadron at Warboys: Flying Officer S. H. Johnson RAAF, navigator / radar-set operator; Squadron Leader Les Glasspool DFC, navigator-plotter; W. H. J. Love RAAF DFC DFM, rear gunner; Sergeant Truman, flight engineer; Arthur Irwin, mid-upper gunner and Squadron Leader D. M. Walburn DSO DFC. (S. H. Johnson)

Top right: Sergeant Sidney Lipman, flight engineer on New Zealander Alan Gibson's crew on 166 Squadron at Kirmington.

Right: Sergeant Robert D. Dack the 33-year old wireless operator on twenty three year old Flight Sergeant Thomas William John Hall DFM's crew on Lancaster JB586 'C-Charlie' on 106 Squadron. Dack and Sergeant C M Beston were taken prisoner.

Below right: Nineteen year old Flight Sergeant Gilbert A. Poole the son of Frederick and Charlotte Poole (right) of Sleaford, Lincolnshire, was known by his three brothers as 'Tony'. A gunner on Flight Sergeant Hall's crew, he and his pilot, of Wraysbury, Bucks, who had been awarded an immediate DFM 'for showing outstanding skill and perseverance' during the recent raid on Berlin were killed. Flight Sergeant's Ronald Henry George Parker RAAF of Naremburn, NSW, Joseph Thomas Gill RAAF of Sandgate, Queensland and Sergeant George Smith Robertson of Carlisle, Northumberland also died.

Left: 22 year old Pilot Officer Jimmy Batten-Smith DFC pilot of Lancaster III DV276. (via Jane Crossley)

Top Left: Sergeant Russell Margerison the Lancastrian mid-upper gunner on 1st Lieutenant Max E. Dowden's crew.

Top Right: 1st Lieutenant Max E. Dowden USAAF.

Centre: Sergeant Ronald Alfred 'Ginger' Hammersley the wireless air gunner on Sergeant Ronald E. Walker's crew on 'N-Nan' on 57 Squadron.

Below: The crew on 101 Squadron Lancaster LL861 SR-H which was shot down without survivors on the outward flight to Nuremberg. From left: Flight Sergeant John Bede 'Jack' Newman RAAF age 20, mid upper gunner; Flight Sergeant John Alfred Noske RAAF, bomb aimer; Sergeant Frank Phillips RAFVR, flight engineer; Pilot Officer Donald James 'Shorty' Irving RAAF; Flight Sergeant Norman Grenfell Huggett RAAF, wireless operator; Flight Sergeant George King RAAF; (in front) Flight Sergeant Walter Joseph Adam RAAF rear gunner. Absent from photograph is the Special Operator, Flying Officer Ralph Frank Litchfield RCAF.

Top: Lancaster LM457 'G for George's crew on 101 Squadron at Ludford Magna. Back row, left to right: Sergeant Jock Laws, rear gunner; Sergeant Dennis Goodliffe, flight engineer; Sergeant Phil Medway, wireless operator; Flying Officer Stan Licquorish RCAF, navigator; Flying Officer Ken Fillingham, pilot; Sergeant Jack Salisbury, mid upper gunner. Front Row: Ken Connell RCAF, bomb aimer; Flying Officer Adrian Montague Marks RAAF, Special Operator, who is wearing his lucky scarf, which was knitted by his girlfriend in Australia and which he wore on all his 31 operations between February and July 1944.

Below, left: Pilot Officer Donald James 'Shorty' Irving (26) from Bondi, New South Wales. He was one of six Australians on the crew of Lancaster I LL861 'H-Harry' on 101 Squadron.

Bottom right: 20-year old Pilot Officer Russell 'Rusty' Waughman on 101 Squadron.

Left: Sergeant 'Chris' Panton the flight engineer on 19-year old Pilot Officer Jens Paul Christian Nielsen RCAF's crew on HX272 *Nielson's Nuthouse* on 433 'Porcupine' Squadron RCAF.

Below: Pilot Officer Jens Paul Christian Nielsen RCAF.

Left: Squadron Leader William L. Brill.

Squadron Leaders William L. Brill (right) and Arthur W. Doubleday, at the Doubleday's wedding. The two farmers were from Wagga, New South Wales, their war careers marched almost in step, typifying many famous Australian air partnerships. After volunteering for the RAAF they were called up together in 1940 and thereafter their promotions were simultaneous. When they became wing commanders, Brill commanded 463 Squadron RAAF and Doubleday 61 Squadron RAF. Each was awarded the DFC and DSO. Brill added a Bar to his DFC later. Both were original members of 460 Squadron RAAF.

Left: Bruce Buckham in the cockpit of *Whoa Bessie!* on 467 Squadron RAAF at Waddington.

Top right: The Path Finder Force heading to Nuremberg was led by 23-year old Wing Commander Sidney Patrick 'Pat' Daniels DFC* RAFVR, Commanding Officer of 35 PFF Squadron at Graveley, in 'S-Sugar'.

Left: From early in 1942 the Boomerang Club' - motto: 'I go out to return' was a favourite haunt of Aussie airmen, just north of the Strand on the Aldwych curve leading into Kingsway. The Club took up two floors of Australia House and served all Australian services and ranks.

Right: RAAF members of a Glee Party performing at a concert at Australia House, London on Australia Day 1943. Third from the right is Sergeant George Claude Notman, observer from Skipton, Victoria who flew on the Nuremberg raid on 'R-Roger' on 550 Squadron.

Top left: Pilot Officer 'Rusty' Lloyd's crew on Lancaster LL842 at Skellingthorpe. Top: Flight Sergeant 'Maxi' Bacon, rear gunner; Left to right: Flight Sergeant Hewson, wireless operator; Pilot Officer Don Richardson, navigator; Flight Sergeant Pat Dewhirst, bomb aimer; Sergeant Monty Avenell, flight engineer; Sergeant Alan McCarthy, mid upper gunner.

Top right: Pilot Officer 'Dick' Starkey who skippered 'Q-Queenie' on 106 Squadron.

Right: Crew of 'Q-Queenie' on 433 Squadron at Skipton On Swale. Back Row, left to right: Sergeant mid-upper gunner (unknown) RCAF; Sergeant D. H. 'Taffy' Williams, WOp/AG; Sergeant A. R. W. 'Johnny' Hardes, navigator; Pilot Officer Ronald Reinelt, pilot. Front Row, left to right: Sergeant J. E. Peppercorn, flight engineer; Pilot Officer G. Dykes RCAF, rear gunner; Flying Officer George 'Geordie' Wade, bomb aimer.

Top: Lancaster LL744 VN-B on 50 Squadron, otherwise known to the crew as 'VN-B-Beetham' at Skellingthorpe in the winter of 1943-44. Michael Beetham flew this aircraft on 21 operations. (Les Bartlett)

Centre: Michael Beetham.

Below: Michael Beetham's crew on 50 Squadron at Skellingthorpe. (Les Bartlett).

Top Left: Oberst im Generalstab Johannes J. Janke.

Top right: Generalmajor Walther Grabmann a former policeman in the Luftpolizei (Air Police) before the war.

Below: Jägerleitoffiziers (JLOs or GCI-controllers) in their 'Battle Opera House' where they orchestrated Nachtjäger movements and pinpointed individual target aircraft in the Himmelbett Räume.

Above: General Josef 'Beppo' Schmid (front) with his chief of general staff, Colonel Heiner Wittmer.

Above: 'Light Spitter girls'. These women were highly-trained and they made up about 75 per cent of the personnel of the aircraft-reporting service.

Left: High tiered rows of Leuchtspukers or 'Light Spitter girls' wearing headphones and laryngophones received curt, precise orders which came through their headphones and using bold arrow symbols, copied the information onto a huge transparent glass screen for them while operators moved the plots on the Seeburg plotting tables.

Left: Flying Officer J. H. 'Johnny' Nicholls DFC RAAF pilot of Lancaster III JB706 'T-Tommy' on 635 Path Finder Squadron.

Centre: Sergeant S. A. C. 'Sid' Smith the flight engineer; Flight Sergeant Jack Gardner the wireless operator, Warrant Officer Kenroy Alfred 'Bomb Doors' Jolley DFC and Flight Sergeant William Donald 'Oggy' Ogilvie the 23-year old mid-upper gunner.

Below: Sergeant S. A. C. 'Sid' Smith the flight engineer: Flight Sergeant Jack Gardner the wireless operator: Warrant Officer Kenroy Alfred 'Bomb Doors' Jolley DFC; and, 28-year old Flight Sergeant Alfred Whitehead the rear gunner on Lancaster III JB706 'T-Tommy' on 635 Path Finder Squadron.

Top left: Pilot Officer Oliver V. Brooks crew on XV Squadron at Mildenhall. Left to right: Sergeant Ken Pincott, navigator; Sergeant 'Whacker' Marr, rear gunner; Oliver Brooks; Sergeant 'Chick' Chandler; Sergeant Les Pollard, WOp/AG; Sergeant Ron Wilson, mid upper gunner; (partly obscured); and Sergeant Alan Gerrard, (Chick Chandler) bomb aimer.

Top right: Sergeant Cecil Harry 'Chick' Chandler on XV Squadron the flight engineer on 21-year old Pilot Officer Oliver V. Brooks crew at Mildenhall.

Below left: Sergeant Donald Stewart RAFVR, a 20-year old wireless operator from Finsbury Park, Middlesex on 424 'Tiger' Squadron RCAF at Skipton-on-Swale.

Below right: Sergeant Donald Stewart on the day of his marriage to Joan. He was promised leave for his honeymoon if he volunteered to fly the Nuremberg operation.

Top left: Unteroffizier Bruno Rupp of 4./NJG3. He is credited with 16 Night Victories including one Fortress and 15 Lancasters and a Halifax. He was awarded the Iron Cross, first and second class and the German Cross in Gold.

Top right: 25-year old Pilot Officer Leslie George Kellow pilot of Lancaster III JB314 on 49 Squadron whose crew were on their first operation.

Bottom: Left to right: Hans Eckert; Bruno Rupp and his bordmechaniker, Albert Biel.

'I groped about on the floor, found my parachute and clipped it on. After Berlin I hadn't kept it on the rack. That's what saved my life. All the practising for bailing out and following the drill I knew was useless because in an emergency you had no time. I switched on the intercom and heard a babble of voices. Tony Poole, the mid-upper shouted: 'The whole ruddy port wing's on fire.' I looked out and saw it blazing from root to tip, with a great flood of flames pouring out.

'Amidst the confusion I heard the skipper shouting: 'Bail out, everybody! Bail out!' I unplugged some equipment, including the oxygen line. We were at 23,000 feet. I knew we'd only got seconds without oxygen. Officially, I was supposed to walk down the fuselage, help out the rear gunner then jettison the rear door. But when I looked back the flames were coming up through the fuselage floor with the metal burning like a sheet of newspaper. At least one shell had gone through a canister of phosphorous incendiaries. Others had been within a few inches of cutting me in half. The whole fuselage to the rear was a solid wall of flame and in the middle of it I saw the silhouette of Tony Poole. My only way out was through the escape hatch in the bomb aimer's compartment.

'Worried about oxygen I turned to go. The navigator was standing beside me and I tapped him on the shoulder, pointing forward. But he hadn't got a parachute on and was in a complete daze. Still on intercom, I heard the skipper screaming: 'Get out quick! I can't hold her, she's breaking up.' At that moment the aircraft seemed to collapse as the wing broke off. Rolling over and over we hurtled towards the ground, the engines, still working, pulling us down at a tremendous speed. First the engines were roaring. Then they screamed and then howled. The howling was almost too much. I'd been swept off my feet and was pinned with poor little Ronnie against the side by G-force. There was nothing we could do about it.

'The big bomb was supposed to go off on impact. I was worried about that Cookie, although it wouldn't have mattered if the bomb bay was empty. Hitting the ground would kill us all just as well. An eternity of time passed, although I knew that within seconds we would hit the ground. My mind was working furiously: how do I get out of this one? But I had no answers.'

Before the wing fell off, Cyril Beston, his parachute on, had dived down two steps to the escape hatch. To his surprise the hatch was open. He reached forward to pull himself out as the Lancaster began falling and to his horror, was unable to move. 'Then there was an almighty explosion and I was outside the aircraft, spinning rapidly over and over, but going up, not down, with my legs wobbling about. As I was wondering what had happened, I started falling. I pulled the ripcord and remember the little pilot 'chute swishing up by my face. Later, I was swinging gently, as if I was playing on a child's swing. The moment my parachute opened, alone in the sky, I heard a voice and suddenly realised it was mine, shouting: 'I'm sorry Anne; I shan't be coming home on leave.' I heard a mighty boom from below, the parachute flapped wildly above and there was the sound of things whistling through the air around me. My aircraft had struck the ground.'[67]

Only Dack and Cyril Beston, who had landed in a tree about fifty yards away from the wireless operator, but had fallen fifteen feet, spraining both ankles, survived this explosion which occurred near Berghausen. Dack sat down at the foot of the tree he had just come down, looked for his pipe and some Four Square Green tobacco that he had just bought in the Mess. His boots and socks were gone but his pipe and tobacco were there so he sat there and smoked at least two pipe-fulls, trying to think out what to do next.[68] Both men were rounded up and eventually incarcerated in Stalag Luft VI at Heydekrug on the Baltic. Tom Gill, the bomb aimer, had been desperately close to getting out. Virtually lying on the escape hatch in the nose he was in the ideal position. It was clearly Gill who had opened the hatch before hurrying a few feet for his parachute. It would have taken him seconds; too many seconds. He might even have had the 'chute in his hands, an eye blink away from clipping it on, when the wing fell off and he was cruelly trapped by G-force. The body of the pilot was found near the wreckage with his hands still gripping the control column. This brave young man's operational career had lasted less than a week. He never knew that he had been awarded the DFM for his good work on the Berlin raid.[69] Hall's DFM, an immediate award for showing outstanding skill and perseverance during the raid on Berlin, was Gazetted on 18 April 1944. Beston arrived back in England three weeks before Dack who was flown home in a Lancaster on 106 Squadron.

Sergeant Edgar Charles Hazelwood the London-born navigator and one of six Englishmen on Flight Sergeant A. C. McQueen's crew on 'U-Uncle' on 'B' Flight on 15 Squadron almost always kept himself shut off from activity outside the Lancaster so that he could concentrate on his navigation, a task which he did not find any easier when he was suffering from air-sickness as a result of evasive corkscrewing by his pilot to escape enemy attack. But near Bonn on hearing the crew's comments on intercom, he left his navigation table for once to see what was happening. Flying Officer Burnett the Canadian bomb aimer remarked how bright the moon was and that he could see 'for miles'. The gunners and the rest of the crew who were looking out all agreed that it was 'a lovely night' with nobody voicing the thought that was in all their minds, 'for German night fighters'. When Hazelwood looked outside the aircraft the sight he saw surprised him. 'A lot of our aircraft seemed to be drifting north into the Ruhr defences as I saw a lot of activity with searchlights and gunfire. I thought at the time that the winds might have changed and drifted a lot of the aircraft off track. In front of us anti-aircraft shells were being shot into the air and on exploding, looked like aircraft being shot down. I suppose this was to upset aircrew morale.' On several occasions Sergeant Quinlan the mid-upper gunner and Flight Sergeant Chivers the rear gunner saw enemy aircraft but held their fire in case the muzzle-flashes from their guns betrayed 'U-Uncle's position in the bomber stream. 'Our orders were to bomb the target, not to engage in fighting enemy aircraft,' Hazelwood recalls. On the long leg eastward and on to the target, the gunners were to see many more enemy aircraft.[70]

'Enemy fighter activity had increased until it reached its highest intensity at the Rhine' recalled Pilot Officer Robert McHattie on 101 Squadron. 'Numerous combats broke out on both sides and to our rear. Tracer criss-crossed the sky as fighter attacked and bomber replied. The path of the bomber stream, on the ground, was strewn with the burning wrecks of crashed bombers. A rocket-firing Junkers Ju 88 attacked us from extreme range but evasive action enabled me to watch the salvo go streaking harmlessly past us. Far away to port I could see a number of aircraft, away off track, coned in searchlights. It was probably Mainz. I saw one shot down. Fifty miles from target a Lancaster corkscrewed downwards past my nose closely pursued by a Messerschmitt Me 110. Neither aircraft opened fire although the range was close. The intensive fighter activity seemed to have diminished as we approached the target'.

McHattie's wireless operator Sergeant John Allison also noted that it was bitterly cold when SR-E reached operational height. Even in Allison's radio position which was one of the warmest crew stations in the Lancaster, the cold was almost unbearable. 'As soon as we got over German territory it was clear that it was going to be a big night. Swarms of enemy fighters took full advantage of the bright moonlight and all the way into the target... tracer from air combats streaked the sky around us. We strained our eyes in the darkness, expecting attack at any moment ...about halfway to the target, a rocket tore towards us and Ken in the rear turret gave Mac, the skipper, directions for evasive action and we avoided it successfully. These rocket missiles looked like big balls of light leaving a trail of sparks behind them. They travelled fairly fast but it was usually possible to dodge them. Sometimes they seemed to follow you even if you took evasive action - rather shaking! Soon afterwards, Junior's mid-upper turret electrics packed up and with it his electric heating. Without this he was practically comatose in the intense cold so the skipper ordered him to keep watch from the astrodome beside me where he could have the benefit of the cabin heating.'

Flight Lieutenant Robin Knights, another 101 Squadron pilot on 'Airborne Cigar' special duties recalled seeing a few flares of the type then believed to be dropped by the German night fighters along the route of the bomber stream but he did not see any of the flares customarily dropped by Path Finder aircraft to mark navigational turning-points for the main force. 'There was a feeling that forecast winds were wrong and that navigation was awry. Turns on track were made on DR (dead reckoning) and at the elapsed ETA for the target nothing was seen of PFF flares or of fires. We 'stooged around a bit'. This was when we began to see other aircraft, mostly going in the opposite direction. This, I think, was where the night fighters began to take effect as we began to see combats taking place. After a short while a fire was seen to be started some way off and the place had a cone of searchlights over it. This, we thought, might be Nuremberg and I headed towards it. So did a few hundred other Lancasters and there were some good fires going by the time we began a run-up.

At a quarter to one, the leading bombers reached the end of the Long Leg at Fulda and started to turn south to Nuremberg. The 220 miles from Liège to the last turning-point was by now clearly marked by the blazing remains of 41 Lancasters and eighteen Halifaxes. It is unlikely that a single hour, before or since, has seen a greater rate of aerial destruction. By the time the Main Force reached the target area they would be missing 79 aircraft, a figure exceeding the Leipzig total of six weeks earlier.

'Night-fighter opposition became very heavy about thirty minutes from the target' recalled Ted Shaw on 12 Squadron 'and numerous attacks on our aircraft were sighted. One I remember in particular: a Lancaster flying straight and level was being attacked time and again. Apparently those on board were either dead or wounded because there was no evasive action being taken and no opposition from the gunners. The moonlight and the reflected light from the snow on the ground made it almost like twilight. A few minutes later we were attacked by a Focke Wulf 190 which made a pass at us from slightly below port. I called to the skipper to turn hard to port just before he opened fire and he missed us. By this time we were perhaps six or seven minutes away from the target which was burning very well. All of a sudden there was a tremendous pounding and vibration. Another fighter had attacked us from below and we had flown through its fire. Both the mid-upper and I hose-piped it as it turned away and it appeared to have been hit. This attack caused considerable damage to the aircraft and started a fire in the bomb-bay. One of the blades of the starboard inner engine was holed and bent causing the skipper considerable trouble in controlling the aircraft.

'The third attack happened about a minute later. All I remember of this attack was glimpsing the tracer coming at me. One of the shells hit the gun stanchion in front of me and exploded. The explosion blinded me, blackening both my eyes and some of the fragments entered my left eye. This attack cut off the intercom, oxygen and hydraulic systems to my rear turret. The aircraft was taking violent evasive action and I did not know whether or not it was out of control.'

The target was now 75 miles to the south; without the tail wind, this would be a twenty-minute flight. The turning-point was a tricky one, above the forests of Thuringia with no recognizable feature or nearby town. Most of the aircraft turned well to the north of the right place and slightly short of it. As the leading Path Finders flew past the searchlights of Bamberg, thirty miles north of Nuremberg, they were confronted by a thick blanket of cloud, less than 2,000 feet at base and extending up to 11,500 feet. The plan called for the raiding force to pass through the target in a seventeen-minute period, which meant that, at the bombers' 220 mph still-air cruising speed the stream was to occupy a strip of sky 64 miles long and one mile (5,000 feet) deep... the raiders were divided into six separate waves, which were to follow each other, snake-like, through a succession of turning points.[71]

Lancaster III JB706 'T-Tommy' on 635 Path Finder Squadron flown by Flight Lieutenant 'Johnny' Nicholls DFC RAAF and crew, some of whom were on their 35th operation, was hit by flak fired from an isolated battery near Westerberg. Flight Sergeant William Donald 'Oggy' Ogilvie the 23-year old mid-upper gunner, who was on his 34th operation, recalled: 'Our function was a blind (target) marker - illuminator. We were at the head of the stream so we were not protected by 'Window' and we were also a 'Wind Finder' so we got it when we were flying straight and level for an exact fix to calculate the winds. The flak battery got three of us in quick succession.'

The TI flare in the bomb-bay ignited and burned through the metal control rods to the elevators and rudders. Further aft, beyond the bomb-bay, the bomb-sized photographic flash flare exploded in searing white light, burning a large hole in the fuselage. Aglow with the lurid light of its own pyrotechnics, the Lancaster had itself become a target. Petrol was streaming from ruptured wing tanks when Nicholls ordered his crew to bail out. The rear gunner, 28-year old Flight Sergeant Alfred Whitehead, husband of Freda Whitehead, of Sheffield was killed in his turret. The bomb aimer's parachute did not work - he may not have had his leg straps fitted - and 22-year old Warrant Officer Kenroy Alfred 'Bomb Doors' Jolley DFC of Plympton, Adelaide in South Australia was killed. The aircraft subsequently blew up when the 'Cookie' went off. The skipper and Sergeant S. A. C. 'Sid' Smith the flight engineer, Flying Officer Ron Easson the Australian navigator, 'Oggy' Ogilvie and Flight Sergeant Jack Gardner the wireless operator landed safely in Germany. Thirteen was 'Sid' Smith's lucky number. His parachute was numbered '13'; no one else would have it!

Upon landing 'Oggy' Ogilvie suffered a fractured ankle. 'I received initial treatment at Hohe Mark (Oberusel) where we were housed in the mental block for security. I was then sent to Obermassfeld Lazarett in Stalag Luft IX with British doctors and then on to Meiningen for convalescence and to receive some most excellent physiotherapy. We could never escape so my walking and ankle became 100% again. I arrived at Stalag Luft VII on 20 June and remained there until we started the forced march to Stalag IIIA Luckenwalde south of Berlin.' Nicholls and Easson were PoWs at Stalag Luft I, while Smith and Gardener went to Luft VI and 357. Sidney Smith was one of the many who were seriously injured on 19 April 1945 when they were attacked by Typhoons at Gresse while on the march westwards when 25 airmen PoWs, at least twelve British soldiers and six German guards were killed. Eight more airmen were seriously wounded and a further twelve less so.[72]

'I wish to forget' 'Oggy' Ogilvie said many years later. 'The sooner we all forget the better. It was a bloody business.'

His pilot would agree. On 'Black Thursday' 16/17 December 1943 Johnny Nicholls and crew were flying 'H-Harry' when they were diverted to Graveley to land with FIDO, desperately low on fuel. They were letting down and suddenly spotted the runway at an angle with no time to call 'Funnels'. Nicholls pulled the Lancaster round tight, keeping the runway in sight and came straight in. They landed long, finishing at the far end of the runway. As they taxied to a strange dispersal one of the outer engines quit, starved of petrol. The following morning Nicholls went to the shower-wash room and with no warning was confronted with the sight of several mangled dead crew laid out on the floor. The mortuary must have been full. Flight Sergeant Ian Macdonald Scott and crew who he had been with in the Sergeants mess at Bourn the day before had crashed one and a quarter miles north-east of Graveley. There were no survivors.[73]

Endnotes Chapter 7

63 See *Bomber Squadron: Men Who Flew with XV* by Martyn R. Ford-Jones (William Kimber 1987).

64 *Sky Battles! Dramatic Air Warfare Actions* by Alfred Price (Arms & Armour Press 1993).

65 It was Brill alone, also, who first reported sighting Ju 88s with their 'Schräge Musik' cannons projecting from the top of the fuselage behind the cockpit for attacks from below. At Waddington this was thought to be the first occasion that the tactic had been used in a major way, not only on Ju 88 aircraft but also on the newer Me 410 twin-engine night fighters. *The Nuremberg Massacre* by Geoff Taylor (Sidgwick & Jackson 1980).

66 *Into Battle With 57 Squadron* by Roland A. Hammersley DFM (Privately Published, 1992).

67 *Quoted in Flying Into Hell* by Mel Rolfe (Grub Street 2001).

68 *Quoted in The Nuremberg Raid* by Martin Middlebrook.

69 As quoted in *Winged Victory; The Story of a Bomber Command Air Gunner* by Jim Davis (R. J. Leach & Co, London, 1995).

70 Sergeant Mattingly, flight engineer and Sergeant Blakes, wireless air gunner were the other two members on the crew.

71 *Sky Battles! Dramatic Air Warfare Actions* by Alfred Price (Arms & Armour Press 1993).

72 Quoted in *The Long Road* by Oliver Clutton-Brock.

73 Ken Smith, son of Sergeant S. A. C. 'Sid' Smith, Nicholls flight engineer.

Chapter 8

At Laon-Athies in the Aisne department of France, 24-year old Oberleutnant Dietrich 'Dieter' Schmidt, Staffelkapitän, 8./NJG1 vacated his billet in the 'noble if somewhat dusty accommodation' at Palais Marchais, which belonged to the Princess of Monaco and left for the airfield and his Bf 110 for 'Sitzbereitschaft' (cockpit readiness). Originally a grass civil airdrome the airfield was seized in June 1940 during the Battle of France. The Germans improved the facility by expanding the support area with numerous maintenance shops, hangars and laid two 1600 metre concrete all-weather runways, numerous taxiways and dispersal aircraft parking areas. Schmidt, who was born at Karlsruhe on 17 June 1919, had joined 8./NJG1 in September 1941 at Twente airfield near Enschede on the Dutch-German border. As with many young and enthusiastic but inexperienced night fighter crews - his bordfunker was Kurt Schönfeld - he only got a few opportunities to prove himself in the 'Himmelbett' night fighting system - the most experienced and successful crews were usually assigned to the 'best' Himmelbett zones where they kept accumulating their 'Abschüsse'. Keen but green men like Schmidt had to wait or patrol in those zones which were seldom flown through by the RAF bombers. One night in March 1943 he had claimed his first victory - a Special Duties Halifax on 138 Squadron which he shot down into the waters of the Zuider Zee.[74] A few months later 'Dieter' Schmidt was appointed Staffelkapitän. His Star rose rapidly and by mid March 1944 he had seventeen Abschüsse.

Twenty-three year old Leutnant Wilhelm Seuss, pilot of a Bf 110 in 11./NJG5 at Erfurt near Weimar in Saxony had been due for leave and had packed his suitcase because he thought that he would not be flying at all that night. The moonlit night had seemed to confirm it but he and his comrades had been ordered off at 2317 hours with orders to fly west. With him in his Bf 110 were bordfunker, Bruno Zakrzewski and Fritz Sagner his bordschütze. At an altitude of 6000 metres the fighters levelled out in the neighbourhood of Frankfurt where anxiously watching their fuel gauges, the pilots orbited for fifteen minutes. Then at about 0015 hours they noticed lights in the sky. Seuss estimated that it was in the region of Giessen that the bombers had a turning point where they would change course. Visibility at the altitude at which they were flying was so good that they could even see burning aircraft a great distance away. Seuss flew for about ten to fifteen minutes in a northerly direction and reached the main bomber stream. The heading on which they were flying was readily distinguished because some were burning on the ground.

Bruno Zakrzewski obtained a number of good fixes but each time Seuss had to break off the action as other night-fighters were attacking the same aircraft and then at about 0052 hours north of Fulda Zakrzewski got another contact on his radar screen. Zakrzewski nursed his newfound quarry on his set and called out, 'Target ahead... climb a bit... steady. Left... left... a little higher. Easy…1000 metres... 800 metres... 600 metres...' At 400 metres north of Fulda Seuss saw the Viermot ahead. It was a Lancaster. He brought his Messerschmitt below and to the port of his target until the port wing was ringed in the sights of his side guns and he fired. The Lancaster caught fire slowly. Seuss assumed that at least some of the crew were able to save themselves by parachute.[75]

Keeping a sharp look-out, Seuss flew quite near to the searchlights and his crew was able to see another bomber catch fire and dive to the ground. It had been caught in the beams. Later, they learned that it was one of two Lancasters that had been shot down by their Kommandeur Hauptmann Gustav Tham. Seuss then called Sagner and told him to change the ammunition drums on the oblique guns. Meanwhile, Zakrzewski was able to lead his pilot on to another 'Dicke Auto' ('Fat Car') approaching the turning point on to final leg at 22,000 feet. It was another Lancaster, a 514 Squadron aircraft (DS836), which was flown by 29-year old Pilot Officer Donald Charles Cameron Crombie of Ascot, a suburb of Brisbane and his crew who were on their 14th operation. Flight Sergeant Claude Charles Payne, a Londoner from Stratford in the mid-upper turret and rear gunner Sergeant Roy Hill, saw what they believed to be a Ju 88 flying parallel to their own aircraft with its navigation lights on. They alerted Crombie and aimed a short burst at the German aircraft, which turned its lights off. For the next half a minute, calm was restored but suddenly there was a succession of loud bangs and the starboard inner engine caught fire.

In his excitement Sagner took longer than usual to change the drums and Seuss had to shadow the Lancaster, keeping 120 metres beneath it while he followed all its movements. Without warning, Crombie corkscrewed, although Seuss was certain the crew had not seen them. At that moment he decided to attack from behind using the horizontal guns. Sagner reported that the oblique guns were now working. Seuss tried again to land his shots between the two port engines but the Lancaster suddenly swerved to port so that his fire landed in the port and starboard wings. Both wings burst into flames and the Lancaster dived sharply. This shooting-down was probably south-east of Schweinfurt.

Sergeant Jim McGahey, the new flight engineer replacing Sergeant Ben Le Neve Foster, tried to extinguish the flames, but the fire could not be contained and indeed it was soon spreading towards the fuel tanks. McGahey, who was from Exeter, died going to the aid of Sergeant Roy Hill who was trapped in his rear turret. McGahey was deeply religious and also a scoutmaster and carpenter and he worked on churches and cathedrals in the Devon area. A talented musician, he played the piano and accordion amongst other instruments. He surprised his whole family when he volunteered for the RAF, as they were expecting him to be a conscientious objector. His brother, Frederick, remembers the whole family being shocked when Jim once came home on leave wearing sheepskin flying boots, a breach of regulations but the winter of 1943-44 was the coldest on record and he was determined that his feet shouldn't get cold! Frederick believed that Jim was 'led astray' by another regular member of the crew, William Earle Brown, from Calgary, Alberta, the bomb aimer who, apparently, was a bit of a rascal!

Pilot Officer Harry G. Darby, flying in place of Earle[76] heard Roy Hill say that he couldn't free himself from the rear turret, but was unable to make his way the whole length of the Lancaster to try and help his comrade. As Darby was right on top of the escape hatch in the nose, Crombie ordered him to get out to allow access to freedom. Sergeant Morris Joseph Tyler, the wireless operator, was killed. Darby and Flight Sergeant Andy 'Jock' McPhee the navigator were the only members of the crew who managed to get out of the aircraft before it crashed with a full bomb load just outside the Bavarian village of Eichenhausen, a district of Bad Neustadt. Crombie left a widow, Ilma Roslyn Crombie, who received one of over 721 telegrams sent out by the Air

Ministry to next-of-kin on Friday morning, 31 March. Telegrams which had gone out to families and loved ones during the Battle of Berlin had totalled nearly 9,000. [77]

Harry Darby was immediately overcome by a feeling of profound relief that never again would he have to run that gauntlet. 'I experienced a distinctly warm glow, almost of elation. I had done my bit and now, given a shade of luck I would survive and live to a ripe old age. I swore a solemn oath that I would never go in the air again.'

Seuss's third shoot-down was another Lancaster, 'which appeared to be just sitting there under the bright crescent moon waiting for the inevitable'. It was either ND425 BQ-C on 550 Squadron skippered by Flight Sergeant Charles Grierson Foster RNZAF, which exploded over Unterspiesheim with no survivors or Lancaster II LL633[78]'L-London' on 408 'Goose' Squadron RCAF piloted by Flying Officer J. G. White RCAF who was on his 18th operation with a scratch crew, some with twenty to 25 operations flown. The only exception was his fellow Canadian, Flight Sergeant John Robert Hughes, the 'second dickey' who was aboard to gain operational experience. For Hughes, it was hell. The Lancaster rocked three times in the barrage. 'We were now limping along, losing altitude. At the last attack a shell had smashed the instruments and windshield and possibly two engines on the starboard side were not working. I asked the pilot if he had jettisoned the bombs and he pointed down beside his seat and there was a gaping hole in the side of the aircraft where the bomb bay lever had been shot off. So we were riding on a 4,000lb bomb.' On orders to bail out, Hughes scrambled. The ring on his parachute ripcord caught against something. 'I was appalled to see a billow of white silk burst forth.' In desperation, he gathered up the loose chute in his arms and jumped. His harness jolted. 'I thought the parachute had been hooked on the aircraft. I looked up anxiously and saw the most beautiful flower I had ever seen - a white blossom with orange segments. I remember thinking that 'for you the war is over - I hope.'

For Bob Hughes the war was not over. After navigating a 20,000-foot, fifteen-minute descent into trees, his only injury, a face scraped by the violent snap of the parachute shrouds upon opening, Hughes took a bearing from the North Star and attempted his escape from enemy territory. Apprehended the next night, Hughes became a prisoner of war and was incarcerated in Stalag Luft VI.

Seuss, who was again led on to the target by his bordfunker, Bruno Zakrzewski, believed that he must have hit an important point in the fuselage, because the aircraft burst into flames and threatened to drop down upon their 110. He immediately threw his fighter into a steep dive and lost at least a thousand metres before the machine answered to the controls again. The shooting-down took place south of Bamberg and the Lancaster crashed in the village of Simmershausen, three kilometres northeast of the small town of Hilders with the loss of the wireless operator, Flight Sergeant Frank George Leahy of Reading, Berkshire and the two Canadian gunners, Pilot Officer Alvin Alston Patton of Winnipeg and Flying Officer John Irvin Labow who was from Beachburg, Ontario.

Flying Officer White reported: We took off at approximately 2030 hours. Aircraft all okay. Fighter attacked approximately 0108 hours. Wounded bomb aimer and pilot (left arm). Attack broken off and attack reported. The flight engineer reported fire in starboard wing. Dived to put out fire and used usual fire procedure. Fire died down but continued burning. Believe mid-upper gunner killed then. After third attack starboard outer quit and port inner running rough. Ailerons unserviceable. Believed wires cut. Gave order to bail out over intercom (which kept cutting out) and also used call light. Fourth attack but no damage. Saw bomb aimer, flight engineer, second pilot and navigator go out. Aircraft went into spin on fifth attack so I also abandoned aircraft. Landed near Schweinfurt.

Flying Officer Gord Schacter the Canadian navigator who was on his 19th operation, reported later: 'On last leg to target 20,500 feet Schweinfurt on starboard bow. Rear gunner said 'evasive action skipper'. As he was saying this the aircraft was raked by cannon shells. Time 0107 hours. Bomb aimer said 'I'm hit'. Skipper also hit. Gee receiver unit hit. Second attack followed almost immediately - believe it to have been a second fighter. Aircraft on fire - bomb jettisoned - ordered to abandon aircraft. Third attack as I was leaving. Rear gunner still at his guns and firing. Believe mid-upper gunner killed in first attack. Saw wireless operator leave his desk and go towards rear door with parachute on. I left via front hatch after pushing navigator's detonator buttons. Diving steeply and in circle but not too bad to get out.' Hughes and Sergeant J. E. Bates the flight engineer both went to Stalag 357 with White. Schacter and Flying Officer G. L. Wood the bomb aimer were incarcerated in Stalag Luft I. Flying Officer White's Lancaster was the only one of the dozen dispatched from Linton-on-Ouse that failed to return.

'We were evidently a couple of minutes late getting to the target,' said Sergeant George Dykes the rear turret gunner on Halifax 'Q-Queen' on 433 'Porcupine' Squadron 'and no target indicators were visible when we arrived. However, in spite of quite a lot of cloud the fires could easily be seen and I believe our bomb aimer, George Wade, bombed on these fires immediately after the 'bombs gone' call I spotted a twin-engined aircraft astern, to starboard and slightly below us. I called for evasive action and opened fire together with the mid-upper gunner, Douglas Carruthers, another Canadian. The enemy fighter evidently had two 20-millimetre cannon. He broke off his attack quite close to us but got no hits on us. He went right through our .303 machine gun fire from both turrets and disappeared to port. We had just straightened away for home again when the same type of fighter was seen to be coming at us from a starboard bow, below, position. On this pass he put several shots into our starboard outer engine which immediately quit. Ronald Reinelt and the flight engineer were unable to feather the dead prop and the aircraft became very difficult to control. At the same time fire broke out in one of the wing tanks beside the wind-milling prop of the dead starboard outer motor. I believe our flight engineer switched the other three motors onto the burning tank and after about thirty minutes the fire burned itself out. The fighter may have been hit by our return fire on his second pass as he did not return to the attack although we were very vulnerable and could not take any further evasive action due to the drag of the still wind-milling starboard outer prop.'

Reinelt flew 'Q-Queen' towards home at about 11,000 feet and at reduced speed with a dead starboard outer motor, a wind-milling prop and the prospect of fire reoccurring in the starboard wing fuel tanks. It was almost daylight as the Halifax limped across northern France and although several airfields were passed where enemy aircraft were seen to be circling, they were not intercepted and the French coast was reached without incident. Heading out over the English Channel the crew were delighted to have two RAF Spitfires join them, one either side, for the Channel crossing. Reinelt had flown his Halifax for nearly two hours with a raging fire in the starboard wing. He only just made it to Manston where 32 square feet of the wing's aluminium skinning had been burnt away. The pilot was awarded an immediate and well-earned DFC on return to Skipton-on-Swale.

No word had been received from Pilot Officer Chris Nielsen's crew on Halifax HX272 'N-Nan' in 'B' Flight; most of whom were on their last trip and on landing back at Skipton-on-Swale would be screened from operations. Crossing the English coast and then the French coast, Pilot Officer John McLauchlan in his rear turret scanning from side to side of the sky. On the way to the target he had seen many combats but witnessed only about six bombers going down out of control. With the bomb-doors open for the run-in to the aiming-point at the target and with the intercom silent except for the voice of the bomb aimer Les Milward giving Chris Nielsen corrections on the bombing run, McLauchlan was totally unprepared for what happened next. His Halifax was attacked just before the bombing run south of Bamberg by Leutnant Wilhelm Seuss who had got under the Halifax but his 'Schräge Musik' was out of ammunition and Obergefreiter Bruno Zakrzewski his bordfunker had to change the drum. This took three or four minutes and at 0112 hours at Friesen Seuss remained under the Viermot, which did not spot his Bf 110 below. Then, just as he fired, *Nielsen's Nuthouse* dived to one side and flew through the burst of cannon fire and began to burn immediately.

Seuss recalled: We must have hit an important point in the fuselage. The aircraft threatened to drop down upon us so I went into a steep dive. It was with great difficulty that I managed to regain control.'

Nielsen's Nuthouse was the German's fourth and final victim of the night. Flight Sergeant Rost, the 'second dickey', reported that there was a fire in the starboard inner engine. 'Didn't I know it,' said McLauchlan. 'The flames were streaming aft and licking at my turret. I was getting burned. I heard our pilot tell the 'second dickey' to feather the prop on the starboard inner. The next thing I knew we were in a spin and heading down fast. I reached for my parachute in between being either pinned down or thrown from side to side of my turret. I couldn't get the bloody pack clipped onto my harness. I was all thumbs and still being thrown about and being burned. Rather than stay there and be roasted I decided to bail out. One last try and then something caught. I'd practiced this many times before but never in a spin. I pulled the rip-cord handle and was immediately plucked out of the aircraft. I had not pulled out the connections for my oxygen mask or the heater cords for my gloves and shoes and so smashed my head against the aircraft. Down I went, though, covered in blood. I could see the bombs dropping on Nuremberg and the flak rushing up. I landed beside a church on the outskirts. I remember thinking how close I had come to being spiked by the spire. People came running. Six or seven of them grabbed me and began all tugging in different directions. Eventually we got all sorted out. I was placed in a school for Hitler Jugend and my wounds were tended by a lady of the area.'

Seuss was feeling very exhausted and had to look for a landing strip. 'We had been two hours in the air. At 0155 hours we landed at Erfurt. Later that night a long-range Mosquito Intruder raked the hangars with long bursts of gunfire. My Messerschmitt - unscathed by its four combats - was hit, damaging its cooling system and propeller.'

Having narrowly escaped being impaled on the steeple of a medieval church as he parachuted into Germany, McLauchlan was to spend the rest of the night in a local Gestapo jail. Next morning he saw the wreckage of numerous British bombers still burning and smoking in and around Nuremberg so he was not unduly surprised when an interrogating officer at Dulag Luft subsequently told him that the Luftwaffe had shot down 178 British aircraft during the battle. He was even less surprised to be told that the Germans had known in advance not only the target but also the track of the bomber stream. Of the nearly seven hundred British aircrew shot down, McLauchlan encountered less than twenty fellow survivors during his stay in the transit camp at Dulag Luft. This could have been due to the fact that British survivors of combats during the running air battle had been scattered along the bomber stream's route for at least five hundred miles. After interrogation at Dulag Luft, Frankfurt-on-Main and subsequently a prisoner at Stalag Luft VI Heydekrug and Stalag 357, McLauchlan survived a lengthy march across Germany towards the war's end. Chris Nielsen, 'The Mad Dane' and Warrant Officer Harry Cooper the Canadian wireless air gunner who were blown through the side of the aircraft when it exploded at around 15,000 feet were taken prisoner also. Pilot Officer Don Awrey, navigator, Warrant Officer Les Milward, bomb aimer; Flight Sergeant Rost; Sergeant Thompson the mid-upper gunner and Sergeant 'Chris' Panton the flight engineer who had wanted one day to become a pilot, were killed.[79]

424 'Tiger' Squadron, which shared Skipton-on-Swale with the 'Porcupine' Squadron lost two Halifaxes and one aircraft damaged. On the outward journey Halifax III LV879 QB-A captained by 31-year old Flying Officer John Doig of Winnipeg, Manitoba was attacked by a night-fighter and crashed at Alten-Buseck, a small town, six kilometres north east from the centre of Giessen. Flying Officer Marsh the Canadian navigator was the only survivor and became a prisoner of war. Twenty-year old Donald Stewart the WOP/AG the only married man on the crew having married Joan Celia Helen of Finsbury Park, Middlesex just two weeks earlier and who had been promised leave to have a honeymoon when he returned was killed, along with Sergeant John Stanley Bolton the flight engineer, Flight Sergeant Alfred Hirst Crosland RCAF the 22-year old air bomber of Pickering, Ontario and the two air gunners, 27-year old Sergeant Robert James Atkins RCAF of Petrolia, Ontario and Sergeant Thomas James Rogers of Kidwelly, Carmarthanshire. All were interred at Hanover War Cemetery.

Halifax III LV944 OB-D flown by 30-year old Squadron Leader Harry Warren Metzler RCAF from Thunder Bay, Ontario, was brought down possibly by flak near Schweinfurt while running towards the target, crashing at Falkenstein, eleven kilometres southwest of Hassfurt. All seven crew were killed. The 35-year old flight engineer, Sergeant George Myles was from Liverpool; Flight Lieutenant Roderick Joseph Digney RCAF the 29-year old navigator was from Edmonton, Alberta; Flying Officer Felix Frederic Florent Paquin RCAF the 24-year old bomb aimer was from St. Boniface, Manitoba; Flying Officer Norman Alexander MacAulay RCAF the 26-year old wireless operator was from New Westminster, British Columbia; Sergeant John La Pointe Berry RCAF the 21-year old mid-upper gunner was from Roland, Manitoba and Sergeant Jack Beatty Allen RCAF the 20-year old rear gunner was from Toronto.

Flying Officer Frank Fletcher Hamilton DFM born on the family farm at Mazenod, Saskatchewan on 3 April 1921, was a pilot on 424 'Tiger' Squadron who remembered the Nuremberg op as the worst of his career - a 'horror trip.' An indication of the remarkably clear conditions was the fact that a night fighter attacked his Halifax head-on. 'All I could see was white tracer getting nearer and then Bang! It all happened in one or two seconds. The attack set one engine on fire and I knew we probably had about ten seconds to get out. A small panic developed among the boys trying to get the hatch open but there always seemed to be at least one guy standing on it. We were hit again from above and behind.' This second burst shot the burning engine completely out of the wing. It tumbled away taking the fire with it. To his surprise, Hamilton found the Halifax responded to the controls, despite the huge hole in the wing so he ordered 'Hold everything' and no one jumped. 'We were hit a third time and had lost a lot of height. We jettisoned the incendiaries and continued on our happy way with the main stream across Nuremberg. The aircraft would only fly at just above the stalling speed and so we rapidly fell behind. We were sharpened up by flak several times and only by the grace of God reached England, landing at West Malling.'[80]

Out of his little port window on Halifax MH-L on 51 Squadron Bill Stenning could see flak coming up. 'It seemed very light with all the flares around us. I was now studying 'Fishpond' very closely and imagining all sorts of blips coming but they were probably interference at that stage.' Several of the bombers had been installed with 'Fishpond' - a radar-set operated by the wireless operator and capable of locating enemy aircraft with a five-mile radius. 'Soon there were reports from the flight engineer and the gunners of activity above and below. They hadn't seen any fighters yet but it was obvious that they were about. I saw a lot of flak ahead and to port followed by two very big explosions in the air. I could see an aircraft falling away in pieces. This was the first I had ever seen shot down but the feeling I had was that it just couldn't happen to us.

'We were heading towards the target on time with regular broadcasts coming in on W/T at fifteen minutes and forty-five minutes past the hour when a signal came through warning all aircraft to listen out on the 'Tinsel' frequency. I tuned in and heard German controllers saying 'Victor, Victor' or something similar.

'As briefed, I banged away on the Morse key, using the carbon mike in the engine nacelle. I could hear our operators in other aircraft sending out a sort of distorted message in Morse. I picked up one - John, from Nottingham - and sent back - Bill, from Guildford - and we exchanged OK signals. I wondered if this really disturbed the German night-fighter frequencies.

'Soon after this I could hear 'Nobby' Clark the navigator telling Joe Pawell to turn starboard towards the target. We were now at about 18,000 feet and I could see some fires on the ground, to port. Night-fighter activity was increasing with tracer appearing in the bomber stream. About 0100 I went around with coffee for the crew and checked that the photoflash flare was OK and ready to go as we bombed.

'So far, it had been a fairly quiet night and I settled down and, as briefed, began dropping window.'

From the nose, Bob Burgett the prone bomb aimer reported sighting the target. The radio was switched to 'Master Bomber' frequency.

'It would not be long now.'

Ten Mosquito B.IVs on 627 Squadron at Oakington four miles north-west of Cambridge opened the activities of the Primary Marking Force at two minutes to one, off-loading 500-pounders and 'Window' at the rate of four bundles a minute to disrupt the 100-plus radar-predicted flak guns known to be defending the city. Flying Officers Allan Brown and Harold Barker DFC RAAF on Mosquito IV 'V-Victor' on 139 (Jamaica) Squadron at Upwood were both dropping bombs and observing the success or otherwise of the attack. 'We arrived over the target on time after following a devious route and large fires were soon evident,' said Barker. 'We bombed from 25,000 feet. A layer of cloud approximately 5,000 feet below us veiled the target area. It was thin stratus cloud though and the markers and fires could be seen through it. However, it acted as a huge reflector and the Lancasters were easily seen as they made their bombing runs and continued on. We stayed in the target area for about half an hour and observed dozens of combats between fighters and Lancasters. There were many explosions in the air as the Lancs blew up. We could see many German fighters around us and below, making their attacks on the lower flying Lancs but we were not attacked as there were too many easier targets to be seen.'

On the way home Brown and Barker received two warnings of enemy aircraft approaching from astern. Diving quickly, Brown soon lost them. They returned to Upwood without further incident having spent 4.35 hours in the air. Reporting at debriefing on combats which they had seen taking place in the bomber stream, Brown and his navigator agreed that the layer of cloud lit up by the fires in the target area below had made the heavy bombers an easy target for the swarms of fighters seen to be operating.

Flight Lieutenant Ronald George 'Tim' Woodman, an experienced 'Intruder' pilot on 169 Squadron flew a Mosquito II on Bomber Support on the night of the Nuremberg raid accompanied by his radar operator, Pat Kemmis. Woodman recalled: 'When the intelligence officer revealed details of the raid on the map, I was appalled. I said that if the bombers took the route indicated, there would probably be disastrous losses, possibly reaching the 70s - which had already occurred. I had discovered on the night of 24 February [when he destroyed a Bf 110], one of the German night-fighter beacons, indicated by a low-powered searchlight. It was southwest of Mannheim. The Resistance had subsequently sent us a captured map from a German night-fighter which gave the positions of all such beacons. Now Bomber Command was sending their main force right between two of them. We voiced our views to Group. Air Commodore 'Rory' Chisholm, the Senior Air Staff Officer, passed them on to Command. No change. Then I asked that two of us should go ahead of the bomber force and get stuck into the German night-fighters before the bombers arrived. Again Bomber Command refused. Instead, I was ordered to fly across the head of the bomber stream as it climbed into Germany and take up a patrol ten miles to the south of its flank; idiotic and stupid beyond reason - comparable to a destroyer taking up patrol alongside a convoy. I resolved that come what might I would head for one of those beacons when I got into Germany.

'I was late arriving [because of engine trouble] and the bombers were ahead of me as they flew east. They were already being shot down. The Germans couldn't go wrong. The massed night-fighters around the beacons pounced, calling in others like the Munich wings. As I nosed up to it in my Mosquito at 20,000 feet, I obtained a number of AI contacts of German night-fighters orbiting it, awaiting instructions from ground control as to the whereabouts of the bomber force which was on its way to Augsburg. I selected one of the contacts and gave a Ju 88 a burst.

'I crossed through the stream, which instead of being five miles wide, it was more like fifty. Before I reached to the far side of the stream, bombers were being shot down on my left. Masses of 'Window' were being tossed out of the bombers, which also jammed our radar. We tried three times but each time came up below a bomber, the rear gunner spotting us the third time, his tracer coming uncomfortably close whilst his pilot did a corkscrew. It was hopeless; we were doing more harm than good. Ahead the bombers were being shot down one after another, some going all the way down in flames, some blowing up in the air, the rest blowing up as they hit the ground. We counted 42 shot down on the long leg. Then my engine caught fire again and I came back on one. What was happening behind I could only guess. I was inwardly raging at the incompetence of the top brass at Bomber Command.'

Flight Sergeants J. Campbell DFM and R. Phillips on 239 Squadron who picked up a Ju 88 on AI near beacon 'Ida' attacked once but missed and lost their contact. A few minutes later they again found and attacked a Ju 88C-6 piloted by Oberleutnant Ruprecht Panzer of 4./NJG3. His rear gunner was alert and put just seven bullets into the Mosquito, setting one of the engines on fire. But this time Campbell and Phillips had not missed. One of the Jumo engines exploded and the Mossie crew were able to see the 88 fall all the way to the ground where it crashed and exploded ten kilometres Southwest of Bayreuth and only a short distance from beacon 'Ida'. The Mosquito's engine fire was extinguished and the fighter nursed safely to West Raynham on one engine. Panzer, who was wounded in action and his bordfunker and bordschütze, all bailed out safely. [81]

Flight Lieutenant D. F. Gillam on 100 Squadron reported an unexpected hazard caused by freak weather. 'We started leaving contrails at our allotted height of 19,000 feet. I decided to 'misinterpret' orders and get as much height as possible. We got up to about 22 000 feet, which was as high as we could get fully loaded. From there I could see a mass of contrails below us; they looked like a formation of American daylight bombers.' Another Lancaster pilot said, 'As I looked down from my bomber, I could see the vapour trails of about a score of other bombers flying below me. That was the sort of night it was. Not only was there a moon to help the enemy but also their pilots could occasionally track us down from our vapour trails. We knew then that we would have to blast our way through to Nuremberg. All this was fairly early in the flight. Then to our port we saw our first combat. Tracer darted across the sky and an aircraft began to glow red in the night. Down it went in flames and my mid-upper gunner was sure that it was a fighter. Most of the fighters seemed to have been waiting for us on the outskirts of the Ruhr and it was here the battle began in earnest. While enemy searchlights raced across the gaps in the cloud in the hope of picking up any bomber that might have strayed off course, the fighters flew in to the attack. We found that they had already started dropping their flares; most of which were going down in clusters of three; and the fighters were laying them as close to our route as they possibly could. It wasn't safe to relax for a single moment.' [82]

At briefing Warrant Officer Alan Strickland had noted mainly that the weather forecast indicated the crews could expect cloud cover over most of the route and over the target area. 'In fact', Strickland recalls, 'there was cover for only about two-thirds of the track in, the last third and the target itself was clear. I consider this resultant visibility, together with radar aids, enabled the enemy to track and vector his aircraft onto us. The heavier armament carried by his fighters enabled them to stand off and shoot down our aircraft as their effective range was 200 to 700 yards in excess of ours. Our meteorological forecasts were in error regarding winds and many of our aircraft found, on breaking cloud cover, that they were twenty to thirty minutes ahead of track. The resultant milling around of 200 aircraft gave the enemy some indication as to our target. Again, some of our aircraft (who had failed to check their position after breaking cover) were now approaching Nuremberg and the choice of target was plain to the enemy.

'Our duties over the target were to be special blind markers. We had a good run in and dropped on radar, checking visually. Some of the first wave of Main Force had already arrived and were bombing the preliminary markers. We dropped at zero minus one and the first markers were dropped at zero minus five. I estimate that general bombing commenced at zero minus two. This distracted attention from us and our run in was simple. We dropped a double colour (reds and yellows) and as ours were the only double colours on the target-marking for the attack they could be readily identified. Having dropped, we observed sticks of bombs falling across our markers which were well backed up by other Path Finder aircraft. Over the target, flak was not particularly heavy and I estimate there were only forty heavy guns. However, searchlights co-operated with fighters and caused some losses in this area.'

At 0105 hours the first of the Path Finder 'Wanganui' vivid red sky-markers went down on their parachutes and were interspersed with clusters of emerald-green stars and red TIs and then came more red flares, which fell over the city 'like fiery Christmas trees.' These were followed by more red flares, while down below anti aircraft guns blazed away with red-orange flashes. It looked like the clouds were on fire. A minute later, more red flares were released, 'this time shooting out clusters of yellow stars from their centres.' And at 0107 hours the six 'visual' PFF Lancasters swept in and released ground markers through the centre of the 'Wanganui' flares, followed a minute later by a strong formation of blind-sky marker Lancasters which dropped its candelabras among the still-twinkling illuminators of the leaders. Behind them came more visual markers, who unloaded further clusters of TIs and at 0109 hours both sky and ground were exposed to yet more flares as the PFF force droned over the target.[83]

By 0108 hours 65 Path Finders and Supporters had done their best but the conditions were hopeless. Instead of a clear and vividly marked target for the Main Force bomb aimers due to arrive at 0110, there was one group of sky-markers over Nuremberg and another group ten miles to the north-east near Lauf on the western edge of the Black Forest, both being blown eastwards and falling towards the clouds. Seeing two groups of markers, the Main Force crews were understandably confused; so were the Backers-up among them whose duty it was to renew the sky-markers. They managed to re-mark the group over Lauf, which now gave off the most light and attracted by far the greater number of bombs. Some of the later Path Finders placed their markers accurately but the damage had been done and soon there was a ragged line of sky-markers more than ten miles wide. The wrecks of nine aircraft shot down on their bombing runs formed a long straight line from Bamberg to Lauf. The creep-back started early and soon measured fifteen miles.

Wing Commander 'Pat' Daniels arrival over the target was to prove to be something of an anti-climax. 'As soon as we crossed the enemy coast there was evidence of the greatest fighter opposition I had ever contacted. Fighter flares were being dropped to mark our route and scarecrows, simulating exploding aircraft, were being fired into the bomber stream. My crew, who were not very experienced, were rather shaken by the sight of large numbers of our aircraft being attacked and shot down. Since I always insisted on no intercom chatter and strict silence so that our gunners could give warning of attacks on ourselves I instructed the navigator to stop logging sightings of aircraft being shot down as there were so many occurring that he would not have been able to carry out his normal work of navigation. We were attacked once by night fighters on the way into the danger area. I did a lot of cork-screwing up and down, four or five hundred feet, with continual steep banking, for periods of four or five minutes, whenever I felt fighters were near.'

Daniels was the first in the Path Finder force to orbit the target, which was covered in seven-tenths cloud. Not only was Nuremberg covered by heavy broken cloud but the winds from the west had suddenly increased in velocity and were blowing the big bombers sideways to the east. So, instead of flying over Erlangen and on to Nuremberg, some of the Path Finders had crossed another small town (Forcheim) and then approached Lauf, much smaller than the real target but with similar characteristics on the H_2S radar screens, being situated on a river and surrounded by woods. Daniels made three orbits of Nuremberg in all. He saw that some of the Main Force bombers, which had arrived earlier than they should have, were levelling out for their bomb runs. At 0110 hours the first wave of the Main Force Lancasters and Halifaxes fanned out over Nuremberg on a broad front. Some of the bombers were operating on misjudged wind-speeds and their bombs overshot the city. Others completely missed the city with their bombs. During the first five minutes only 33 aircraft bombed. As Daniels swept 'S-Sugar' across the city for its third circuit of the target he noted with anxiety that the bombing was becoming increasingly erratic. Whirling mists and curling peaks of dense vapour were obscuring the markers and spoiling the accuracy of the bomb aimers. Altogether, 512 aircraft bombed in the Nuremberg area; what had happened to the other 119 bombers that should have done so? Forty-eight crews would take back clear bombing photographs - of Schweinfurt! Damage was done to all three of the ball-bearing plants. Thirteen other bombers released their loads when they realized they were lost; these fell on unspecified targets, including Bamberg and a small town sixty miles north. Daniels, having spent nearly 25 minutes over Nuremberg, swung 'S-Sugar' in a broad arc and headed for home. There was nothing more that he could do and he needed every precious drop of fuel if he were to make Graveley.

Like his CO, Squadron Leader Keith Cresswell, the leader of the primary visual markers, had a strong feeling that the attack was not as successful as it might have been. On his first quick circuit of the city he knew that the 60 mph winds encountered had dispersed many of the sky-markers and as a consequence, the bombing 'was poorly concentrated and very spasmodic.'

Cresswell was shocked by the number of flaming bombers he saw dropping from the sky and equally disturbed to see the 'bright sickle moon being reflected by a carpet of cloud directly beneath him, which exposed his Lancaster to all and sundry. 'One would have been less embarrassed in Piccadilly Circus with one's trousers down,' he wrote later. 'The route was marked by burning or exploding aircraft and for the first time I was aware that great losses were taking place. I considered that my chances of returning were slim.'

Knowing beyond doubt that 'B-Beer', which had been holed in one of the petrol tanks by a shell, could never make Graveley, Cresswell was ready to land anywhere and so his only option was to head for the nearest coastal airfield, the Fleet Air Arm station at Ford. As if things were not bad enough, mist and fog now engulfed them in swirling eddies. When he reached the airfield, there simply was not enough fuel for circling first: it had to be a straight, flat approach. 'We left a rather badly damaged aircraft on the runway,' he wrote afterwards, 'with a burst tyre, half the elevator shot off and a hole one could crawl through in the port wing. Why she didn't blow up I shall never know. I found out later that a cannon shell had lodged in the armour-plating of my seat, the firing pin having been bent over during its passage through the fuselage...How lucky can one be!' In fact Cresswell had been doubly lucky. During an attack by a night-fighter he had had an intuitive flash, ignoring his gunners' call to corkscrew to port when the fighter attacked them. Cresswell said, 'I suddenly thought that the bastards always reckoned on one turning to port, so I whipped the aircraft over to starboard. It just goes to show how thin one's life-thread is.

'We did not consider the raid very successful,' was his comment.

Endnotes Chapter 8

74   See *Raiders of the Reich* by Martin W. Bowman and Theo Boiten (Airlife 1996).

75   According to research by Theo Boiten his victim was either ME721 'M-Mother' on 103 Squadron or ME629 'R-Robert' on 44 Squadron; or Lancaster III LM470 on 576 Squadron. ME721 which was being flown by 20-year old Pilot Officer Robert Richard Jack Tate of Loughton, Essex whose crew were flying their first operation Tate, Pilot Officer Allan Conway Bellyea the 21-year old Canadian navigator of Vancouver; Sergeant William Vernon Ford the 31-year old wireless operator of Banbury, Oxfordshire; Sergeant Patrick Joseph Lynch rear gunner of Bletchley, Buckinghamshire; Sergeant Ronald James McDonald, flight engineer of Wembley, Middlesex; Sergeant Edwin McCully bomb aimer of Darlington, County Durham and Sergeant John Norgrove, mid-upper gunner of Handsworth, Birmingham were interred in Hannover War Cemetery.

ME629 was flown by Pilot Officer Charles Albert Frost who was from Birkenhead, Cheshire and his crew who were on their sixth op. There were no survivors. Those who died were: Flight Sergeant Tom Ashton, navigator of Huddersfield, Yorks; Sergeant James Henry Carr, mid-upper gunner of Aglionby, Cumberland; Flying Officer Harold Alan Devon, bomb aimer of Dalston, London; Sergeant John Hamlin, rear gunner of New Malden, Surrey, Sergeant Arthur James Johnson wireless operator of Kettering, Northants and Sergeant Fred Stanton, flight engineer of Evesham. The crew were on their sixth operation.

LM470 was piloted by Flight Lieutenant P. E. Underwood whose crew were on their sixth operation. Underwood was flying at 20,500 feet when they were shot down by a night fighter at Oberweid, 25 kilometres ENE of Fulda. The skipper and Sergeant A. E. Evans the wireless operator bailed out successfully. Sergeants Roy James Alfred Boon, flight engineer of Slough, Berkshire, John Angus Hildreth, navigator of Greenock, Renfrewshire and Flying Officer Eric Charles Espley, bomb aimer of Rhyl, Flintshire and Sergeants Harold Raymond Lawrence, mid-upper gunner of Spring Bank, Hull and Leonard George Washer, rear gunner from Southville, Bristol were killed.

76   Warrant Officer2 William Earle Brown was KIA on 21/22 May 1944 on the operation on Duisburg.

77   *The 4T9er*; 49 Squadron Association Magazine, May 2015.

78   According to research by Theo Boiten.

79   Chris Panton had two younger brothers, Fred (13) and Harold (11). They were forbidden from visiting their brother's grave for thirty years because their father wanted 'nothing more to do with the war'. In 1981 the Panton brothers bought the airfield at East Kirkby and seven years later purchased Lancaster X NX611. Fully restored, *Just Jane,* as the aircraft is named can be taxied on all four engines and may be viewed at the Lincolnshire Heritage Centre.

80   See *Reap The Whirlwind; The Untold Story of 6 Group, Canada's Bomber Force of World War II* by Spencer Dunmore and William Carter Ph.D. (McClelland & Stewart Inc. Toronto 1991) and *The Nuremberg Raid* by Martin Middlebrook. Hamilton received a DFC for his action.

81   See *Confounding The Reich* by Martin W. Bowman. (Pen & Sword 2004) and *The Nuremberg Raid* by Martin Middlebrook. (Allen Lane 1973).

82   Air Ministry Bulletin broadcast on 31 March.

83   *The Bombing of Nuremberg* by James Campbell (Futura 1973).

Chapter 9

Canadian Flight Lieutenant Reuben William Wright DFM on Lancaster JB344 'V-Victor' on 'B' Flight on 405 'Vancouver' Squadron RCAF of the Path Finder Force lined up Nuremberg in his bomb-sight to drop the one 4,000lb 'blockbuster' bomb, five 1,000lb bombs, one 500lb bomb and four hooded Path Finder flares. No fighters had been seen on the way in to the target but Flying Officer J. D. Routledge the Canadian rear gunner on the crew had at one time counted thirteen Lancasters or Halifaxes going down in flames south of Bonn. For Reuben Wright this was to be the 48th target out of what was finally to be a total of sixty-two operational trips. The experienced crew was skippered by Flight Lieutenant J. R. McDonald DFC (later promoted to Squadron Leader and awarded the DSO). Pilot Officer G. G. Bellamy DFM was the navigator; Flight Lieutenant E. R. Wright, flight engineer, Flying Officer J. C. Gibbs RCAF, wireless air gunner and Flight Lieutenant T. R. N. Duff DFC RCAF was the mid-upper gunner. Wright found the target covered by heavy overcast with moonlight above the cloud. 'The flares and target-indicators were fairly widespread' he said 'and I believe the bombs were rather dispersed - whether on the target or not I do not know.' Back at Gransden Lodge, the Path Finder bomb aimer logged the fast time, for a Lancaster, of 6.50 hours.

'Vancouver' Squadron had put up fourteen Lancasters and suffered no aircrew casualties and just two aircraft damaged. Group Captain Gerry South was one of a select number of pilots who flew three, tours on the Path Finder Force. 'I suppose the chance on our trip to Nuremberg was that we had no navigational problems, were not intercepted by night-fighters nor were we damaged by flak. Luck must have been on our side. But how much was pure chance and how much due to the good work of the ground crew who produced an aircraft in a perfect state for operations? And again, ill luck was, perhaps, countered by accurate navigation. Our little Yorkshire radar operator, Norman Kaye, was a real expert and the accuracy of track-keeping was largely due to him. This skill enabled us, as a Path Finder crew, to be selected as openers of an attack. We were 'Primary Blind Markers' and so at the head of the stream. This was usually considered to be a good position as the enemy might not, by then, have had time to assess the nature, strength and location of the attack.'[84]

Pilot Officer Frank Collis piloting 'V-Victor' on 207 Squadron at Spilsby, still ahead of the first wave of bombers, arrived at Nuremberg at 0110 and bombed from 21,000 feet. The former policeman flew his still undamaged Lancaster south for eight minutes after leaving the target and then turned west to track between Stuttgart, Karlsruhe and Strasbourg. He believed that the Squadron's early start had made it 'a somewhat easier trip than usual' and that for once everything 'went smoothly'. It had kept losses down to just two aircraft. Lancaster III LM436 EM-G, flown by 22-year old Pilot Officer Bertram Challis Riddle RNZAF of Fairlie, Canterbury, New Zealand was shot down thirty-five minutes after midnight in the Vogelsberg area by Hauptmann Gustav Tham of IV/NJG5 flying a Ju 88G-6 for the first of his two victories that night.[85] The skipper and his crew who were on their 5th operation died on the aircraft which crashed at Freiensteinau. Three of the crew were twenty years old: Sergeant David Angus Anderson the wireless operator was from Bideford, Devon; Flight Sergeant John William James Buckland the Australian rear gunner came from Toowomba, in the Darling Downs region of Queensland and Flight Sergeant George Frederick Clulow the navigator was from Bow, London. Flying Officer John Larsenius Larsen the 21-year old bomb aimer resided at Nuneaton, Warwickshire. Sergeant Stanley Jones of Liverpool was the mid-upper gunner; Sergeant Frederick Keightley the 24-year old flight engineer was from Leeds. They were on their fifth operation.

Twenty-seven minutes later, at Fladungen, north of Schweinfurt, Tham shot down Lancaster III ND568 EM-L, skippered by Pilot Officer Jack Hardy Thornton RCAF of Hamilton, Ontario who were on their 11th operation. This Lancaster crashed at Schweinfurt with the loss of all the crew. Sergeant Norman Richard Cottrell the rear gunner came from Coventry; Sergeant Clifford Francis Charles Davis the flight engineer was from Luton, Bedfordshire; Sergeant John Duncan Dyson the wireless operator was from Greenland, Yorkshire; Sergeant Alan Latham the 19-year old navigator came from Barrowford, Lancashire; Flight Sergeant Robert Findye Thompson, the Scottish bomb aimer hailed from Edinburgh and Pilot Officer Gordon Ralston Thorpe the Canadian mid-upper gunner was from Toronto. The crew were on their eleventh operation. The two victories took Tham's total to thirteen Abschüsse. He would finish the war with fourteen.

Pilot Officer 'Rusty' Lloyd, the captain on 'F-Freddie' on 50 Squadron had been able to follow vapour trails streamed in the moonlight by the Path Finders in the direction of the target which the crew was to bomb at 0111 but Don Richardson his navigator had found early in the night that the forecast winds given out at briefing were not as forecast. As a consequence, by 07° East the bomber stream was north of track and perilously close to the Path Finders' diversionary 'spoof' at Cologne and the 'spoof' simulated Luftwaffe fighter flare at 08° East, which had been laid to attract the Luftwaffe's night fighters. 'Maxi' Bacon our rear gunner reported many combats in this area. They were too numerous to log. We altered course to avoid the Ruhr so probably avoided the main fighter activity. We ourselves were never touched.' Over the target the actual winds indicated that his skipper would have to steer 150° for nine minutes. 'F-Freddie' was not fitted with H$_2$S and Richardson had had to rely on forecast and broadcast winds, which had been in error and the cause of poor tracking over Germany. 'About thirty miles accumulated error in wind from the last 'Gee'-fix took us about seven and a half minutes to fly to the target. Errors from this cause were larger than on other raids. I attributed more and more my survival to good luck - similar to winning a lottery. Like many others I said my prayers - of five crews that started war operations at the same time we were the only crew to finish our tour of operations.'

'When we set off we had a sense that something wasn't quite right' recalled Mike Beetham, skipper of VN-B or 'B for Beetham' as it was better known. 'We were to fly south of the Ruhr valley but there were much stronger winds from the south than had been forecast. I kept telling the navigator that the winds were very strong but the bomber force was being pushed into the Ruhr valley, with its thousands of flak batteries, on a clear, moonlit night. We could see aircraft being shot down around us but I think experience got us through that night, because I knew roughly where we were and how to compensate for the winds to prevent us being pushed into the Ruhr Valley.'

'As we drew level with the south of the Ruhr Valley', continues Flight Sergeant Les Bartlett, 'things began to happen. Enemy night fighters were all around us and in no time at all, combats were taking place and aircraft were going down in flames on all sides. So serious was the situation that I remember looking at the other poor blighters going down and thinking to myself that it must be our turn next, just a question of time. A Lancaster appeared on our port beam converging, so we dropped 100 feet or so to let him cross. He was only about 200 yards or so away on our starboard beam when a string of cannon shells hit him and down he went. We altered course and I looked down at the area over which we had just passed. It looked like a battlefield. There were kites burning on the deck all over the place, bombs going off where they had been jettisoned by bombers damaged in combat and fires from their incendiaries across the whole area. Such a picture of aerial disaster I had never seen before and hoped never to see again.

'On the way to the target the winds became changeable and we almost ran into the defences of Schweinfurt but we altered course just in time. The defences of Nuremberg were nothing to speak of; a modest amount of heavy flak, which did not prevent us doing our normal approach and we were able to get the Target Indicators dropped by the Path Finder Force in our bombsight to score hits with our 4,000lb 'Cookie' and our 1,000lb bombs and incendiaries. With our eyes peeled we were able to successfully get out of the target area, which was always a dodgy business and set course for home.'[86]

Although Frank Swinyard the navigator's calculations were suggesting that they should turn to port Beetham kept turning starboard, away from the known defences and because the visibility was good enough for him to see the defences on his left and other aircraft being shot down. On reaching the target Beetham found the area covered by cloud and the defences were not causing any real problems. They bombed as best they could and on the way home managed to avoid any night fighters and other local defences. They eventually returned to Skellingthorpe unscathed. [87]

Pilot Officer J. R. E. Howell of Hobart, Tasmania on 460 Squadron RAAF said: 'We could see combats going on all round us. We spotted a FW 190 on our port side. It started to turn in underneath us but our mid-upper gunner had it well covered as it made a diving turn. Then the fighter tried again from the other side but before it could make the attack we cork-screwed into it and gave it the slip.'

Twenty-four year old Flight Sergeant Robert Ford 'Bob' Whinfield of Newcastle-upon-Tyne, on his thirteenth trip as a Lancaster pilot on 619 Squadron at Coningsby, which had dispatched sixteen Lancs, was fascinated by what he believed to be 'scarecrow rockets'; but they were Lancasters exploding, of which he said, 'They came up like flares and hung in the sky. Then they burst and scattered on the ground, like clusters of incendiaries. The explosion of one of them as it hit the ground looked almost as if a one-thousand-pounder was going off. There was just one damned thing after another, all the way to the target and on the journey home. Tracer showed that air-combats were going on all the time and still more lights of various colours were being shot up as signals from enemy airfields as we passed overhead.' [88]

The crew on 'D-Don' on 103 Squadron skippered by 32-year old Flying Officer

Leonard Young, a post-office clerk from Hull were on their 19th operation, ten of which had been to the 'Big City'. 'Everything was fine until we left the coast' recalled Flight Sergeant Ronald Gardner the 19-year old wireless operator from Tooting, London who picked up on his 'Fishpond' set some blips which looked suspiciously like those made by night-fighters and he warned the gunners that one blip astern and the other was in the supper port quarter. Gardner further recalled. 'The clouds we had been flying in suddenly broke and the sky was absolutely clear and it was full of Me 109s and 110s. They were waiting for us as if they already knew our target and route. And they were in force. Never have I seen so many gathered at one point during my tour of operations. We were attacked about three or four times but as soon as the fighters knew by our evasive action that we were alert they seemed to sheer off to look for less vigilant crews. '

Sergeant Clem Storey the 18-year old rear gunner of Southend, guided by directions from 'Fishpond' was the first to sight a fighter coming in. A staccato shudder rattled along the fuselage as he opened up with his four Brownings and a few seconds later Paul Hawthorn the mid-upper gunner of Hendon, Middlesex - also eighteen - fired his machine guns at their attacker. Flying Officer Young shoved forward his control column, jammed on full left rudder and threw 'D-Don' into a corkscrew to port. Bursts of cannon fire and heavy machine-gun trace flashed above, missing them by seconds. Storey reported that they had lost the fighter and Young levelled out of the corkscrew - at which point Warrant Officer Alfred Shields, the 30-year old navigator, a clerk from Finchley in North London, groped under his chart table for the navigation instruments, which had been scattered when the bomber plunged into its wild dive. Flight Sergeant George Hatherway the bomb aimer - also thirty - was a motor mechanic from Handley, Birmingham. Suddenly there was an almost simultaneous shout of 'Corkscrew star'd go!' from the gunners. Young kicked on full right rudder and slammed the control column forward, throwing the Lancaster into a steep diving turn to starboard as tracer shells zipped over their port wing. Checking with the gunners, he learned that the enemy fighter - a Bf 110 - had now disappeared.

Young swung the Lancaster back on course and began to climb. 'D-Don' responded well and he was certain that if they had suffered any damage it could only be slight. The skipper was more concerned about the crew and was relieved to discover that no one had been wounded in the two attacks. Ahead of them two more bombers rose almost vertically and then turned over on their backs to plunge to earth in flames.

'Normally, flying in the leading wave, we were seldom attacked by fighters until well into France or Germany' Ron Gardner said. 'This raid was the only one in thirty operations when I could see in large numbers our fellow bombers. I counted fifteen of them being shot down within fifteen minutes of crossing the enemy coast. The losses I think were increased by pilots ramming their throttles through the gate to get more speed and burning their exhaust stubs off. Then they were lit up like Christmas trees and easy targets. Usually the fighters took at least half an hour to get amongst us. But this time they seemed to be waiting in strength...'

'It was obvious that losses were going to be high', recalled Len Young on 103 Squadron; 'one could navigate on the blazing wrecks below and this was one occasion when I was really convinced that we had 'had it' as there was still a long way to go. Others evidently thought the same as another Lanc practically formated with us for quite a time for moral support.'[89]

Pilot Officer William John Taggart RAAF and crew on Lancaster 'F-Fox' on 156 Squadron at Upwood were even more of an eclectic mix. Flying Officer William John Barclay the Australian navigator was from Melbourne, Victoria. Canadian Flight Lieutenant Nathan Crawford was second navigator; fellow Canadian, Pilot Officer Wray Paterson the bomb aimer; Flight Sergeant Hart the English flight engineer; Pilot Officer Alan Robb the Australian wireless air gunner; Flight Sergeant Derek Hughes the English mid-upper gunner and Pilot Officer J. H. de Tores, from Lismore, a subtropical town in north-eastern New South Wales was the rear gunner. It was the crew's third Path Finder Force operation since transferring to 156 Squadron from 460 Squadron RAAF where they had flown nineteen trips.

As one RAF air crew member once said, 'The crews on the squadron consisted of Australians, New Zealanders, Canadians and British. The Aussies were a revelation. They were wild but loveable. On the ground whilst the British saluted all officers, the Aussies regarded everyone the same no matter what their rank and saluted nobody. They treated privates up to air marshals in the same fashion. They were friendly and fair to everyone. The Aussies had an effect on all the British aircrew. They showed them how to relax and how to really enjoy themselves. They gradually started to live, think and act as they did; while they never did become as delightfully wild and classless as the Aussies, but they showed them that they did not give a damn about 'Red Tape'. They simply ignored it. They kept the camp happy and were a delight to live and fly with. As a crew RAF air crewmembers were lucky to belong to a squadron that had so many Aussie and Canadian crews. They, above all, made it a happy squadron.'

Flight Sergeant C. P. Steedman a Lancaster bomb aimer of Parry Town, Ontario, Canada on his 26th operational flight, recalled. 'We were on our run-up when we saw one particularly large explosion in the target area. At the time, the whole area was covered by cloud and the target was further obscured by the condensation trails left by our bombers; which criss-crossed over the target and caused a layer of haze through which we had to fly - but the light of this explosion flashed up in a bright orange glow. It lasted for some seconds.'

Twenty-four Lancasters on 460 Squadron RAAF had taken off from Binbrook on the windswept Lincolnshire Wolds (which to the Aussies were not really hills but 'rises'). ND361 AR-R was skippered by 30-year old Squadron Leader Eric Arthur Gibson Utz DFC* RAAF, a grazier from Armidale in the 'New England district' of New South Wales. Sergeant Kenneth Edwin Green, flight engineer, was from Mitcham, Surrey; Pilot Officer Jack Hamilton Thomson DFC RAAF the 28-year old bomb aimer came from Forest Lodge, a small, inner-city suburb of Sydney, Flight Sergeant Tom Dawson the Scottish wireless operator was from Tillicoultry, Clackmannanshire; Flying Officer John Howarth the mid-upper gunner who came from Grimsby had been awarded an immediate DFM while on 142 Squadron, on a sortie to Hamburg in July 1942. Pilot Officer Arthur George Jackson Chadwick-Bates DFC the 33-year old rear gunner was from Cammeray, a suburb on the lower North Shore of Sydney. Pilot Officer Ronald James McCleery RAAF was the navigator. Most of the crew were on their 18th operation of their second tour.

Pilot Officer Carlos Patricio 'Paddy' Gundelach on 'B' Flight was the skipper on Lancaster 'M-Mike'. His crew comprised a New Zealand navigator, Warrant Officer 'Mac' McFarlane; a Canadian bomb aimer, Flying Officer Dough Williams; the Canadian rear gunner, Flight Sergeant Bill Rendall; flight engineer and Sergeant 'Red' Akers; wireless air gunner, Flight Sergeant Tommy Tucker and mid-upper gunner, Sergeant Ray Warton. ED750 was captained by Pilot Officer Peter Robert Anderson, an Australian from Halbury, South Australia whose crew were on their 5th operation. Sergeants Douglas Graham Lax, the flight engineer came from Torquay, Devon; Albert Stanley Pitfield the wireless operator was from High Wycombe, Buckinghamshire and Richard Sydney Parmenter the rear gunner was from Outwood, Surrey.

ND738 was flown by 20-year old Flight Sergeant Charles Haley Hargreaves RAAF of Gordon, on the Upper North Shore of Sydney. All of the crew were on their fourth operation. Sergeant Donald Frank Siddall the flight engineer came from Waverlee, Liverpool; Flying Officer John Edward Beaumont the navigator was from Mansfield, Nottinghamshire; Flight Sergeants William Henry Spargo RAAF the bomb aimer came from East Preston, just north of Melbourne and George David Moody the wireless operator was from Galashields, Berwickshire. Sergeants Glynn Jones of Bentley, Yorkshire and Alfred Edward Leggett of Walthamstow, London were the mid-upper gunner and rear gunner respectively. An ordinary schoolboy at Doncaster Grammar School in the 1930s, Jones excelled at football, cricket, athletics and boxing, winning virtually every sports prize the area had to offer. Indeed, he might have had difficulty deciding which sport to pursue had not a talent scout working for Charlton Athletic's legendary manager Jimmy Seed spotted him early in 1939 and persuaded him to pack a bag and get on the train to London. Seed knew a potential star when he saw one. The 16-year-old signed for Charlton as a centre forward on 28 June 1939. He must have felt like the sky was the limit, the Addicks having just finished fourth in the First Division.

Pilot Officer V. H. 'Vic' Neal's crew had not been fooling themselves that the run-in would be easy, but they were comforted by the knowledge that their aircraft had had the phenomenal luck to come through 86 operations so far, trusting that Nuremberg would be the eighty-seventh. When Neal's crew found that 'K-King' their regular aircraft, was undergoing a major overhaul they had raced another crew around the perimeter track in crew buses to the veteran W4783 'G-George' the spare aircraft. Neal's crew won and scrambled aboard for their eighth operation. If 'G-George' survived to do this and two more operations it would then be flown to Canberra to be exhibited in the Australian National War Museum. Neal, who came from Melbourne and his navigator, Pilot Officer Willam A. Gourlay of Tasmania were the only Aussies on the crew. The rest were Englishmen. Gourlay thought later that if they had known of the trip ahead they might not have been so keen to get there first! 'George' was imbued with a 'dreadful' vibration and Gourlay was driven 'to utter desperation' on the flight with this affliction and his navigation instruments spread all over his table continually worked their way onto the floor!

Remembering the operation, Sergeant R. E. Holder the flight engineer recalled: 'As we crossed the coast at a height of 18,000 feet, climbing towards our operating band of 22,000 feet we saw a vast change in the weather. The sky in front of us was clear with hardly a trace of cloud. We expected the usual anti-aircraft fire from the coastal batteries but there was none. And we spotted many other bombers cruising alongside of us, though normally we never saw them until we neared the target. It was a story of the perfect air ambush and Germany's greatest single defensive success in the grim cat-and-mouse game that was played out for nearly six years between the bombers and the fighters. The ground controllers had to guess where we were heading for and they guessed correctly. We were heading for the Stuttgart 'gap' - a small opening in the great flak belt. When we reached it there were hundreds of German fighters waiting in the brilliant moonlight to shoot down our heavily-laden bombers and they downed us by the score. Fifty miles from the target all hell was let loose. There were enemy fighters everywhere. We were sitting ducks with no cloud cover to shield us. We counted twelve of our aircraft going down in almost as many minutes, all of them in flames. Sometimes we could see two or three night-fighters peeling away from one of our crippled bombers. Usually when we saw an aircraft going down or blowing up we reported it to the navigator, who made a brief note of the time and position; but on this raid it would have been a full-time job for him, so he told us to forget it.

'During the heat of the battle we began to wonder when our turn would come. All the time, tracer fire was criss-crossing the sky. Bombers were taking violent evasive action, so one didn't really know what was actually happening. But if a red glow appeared, we knew it was one of ours. Over the target it was chaotic. Bombers were sweeping in from all directions, unloading their bombs and getting out as fast as they could. It was obvious that the stream was disorganised before it ever reached Nuremberg. The run-in was nerve-racking as we had to watch for other bombers suddenly swerving across our track. But with luck, or perhaps skill on our bomb aimer's part, we made a perfect run over the target. The ack-ack was fairly intense, but I thought they were firing at random. Yet even over the city the fighters were mixing it with us. After we dropped our bombs, our pilot shouted over the intercom for us to get the hell out of it and rammed the throttles through the gate. He screamed into a dive and the Lancaster shuddered with the speed of it. This worried me as I had to watch our fuel consumption and such action burned it up.

'The bomber gunners put up a brave show against terrific odds. At one period near the target we saw one Lancaster on fire from nose to tail, yet the gunners were still firing until it eventually blew up. I was amazed that there were not more collisions over the target. One bomber missed our tail by inches and our rear-gunner coolly remarked that if he had thrust out his hand he could have shaken hands with its pilot. Before this hellish action we had bombed many big German cities such as Berlin, Essen, Frankfurt and Stuttgart - but this was our first real experience of encountering the full fury of the enemy's fighter force...and it was terrifying.'

Twenty year old Flight Sergeant Edgar Oberhardt RAAF of Maryborough on the May River in Queensland, a rear gunner on a Lancaster on 460 Squadron RAAF reported: 'We were going in to bomb when we saw a Junkers 88 about 350 yards away. I warned my Skipper and gave the fighter a burst as it came in from the port side. Then it went over to starboard. I had my guns trained on it as it snooped below. I saw tracer going through its fuselage and it soon made off. Other combats were going on near us at the same time. A shell from the Junkers went through our starboard wing, near the starboard inner engine and left a very large hole. A few minutes later, the engine began to get troublesome and we had to feather it. In the end it stopped altogether. We made our way home on three engines.'[90]

Another Queenslander, 30-year old Flight Sergeant Norman David Livingston Lloyd, a Lancaster skipper on 460 Squadron RAAF, of Winton, Northern Queensland, recalled: 'During our run-up, I was told that a fighter had seen us. It kept away until we had dropped our bombs and then came for us. It was a FW 190. My gunners were ready for it and after a sharp exchange of fire it made off. A few minutes later, another fighter took up the challenge. It was a better stayer than the first one and we didn't shake it off until it had followed us for about ten minutes.' Promoted Pilot Officer, Lloyd's luck and that of his crew were to run out on 3/4 May when they were shot down and killed coming home from Mailly-le-Camp.

Flight Lieutenant T. R. Donaldson of Brighton, a beach-side suburb of Melbourne, piloting 'P-Peter' said: 'There were fighters all the way and they were making the most of the bright moon. I watched tracer flashing across the sky as, bomber after bomber fought its way to the target. The Germans were doing their damnedest to beat us off. Searchlights...flak and fighters...' Crouched over his chart table for eight hours and fifteen minutes of navigation in the cramped tunnel on 'P-Peter' Flight Sergeant John Gordon Earl RAAF recalled only that 'the volume of attacks was considerably greater than we had experienced on any other trip' and there was ten-tenths cloud over the target.' It was the crew's seventh operation.

Flight Lieutenant C. G. Broughan, a Halifax pilot from Sydney reported, 'There was cloud over the city but it was broken. Through the gaps we saw fires getting a firm hold. The Path Finders had marked out the area with sky and ground markers and though there had been scores of fighters along the route, there were not enough of them over the target to interfere seriously with the bombing.'

More and more shoot downs were being logged with each minute it seemed to Ernest Rowlinson on 'H-Harry' on 50 Squadron. He had never seen a bomber blown up before so he eventually decided to leave his radio compartment on the port side of the aircraft for a moment and take a look to satisfy his morbid curiosity. He had hardly stepped into the astrodome when a bomber ahead of him exploded in flames and commenced its death dive. Severely shaken by what he saw Rowlinson hurriedly returned to his compartment and quickly busied himself with his 'Fishpond'. At once a blip appeared on the 8-inch diameter radar screen, small at first but growing bigger by the second. It was closing on 'H-Harry'. Rowlinson alerted Startin on intercom to tell the Australian that a fighter was approaching fast from 4 o'clock on their port quarter. Sergeant E. Hopkinson the rear gunner shouted for them to corkscrew to port. He had seen the enemy night-fighter clearly enough to identify it as a Bf 110. The blip now filled Rowlinson's screen and he jumped nervously as Hopkinson fired his four Brownings, quickly followed by those of Sergeant Ernest McIlwine, 'H-Harry's short and stocky Irish mid-upper gunner from Armagh. Hopkinson informed Startin that the 110, possibly hit, had broken off the attack. Startin brought the Lancaster back on course and warned the crew to keep a sharp look out. He then asked his Canadian navigator, Pilot Officer T. Evans who was standing in for the regular navigator who was on the sick list, to give him a new course to the target. Dismayed, Startin noticed that the moon was getting brighter.

Rowlinson's 'Fishpond' now decided to go out and the screen went completely blank but he knew that the picture would fade if the rear escape-hatch accidentally opened and let in cold air to blow on the transmitter and cool the valves, so he went back to check. Sure enough, the escape-hatch door was wide open. Twice he tried to grasp the open door, missing it each time because the Lancaster lurched. The exertions of clambering around the weaving Lancaster to the hatch door and trying to shut it while using a portable oxygen bottle made it heavy going and he had left his parachute in his radio compartment, so one false move and he would have been whisked away into the night. On the third attempt Rowlinson got the door shut but the effort had exhausted him and he had to rest before returning to the nose of the aircraft.

He was relieved to see the target when they arrived over Nuremberg shortly after 0109 hours. Flight Sergeant Keith Gilbert 'Ben' Lawrence the 22-year old bomb aimer brought 'Harry' on to the bomb run at a height of 19,000 feet but 'Harry' was coned and Startin immediately dived. They went left and then right and everything that was not bolted down flew around inside the Lancaster. By the time Lawrence called on Startin to open the bomb doors 'Harry' was down to 8,000 feet!

'There it is Skipper - straight ahead. Keep her steady. Steady - right; right; hold it - ste-ady.'

Eight seconds to go. With only three seconds to go Lawrence called 'Steady - hold it...' and then, 'Bombs gone'. There was relief in his voice.

Rowlinson meanwhile was watching his 'Fishpond' when another blip showing a fighter approaching from the port quarter, appeared on his screen. He alerted the gunners and Hopkinson in the rear turret spotted the fighter almost at the same instant and he and McIlwine in the mid-upper turret fired immediately. The fighter disappeared and Startin weaved and corkscrewed 'H-Harry' until they were well clear of the target.[91]

By the time Squadron Leader Thompson and the crew on 'Z-Zebra' reached the target it was well lit up, with conditions ideal. Numerous bombers and German night-fighters were sighted. The run in was normal and very steady with the bomb aimer sighting on red TI markers which were visible burning on the ground. 'Unfortunately the first run was not satisfactory,' says Stephen Burrows the flight-engineer. Bill Clegg had just stretched himself along his bombing mat when he realised that it was going to be tricky to bomb - for above, below and on each side of his Lancaster other bombers were making the run, their bomb-bays open. Around him, the glaring flashes of their camera flares were proof that they were ignoring their bombing heights. He could see some of the red target indicators burning on the ground, but before he could level them in his sights other aircraft recklessly swung on to them, seemingly oblivious to the collision risks they were taking.

Clegg was an experienced bomb aimer who had been through too much to let his bombs go at random. The 'panic' crews could drop theirs heedlessly and get the hell out of it. He didn't really blame them. But there would be other nights - and if panic got him tonight, it might get him again in the future. It just wouldn't be worth it. He called for another orbit of the city and heard someone groan over the intercom, but Thompson hauled the Lancaster into a shallow turn and cautiously began the circuit. As the second run began, Clegg noticed that the cloud veiling the city was now gradually thinning. And then he saw a dying target indicator winking teasingly at him from below. It was just what he needed. He thumbed forward the drift handle of his Mark 14 bombsight, slapped down his selector switches and fused his bombs. Thompson had just seen the light appear on his panel to confirm that the bomb-doors had opened when out of the night another bomber side-slipped in front of 'Z-Zebra'. The Wing Commander jabbed on right rudder, dropped the nose of the Lancaster and cursed the black shape that now flashed past above them. It appeared to him that the bomber crews now had only one thing in mind - to get quickly away from Nuremberg regardless. For the third time 'Z-Zebra' made its bomb-run and this time the approach was clear. But although the crew breathed heavily in relief as the bomb-load left them, they could not now thrust on full throttle and, like the other bombers, dive away from the target. During the crew's prolonged stay over the target - they were one of the last to leave the area and head for home - it was noticeable how quiet all was.[92]

'Then we had the painful job of trying to take pictures and assess damage' continues Stephen Burrows; 'losing height to about 10,000 feet to carry this out. I happened to glance to starboard and found to my horror another Lancaster coming straight at us at exactly the same height and I screamed 'Dive, dive, dive!', the skipper doing so immediately. How we missed each other is something we would discuss every time we met.'

Thompson swung 'Z-Zebra - one of the last of the Lancasters to leave Nuremberg - on course for England; its mission accomplished. During the summer Thompson was awarded the DSO.

'Eventually, a glow in the distance came into sight and I knew it was fires burning at the target' recalled Sergeant Eric Morrey, flight engineer on Lancaster JO-B. 'As the sky came brighter with the glow from these fires, other aircraft became visible above us and on each side of us, all flying in the same direction and from now on a special check was made to see if any aircraft were above us and directly in line with us as we were quickly approaching the target. Flight Sergeant Tom Morris RAAF got his bombs away on the first bombing run. As the bombs went, the aircraft lifted slightly and began to climb to 21,000 feet. The flak was considerably heavier now and our aircraft was buffeted about to some extent. Soon the Lancaster was flying in smooth air and Charlie Cassell was getting a bit more speed out of the Lanc. Vic Brill soon gave us our new course for home and we gradually lost height on the way out to the French coast.'

'It turned out to be a lovely night with a good moon and no cloud over France,' recalled Flight Lieutenant Dan Conway, the pilot of Lancaster 'K-Kitty' on 467 Squadron RAAF.

'Almost as soon as we crossed the coast we were made aware of the terrific enemy aerial activity which was only too apparent in the sight of bombers bursting into flames' recalls Wesley. 'As navigator it was part of my duties to record in my log any activity reported by the remainder of the crew - combats, aircraft shot down, with estimated positions. Within a very short time the reportage became excessive and we were made positively aware that this was going to be a night to remember.'

'We now turned onto an almost easterly course' continues Wesley 'which took us south of Aachen for approximately 240 miles to a position about seventy miles north of the target where we altered course to an almost southerly heading for the target.'

'Approximately south of Aachen the combats began in earnest' adds Dan Conway 'and it was soon obvious that the enemy fighters were out in good strength. I had to warn my crew not to comment on the combats but rather to maintain a good look-out. My engineer did, however, at one stage count seven aircraft falling in flames and a further eleven wrecks burning on the ground.'

Sergeant Joe Wesley would normally record on his navigation log any reports of aircraft going down, but not on this night. Conway had told the crew to stop mentioning them: 'We could not afford to have the intercom overloaded with reports when at any second one of them might call up to report a fighter. Self preservation overruled statistics and I did not propose to become one.' Earlier they had seen a Lancaster drifting across their path only 200 feet above them. 'We could have shot it down ourselves with no trouble' Conway said. Most aircraft one saw exploding in mid air did so after a short burst of tracer fire which, in the darkness, looked only a matter of feet long. These sightings were one-sided sudden death and were increasing in frequency. Certainly different to the criss-cross of fire across the sky, which marked the standard approach of a fighter from the rear.'

'Now I know how those poor bastards in the Light Brigade felt' Conway thought to himself.

'Just when we were complimenting ourselves on being out of trouble on what we already knew to be a very bad night for the bombers, we were attacked by a Ju 88' says Joe Wesley. 'Fortunately the gunners were on the job and we counter-attacked, but the Ju 88 persisted. Our pilot took evasive action, really throwing the aircraft around violently but, in spite of this, cannon shells came through the fuselage, without causing serious damage, until the port outer engine was hit and feathered out of action. I was beginning to think 'this is it' and that our luck was running out when suddenly the attack ended and the Ju 88 disappeared. 'He's gone' was the most welcome sound and an eternity that had been compressed into minutes was over.'

'The fighters seemed to know our course as, when we did alter course, they turned with us' added Dan Conway. 'It was at this stage, twenty minutes before our time-on-target that a series of bright flashes like a giant sparkler appeared close to port. At the same instant both gunners called 'Dive port.' I think I was already on my way. As the port outer motor was on fire I maintained the dive in the hope that the speed would help extinguish the flames and I also checked that the flight engineer was feathering the airscrew of the correct motor. The fire in the port outer motor went out as I continued rolling the aircraft into the standard corkscrew evasive manoeuvre as we were again under attack by night fighters. Both my gunners were firing back but they observed no hits. [They saw smoke coming from one of its engines so they claimed it as 'damaged']. The fighter then broke away.

About five minutes later we were attacked again but no damage was done. A crew check revealed no injuries and no observable damage to the aircraft apart from the port outer motor. We were now down to about 17,500 feet having been attacked initially at about 21,500 feet.'

'With the three sound engines we resumed course for the target area which we could now see well lit up.' said Wesley.

'It took a lot longer to reach the target than its nearness indicated' continues Conway. 'I think it was about this time that the air-speed indicator began to play up. We had been plagued with icing trouble at the pitot head and on several previous occasions had flown to and from the target with no indicated air speed. This trouble seemed to occur mostly when flying in mist or vapour trails at altitude and we now were in a slight haze. Sergeant Joe Wesley gave me a course for the target where the attack was now developing. Fortunately, the target was quiet when we arrived, with few searchlights.' The raid had been scattered and we had trouble locating our target-indicators through the smoke. We found the TIs after some exploration and did a good run at 16,500 feet. We seemed to have the whole place to ourselves at this stage which we didn't regard as a good thing. Having brought our bombs so far and having lost so many of our mates we didn't intend to waste them. Although we were about twenty minutes overdue on our scheduled time for bombing, quite a few of the bomber force were still backing up the markers and our bombs were dispatched on them on our correct heading.'[93]

They were the last aircraft over Nuremberg, bombing at 01.35 - thirteen minutes after the attack had been scheduled to end. 'We set course for home on three motors said Wesley 'and with airspeed indicator definitely unserviceable.'

'This handicapped the navigator as I couldn't give him an air speed' says Dan Conway. 'I therefore asked the wireless operator to obtain a fix. He reported that his set was unserviceable. He suspected the generator operating from the damaged motor. About forty-five minutes after leaving Nuremberg, flight engineer, Sergeant Tanfield, reported that oil temperatures and pressures on the remaining port motor were 'off the clock'. He requested permission to feather the airscrew of the motor but as it still seemed to be running sweetly I decided that the gauges might be at fault. Particularly as flying on two motors all the way home didn't look like a proposition. I was right. We seemed to have plenty of petrol although here again the gauges were not registering.'

Conway saw very little activity on the way home apart from the usual searchlights. With the port outer stopped and the airscrew feathered, 'K-Kitty' lagged well behind the Main Force Bomber stream and anticipating a fighter attack at any time, he and his crew kept a good lookout. Conway's flight plan called for him to cross the enemy coast on the way out over northern France and to make his English landfall near Beachy Head. When Joe Wesley tried to get a positional fix by radar on his 'Gee'-set he found that this also was unserviceable. All that Conway could do was maintain the dead reckoning course given him by Wesley, keep the Pole Star on his right and hope that they were on track with the rest of the bomber stream ahead of them. Shortly afterwards two fighters flew at them 'aggressively', but once they were recognised as Spitfires and the colours of the day had been fired off, the two aircraft formated on the struggling Lancaster and provided an escort until they reached the coast.

By the time Pilot Officer Raymond Curling and the crew on 'A-Able' on 622 Squadron reached the target and bombed at 0125 the Australian estimated that he had about six- to seven-tenths of cloud cover at 20,000 feet. 'It was a hot target with huge fires burning below. On our bombing run a FW 190 attacked us. It closed to 400 yards. Our rear gunner fired a three-second burst which appeared to hit the fighter which dived away and was not seen again. We got our bombs away and turned for home. By this time we had seen a total of approximately twenty of our own aircraft going down. We were feeling more scared that night than on the previous trip to Berlin.

'The way out of the target was quite a sight. We didn't need a navigator. The moon lit the sky like daylight and vapour trails of aircraft ahead of us left a road like a modern highway. I just kept above this roadway in readiness to dive into its cover should the need arise. Fighter attack seemed to have eased off considerably. We were not permitted to land at our base at Mildenhall and were diverted to the emergency airfield at Woodbridge on the coast. Landing there was no problem. There were plenty of other aircraft badly shot up. The various other air crews we spoke to, confirmed our opinion that it had been a shocking raid.' Curling's aircraft was undamaged. It had been airborne eight hours. The reason they had been diverted to Woodbridge was because their base was blanketed by ground fog. Not only did Curling survive the war but also a Court of Inquiry charged him with flying a Lancaster below Blackpool Tower and down a street in Clevelys.

Endnotes Chapter 9

84   *Out of the Blue: The Role of Luck in Air Warfare 1917-1966* Edited by Laddie Lucas (Hutchinson, 1985).
85   From research by Theo Boiten.
86   Diary entry quoted in *The Lancaster Story* by Peter Jacobs (Cassell 1996)..
87   *Stay The Distance: The Life and times of Marshal of the RAF, Sir Michael Beetham* by Peter Jacobs (Frontline Books 2011).
88   Air Ministry Bulletin broadcast on 31 March. Flight Sergeant Robert Ford Whinfield was KIA on 26/27 April 1944 on the operation to Schweinfurt.
89   Quoted in *The Nuremberg Raid* by Martin Middlebrook.
90   Oberhardt was KIA on 9/10 April 1944 when Lancaster JB734 flown by Pilot Officer Robert John Proud RAAF was lost on a 'Gardening' operation to lay mines in the Baltic. All of the crew, five of whom were Australian, were killed.
91   *The Bombing of Nuremberg* by James Campbell (Futura 1973).
92   *The Bombing of Nuremberg* by James Campbell (Futura 1973).
93   Dan Conway, *The trenches in the sky*, Hesperian Press, Victoria Park, 1995.

Chapter 10

The hands of the clock wandered towards 2300 hours. Tired and sleepy, the crews in the readiness room at Langendiebach, two kilometres NNE of Hanau in Hesse slumped in their armchairs. Chess boards and suits of cards lay abandoned; only soft music could be heard on the wireless during the night hours. Twenty-three year old Unteroffizier Bruno Rupp and a few crews in 4./NJG3 had returned to their bunks in full flying kit, ready at any moment to run to take off but with the full moon turning night into day they expected to be stood down. After dining on sausage and potatoes, Rupp, born in Stuttgart on 1 August 1920, had peremptorily broken off a game of 'Skat' with three other pilots to take a breath of fresh cold night air. He pulled out his packet of Overstolz cigaretten, lit one up and glanced at the rows of night-fighters bathed in the moonlight. Returning to the ready room there was a slight crackle in the telephone. This barely audible noise roused some of them. Still half drunk with sleep a messenger took up the receiver. His features hardened. It was General Max Ibel's 2 Jagddivison headquarters at Stade near Hamburg.

'Jawohl, Herr Oberst.

A pause and then: 'Bomber formations are reported assembling in Map Square 23. Strength, 900 aircraft. Altitude 4600 metres. All aircraft proceed to Beacons 'Bonn' and 'Osnabrück'!'

Without stopping to put down the receiver the messenger announced; 'Sitzbereitschaft' (cockpit readiness)!

Outside again Rupp stubbed out the butt of his half smoked cigarette into the earth with the toe cap of his flying boot. His two bordfunkers, Hans Eckert and Gerd Gerbhardt - who shared his birthday - and the bordmechaniker, Albert Biel joined him at the Ju 88G-6. Putting on the inflatable Mae West and parachute, helmet and throat microphone and the fastening of the harness was done in oppressive silence. Cockpit readiness was a nerve-wracking business. Mosquito intruders could appear at any moment and the more unfavourable the weather conditions on take-off and landing were, the stronger the tension and the greater the pressure on the nerves. All of a sudden, the green lamp on the front edge of the hangar was blinking: the order to take off! The NCO Schwarzemänner jumped up and shut the cockpit roof; Rupp locked it from the inside. On the seat of his pants, the 'black man' (so-called because of the colour of his tunic) slid down from the wing and ran toward the battery trolley, which he plugged in. One after the other, the engines burst snorting into life. Cable removed, battery trolley rolled aside; chocks away, Rupp cautiously taxied out and turned off towards the taxi track whilst applying a bit of extra power. The engines roared and a dense rain of sparks swirled in the slipstream behind them making the Schwarzemänner shield his eyes. After lifting off and the props were turning quietly and smoothly, the pressure Rupp had felt was gone - left behind on the ground.

Rupp had to change over to flying on instruments immediately in order to have his eyes and brains free for blind flying. This done, he turned on course without making a circuit round the airfield, switched off his navigating lights and his Ju 88 was swallowed up in the darkness. A clear starry sky overhead signalled ideal weather for night fighters. Rupp climbed rapidly and the ground station reported other night-fighter gruppen in the air. 2nd Jagddivision's night-fighters commanded by Generalmajor Ibel's headquarters were being switched in by 'Funk Feuer' (radio beacon) 'Frankfurt' (which also directed single-engined units from Oldenburg, Rheine and Bonn) to Funk Feuer 'Nürnberg'. 1st Jagddivison commanded by Oberst Hajo Herrmann at Berlin-Döberitz was brought near via FF's 'Bonn' and 'Hartz' and switched in by radar north of Frankfurt, as was 7 JD commanded by Generalleutnant Joachim Huth at his headquarters at Schleissheim near Munich. Night fighter units from Ludwiglust, Zerbst, Jüterborg and Wiesbaden were led directly to 'Funk Feuer' 'Nürnberg'. All units of Generalmajor Walter Grabmann's 3 JD were switched in over FF 'Bonn'. Altogether, 246 night-fighters were engaged.

Rupp had claimed a B-17 Flying Fortress at Hannover on 11 January and by now had six confirmed 'Dicke Autos' or 'Fat Car's as the bombers were known. He respected his enemy and their bravery and usually aimed for the bomber's fuel tanks to give the crew a fighting chance.

At 0036 hours one of Rupp's bordfunkers picked up scores of blips on the cathode ray tubes. Normally contacts were few and far between but bombers were everywhere. Miss one and another would soon appear. Wild with excitement the first bordfunker immediately gave his pilot a change of course. As he turned the Ju 88 Rupp knew from the altitude and distance tubes that a bomber was directly ahead. His nerves were at breaking point. The enemy pilot took no avoiding action and he gave full throttle. Cautiously Rupp throttled back and then saw his quarry clearly. It was a Lancaster, possibly 'X-X-ray' on 635 Squadron but most probably LM463 'K-King' flown by Pilot Officer Albert E. Lander RNZAF whose crew was on only their second operation on 101 Squadron. Outbound at 18,000 feet 'King' was well north of the planned track. To ground control Rupp announced: 'Making Pauke-Pauke! ('Kettledrums, Kettledrums' - going into attack).

Near Dillenburg, a town 23 kilometres south east of Siegen, a burst of 'Schräge Musik' caused a series of small explosions in the wing and the engines and petrol tanks exploded with a bright scarlet flash. Lander fought to keep his blazing aircraft straight and level to give his crew a chance. As the flames reached the cockpit he lost control and 'K-King' entered a spin. The New Zealander found himself pinned against the canopy by the increasing G-force with his clothing beginning to burn. He put his feet against the pilot's seat and, by straightening his legs, managed to push himself out through the window and flip out over the wing into the night. Seriously injured, he nevertheless survived. Five of the crew including three New Zealanders were killed. Flight Sergeant Raymond Leonard Cato the bomb aimer of Takapau, Hawkes Bay; Flying Officer Mervyn Gillard Hutchinson the navigator from Christchurch on South Island and Flight Sergeant Cyril Robert Parkinson the rear gunner of Te Awamutu, Hamilton on the North Island and the two English Sergeants, Erod Gordon Johnson the mid-upper gunner from Halifax in Yorkshire and Alexander Oliver Johnston the flight engineer from Bristol were laid to rest in Hannover War Cemetery. Sergeant W. G. Clapp the wireless operator was seriously injured but was thrown clear, as was the Special Operator Alfred James Herbert Clayton, from Edmonton, London who later was probably tortured to death for information on the SOs.

Rupp claimed his second Abschuss when he destroyed Lancaster III JB314 on 49 Squadron skippered by 25-year old Pilot Officer Leslie George Kellow whose crew were on their first operation. Kellow, whose parents lived in Victoria, British Columbia died instantly. Sergeants Stanley Gordon Silver, flight engineer of Woodford, Essex and two Londoners, Terence Charles Baker, the 22-year old bomb aimer of Brentford and Leonard Ernest Walford, wireless operator of Shepherd's Bush; and Pilot Officer Jim Latham the 19-year old Canadian tail gunner from Windsor, Ontario also died. Only two men got out of the doomed Lancaster. Sergeant A. J. McAvoy the mid-upper gunner, his face badly burned and crusted, crawled around for two hours bumping into trees until villagers found him. He was then left in a coal cellar for twelve hours without any attention at all. Cold and in great pain he was placed in a cart with the 21-year old navigator, Sergeant David Rowcliffe of Wolverhampton, who could not recognise McAvoy. At the local hospital, both received devoted nursing attention but Rowcliffe died of his injuries on 1 April. McAvoy underwent thirty surgical operations for his burns. In time he was repatriated, arriving aboard the *Arundel Castle* at Liverpool on 6 February 1945.

At about twenty kilometres north of Bamberg at approximately 0120 hours, Bruno Rupp came upon another Lancaster. It was EE174 'A-Apple' on 50 Squadron skippered by 'Jimmy' Waugh. In a brief engagement, Rupp aimed at the right wing, quickly setting it on fire. Sergeant 'Jack' Dunn the WOp/AG had just switched himself from the intercom to take a broadcast message from base when he felt the aircraft give a sickening lurch. Dunn looked up to see 'Chas' Chaston the navigator standing up with his parachute on his chest, silhouetted against a mass of flames which were blazing past the starboard portholes from the outer engine and waving frantically to him. The skipper gave the order for an emergency 'bail out'. Dunn had switched back on to the intercom in time to hear the two gunners acknowledge the order to 'bail out' and the bomb aimer shouting 'I can't get this bloody hatch open'.

'Not waiting to hear any more, I tore off my helmet and clipped on my 'chute, which was stored behind me. I scrambled to the rear of the fuselage following the navigator, who, probably feeling that his best chances lay in escaping via the rear exit was ahead of me clambering towards the rear. I had cleared the main spar and was standing more or less upright and could see both gunners at the rear door - they were struggling and appeared unable to open the door. Almost immediately there was a violent explosion that threw me off my feet and I was trapped, pinned to the inside of the fuselage of a blazing aircraft at 21,000 feet with nearly 12,000lb of incendiary and high explosive bombs. My limbs were weighted, I seemed too heavy to move even a finger and the aircraft was gyrating madly, obviously in a dive. Suddenly, I saw a gaping jagged hole, through which the moon shone - the aircraft had broken its back at exactly the point at which I was pinned - and gave its last dying lurch. But in that instant and before I knew what was happening, I was catapulted into the clean, cool night air above the Bavarian slopes. The aircraft suddenly went into a steep dive which followed an explosion.[94]

'My parachute responded as soon as I pulled the rip-cord and as I fell, everything seemed strangely silent and still - even the sound of aircraft had disappeared. It was like being in another world, for only a short while previously I had been trapped in a doomed aircraft, heading for the hereafter and now by an amazing twist of fate that had saved me from certain death I found myself floating down on my parachute. On my descent I wasn't sure if I had seen any other parachutes, but because of the bomb aimer's call prior to baling out, plus the obvious difficulties being experienced by the two gunners, I concluded that I had been the only survivor. I could see the landscape

below me bathed in moonlight and it appeared that I was heading towards the centre
of a large lake. This made me take a grip of myself. I was alive and my thoughts were
now for survival. It looked as if I was heading for some water and being a non-
swimmer I began frantically pulling on the lines to alter my drift as I had been
instructed, to spill air from the 'chute and attempted to direct the drop towards the
shore. I afterwards realised that I was spilling air from the 'chute in the wrong direction,
but fortunately it wasn't a lake but merely a large moonlit clearing on the edge of a
pine forest. Had I correctly handled my 'chute, I should have undoubtedly landed in
the pine trees. As it was, I landed in the clearing close to its edge.

'The landing was perfect and I even kept my feet. Within seconds I heard the
aircraft explode nearby and realising it was still fully laden, I hastily hid my parachute
under a pile of dead branches and found my escape compass. I recall laughing to
myself as I thought of the breakfast I was going to miss, but no doubt the laughter was
a trifle hysterical. As I set course for the south west, I heard the sound of small arms
fire and at first thought I had been seen, but soon realised that it was the ammunition
from the aircraft exploding. It wasn't very long before I realised I was heading in the
opposite direction to the one I wanted, having taken a reciprocal bearing. I circled back
in a wide sweep to avoid the burning aircraft and headed, optimistically towards
Switzerland, which I thought to be about 200 to 250 miles to the south west. It was
unlikely that I should get that far without some assistance. We had been in sight of
the fires burning in Nuremberg to the south as I was taking the Group broadcast and
I knew that I was well and truly inside enemy territory and on my own.

'Using the stars to give me some guidance I began to make my way in a general
South Westerly direction, hearing the last of the bomber stream droning away above
me, I knew I was going to miss my breakfast this time. Suddenly there was a burst of
what sounded like machine gun fire, but I later realised that it was probably the
ammunition in the burning aircraft and not someone pursuing me.

'It was bitterly cold and on some slopes there was an accumulation of snow and
the water in the ditches had ice over it. I tried to fill my water bottle with water, adding
the tablets from my escape kit to make it safe to drink, but although I tied the bottle to
my belt, the contents soon turned to slush. I was without my Irvin jacket - being near
the main heat source of the aircraft I had been sitting on the jacket instead of wearing
it and I soon became aware of the intense cold.

'Keeping to the fields and away from paths, roads or signs of any habitation, I kept
on the move. I noted the absence of hedges or field fences but found, to my dismay
that the field boundaries consisted of water filled ditches which had a light film of ice
over them. Having fallen into these on more than one occasion, I decided to gain some
sleep until there was some light to enable me to avoid them but the cold prevented
this, although I tried to gain some shelter under bushes. I continued my walk and
eventually, as the light was breaking, I found myself walking down a small valley
which eventually met up with a road and a hamlet. Having been discouraged by
constant falls into water filled ditches, I decided to keep to the road and commenced
to walk between the houses down the village street. On passing a row of cottages,
some men emerged dressed in a uniform type cap, obviously leaving for their
employment. I kept on the opposite side of the road, but the womenfolk appeared a
bit suspicious as they watched the men go off.

'The only words of German I knew were 'Guten Morgen', so I muttered this as I passed and received a reply, to my surprise. I had gashed the little finger of my left hand which was bleeding badly and I had used the tail of my vest as a bandage, so I kept this hand in my pocket. On leaving the village, I discovered the road ran parallel to a railway line, beyond which was a wide, fast flowing river, which I surmised was the River Main. Although I wanted to continue in a South Westerly direction, I decided to continue on a more easterly course to see where it was possible to cross and resume the direction I wanted.

'Leaving the road and crossing the railway line, I continued along the river bank until I saw signs of a town on the opposite bank and in a short while I came to a bridge. As I started across towards the town, a young lad on a pedal cycle overtook me and continued to look over his shoulder at me in a suspicious manner. I had removed all insignia from my battle dress, but was obviously looking very disreputable. On the far side of the bridge I noticed a group of men lounging against the parapet and the lad on his cycle stopped to speak to them, at the same time glancing in my direction. I was committed and put both hands in my pocket - to hide both my water bottle which had frozen to my belt and the bandage on my little finger, I slouched past them and to my surprise they made no comment. I turned immediately to my right and to my consternation a squad of soldiers was being marched towards me but again they too ignored me.

'Still suffering from the shock of seeing the marching German soldiers, immediately I was out of sight of any buildings I left the road and climbed up the steep side of the valley, regaining my general south-westerly route. After avoiding a gun emplacement which I almost stumbled on and hiding from a group of children playing in the woods. I was descending into a valley following a path when I became aware of a group of people at the top of the path. At least one seemed to be carrying a rifle or shot gun and not wishing to encounter anyone at close quarters I changed direction on a branch path which led me further away from them, but not too abruptly. As I continued up the side of the valley, a voice shouted to me and I looked across and decided that discretion was the better part of valour.

'As they approached me I realised that what I had thought to be a rifle was, in fact, a felling axe. Feeling the game was up, I said to him 'RAF'. I think he was more scared than I was as he stuck his axe into my chest and insisted I put my hands over my head. The group, which included two or three women, shepherded me to their village, some distance away and I was placed into the custody of the local schoolmaster who seemed to be a sort of deputy mayor. Followed by most of the inhabitants of this small hamlet, the schoolmaster took me to the next village which had a burgomeister. The womenfolk were very wary of me en route and ensured their children didn't get too close to me. He contacted the military who sent an escort. Whilst I was waiting, a nun in the mayor's household made me a cup of coffee and cut me a slice of 'seed' cake which I did not like.

'An SS Feldwebel came for me in a Volkswagen with a civilian driver and took me back to the town I had passed through earlier, to an official looking building at the end of the bridge. He was surprised when I told him that I had crossed the bridge early that morning, saying it was always under military guard. I was cursorily searched, but none of my maps, compasses were found and eventually a lorry with a number of RAF, RAAF and RCAF aircrew in the back collected me and conveyed us all to an aerodrome at Schweinfurt. We now totalled about 23 and were held in a large room for the rest of that night and the whole of the next day. To my joy, I saw among the aircrew, but kept to one end away from us, were three of my crew; the skipper, bomb aimer and engineer. I had never expected to see them again. We were searched but again I managed to keep my compass and map, placing them on a ledge in the room during the searching and retrieving them after we were locked up for the night. Words were not needed to exchange our relief to each other. This gave me time to rest-up a little and talk with them. I learned that Jerry Lynch had at last managed to open the front hatch and all three had bailed out. They saw the explosion which had blown the starboard wing off and then the aircraft went down in the steep dive. They saw no other 'chutes emerge. It seemed to them that just prior to striking the ground the aircraft pulled out of its dive and broke in two before finally plunging into the ground. It was obviously at this point that I found myself flung out of the aircraft, being lucky enough to have been pinned to the inside of the fuselage near the mid-upper turret at the precise point the aircraft broke in half. I was in the air only a very short time before landing, perfectly on my feet and it was only several seconds before the explosion of the aircraft and its load showered me with debris.

'The skipper was unfortunate to land on a cottage roof and was soon captured before he was able to recover from his ensuing fall. The bomb aimer landed in pine trees and found himself swinging some distance from the ground. His release knob had jammed and he was some time in getting free. At daylight his position was given away by some small boys who were on their way to school and were over curious. Jerry was hooked up in a pine tree, but later had been seen by schoolchildren who had given him away. George Prince was very unfortunate as his 'chute caught in a projection as he jumped and the fabric was badly torn, which resulted in a descent much faster than was safe. As a result he was badly bruised about his face and body and was unable to make much progress so he was caught fairly quickly.' They had seen only their own parachutes coming down after they left the aircraft and had thought the remaining four had perished. They had seen the starboard wing break off prior to the aircraft diving into a spin, followed by the aircraft breaking in two, just aft of the mid-upper turret, before plunging to earth. This was when I was catapulted out into the night air.

'After two or three days we were taken to Schweinfurt railway station by bus, from which we could see the damage inflicted by earlier raids and from there by train to Frankfurt-on-Main. A tram took us to Dulag Luft, the interrogation centre for aircrew. We were put into solitary cells for several days, only coming out to be interrogated. I was eventually released into the compound where aircrew were kept pending transport to a PoW camp and there met Flight Sergeant 'Jock' McPhee, a fair haired Scotsman who had been on the same raid as myself. We spent a part of Easter period waiting for our move and eventually spent several days in a cattle truck on a journey to Heydekrug in Lithuania. We spent one night in the Berlin goods yard listening to the RAF bomb the area and trusting that we weren't going to receive any bombs ourselves. I spent the next thirteen months in captivity, in Lithuania, Poland and Germany.'

From his rear turret on Lancaster 'V-Victor' on 49 Squadron Flight Sergeant Walter Morrisby had a brief but vivid view of the target: 'The whole of our bombing run was between fighter flares and the entire area was extremely bright... on the run in, flak was heavy but not as heavy as one would expect. Searchlights were numerous although most aircraft that I saw coned over the target area appeared to be shot down by fighters, not flak. During the entire operation we had not suffered any damage by flak nor attacks by fighters. Two FW 190 fighters were observed just after 'bombs gone'; the first appearing below our aircraft heading in the opposite direction and the second, travelling from port to starboard, about a thousand feet below our own height.'

Morrisby reported that the first outward leg from the target was subject more to flak than to fighters. Although, from the flight engineer's jump-seat alongside Pilot Officer Frank Clark, he observed that German fighter flares by then were not as concentrated as before; he also observed fighter activity on the first long leg away from the target, south of Stuttgart. The rest of the flight home was uneventful although the French coast was not crossed as flight-planned, due to incorrectly forecast winds. The crew landed back at Fiskerton in Lincolnshire after 7.25 hours in the air.[95]

There was no word from Pilot Officer Kellow's Lancaster which had been shot down at about 0036 hours and none either from JB466 skippered by 25-year old Flying Officer William Andrew Lawrence Colhoun, which had taken off from Fiskerton at 2206. Colhoun, an Irishman from Belfast, was shot down by a night fighter practically on the turning point for the final leg into Nuremberg and crashed at Schleusingen in Thuringia. Sergeant A. W. Black the flight engineer and Flight Sergeant R. Prinn the navigator bailed out and were taken prisoner. The skipper and Sergeant Leslie Henry Broad the mid-upper gunner from Finchley, London were lost without trace and are commemorated on the Runnymede Memorial. Sergeant Hector Hugh Watson Anderson the 31-year old bomb aimer from the Taranaki region of New Zealand's North Island; Sergeant Kenneth Ellam, the wireless operator from Coventry and Sergeant William Albert Simmons the rear gunner from South Hackney, London are buried in the Berlin 1939-45 War Cemetery.

Returning on one of the fourteen Lancasters that landed back at Fiskerton the diary entry written by Sergeant John Patrick Hennessey a flight engineer simply said 'The greatest mistake the RAF has made: for we went to do the attack in moonlight. Fighters intercepted us as soon as we crossed the enemy coast and kites were being shot down all around us.' Next day Hennessey went home on leave to see his wife and baby son, returning in time to fly the trip to Aachen from which his aircraft failed to return. Just eleven nights after returning from Nuremberg, Hennessey and all his fellow crewmembers lay dead in a Belgian meadow amongst the wreckage of their shattered Lancaster bomber.[96]

Towards the rear of the Bomber Stream, Sergeant 'Andy' Wiseman on Flight Sergeant Barry Casey's crew on 466 Squadron was restless as usual and kept himself occupied maintaining a ceaseless vigil for night-fighters but an hour from the target an unseen German pilot attacked without warning and his cannon shells set a port engine on fire and damaged one of the starboard engines. The Halifax began diving out of control and Wiseman watched Casey wrestle manfully with the steering column, eventually bringing the ailing bomber level. Fortunately the fire went out but with only two engines still functioning Casey shouted to the navigator for a reciprocal course home. The bombs were jettisoned and Casey nursed the devastated Halifax towards England where he put down at a US base in the south of England. They were issued with railway vouchers for their journey back to Leconfield - third class.[97] On 19 April Barry

Casey and the crew on Halifax LV956 failed to return from the operation on the rail marshalling yards at Tergnier in France. Andy and the crew were caught by Oberleutnant Martin Drewes just after bombing the target. As the aircraft caught fire Andy was forced to parachute out into the darkness and confusion of occupied France. Barry Casey, the rear gunner and the flight engineer died in the crash. Briefly on the run 'Andy' Wiseman was betrayed and captured, spending the next twelve months as a prisoner of war in Stalag Luft III, using his knowledge of Russian, Polish and German to act as one of the principal camp interpreters and working as a 'scrounger' for the 'X' committee of escapers.

Flight Sergeant 'Spider' Webb in the mid-upper turret of Halifax 'D-Dog' on 640 Squadron helped fight off five German fighter attacks in the thirty minutes before commencing the run in to the target. On the way out to the enemy coast he had seen only a few lights and some occasional flak. Over the enemy coast 'slight anti-aircraft fire' was encountered. 'We flew at 22,000 to 23,000 feet, he said, 'the night being clear with low temperatures. When we were about thirty minutes from the target a Path Finder Force aircraft was shot down to the port of track. Due to the exploding of its target indicators and markers on the ground, many aircraft in the Main Force stream bombed these markers thus splitting up the compactness of the stream. At this stage, night fighters attacked us. After the first attack all our guns became unserviceable. Due to the freezing temperatures the breechblocks of the guns had frozen in the forward position. We were an experienced crew and did not bomb the wrong PFF markers but carried on to the main target. Four more times we were attacked by fighters. Each time we took evasive action, only suffering a few bullet holes in the second and third attacks.'

Webb was prepared for the worst as the bomb-doors opened. Strangely, nothing happened.

'We bombed the main target,' he reported briefly. 'Later, the camera photos showed that the bombs had been bang on the TIs.'

Just thirteen weeks later, Flight Sergeant, now Pilot Officer, D. Johnson and crew were one of two Halifaxes shot down on the night of 10/11 August during an attack on railway objectives at Dijon, a comparatively lightly defended, short-range target. All of the crew bailed out and evaded capture. Flight Sergeant 'Spider' Webb and Flying Officer R. F. Lane RCAF were flown home to England in an Anson and were back at Leconfield eight days after being shot down.

Flight Lieutenant Robin Knights piloting LL773 'D-Dog' on 101 Squadron was among the aircraft destined to wait; milling around over the assumed target on ETA. He was not impressed with the results of the attack:

'It was nothing like the size of conflagration normally seen on these occasions but there was enough light to see other aircraft when running over the target. They were coming in all directions, from dead ahead and at angles from both bows and quarters. Some were above and some below. Those above were the most unhealthy as with their bomb doors yawning open and bombs falling away, the danger of being hit was very great. Several times I took violent evasive action both to avoid being bombed from above and also to avoid aircraft coming in the opposite direction. It was an absolute free-for-all mêlée and the bombing run was hardly straight and level. The bomb aimer (Sergeant Morgan) claimed to have seen a coloured flare so there may have been a

Path Finder to start if off. I personally think that a very large percentage of the losses were collisions as I had so many near misses in a comparatively short period.'

Knights was glad to get his Lancaster on a homeward heading. By then the unpredicted winds had scattered the bomber stream and with a long return flight over enemy territory it could be assumed that the German ground control interception controllers would be finding it easy to pick up stragglers. Certainly, Knights' gunners, Hart in the mid-upper turret and Murphy in the rear turret, kept him corkscrewing his Lancaster most of the way back to the coast so as to frustrate enemy fighters, whether real or imagined. 'Back-plotting the navigator's log afterwards seemed to indicate that we had bombed Schweinfurt,' Knights said. 'I have my doubts as Germany is a big place on a dark night with no aids and the winds 'up the spout'. In retrospect, I wished that I had brought my bombs back.'

For the farm worker turned regular soldier turned officer and pilot it had been an exhausting eight hours of night flying with three of them on instruments in turbulent cloud. It was all the more disappointing therefore not only to have missed the primary target, but also to finish the night with doubts about having hit Schweinfurt.

Flying Officer Robert McHattie found that the attack had not long begun when he arrived over Nuremberg.

'The searchlights and anti-aircraft fire seemed only moderate to me,' he said. 'The target was well marked and numerous fires had already broken out. We had a smooth, uninterrupted bombing run and we got the bombs away first run and turned for home. For a short distance before reaching the target, contrailing at 21,000 feet had become intermittent but almost as soon as we left the target a pretty solid contrail appeared in front of me - same height, same track. Reasoning that this might afford a measure of cover in the bright moonlight and that one contrail would be less easily seen than two, I entered it and flew along it for about fifty miles.'

His wireless air gunner, Sergeant John Allison noted that despite the defences...'the attack was a success and we left the target blazing.'

From his mid-upper turret on Lancaster VN-N on 50 Squadron flown by Pilot Officer David Jennings RAAF, Flight Sergeant Brian Hayes was to see plenty of action before they had left the target behind, for their arrival over Nuremberg was the climax of a running air battle with up to three night fighters at a time. It started with a Ju 88 passing his aircraft on a reciprocal heading and at a slightly lower altitude. With the rear gunner, Flight Sergeant A. C. Mathews, he tracked it for about 900 yards when it turned and commenced an attack. 'The next forty-five minutes was a series of running battles,' Hayes recalls, 'as we corkscrewed and fought our way into the target, dropped our bombs and fought our way out again. It appeared as if we were attacked by three Ju 88s taking it in turns to run in from the port or starboard quarters. Fortunately, they always followed a normal curve of pursuit so we had the advantage of having practised our commentary patter, our corkscrews and our deflection-shooting time and time again against this very type of attack. This enabled us to destroy two of the Ju 88s and we either damaged or perhaps discouraged the third. During this time we were only vaguely aware of the magnitude of the battle going on around us which was evidenced from time to time by corkscrewing bomber aircraft with fighters in pursuit, spraying tracers in the sky and the awful red glow of burning aircraft in the air and on the ground. The combination of the moon period, flares, burning aircraft, fires and tracer made visibility far too good for the bombers and those of us who survived did so mostly by the grace of God, I feel.'

John Chadderton piloting 'E-Easy' remembered that at briefing at Dunholme Lodge 44 Squadron had been promised cloud on the outward route but: 'This trip was definitely not normal. Conditions were all wrong! Here we were in bright moonlight, feeling very conspicuous and flying a long straight leg, 270 miles long in fact, with none of the jinks and deviations that might cause the night fighter controllers to make the wrong decisions about our destination. We were, however, the lucky ones at the front end, having managed to slip through the deadly gap before the wolves gathered. We had ploughed on towards turning point 'C' where we made a right-handed turn, almost due south, towards Nuremberg seventy-six miles away. Normally, a steep turn like this would have thrown off many fighters, but conditions this night so favoured them that they were able to follow round the corner and shoot down another thirty bombers. In the perfect conditions it was easy to follow the bomber stream and the aces among them managed to shoot down six or seven apiece before they had to break off and refuel.

Chadderton was about to make a routine intercom check on the crew when suddenly the mid-upper gunner came on. 'Bill Campion, an 18-year old Canadian of an excitable nature, but possessing the sharpest eyes on the squadron, bless him, 'Hey, Skip! Are the engines OK?' There seems to be smoke coming from them!'

'The rear gunner, a phlegmatic Glaswegian and the perfect foil to the eager Canadian, said, 'Wheesht yer bletherin' Champ - they're contrails!'

'Contrails! How did he know? We had never made them before, although we had often admired the pretty patterns left by the USAAF on their daylight raids 10,000 feet above us. Everyone craned their necks to look behind them through side blisters and astrodome but without much success, when Ken the flight engineer nudged my right arm and pointed down, where a thousand feet below another Lanc was leaving four long white fingers which were twisted into a cloudy rope by the slipstream - a perfect invitation to the night fighters. I decided to climb out of the layer of humidity, but 'Easy' was very reluctant and Ken had to put the revs up to 2,750, the throttles being already fully open. However, by now we had used about a third of our 7½-tons of fuel, so with much mushing she was able to heave herself up another few hundred feet, as the clutching fingers of fog snapped on and off a few times and finally disappeared. While Ken was synchronizing his propellers again I called the nav: 'Pilot to navigator, how much longer on this leg Jack?' As usual, his calculations were right up to date and he immediately replied, 'I've just got a fix on Giessen. We are about two thirds of the way along, about twenty minutes if you can manage to stay on course.'

'I grinned to myself, which was a mistake as the slight wrinkling of the oxygen mask allowed some icy condensation to trickle down my chin - after all it was minus 35 degrees outside and the cockpit heating on 'Easy'; was on a par with the rest of her. The wry smile was a tribute to all navigators, sitting there behind their curtains, at a vibrating plotting table where just hanging on to pencils and protractors was a work of art, precise mathematicians, who couldn't really understand why ham-handed pilots were not able to hold a course to one degree. Our crews appreciated that we had got one of the best. Using 'Gee' until it was jammed at the Dutch coast and H2S,

Jack worked swiftly to calculate winds which were then transmitted back to Group by the WOp, Jock Michie, who had to risk breaking the radio silence that all bombers observed. At Group the winds from all sources were averaged out and re-transmitted back to the bomber stream in the half hourly 'group broadcast'. The wind-finders complained that Group were far too conservative and always played safe with the averages. Jack was still disgruntled about the last Berlin raid when he had found winds of well over 100 knots due to freak weather conditions (since known as 'jet stream'). Group would not accept them, which badly upset the planned time over the target. The intercom crackled again, 'Nav to pilot. Group has done it again Johnny. They are still using the forecast winds which will put everybody north of track.'

'Unwelcome proof of this came from both gunners who had been reporting unusually large numbers of 'scarecrow flares', mostly off to the port quarter and quite a way behind. 'Scarecrow Flares' had first been mentioned at briefing some weeks earlier with the explanation that the Germans were sending this impressive firework up to 20,000 feet to look like exploding aircraft and lower our morale. We hardened cynics were pretty sure that they WERE exploding aircraft, but knowing nothing of the night-fighters using upward firing tracer-less cannon we could not understand why there were not the usual exchange of tracer in the normal 'curve of pursuit'. What the gunners were reporting were the deaths of over fifty bombers. This was the night that the German controllers got their calculations right and ignored a 'spoof' attack in north Germany, deciding that the bomber stream would use a favourite flak gap just south of Cologne to penetrate into the hinterland and maybe turn left to Leipzig or Berlin. Me 110 and Ju 88 squadrons had been pulled in from the north and south to orbit fighter beacons 'Ida' and 'Otto' near Bonn and Frankfurt. They could hardly believe it when they found the bomber stream flying en-masse between the two beacons and into their waiting arms, like the gentlemen guns in a partridge shoot waiting for the coveys to sweep over them. The resulting slaughter was much the same.'

Endnotes Chapter 10

94 'Chas' Chaston, Donald Sehlin and Roy Thibedeau were killed, the Lancaster falling at Mauschendorf, seven kilometres south of Ebern. All of Rupp's claims here are the result of research by Dr. Theo Boiten.
95 Frank Clark and his crew were killed on the night of 24.25 April on Munich. Morrisby's place on the crew was taken by another gunner.
96 *Beware of the Dog At War* by John Ward.
97 *The Red Line* by John Nichol (Collins 2013).

Chapter 11

One of the advantages of only being five feet six inches tall meant that Ron Buck on Lancaster 'B-Baker' on 97 Squadron could take up a standing position in the rear gun turret because most attacks on Lancasters by night fighter come from dead astern and below; that was the blind spot. By standing up he could see down and astern through the clear vision panel cut out of the perspex of the turret. As he glanced back through the dark sky he could see that they were giving off contrails from the engine exhausts.

'Skipper, what height are we?' he said in his Cockniest of cockney voices.

'18,000 feet Ron' came back the reply from Peter Drane.

'Why?'

'We are leaving contrails behind.'

'I was interrupted as Trot the navigator broke into the conversation. 'Not surprised; it's minus 57 bloody degrees outside'.

'I unclipped my oxygen mask and spat on the barrel of the nearest gun, it was solid as soon as it landed.'

The Lancaster droned on at a height of 19,000 feet. They were briefed to bomb at between 18,000 and 20,000 feet.

'One and a half hours to target', crackled the navigator's voice over the intercom.

Ron continued standing, revolving the turret through 180 degrees searching the clear dark sky when suddenly to the port quarter a burst of cannon fire; tracers shooting through the darkness - an explosion - a big flash and burning metal falling out of the sky. He carried on searching the sky and behind him he counted a dozen blazing bombers falling in quick succession. He had never seen twelve aircraft going down together before. Running battles began breaking out in all directions and he must have witnessed sixty or more go down behind him before he gave up reporting them to the navigator who usually logged them and concentrated hard on watching the dark sky in front and below. Suddenly, at 400 yards or so he picked up a fighter in the darkness.

'Fighter! Fighter port quarter. Prepare to corkscrew port', he shouted over the intercom. 'Got him Johnny?'

'Not yet' replied Johnny Henderson from the mid-upper turret.

'Standing by' came the quiet voice of Flying Officer Drane.

'Corkscrew! Go!' shouted Buck. 'The nose of the Lancaster dropped so sharply that for a few brief seconds the fighter was lost but as we pulled out of the dive I picked him up again and closed in. Then Johnny called.

'I've got him, Ron'.

'Good'. Let's go together. Ready, Ready, Fire!'

'The fighter was now well in range of our .303 Brownings and I squeezed the triggers. I expected to see the tracers streaking into the Me 410, which I had now identified, but instead nothing happened. I froze, my mouth went dry and I waited for death, expecting a burst from the night fighter. Over the intercom Johnny's voice screamed, 'My guns won't fire'. The fighter held off not more than 100 yards away. As he did so, I checked the safety catches, which were all on 'fire'. Why didn't the guns fire? During all this time the aircraft carried on corkscrewing and I gave out a running commentary as the fighter followed us casually through our evasive action. He seemed to be biding his time. I called to Jock Donald, the wireless operator, to bring me a Very pistol. At least I could have a go at the fighter and it might put him off if a Very cartridge burst in his nose. I kept up the running commentary, mainly to take my mind off dying. I expect the rest of the crew would have preferred not to have heard, for five of them could not see what was happening.

'The fighter closed in for the kill and I took a deep breath. Closer, so close I could now see the outline of the pilot's head in the cockpit, for he was within twenty feet of my turret and as Jock had not reached me with the Very pistol, I shut my eyes and waited for a quick death. After what seemed an age I opened them and as I did I was just in time to see his nose drop and he was gone. As the Me 410 vanished into the darkness below I offered up a short prayer - 'Thank you, God. Thank you'.

'He's gone, Johnny'. 'All clear behind Skip'.

'I felt the sweat cooling under my flying clothing and I felt cold and clammy all over. I could find no satisfaction from the outcome, only relief. I had wanted to see the tracers steaming from my guns and the German night-fighter disintegrate as the bullets smashed home. It was both frightening and disappointing at the same time.

'Target five minutes Skip' came Charles Trotman's voice over the intercom.

'OK Trot'.

'Going down into the nose Skip' said Flight Sergeant Leslie Wagner the bomb aimer.

'OK 'Wag'. 'Ready when you are'.

'There was silence as 'Wag' made his way down into the nose of the aircraft. The gunners continued searching the dark night sky.

'Selecting bomb switches Skip'.

'OK 'Wag'.'

'Two minutes to target' said Charles Trotman.

'In position Skip', announced Flight Sergeant Wagner.

'From this point on, the navigator took over as our operation was blind backing-up and we were to bomb on instruments. As we ran up to the target the navigator relayed the course heading to the pilot.

'Bomb doors open' said a voice over the intercom.

'Bomb doors open' replied the pilot.'

'Bombs gone Skip, bomb doors closed. Get weaving.'

Peter Drane placed a gold-braided naval hat on top of his helmet, switched on the intercom and as he began to weave the Lancaster from side to side, started singing *A Life on the Ocean Wave*. This ritual had taken place ever since the hat was acquired from the 'White Hart' in Boston, Lincolnshire after a night on the town. However, on this night the ritual was half-hearted for there was very little to celebrate. Ron Buck called to the pilot as they turned for home and explained the situation about the guns being iced-up because they faced a long trip home without any armament and the thought was not a happy one. They decided to go for height and get out of the main stream and any night fighters. 'B-Baker' climbed and on reaching 27,000 feet, levelled off. As he swung the turret through its 180 degrees, taking the slipstream through the clear vision panel, his eyes above the oxygen mask felt like hot coals as the cold air hit them and they watered and felt raw, making the searching very hard. Soon over the intercom crackled the navigator's voice: 'Crossing enemy coast'.[98]

Elsewhere on 97 Squadron Henry Van Raalte was at the controls of 'O-Oboe' and was on his way to the target with four red/yellow TIs, a 4000lb 'Cookie' and 762 x 4lb and 48 4lb 'X' incendiaries nestling in the bomb bay and 5 to 6/10ths cloud below and visibility clear above with moon. Searchlight activity in vicinity with fighter flares close on starboard quarter. Sergeant Bill Benfell, his rear gunner, reported unidentified aircraft dead astern at 900 yards range on same level and burning navigation lights. The aircraft - a night-fighter - then moved to starboard quarter and attacked, but a corkscrew to starboard was made and aircraft was lost. One minute later the same aircraft started another attack from the port quarter at 800 yards range but discontinued attack and moved over to starboard quarter coming in at 600 yards range. Van Raalte, who was preparing to turn to port then corkscrewed starboard and the night-fighter then broke away up port. Two minutes later Benfell reported the same aircraft at 150 yards range immediately below his rear turret being then identified as a Bf 110. A diving turn to starboard was made and the 110 was lost to sight. After a period of a minute or two the same enemy aircraft attacked from port quarter at 700 yards range. Benfell then ordered Van Raalte to corkscrew port and as enemy aircraft closed in to 500 yards. Benfell and Sergeant R. G. Davis the mid-upper gunner both opened fire, pouring 150 rounds in to the night sky. The enemy aircraft was last seen diving to port but no claim was made.

The usual business of briefing over, the crew on 'Q-Queenie' on 61 Squadron piloted once again by Pilot Officer Denny Freeman whose crew was flying their third 'op', were soon clambering aboard their Lancaster at the dispersal on the edge of Coningsby airfield. But first the crew had all gazed up into the open bomb bay to have a good look at the bombs hanging there. 'We had seen them or similar ones before' the Norfolk born bomb aimer, Sergeant 'Pat' Patfield recalled, 'but they always fascinated us just the same. And so in we climbed and were soon making ourselves as comfortable as the cramped crew positions permitted. As we plugged in our intercom we ceased our somewhat idle chatter about girls and got down to the serious job of checking equipment, controls, guns and radio etc and waited somewhat nervously for the four engines to burst into life. We didn't have long to wait before we were rumbling round the perimeter track towards the end of the runway, accompanied by other Lancs of our squadron, which in the rapidly fading daylight gave the appearance of large, dark birds of prey. On to the runway, engines revving hard. A green light from the caravan. Brakes off. We were away.

'As usual, I sat in the nose of the aircraft on take-off (rules are made to be broken) and got settled down with maps spread out, parachute stowed near - very near, the numerous fairly heavy and bulky brown covered parcels of 'Window' stacked all around me. In a few seconds, which were only broken by the orders of the pilot and acknowledgment of the flight engineer, with engines straining to get the over-laden aircraft into the air, the jolting ceased and, with the engineer's 'Undercarriage Up', we knew we were really on the way. With a remark from one crew member, 'And to think I had a bloody date in Boston tonight', we settled ourselves to our allotted tasks, en route to Nuremberg. We did not know it then of course, but this was to be the last time that we flew together.

'Gaining height, we flew off to the rendezvous where we could see the dim shapes of other Lancs turning on to course. Taking up our position, we joined in the gaggle for we didn't fly in formation. Indeed it would have been extremely dangerous to attempt to do so. We headed for a point on the southeast coast of England on the first leg of the flight plan. Looking down through the perspex blister in the nose, the ground, what could be seen of it, looked strangely quiet and I often wondered how many people stopped and peered skyward as the drone of the bombers disturbed the peace of the evening sky. I know I had many times during training, wondering whether I would join them one day. Where were they going and how did they feel? Well, now I was here and the main thought in our minds was not whether we would get back OK - you just didn't think of that - but what it'll be like at the target. Hope we could find it and then let's get back to that egg and bacon and bed.

'There wasn't much chatter over the intercom, just the odd remark or two, which usually concerned the opposite sex. The flight engineer took his instrument readings, the navigator was busily working intently at his small table working out the next course for the pilot, the wireless operator getting his set lined up and listening for messages and the numerous other things a wireless operator did. The two gunners, who always seemed so remote from the rest of the crew, were busy swinging their turrets around and peering into the darkness for anything, which shouldn't be there. The pilot as ever, intent on his instruments and usually oblivious to what was happening elsewhere. Having put the correct settings on the bombsight computer, I was now gazing downwards in the hope of picking up some recognizable landmark which, after checking with a map, would be passed to the navigator as a 'pinpoint' to check against his calculated position. Map reading was the bomb aimer's primary job, next to actual bombing and even at night it was surprising how many geographical landmarks could be seen. The hardest part was reading maps as in the nose no lighting was permitted and the only source of light was from a 'blacked-out' flashlight with a few tiny pinpricks to allow a very small percentage of light to pass through. At last the Suffolk coast appeared and crossing it we really felt we were on our way. The usual instruction from the pilot to both gunners: 'OK gunners, keep your eyes skinned!'

'Over 10,000 feet we went on oxygen. On a lot of flights, when we were flying high, the moisture from our breath froze in our oxygen masks. We had to keep squeezing our oxygen mask and the corrugated pipe that came down to break the ice. It wasn't a very nice smell but we had to be on oxygen all the time over 10,000 feet. Our oxygen masks had a microphone on the end, so it was quite a lot of weight hanging down. We didn't have steel helmets and flak vests like the Americans; just a leather helmet and canvas flying suit.

'Usually the pilot was strict on intercom silence. We kept quiet unless we had something to report. It would be quiet and all of a sudden I'd say, 'Bomb aimer to navigator, we're just crossing the coast.' He would acknowledge it and it would go quiet again.

'We had as many as four or five maps, on which we marked out the route and turning points. These had to be checked with the bombing leader and each one of us to make sure they were accurate. We had a target map as well. We had to 'Window' at a certain rate depending on our point on the route. If an area of radar-controlled searchlights and guns were coming up, I'd just chuck bundles out as quickly as possible. They were brown paper parcels done up with string. I had to pull the string off and then I'd have all the individual bundles of 'Window'. Each individual bundle had a piece of brown paper wrapped round with an elastic band or piece of string to pull off and then I shoved it down the chute beside me. Before long you were just mixed up with paper, string and 'Window'. That got a bit tiresome.

'You could not see much at night. If we had to come down and make a forced landing I couldn't see if it was a wood or a field or houses below. It was awful being unable to see what was happening. We even lost some chaps who went to investigate flak damage to the aircraft and went straight out a hole in the fuselage. I definitely preferred daylights. You could see what was happening and we had a fighter escort on some of them.

'It was quite interesting to see aerial combats at night. I could see tracer the bombers fired. It was a different colour to fighter tracer. To demoralize the bomber crews the Germans fired up shells containing Very lights, oil and explosives so, when the shell exploded, it mimicked an aircraft blowing up. They did demoralize us, especially when they were right near. We were told about these shells, but that was all eyewash. They were really aircraft exploding.

'I was in my compartment all the time, unless there was a lot of fighter activity. Then I'd get up in the front turret. There was no bottom to it. It was open. There was a little platform to kneel on when bombing. You stood on that and you were in the front turret. There wasn't a lot of room. I was always glad I was small. Quite honestly I failed to see how you were going to get out in an emergency. I was kneeling on the emergency hatch, surrounded by parcels of 'Window'. If you had to get out quickly, you had to chuck all the bundles of 'Window' out of the way and pull back the rubber pads and then you'd have a job finding the hatch release handle. The rear gunner used to say he was lucky. He saw what he'd been through. At the front you saw all you were going into. I'd identify the target by the surrounding area. You had to be quick to identify flying bomb sites, to get your bombs down in time. They were not self-evident like a big factory or marshalling yard because they were well camouflaged. You just went by your maps and photographs, but we all did our own navigation and bomb run.

'The bomb release point could be one to four miles to the target - depending on our height. I had to release the different bombs in a certain order to keep the aircraft stable and the different sized bombs had a different time in the air. They had to be arranged so they went down at a similar point. I had selector switches and a sweep arm went round, made contact and each contact released a bomb. Lots of things affected hitting the target. I had to set the height of the target above sea level on the bombsight. That came from our maps. If that was wrong the bombs' angle of flight would be wrong and the bombs wouldn't hit the target. I had to take drift and speed and direction into account as well. The winds were given to us at briefing, but we had to check it on the bombsight. Even at night I'd check. It is surprising what you could see at night. Headlands, marshalling yards and railway lines shone if there was a bit of a moon. There was a compass on the bombsight so I could give the navigator a bearing on any pin point and he could check his navigation. He'd start re-navigating on any pin point I gave him. I'd set drift on the bombsight so that the graticule was at an angle. Then I'd bring the aircraft round so the graticule lined up to the target. The aircraft went slightly sideways to allow for drift.

'It didn't do to worry about the people in the towns and cities. As far as we were concerned it was a target and we were interested in pasting the German war machine. That was all we were interested in. At 20,000 feet you were only concerned with hitting the target. I'd think about what we were told when we graduated: You had the station personnel, ground crew and six other blokes all working getting you over the target, with one thing in mind - to drop the bombs on that target. That's the way I thought about it and I always made sure I had got the Aiming Point. That's why I'd have a clear conscience, knowing I got the AP in the graticule of the bombsight and everything was in order when I released the bombs.

'Although briefing had given us 80-knot winds' recalled Warrant Officer Ken Lane on 83 Path Finder Squadron, 'we found when proceeding over the enemy coast at 22,000 feet that the wind was now 120-130 knots! Much of the ground was hidden under heavy cloud, making it almost impossible to obtain a 'fix' and as we made the necessary course adjustment, I sympathised with aircraft of the Main Force that would certainly be experiencing more difficulty.

'Flying in darkness can be very lonely, with little or no conversation between crew members and it was sometimes quite a relief to be almost turned over by the slipstream of an unseen aircraft or to see flames from four belching exhausts spitting at you through the gloom. At least you knew that another aircraft was in front and going in the same direction. However, even this reassurance was lacking on this loneliest of all nights when there was nothing to be seen apart from the occasional glow in the distance. This probably resulted from aircraft being blown off course and drifting over heavily defended areas. Routes were planned with great care to avoid danger spots and to wander off made for a rough flight. We were still above broken cloud over the target, where our function was to drop four flares visually to build up those dropped earlier by other Path Finders and to add for good measure 8,000lb of high-explosive bombs. This we did with only slight interference from flak, which was rather scattered and then came the welcome time to turn for home.'

Thirty-nine bombers were shot down on the final approach and over the target area. The force had by now lost 79 aircraft, exceeding the Leipzig total of six weeks earlier. Of all the aircraft shot down on the outward flight, there was only one from which the entire crew survived; from one crew in every three there were no survivors at all.

Flight Sergeant (later Pilot Officer) Jim Marshallsay DFC an experienced PFF pilot on 627 Squadron at Oakington was aloft in a Mosquito this night, as a 'Window Opener' for the heavies with navigator Sergeant (later Pilot Officer) Nigel

'Nick' Ranshaw by his side as usual. Marshallsay recalls.

'Sometimes just a handful of Mossies would set out for the big German cities, usually in the 'moon period' when it was much too bright for the 'heavies'. If, on these trips, the weather was cloudy, it was possible to take off, climb into cloud, travel to Germany, bomb the target on ETA and return to base, having seen nothing but the runway lights at base on take-off and landing. If however the night was clear, with moonlight and stars, then you could get a hot reception from predicted flak and from the massive searchlight cones, especially at 'Whitebait', the code name for Berlin. If you saw one of the attacking Mossies coned over the target, you took your chance, slipped in, bombed and slipped out again while the poor unfortunate in the cone was dazzled and blasted. When you got back for interrogation, if you had been the one in the cone, you got no sympathy from the other crews, just a lot of banter like, 'Brave lads, taking the flak from us.'

'The 30 March operation had started quite normally. We were airborne at 2300 hours. 'Window Opening' meant that we had to be over the target before the first of the Marker aircraft and scatter 'Window' to confuse the radar defences. The Lancs on 7 Squadron had taken off from Oakington about half an hour before us. The track to the target was past Brussels, then almost East between Koblenz and Bonn, on the so-called 'long leg', then south to Nuremberg. As we turned onto this long leg we realized that something was going badly wrong. The moon was much too bright for the heavies. The expected cloud cover was not there. The Main Force was leaving persistent condensation trails, so there was a great white road in the air, leading into Germany. Combats soon broke out below us. As this was our 38th trip we knew what was happening to the heavies. First a long burst of tracer from the night fighter, then a ripple of flame from the wings of the Lanc or Halifax. A short interval and then a massive explosion and fire on the ground. Nick logged the first few crashes, but after we had seen sixteen go down in six minutes, he stopped, preferring to use his time and eyes searching for fighters. We later learned that over fifty heavies had gone down on the long leg. Nuremberg, when we reached it, was covered in cloud. We threw out our 'Window', dropped our bombs and circled to watch the attack develop, but little could be seen except for a few 'Wanganui' flares. Nick said 'we're going straight home' and that is what we did. We turned the aircraft's nose towards Oakington and left at a great pace, landing at base at 0317 hours; a trip of four hours seventeen minutes. After interrogation we had our operational egg and as we left the mess to go to our beds, the first of the 7 Squadron Lancs were circling to land. The cloud base had lowered and there were flurries of snow in the air. Whereas we had taken the direct route to base from Nuremberg, the heavies were routed north of Paris, to Dieppe, Selsey Bill and home. The difference in flying times shows how fortunate we were to be operating in Mosquitoes.'

Basil Oxtaby on 467 Squadron RAAF said that 'it was common to see four or five Lancasters or Halifaxes going down in flames, sometimes with three or four engines on fire, exploding on the ground. That made it even worse because when the aircraft exploded, there was a pool of light for hundreds of yards and the fighters above could see bombers silhouetted against that light.'

It was 'like shooting fish in a barrel', recalled Freddie Watts, a pilot on 630

Squadron. 'With full strato-form cloud and the moon behind them, the Main Force was silhouetted perfectly against the cloud, which covered the whole of Western Europe. After the gunners had reported something like twenty going down, I told them not to report any more because I didn't think it was doing very much for the morale of the crew, especially those poor boys, the navigator and the wireless operator, who were just sitting there and couldn't see out... I also noticed that on the track we were keeping... most of them were going down over on our port side. So I altered course just a few degrees away and then paralleled my course with the navigator's assistance. I like to think we just kept out of the main stream where everybody was going down. And then when we got nearer to Nuremberg or what we thought was Nuremberg - because it was all under cloud - we eased over and went through and bombed what we hoped was the target.'

John Geddes, who had been a Metropolitan Policeman serving in London's dockland during the Blitz before being allowed to volunteer for aircrew duties in 1941 and became a navigator on a 428 'Ghost' Squadron Halifax, recalled: 'We flew across the North Sea and then turned just south-south-east on a long leg over Germany to the target. The Halifax got to max height, but there was a tail wind of 100 mph. I was expected to record any incident a crew member wished to report and was getting numerous reports of shot-down aircraft, until I had to say that that was enough. It was clearly getting hectic outside, but all these interruptions were interfering with my calculations.'[99]

Ken Pincott the navigator on 'O-Orange', flown by Oliver Brooks, was advised by his Skipper to stop recording the number of aircraft being shot down. 'I believe' says Pincott 'that I logged fifty such positions before reaching the target.' Flying Officer George Foley, sitting in his curtained-off and isolated H_2S position of a Path Finder Lancaster, was shocked to hear his pilot call over the intercom: 'Better put your parachutes on chaps, I've just seen the forty-second one go down.'

Squadron Leader G. D. 'Bluey' Graham AFC DFC 'B' Flight commander on 550 Squadron, who was probably flying LM455/T with a kangaroo dropping a bomb and the nose adorned with the words, 'Jenny's Pent house',[100] recalled: We went in south of Cologne and were immediately met by the German fighters - I could say hundreds. It was a fantastic sight in the clear moonlight - aircraft going down in flames and exploding everywhere.'

And the feelings of Lancaster pilot Flight Lieutenant Graham Ross were similar to those of many a bomber captain that night: 'I was very shaken at seeing so many aircraft going down in flames. I was scared by that, but still more scared at the thought that my own crew might be scared by it all. [101]

Flight Lieutenant W. D. Marshall on 467 Squadron reported: 'We were late getting to the target and I don't think we've got a good bombing photo because we were chased by a German fighter and then a very twitchy Lancaster gunner tried hard to shoot us down.' B for Baker' had a close call when a night-fighter shot down another Lancaster five hundred yards behind and to one side of them, the bomber exploding in the air. 'I thought my time was up,' wrote wireless operator Dale Johnston to his brother later, 'and how I thought of you…' Lancaster ME580 Q-Queenie' skippered by Pilot Officer Keith Schultz was attacked by a Ju 88, but his gunners drew hits on its wings and fuselage and they claimed it as probably destroyed. Pilot Officer Dave Gibbs on 467 Squadron, flying PO-W

DV277, was threatened by a Messerschmitt Me 210 soon after passing Cologne. The fighter was driven off by the mid-upper gunner after the guns in the rear turret failed. Warrant Officer Jim McNab, a Scot among the Australians on 467 Squadron RAAF was not alone when he realised that the meteorological forecast was wrong. 'There was no cloud. It was so light that I could clearly read the squadron letters and identification numbers on the Lancasters flying next to us. One of our chaps said we were for it and he was right! I don't think there was any question of a leakage of information. As far as we could make out, it was the bright moon which was the death-blow for our planes. Nuremberg was the only place covered by cloud. I saw Lancasters being shot down by anti-aircraft guns as well as fighters.'

Pilot Officer J. D. Whiteman RNZAF on 10 Squadron told his Group Commander Air Vice-Marshal C. Roderick Carr: 'I did not think we were going to reach the bloody target, let alone return to base.'

'As we approached the target', Pilot Officer Brooks piloting 'O-Orange' recalls, 'Flight Sergeant Harry Marr the rear gunner reported a twin-engined fighter out on our rear port quarter, high. The enemy aircraft turned in towards us and dived, passing underneath us.' 'Chick' Chandler the flight engineer, who had seen the fighter emerge on the starboard side of the Lancaster, quickly warned the gunners over the intercom of the enemy fighter's position. Harry Marr rotated his turret to the starboard quarter and elevated his guns, as the Ju 88 executed a climbing turn into the same area. The enemy aircraft closed in and opened fire with cannon, the beauty of the illuminated stars of light leaving the fighter's nose belying their deadly intent. The Lancaster dipped its right wing as Oliver Brooks flung the aircraft into a corkscrew manoeuvre to starboard but not before some of the enemy shells hit along the main-plane as he recalled. 'We were hit in the number three tank on the port side. That was the small capacity (114 gallons) tank outboard of the outer. A shell went into it and exploded. It was in fact a brand new tank and had not been filled. If it had the results could have been disastrous. The enemy aircraft made just the one attack and disappeared, no doubt to seek other targets of which there were plenty.'

As the Lancaster dived to starboard, Harry Marr opened fire with his Browning machine guns. The Ju 88 continued in towards the bomber and then broke away to port. Sergeant Ron Wilson, whose sighting of the attacking fighter had been· obscured by the Lancaster's tail-plane, saw the enemy aircraft as it broke away. He depressed his guns and fired off a short burst of fifty rounds before it disappeared from view; neither gunner saw the fighter again.

Brooks concludes.

'The target, if in fact it was the target, was not well marked at all. We bombed on a marker that appeared at our approximate ETA but we did not see much in the way of fires. It was clear from the way the bombs were falling all over the place that few people really knew where they were.'

Pilot Officer Cotter, a Halifax skipper on his 30th op; his navigator was only on his first or second trip: 'With the heavy fighter attacks, the navigator could not have had a more unfortunate introduction and eventually he was unsure of his position. Before we were due at Nuremberg, we saw Path Finder markers going down just off our track. We had not been briefed on any diversionary target here and I just thought we were lucky that we'd got to Nuremberg and so we bombed. Not one of us queried the target.'

The navigator on 'M-Mother' on 78 Squadron, one of sixteen Halifaxes that had taken off from Breighton, had given up logging bombers that had been shot down. The pilot was Squadron Leader John Charles Cooper DFC who was on his second tour of operations. Flight Sergeant Ramsden the wireless operator was a veteran of the Berlin raids and during the early part of these operations was usually completely absorbed by crossword puzzles in the *Daily Mirror* but though Nuremberg meant relatively little to him as a target for once he found it too unnerving to concentrate. Then he picked up two blips on his 'Fishpond', a second H_2S cathode ray tube indicator, which showed the other aircraft as spots of light. A night-fighter was obviously circling a bomber. Then the blips disappeared from the radar screen. Flight Lieutenant F. Taylor, the squadron gunnery leader who had replaced the regular tail gunner who had reported sick, confirmed that he had just seen a bomber going down in flames four miles to their port quarter. A little later Ramsden picked up a suspicious contact almost dead astern and it was closing rapidly from a range of half a mile. Ramsden warned the rear-gunner and Taylor fired his four Brownings at the angle given to him by the wireless operator. 'He's on fire! Going down to port!' Taylor shouted. Ramsden jerked back his blackout curtain and peered through the porthole to see a FW 190 as it hurtled under their wing tip in a mass of flames. Ramsden wrote later that 'another five seconds on that course and we could have thrown cream-puffs at him.'[102]

At 0031 hours when flying over Koblenz on 22,000 feet an unidentified single enemy aircraft was seen by Sergeant McCullogh the rear gunner on Halifax LW901 EY-N on 78 Squadron captained by Flight Sergeant Boswell, which was flying outbound at 160 IAS, port quarter up at 900 feet. McCullogh gave the order to dive at 100 feet range. The enemy aircraft opened fire at 600 yards with a long burst and close to 200 feet. He opened fire at 400 feet with only one gun and fired approximately ten rounds because all guns stopped in the No.2 position. Sergeant Chittenden the mid-upper gunner could not obtain a sight to fire. The enemy aircraft broke away to starboard quarter up and was observed to carry a white light. At 0037 hours McCullogh observed a second unidentified single-engine enemy aircraft on starboard fin quarter up at 800 yards range. He gave the order to Boswell to 'corkscrew starboard' just as the enemy aircraft opened fire with a short burst. The enemy aircraft was lost in the corkscrew, so breakaway was not observed.

Sergeant Taylor the rear gunner on Halifax LV795 EY-H 'H-Harry' first observed a FW 190 dead astern and well below at a range of 900 yards. Previous to sighting enemy aircraft, he had notified the pilot that the intercom was cutting out when the turret was turned to port and when Taylor tried to give combat manoeuvre, the pilot was unable to hear the instructions. By the time the rear gunner was able to get through on the intercom and warn the pilot the enemy aircraft had closed to within 600 yards. At 500 yards the Halifax pilot did a diving turn to port and Taylor opened fire with a long burst. Hits were observed to enter the enemy aircraft which climbed vertically and Taylor was able to fire a long burst underside of the FW 190 which immediately burst into flames and dived straight down. Three members of the crew witnessed the fighter go down and explode when it hit the ground.

Sergeant R. C. Corker, a flight engineer on a Halifax on 578 Squadron at Burn was another who experienced a fighter attack. 'Without any warning at all, we were attacked from underneath; there was an enormous bang as a cannon shell exploded in the starboard-inner and four or five pieces caught me in the fleshy part of the bottom. The fighter shot across our nose and attacked another Halifax about 11 o'clock high from us. It blew up. He had made the two attacks in about twenty seconds.'

At Leeming in North Yorkshire, home to two Canadian Halifax Squadrons in 6 Group, sixteen crews on 427 'Lion' Squadron RCAF and thirteen on 429 'Bison' Squadron RCAF were on the Battle Order. Both flight commanders on 'Lion' Squadron were on the Battle Order. Twenty-nine year old Squadron Leader George Johnstone 'Turkey' Laird DFC RCAF of Winnipeg, husband of Elma Laird, would fly Halifax III LV923 'W-Willie' and 23-year old Squadron Leader Jack Montgomery Bissett DFM RCAF from St. Vital, Manitoba, LV898'D-Donald'. Born in Winnipeg and educated at Windsor Park and Norwood schools Bissett left the employ of the Manitoba Power Company to join up in February 1941 and trained at Dauphin, Edmonton, Nanalmo and Calgary. Receiving his pilot's wings at the latter point, he proceeded overseas in January 1942 and flew a tour on 78 Squadron. Now on his second tour of ops, he had volunteered to carry on rather than return to Canada on leave, as was his privilege on completion of his first tour. His crew was on their fourth operation of their second tour.

'Turkey' Laird had received the award of the DFC for his action on the night of 3/4 October when still a flight lieutenant. While en route to the target his Halifax V suffered a devastating attack by a night fighter. 'Jerry raked us from nose to tail underneath with cannon and machine gun and a fire broke out in the bomb bay,' Laird said later. To the mid-upper gunner, Pilot Officer Jim Moffat RCAF of Castleton, Ontario, the attack 'sounded like frozen peas hitting a tin roof.' He later found nine German bullets in his ammunition cans. The attack had killed the rear gunner and the wireless operator and had seriously injured the flight engineer, Sergeant Bill Cardy in one arm and an eye. The 24-year old bomb aimer, Sergeant Joseph Charles Corbally of Toronto, could not jettison the bombs; fortunately, however, the fighter's attack had severed a cable holding the 4,000lb 'cookie'. It fell away, breaking through the closed bomb doors. Laird turned for home. Despite numerous holes in the fuselage, the aircraft handled reasonably well and Laird flew it back to Leeming. During the trip the incapacitated Cardy kept drifting in and out of consciousness. When able, he insisted on checking with Corbally who had taken over as flight engineer, advising him on the operation of the tanks and other aircraft systems.

Over his airfield, Laird found that he could not lower his undercarriage because of hydraulic damage. Fluids such as blood, vomit, coffee spilled from in-flight ration flasks or oil gushing from the ruptured pipelines of a shot-up hydraulic system could make the metal deck above the Lancaster's bomb bay slippery and dangerous to walk on. From the control tower came the order to bail out. Laird refused, knowing that a jump would probably kill Cardy; even if his parachute opened properly, the wounded man might well die before he was found in the darkness. Fortunately, Cardy regained consciousness while Laird was circling

Leeming and was able to 'direct axe and back-saw operations which finally locked down both wheels,' Laird said.[103] He brought the battered, perforated Halifax in to a perfect landing. Cardy received the Conspicuous Gallantry Medal. Moffat had transferred to the rear turret at his skipper's request.[104] Laird took off from Leeming for Nuremberg at 2200 and was followed five minutes' later by LW618 'E-Easy' captained by 23-year old Flying Officer Walter Norval McPhee of Vancouver, whose crew were on their first operation since reporting from 1659 Conversion Unit on 19 March. Squadron Leader Jack Bissett took 'D-Donald' off at 2220.

LV986 'V for Victor' - call sign 'Holdtight' - on 'Lion' Squadron was skippered by 21-year old Warrant Officer Alexander E. 'Rex' Clibbery DFM RCAF of Regina, Saskatchewan. Flight Sergeant Leonard Albert Pratt, the Buckinghamshire-born flight engineer who was the only Englishman on the crew of Canadians recalls. 'We were a crew of eight. The other regular members of the crew were bomb aimer, Norman Nash DFC; navigator, Flight Officer 'Dick' Morrison USAAF; wireless operator-air gunner, Warrant Officer Jimmy Jardine; mid-upper gunner, Sergeant Dick Qualle DFM and rear gunner, Sergeant Billy 'Shorty' Martin, who was screened after a dozen trips. I was regarded as having a good pair of night eyes and was continuously pressured to keep my head in the astrodome and look out. This was because we were a jumpy crew having experienced several fighter attacks. We had the additional job of sending winds. Briefing, to the best of my knowledge, was in the late afternoon or early evening. I don't remember too much about it except that we were carrying an overload fuel tank and this I had already established in the morning visit to the aircraft. The met man told us it would be bright moonlight with little or no cloud cover and a long straight leg in from the enemy coast to the target. Our load was, I think, nine cans of incendiaries and a 4,000-pounder.[105]

'I can remember discussing the pros and cons with 'Rex' Clibbery just after marshalling the aircraft. In fact, Rex was leaning against the starboard wheel at the time. I expressed my doubts about the trip in no uncertain manner but he was quite adamant that it would be scrubbed like a few others had at about that time. Looking back, I feel that this was a bit of bravado and perhaps a little wishful thinking on his part. I had the feeling, as I'm sure the rest of the crew did, that this one wasn't going to be easy, a little different to some of the ops on buzz-bomb sites and railway marshalling yards which had been done quite frequently at about that time. Airborne at 1908, the flight to the enemy coast was uneventful. After crossing and now being at 20,000 feet we were amazed at the terrific range of visibility in the full moonlight. One could see many of the aircraft in the stream. As the met man had said, there was no cloud cover.'

Twelve aircraft on 427 Squadron successfully bombed the target and returned to this country. Returning crews reported numerous night fighters that were aided by the bright moon. 'N-Nuts' piloted by Flying Officer W. J. Weicker was attacked by a fighter. The mid-upper gunner first sighted an exchange of tracers from two unidentified aircraft on the port beam. The enemy aircraft apparently saw this aircraft when he broke away from the other bomber and therefore, opened fire from 600 yards or more. The mid-upper gunner saw this trace coming from the port quarter down and instructed his pilot to corkscrew to port. This was done and the enemy aircraft was not seen after resume course was given. Neither gunner opened fire and no damage was sustained to the aircraft. A number of the pilots actually saw the night fighters shooting down our aircraft and tracers filled the air. Flight Lieutenant A. McAuley, a veteran of twenty-four trips, made his first turn back due to engine trouble.

429 'Bison' Squadron RCAF lost two of its thirteen aircraft that had departed Leeming. Halifax III LK800 'N-Nan' skippered by 22-year old Pilot Officer Keith Hamilton Bowly RAAF was shot down by Oberleutnant Wilhelm Engel of 3./NJG6 at Weiler am Turm at 0238 hours. It was his second victory of the night, having claimed a Lancaster at 0030 hours.[106] The crew, who were on their 17th operation, bailed out. Bowly, of Quirindi on the North West Slopes region of NSW came down in Luxemburg and hid for some time on the edge of an airfield on which were parked many Stuka dive-bombers. He considered the problems of starting one of them but reluctantly abandoned the idea of stealing one in case he was shot down by the RAF if he ever reached England.[107] He walked right through the city of Metz but was later apprehended on the road to Verdun and was later sent to Stalag Luft I. Sergeant J. W. Clowes, flight engineer; Flight Sergeant J. W. A. Myers, navigator; Flying Officer J. Dougall, bomb aimer and Sergeant W. McMahon RCAF, the mid-upper gunner, were ultimately taken prisoner. Flight Sergeant Donald D. Findlay the wireless operator and Flight Sergeant R. Dawson the rear gunner evaded. Dawson was returned to Britain in early September after being taken along the Comète escape line.

Halifax III LK804 'Q-Queenie' on 429 'Bison' Squadron piloted by 21-year old Flying Officer James Henry Wilson RCAF of Moose Jaw, Saskatchewan which had been attacked and badly damaged near Stuttgart on return ditched in the English Channel. It was only the presence of Sergeant H. J. Robinson of Montreal in the newly installed belly-gun position and immediate evasive action by the pilot that saved the aircraft from complete destruction. Robinson had previously served in the Merchant Navy in 1940 before transferring to the RCAF. A violent dive finally shook off the night-fighter but damaged hydraulics left the Halifax with wheels and flaps down. Sergeant Harry 'Hank' Glass the flight engineer of Toronto, Ontario put out a fire by chopping a hole in the side of the fuselage and kicking out two blazing magnesium flares kept there in case of a landing in the sea. Born on 21 April 1921 in Dufferin County, Ontario, Glass had enlisted into the RCAF on his birthday in April 1941 and prior to that had worked as a newsagent and a car mechanic. He originally trained as a member of ground crew as an aero engine mechanic. His action earned an immediate award of the DFM which was gazetted on 2 May.

The Halifax flew on at considerably reduced speed. When the coast failed to appear on time, Wilson and Flying Officer J. C. Hall his Canadian wireless-operator were all for getting a radio 'fix' that would immediately establish their exact position but Flying Officer Cyril William Way the English navigator of Mudford, Somerset was unwilling - his navigation was not that bad! When the coast still failed to appear after a further interval, Wilson ordered the radio fix to be obtained. To the horror of all, they were well south of Paris. The violent dive which had helped put out the fire had probably upset the gyro compass. There was not enough fuel remaining to reach England but the crew were all in favour of flying as far as possible out over the Channel and hoped to be picked up by an ASR launch. Eventually the sea was reached near Le Havre but there was now only a little fuel left. Sergeant Stanley Charles Sharp the wireless operator sent out their distress call and then clamped his Morse key down so that the signal would go out to the very end. In the cockpit, the red light came up showing that the last tank was almost empty and all but the pilot took up crash positions with back to the main wing spar, heads in hands, knees up to chin.

Wilson lined his aircraft up for a landing along the line of the waves but the two starboard engines cut without warning and the Halifax swung into the side of a wave. The whole nose broke off and disappeared immediately, but Pilot Officer Douglas Finlay the rear gunner and the five other crew sitting the main spar in their crash positions were able to walk out along the wing and into their rubber dinghy. After a complicated rescue operation involving Spitfire, Tempest, Sea Otter and Walrus aircraft, the six men were picked up that afternoon only 25 miles off the Normandy coast by two RAF launches from Newhaven.[108] Pilot Officer 'Hank' Glass was killed on 8 August, just before he was due to receive, from HM King George VI, the DFM for dealing with the blazing flares, on the raid to bomb the oil storage depot at Chantilly in the Forêt De Chantilly when the aircraft caught fire at 15,000 feet outbound and broke up at 5,000 feet. Only one of the crew was able to bail out before the aircraft crashed into the sea. Cyril Way who was injured and who later received the DFC was killed on his second tour on 420 'Snowy Owl' Squadron, on 16 January 1945 when Halifax NA192 failed to return from ops to bomb Magdeburg.

Flight Sergeant 'Bob' Furneaux of St. Catherine's, Ontario, a 425 'Alouette' Squadron air gunner, saw about a dozen aircraft shot down. Until some weeks before he had been Squadron Leader Brian Wilmot's mid-upper gunner. Wilmot's aircraft and Wing Commander McNeill's aircraft collided but Furneaux, flying with another crew had been shot down during a raid on Boulogne. He evaded the Germans aided by several courageous members of the French Resistance and returned to England just too late to rejoin his crew. Only one was left, the rear gunner, Harvey Powell of Frankford, Ontario. Powell had missed the fatal flight by minutes, because he had completed his second tour of operations. McNeill himself had screened him that morning, adding that he was not to fly on the forthcoming training flight.[109]

Flying Officer Ronald Beattie Rudd, navigator on 'R-Roger' on 429 'Bison' Squadron RCAF which was skippered by Warrant Officer2 Marco Alfred Fernandez RCAF, a Guatemala-born American, recalled: 'It was a brilliant moonlit night. Rudd, a student from Owen Sound, Ontario, was one of four Canadians on the crew: Flight Sergeant L. M. Shetler, bomb aimer; Sergeant William McGill Stewart, flight engineer, Sergeant Robert Foster Christie, mid-upper gunner. 'I believe we were high and I remember the lane of flares outlining the target area' said Rudd. There seemed to be a definite pattern of flares outlining the run in as well as the run from the target. There was not a great deal of flak and evidence of fighter activity. It seems to stick in my mind that this was one trip where things were very smooth over the target. Our bombing run was uneventful.' The long leg home was remarkable for the mysterious appearance of a Wellington, very close on the starboard side of the Halifax and in formation. 'Both gunners were a bit nervous,' Rudd said, 'but they didn't fire and he (the Wellington) veered off eventually.'[110]

For another Canadian in a Halifax III on 429 'Bison' Squadron that night, the journey to Nuremberg was also strangely uneventful. 'This was our fourth trip over Germany,' recalled Pilot Officer A. Lyle Christner, rear gunner on the crew skippered by Flight Lieutenant A. I. MacDonald, a fellow Canadian. 'I saw fires and explosions all the way to the target. In fact, I reported to our skipper that everyone in the Main Force bomber stream was dropping their loads early but in reality what I had been seeing was our own bombers being shot down. Strangely, we didn't see a German fighter during the trip but then we'd already had our fun on the trip before with fighters at Frankfurt.'

The trip to the target was uneventful for Warrant Officer 'Paddy' Clarke's crew on 10 Squadron also. Denis Girardau the rear gunner recalled. 'However, on numerous occasions I reported to the skipper that there were many flares in the sky behind us, much more so than on previous trips and I suggested that the Germans were using many 'scarecrows' this night'. Later, he was to realize that the 'scarecrows' were actually bombers exploding. His crew arrived on time at the target with the first wave. The bombing run, Girardau remembers, was normal - until Flying Officer Geoff Fenton, the bomb aimer had dropped his bombs. 'At that moment I called for a corkscrew to starboard having sighted a Ju 88 on the starboard quarter. I opened fire and as he broke away; the mid-upper gunner also opened fire. A few seconds later we observed him to be on fire and losing height rapidly. Cloud obscured him quickly.' Within minutes Girardau was glad to hear that his pilot was back on the homeward course. On the way out of Germany there were a number of occasions when Girardau saw other aircraft being attacked although the cloud had built up as had been expected some hours earlier. But neither he nor the Canadian mid-upper gunner, Pilot Officer Don Johnson, had to use their guns again that night.

Flight Sergeant Roger Callaway, the Canadian rear gunner on Halifax 'N-Nan' on 426 'Thunderbird' Squadron RCAF recalled that 'things were fairly quiet until Nuremberg when all hell broke loose. Although we were not attacked I witnessed many aircraft going down and Jerry seemed all around us and it was sure cold... Withdrawal from the contested target area was a quiet affair subsequently complicated only by the urgent need for Flight Lieutenant Shedd to visit the Elsan - literally the can - at the rear of the aircraft. During this embarrassing manoeuvre with the controls of the Halifax in the hands of the flight engineer, 'Nan' got slightly off course over France and flak opened up as we flew over a Luftwaffe airfield. The runway lights were then switched on and I surmised that more night fighters were taking off. After this incident I saw several more aircraft shot down. Other than for this it had only seemed like just another long trip but we were naturally saddened by the number of missing faces at beer call. Our squadron used to buy beer for our missing friends then lean their chairs back against the table and God help anyone who tried to sit in the places of those missing.'

Sergeant Roger Coulombe a French-Canadian of Montmagny, Quebec, a pilot on 426 Squadron known as 'The Berlin Kid' also remembers Nuremberg as 'a hellish night.' Coulombe, who preferred to remain an NCO and had once told his CO, 'You can stick your commission to your arse'[111] completed his operational tour soon after the trip and was the recipient of a wrist watch given by a gentleman from Panama to King George VI to be given to the pilot who dropped the greatest tonnage of bombs on Berlin. Air Vice Marshal 'Black Mike' McEwen presented the watch to Coulombe at 'a sort of investiture ceremony,' as Coulombe describes it, adding that the 'prize' was 'nothing but a cheap Nevada watch ... worth about $20.' He adds: 'I am still wondering how the King of England could have accepted such a ridiculous gift. I am sure he never saw the watch, because he would have ordered the thing thrown away in the garbage!' [112]

In the mid-upper turret of Lancaster 'M-Mike' on 10 Squadron, Flying Officer Fred Stuart RAAF was sweating out his 'spare bod' trip as an experienced gunner with an all-RAF crew:

'Over the target the flak was particularly heavy - the heaviest I had experienced - and that included numerous trips to Happy Valley and to the Big City. Still more fighters buzzed about like flies. The Path Finders had been and dropped their markers and some of the first wave of bombers had already dropped their bombs. 'Bomb the greens' came the voice of the 'Master Bomber' circling somewhere down there.

'Straight and level' said the skipper. 'I've got her,' said the bomb aimer.

'Left, left, steady. Bomb doors open. Bombs away. All bombs gone. Doors closed.

'She's all yours, driver. Let's get the hell out of here. I've got a date for breakfast in York' '

A few minutes which had seemed an eternity had passed.

'Turning off the bombing run we set course for home just a little happier than on the outward journey. Twice more we were hit by night fighters and a cannon shell from an Me 109 punched a hole in the perspex of my turret and the same burst put a few holes in the aircraft fuselage. The main damage was done to the Elsan portable toilet aft of the bomb bay on the port side. There was a big hole blown in the bottom. A messy business. The icy wind whistling through my damaged turret was more than somewhat uncomfortable. However, I was too scared to worry as I kept searching the sky. Every now and then we would see signs of tracer flying through the air and sometimes there would be an explosion and a big ball of flame would tumble earthwards. 'All in all, it was a fairly shaky old do.'

'E-Easy' on 44 Squadron meanwhile, headed for the bomb run. John Chadderton recalled: 'In the perfect conditions it was easy to follow the bomber stream and the aces among them managed to shoot down six or seven apiece before they had to break off and refuel.[113] We, the lucky ones at the front end, had managed to slip through the deadly gap before the wolves gathered and we ploughed on towards turning point 'C' where we made a right handed turn almost due south towards Nuremberg 76 miles away. Normally, a steep turn like this would throw off many fighters, but conditions tonight so favoured them that they were able to follow round the corner and shoot down another thirty bombers.

'At the target 'Scotty' the bomb aimer came into his own. He increased his 'Windowing' rate to the maximum number of bundles per minute and about halfway through the twenty-minute run to the target he handed the job over to Ken with obvious relief and took up a prone position by the bombsight. But now another adverse factor was be-devilling the raid. The Met men, who had promised us high cloud to hide in on the long leg, had also predicted that Nuremberg would be clear of cloud for the attack. The marking force of Path Finders were therefore stocked up with near-ground bursting TIs, which couldn't be seen through cloud and so when they opened the attack five minutes before zero hour these fell useless and unseen. Some of the markers carried a few 'sky-markers', a parachute flare released above cloud so that the bomb aimers could direct their bombs through a theoretical spot in the sky resulting in a fall on the target. Unfortunately, to be accurate, the flare release and bombing runs must be downwind and here we had a crosswind of seventy-five knots, so that when two very lonely red flares appeared dripping yellow blobs, 'Scotty' gave me a stream of 'left, lefts' in an attempt to follow them. This was no way to do a bombing run and I consulted the nav, who agreed that the town on his H2S screen was drifting away to the right. I had to make a quick decision. 'Right Jack, we'll drop them 'on the box'! 'Scotty', abandon bombing run. I'm turning onto 2700M.'

'We headed back to Nuremberg and although the centre of towns gave a mushy picture, Jack was able to pick up the river and gave 'Scotty' the 'now' to drop the load which fell without trace through the cloud. I felt the exhilarating 'twang' under my feet as the straining floor reasserted to normality and 'Easy' surged upwards like a tired hunter taking the last fence after a muddy chase. I held the course for thirty seconds for the obligatory photo flash and camera run, both useless tonight, but which one day would earn the crew an aiming point photograph and forty-eight-hour pass. In the middle of a normal raid this always seemed the longest half minute of my life with searchlights and flak all around and a hideous inferno below. But here at Nuremberg it was quite unreal. A bit of flak about; the odd skymarker still drifting on a reciprocal underneath us and the occasional bump of a slipstream passing at ninety degrees to us. The latter reminded me that it was a bit dicey on a different course to everybody else, so I hastily turned on to 2010M for the thirty-one miles out of Nuremberg to position 'D' where we thankfully took up a westerly heading that would take us home. The gunners reported that the target had livened up a bit after we left, but not very much and after several minutes they called our attention to another target away over to our right which seemed to be cloud free and with a lot of action. Tongue in cheek I asked Jack if he was sure we had bombed Nuremberg and received the expected forceful reply, with added information that the burning town was probably Schweinfurt (we learned later that about one third of the force went there by mistake.)'

'Q-Queenie' on 61 Squadron had crossed the enemy coast and was heading for the 'Otto' night fighter beacon near Frankfurt. It was not long before searchlights probed the darkness and then the crew realised the absence of flak, which meant mainly one thing; night fighters. 'Pat' Patfield immediately started undoing the brown paper parcels of 'Window' and began shoving the small bundles through the small chute in the side of the fuselage to disrupt enemy radar defences. 'It wasn't long before maps, brown paper, string and I began to get mixed up' he recalls. 'The blessed chute wasn't large enough to push the brown paper out as well! For the next half-hour or so very little happened and then there was an exchange of machine-gun fire to our port. Only a short exchange, but suddenly from that direction we saw a glow in the sky, small at first but soon becoming larger, until we could plainly make out the outline of a Lanc, burning fiercely. It continued flying steadily for a while and then turned and went down in a shallow dive.

'Lanc' gone down to port!' I yelled to the navigator, whose job it was to log such incidents. This was our first experience of real air to air combat and with a remark from the pilot, something like 'Bugger me! Did you see that? Keep a look out gunners.' I know we all felt that funny feeling in the pit of our stomachs reserved for such occasions. It wasn't long before we saw more exchanges of gunfire. There we were droning along feeling very much on our own one minute and the next being rudely awakened to the fact that this was definitely not the case and we were the hunted!

'Suddenly the whole sky before and above us was lit by what appeared to be huge fireworks. Fighter flares! We had heard all about these during training. They were the things most feared by bomber crews and here they were. Hanging in the sky like giant magnesium chandeliers, they were being dropped by German planes flying above the bomber stream in lanes three or four abreast and stretching out far in front of us. We then fully realised that we were far from being alone! Other bombers could be clearly seen on either side and ahead of us and it made us feel as naked as the day we were born, exposed to everything! Very soon combats could be seen taking place all over the sky. Sometimes there followed a ruddy glow lasting only a few seconds and ending in a terrific explosion. At others, like the first encounter we had seen, the bomber would burn steadily and begin to lose height. These were the lucky ones, or so we thought, as they were having enough time to bail out. We did in fact see two or three parachutes floating down from time to time.

'Two going down to port and one to starboard' I passed this information back to the navigator for logging. I always admired the navigator in his tiny compartment, not being able to see what was going on but hearing it all over his intercom. In the midst of this, he was working calmly on such things as courses and wind speeds with his charts and protractors etc, while such a commotion was going on outside. Sometimes, 20,000 feet below, a large, solitary explosion marking the end of a plane and perhaps its crew could be seen as it hit the ground. Other explosions frequently occurred on the ground also, an exploding 'stick' of bombs, which had been released from a bomber in distress. Although unavoidable in most cases, these should not have been released until the bomber had turned away from the stream as the incendiaries burning on the ground made the bombers stand out clearly to any fighter as they flew over. The battle raged fiercer, encounters all around, explosions and fires and at one time we counted thirteen aircraft going down all at once.

'Gunners, can you see any fighters?' the pilot kept asking. To which the usual reply was, 'Not near enough to have a go at.' I kept standing up in the front gun turret to man the front guns just above my head, but I did not see anything to have a go at.

'Scared? Of course I was with a horrible sinking feeling in the pit of my stomach, would I see my 21st birthday next week? I wondered, surely we must be attacked!

'Without warning, over the intercom, we heard the gunners firing like mad and a yell from Bill, the rear gunner, 'Look out, skipper' three of 'em coming in!' At the same time there was a terrific explosion. Things whizzed around and there was a sickly smell of smoke and cordite. I was almost thrown on my back as the aircraft tilted at a crazy angle and the nose went down. My first impressions were of small flames around me and my face all wet and sticky. Blood I thought but I seemed to be in one piece and felt no pain. This sticky mess turned out to be hydraulic oil from the gun turret, as a considerable part of it had disappeared and the severed pipes had spewed out their contents over me!

'We were still diving steeply when the pilot yelled, 'I've got her under control but we're in a mess!' The gunners were swearing and I heard three voices saying rather feebly, 'I've been hit skipper'. It was Frank Devonshire, the flight engineer, Tommy the navigator and Jimmy the wireless op.

'In the nose I had already pulled aside the rubber cushioning, on which I knelt, exposing the emergency hatch in readiness to make a quick exit. But the order didn't come, which was just as well, as I discovered afterwards that the hatch had been chewed up quite a bit and was wedged fast! Needless to say I had already hooked on my parachute! 'Come up here as soon as you can Pat,' yelled the pilot. I told him I had a bit of a fire amongst the brown paper strewn around me - the wrappings from the parcels of 'Window' - but fortunately I managed to put the fires out, mainly by sitting on them! Then I clambered up into the main cabin. Frank was half-standing, half-kneeling and beating furiously at a glow by his instrument panel; Tommy was slumped over the remains of his chart table and Jimmy Chapman, the wireless operator, was sitting by his set with blood streaming down his face. With some relief I saw Denny Freeman at the controls and noticed the shattered windscreen in front of him.

'We can still fly', he said, 'We've lost a lot of height. I'm turning north and then making for home. Keep a look out gunners. The engines are still going but one's spitting'.

'Eventually we got the fires out. They were only in the cabin and fortunately they were small.

'Pat, we're over Germany so better get rid of the bombs. If we're going down we don't want to take them with us,' said Denny.

'So clambering back into the nose I pressed the bomb 'tit'. I suppose Denny had opened the bomb doors! Down they went but as the indicator lamp didn't work in the release switches I couldn't tell if they had all gone. I clambered back down the fuselage, still with parachute on and lifted up the small inspection covers over the release hooks of each bomb position. One had hung up. It was the 4,000 pounder! Probing through the small opening with a short hooked length of wire the Air Ministry supplied for the purpose I at last managed to release the 'Cookie'.

'The next concern was for the injured. Jimmy helped me with the navigator. What we took to be a cannon shell had torn a huge hole in his chart table, taking a lot of his hand with it. We tied up his arm as best we could and got him to the 'rest bed' half way down the fuselage. We then discovered that the escape hatch in the roof immediately above the rest bed was missing and an icy blast was coming through, though we didn't give it more thought at the time. We plugged in his oxygen and intercom and gave him a shot of morphia from the first aid kit and went back to Frank. Jimmy insisted that he wasn't badly hurt but he didn't look too good so we decided he had better sit down by his radio to take it easy. He did but he started fiddling with the set and set about getting a 'fix' to define our position.

'When I got to Frank, he was about 'all in' and sitting on the fuselage floor. His right arm looked a mess. His flying suit around the elbow was badly torn and sticky with blood. My knowledge of first aid being limited to cut fingers, I was horrified to see bits of torn flesh and bone sticking out and was rather at a loss what to do. So I tore his sleeve open more and tied a thick bandage near the shoulder as a makeshift tourniquet. I gave him a shot of morphia and tied his arm up in a sling - all this in almost total darkness - then sat him down on the floor behind the pilot.'

Only ten crews on 61 Squadron at Coningsby reported bombing the target. One of them was 'Ted' Stone, who had taken 'N-Nan' off from Coningsby at 2214 hours and brought her safely back and landed at 0627 hours and who now took up his CO's promised flight home. He headed for Bridgewater a few hours after the de-briefing; the interrogation of returning aircrew by Squadron Intelligence Officers, who then had to write-up Forms 540, the Operations Record Books and get these to Group HQ as quickly as possible for inclusion in a consolidated report to Bomber Command HQ. Casualties and general comments on the action had to be teleprinted or telephoned through, in time for C-in-C Harris's 'morning prayers' at 0900 the same morning.[114]

'As we flew south of Cologne at about 26,000 feet' recalled Les Cromarty on *Royal Pontoon* on 61 Squadron, Len Whitehead the mid-upper gunner and I began reporting aircraft going down. Sid Jennings got a bit fed up with logging them after a while and told us that as there were so many they must be 'scarecrows'.'

Whitehead, who flew a tour of operations between 13 December 1943 and April 1944 manning the twin Brownings in the mid-upper turret, first on Sergeant Martin's crew and later, Flying Officer Bernard Fitch's crew, recalled: 'It was normal for the gunners to report to the navigator when we saw an aircraft go down and give such details as to whether we saw any bail out, if it was flak, or if a fighter etc. On this occasion there were so many going down that the skipper told us not to report, just concentrate on looking out for and avoiding attacks. It was difficult not to look at those going down but we knew we had to keep a careful watch. We would sometimes see some tracer fire and then a small flame which would quickly grow until it lit up the whole aircraft and then frequently would finish with a terrific explosion. Sometimes we were rather puzzled because we did not see any tracer fire and no flak, just the aircraft catching fire. I did not learn the answer to this for many years. It was of course 'Schräge Musik'. When using this no tracer was present so that it did not give away the form of attack. When an aircraft went down, or jettisoned the bombs, there would be a long line of incendiaries burning with bright silver and further illuminating the aircraft above.

'I also remember some problem with the forecast winds not being at all accurate and that our navigator instructed the pilot to 'dog leg' (that is to leave the stream at an angle and after a few minutes return so as to lose time) on at least two occasions. However it was not as bad on this raid as it had been the week before on 24 March when we encountered a jet stream for the first time with winds far in excess of 100mph which caused the stream to be spread over a vast area and was responsible for the heavy losses that night.'[115]

'As we began approaching the target area' recalled Les Cromarty 'a Lancaster flew close alongside us. It was upside down and blazing, like a comet. I asked Sid Jennings to come and look at this 'scarecrow'. We tried to turn away from it but it seemed to follow us. Then it slowly dipped and exploded. As we approached Nuremberg we were horrified to see the great spread of the target area. Most aircraft were turning and bombing too soon. We saw the last of the PFF aircraft going down with TIs pouring out of it. I think it was JB722, Flight Lieutenant Stanley Evans on 7 Squadron in 8 Group. We continued turning on to the target but by the time we arrived all the markers had gone out. We began to circle. Sandy Lyons, the bomb aimer, thought he saw either a railway station or yard and so we bombed that and left the target area. We continued to log aircraft going down as we flew along the 'Long Leg'.'

On the way back Bernard Fitch was of the opinion that his luckiest escape happened. 'Suddenly straight ahead I fleetingly but clearly saw the dimly illuminated face of a German fighter pilot as his plane flashed by, perhaps about twenty feet above us. Len Whitehead later told me that the Ju 88 did a 180° turn and flew for several minutes, level with us on our starboard side just out of range of our .303s. He could have picked us off as easy as pie; instead, he just flew away. I have always wondered 'What was it that made him decide to call it a day?'

Les Cromarty had fired a burst to show that he had been spotted. 'Just north of Paris we saw a number of searchlights round a town. We had all been very quiet up to that point and I think the skipper must have thought we were all dozing off because he dived among the searchlights and Len and I had a ten minute shoot out with them. By the time we began approaching Coningsby we were about half an hour late after strong headwinds had delayed our return. We thought that they would be worrying about us thinking we were lost. Our call sign was 'Starlight' and we used to land on the number system. When we called up we expected to get at least fifteen or sixteen and be 'stacked', but instead we got, 'Number one, pancake'. We just could not believe it and so we called again, but got the same reply. We were in fact the first to land, shortly after an aircraft on 619 Squadron crashed off the end of the runway [sic]. One or two more aircraft landed but I think most of the others landed at other airfields.'[116]

The ground crew told Les Cromarty that his friend Flight Sergeant Harold William Pronger the 33-year old mid-upper gunner who was from Bundaberg on the Burnett River in Queensland and his WOp/AG had bailed out over the North Sea while returning from Nuremberg. 'I wanted to go out on a search right away' he wrote 'but the ASR section told me that because the water temperature was so low no one could survive for more than an hour. I think the worst thing about raids was losing one's friends. After a while you just became hardened to it but eventually you just stopped making close friends with anyone outside your own crew.'[117]

'Nuremberg is the one most of us have tried to black out from our mind' said Len Whitehead. 'When we had clear sky and moonlight we knew we were in for trouble. There is little I can say about the raid itself, we were just sitting ducks'.

Endnotes Chapter 11

98   Quoted in *To Shatter The Sky* by Bruce Barrymore Halpenny (PSL 1984).

99   Quoted in *'Ops' Victory at All Costs* by Andrew R. B. Simpson (Tattered Flag Press 2012).

100   FTR 28/29 July 1944, Stuttgart. Roche's crew all KIA.

101   Quoted in *Sky Battles! Dramatic Air Warfare Actions* by Alfred Price (Arms & Armour Press 1993).

102   Adapted from *The Bombing of Nuremberg* by James Campbell (Futura 1973).

103   London Evening Standard, 12 October 1943.

104 *Reap The Whirlwind; The Untold Story of 6 Group, Canada's Bomber Force of World War II* by Spencer Dunmore and William Carter Ph.D. (McClelland & Stewart Inc. Toronto 1991).

105   LV986 was written off on 10 May at Woodbridge and this after a raid to Ghent, Belgium and was replaced by LW161; also ZL-V.

106   From research by Theo Boiten.

107   *The Nuremberg Raid* by Martin Middlebrook. (Allen Lane 1973).

108   See *The Nuremberg Raid* by Martin Middlebrook. (Allen Lane 1973).

109   Quoted in *Reap The Whirlwind; The Untold Story of 6 Group, Canada's Bomber Force of World War II* by Spencer Dunmore and William Carter Ph.D. (McClelland & Stewart Inc. Toronto 1991).

110   Quoted in *The Nuremberg Raid* by Geoff Taylor.

111   *Boys, Bombs And Brussels Sprouts* by J. Douglas Harvey.(McClelland & Stewart Ltd, Toronto 1981)

112   Quoted in *Reap The Whirlwind; The Untold Story of 6 Group, Canada's Bomber Force of World War II* by Spencer Dunmore and William Carter Ph.D. (McClelland & Stewart Inc. Toronto 1991).

113   Oberleutnant Martin 'Tino' Becker, Staffelkapitän 2./NJG6 was the night's top-scoring pilot with seven Viermot kills, six in 'Zahme Sau' fashion on the outward route and, after a short refuelling stop at Mainz-Finthen, one more under 'Himmelbett' control on the bombers' homeward track. These were his 20th-26 night 'Abschüsse', which earned him the award of the Ritterkreuz. Incidentally, his Bf 110 had not yet been fitted with the 'Schräge Musik'; Becker achieved all these kills using his forward-firing armament. (Dr. Theo Boiten).

114   'N-Nan' flew its 100th trip on 29 June 1944 (followed seven days later by ED588 VN-G 'George' on 50 Squadron at Skellingthorpe). While on 61 Squadron 'Nan' completed 105 bombing operations in 14 months before being SOC on 4 November 1944. Ted Stone (who flew a total of 21 operations on 'N-Nan', the last on 21/22 May) and crew decided that the first daughter born to the wife of a crew member would be christened Nan. Ted Stone's wife was first and in late 1944 their daughter was named Jennifer Nan Stone. In 1971 a grand-daughter was born in Sydney, Australia and was christened Nanette!

115   Quoted in *Nachtjagd: The Night Fighter versus Bomber War over the Third Reich 1939-45* by Theo Boiten (Crowood 1997).

116   Lancaster LL 777 was damaged in the air battle of Giessen on the night of 6/7 December 1944. Flying Officer J.H. Byers the pilot and Sergeant Cartwright survived the crash-landing in Belgium. The others, except one gunner, bailed out.

117   On Friday 2/3 February 1945 on the raid on Karlsruhe, Les Cromarty, who was on his 2nd tour, on 189 Squadron, was the sole survivor when Lancaster PB743 flown by Flight Lieutenant John Outram Davies exploded on its bombing run over Weingarten, southwest of Heidelsheim after dropping the 4,000 pounder and part of the load of incendiaries. It may have been hit by a 'Schräge Musik' equipped night-fighter. Cromarty was blown out of his turret and he landed by parachute.

Chapter 12

At Coningsby the loss of two missing Lancasters on 61 Squadron and the deaths of two crew on *Mickey The Moocher* as well as the crash of the 619 Squadron 'kite' were hard to take. *Mickey The Moocher* had made it back after running into problems returning over the North Sea having encountered stormy conditions off the north Norfolk coast. The Lancaster was struck by lightning on the front turret causing 21-year old Pilot Officer John Augustus Forrest RAAF to lose control and the aircraft plummeted towards the sea. While in a blinded and shocked state the Australian pilot ordered the crew to bail out while he tried to pull the aircraft out of the dive. Forrest managed to regain control at 1,000 feet and he immediately countermanded the order to bail out but it was too late to save the lives of Flight Sergeant Pronger and Sergeant Leonard George Darben, a 20-year old Londoner from Walthamstow. They had already taken to their parachutes and they both drowned. Forrest landed safely at Little Snoring at 0600 hours.[118]

There was no word either from 'Q-Queenie'. From the time of being hit, Denny Freeman's crew had forgotten about fighters and the pandemonium. It was just luck that they were not attacked again. All of the able bodied on board were working feverishly to save lives and get 'Queenie' home, even if it meant that some of them had to perform tasks they were unaccustomed to. The bomb aimer being second navigator among other things, the pilot asked 'Pat' Patfield to do what he could about navigating them home. The chart table was a shambles with torn maps, quite a bit of blood about, no protractors or any other navigation instruments to be seen anywhere. This was not a bit like the navigation exercises he had done during training. And the crew was hoping he would get them home! Fortunately, he had the piece of the chart showing their last position worked out just before being hit. Knowing that they had turned north and roughly taking the ground speed of the aircraft and approximate time since turning, he made a guess at the distance they had travelled north. Then he measured this from the scale on the chart with his finger! He was able to put a cross on the chart, which looked all right, made a guess at the drift from the flight plan and passed the course to the pilot. 'Pat' Patfield was still trying to establish their true position when Jimmy Chapman the wireless operator passed him a scrap of paper with a position written on it. 'Thank Heaven he had got his set to work and obtained a fix' recalled 'Pat' Patfield.'

'I took the scrap of paper and had great difficulty in trying to work out which was longitude and which was latitude. I tried to plot this fix but I didn't succeed. The next thing I knew was finding myself under the remains of the chart table and hearing the pilot calling over the R/T: 'Mayday! Mayday!' This was the distress call for immediate assistance. I realised then that we must be over England but what a short journey! Only a few minutes before we had been over Germany, or so I thought! Anyway, what was I doing here on the floor and I attempted to get up. 'Pat's coming round' I heard Jimmy say as I saw him coming to help me up. Oh my head! It was splitting, or so it seemed! 'You passed out', said Jimmy 'and you have been out a long time. You started dancing about soon after I gave you a second 'fix' and then flopped out on the floor. I couldn't see any sign of injury but then I saw that your oxygen mask had two fairly big holes in it (shrapnel or bullets, we found out later), so I guessed you'd passed out from lack of oxygen, but we daren't come down too low at the time.'

'That was it then. No wonder it had seemed a short journey back! Naturally, when safe to descend where normal breathing was possible, the pilot had done so and I'd eventually come round. What a time to have a sleep!

'The pilot was still calling 'Mayday, Mayday'. Then an answer came: 'Searchlights will home you'.

'On my feet now, with nothing worse than a sickly headache, I saw from the cabin windows searchlights wavering from the vertical position almost to the ground, like a giant arm beckoning. Following these we soon saw a cone of three searchlights poised stationary. These marked the 'drome. Shortly, over the R/T the controller called us. 'This is Horsham St. Faith. Another plane is landing. Do a circuit and land'. We almost cried with relief! To me this call made me feel much better. We were over or at least very nearly over, Norwich, my hometown. Horsham St. Faith was in the suburbs. I really felt that I was home.

'Again the controller's voice but not with the message we had hoped for.

'Q-Queenie', runway blocked - proceed to Foulsham aerodrome'.

'Then they gave us a course to fly. We came to the conclusion that the other aircraft landing at Horsham was possibly a crippled bomber from the same raid. Foulsham was only a few minutes' flying time away and we seemed to be flying fairly well so the pilot acknowledged and off we flew. Very shortly we could see another cone of three searchlights and so, as we approached, we called up Foulsham. Answering us, they told us it was clear to land.

'Undercarriage going down' said the pilot. 'Blast, the indicator isn't working!' (This was the green light on his panel, which lit up when the wheels were locked down). The warning horn was sounding, which should have stopped if the wheels were properly locked in the 'down' position.) He looked out of his side window at the port wheel. It seemed down OK. 'How about the starboard, Pat?' he called.

'Well, it was down but it didn't seem to be fully down and I told the pilot so. He swung the aircraft about, as much as he dared in an attempt to make it lock down but it wouldn't.

'Get ready for crash landing. I'm going down,' said the pilot. Jimmy went to the rest bed to hang onto Tommy while I sat down with Frank with my arm around him, behind the pilot's seat. 'Here we go, hold tight,' yelled the pilot. A sickening lurch as we hit the runway, more bumps, but we seemed to be doing OK. The pilot was holding the plane over onto the port wheel, which was apparently locked down. The starboard wheel was flapping about uselessly. As we lost flying speed, the starboard wing began to drop and then the wingtip dug into the ground. This swung us completely round as we grated to a stop. Our fear now was fire!

'Getting up we gathered our wits and made our way down the fuselage to the exit door. The gunners had just opened it when voices outside shouted, 'OK, we'll get you out' and illuminated by the headlights of a jeep and an ambulance, we saw figures clambering in to help us. Fortunately no fire occurred. Poor old 'Queenie' had crumpled quite a bit but didn't catch fire thank goodness.

'Little was said as the injured were taken in the ambulance to sick quarters and we who were not injured were taken in a jeep to the crew room, where a number of officers including the CO flocked round us with cigarettes and soon, mugs of hot tea. 'Put something in it' said the CO. 'I reckon they need it.' And out of the blue came a bottle of whisky and they put a very generous amount in our tea! With apologies they told us they'd have to spend a little time interrogating us about the raid before we could go to bed. This over, we were taken to a Nissen hut where beds had been prepared. Sleep? What an effort. I kept being sick in a pail, which I had asked to be left near the bed. My head was going round and round and I felt as if would burst. Eventually I slept. When we got up at about midday on reporting to the CO, we were told we'd be flown back to Coningsby. We went to the sick quarters to see about the injured but we were not allowed to see them. The MO (Medical Officer) told us that Jimmy had quite a lot of small pieces of shrapnel in his back and just under the scalp. Frank's elbow was badly smashed and he had shrapnel in his side. Tommy's hand was also badly smashed and (I believe) frost-bitten, caused by the icy draught blowing on him from the escape hatch opening. I never saw either of them again.

'We then went to have a look at 'Queenie'. There she was, out there in the middle of the aerodrome, over onto a crumpled wing, her two starboard propellers bent over the engine nacelles. We clambered into her and looked around. What a mess and holes were everywhere. How it was that the engines kept functioning, we'll never know. Those three German fighters had riddled her but she had brought us home though she was now a 'write-off'.'

Later that day the crew of 'Q-Queenie' were flown back to Coningsby and they were interrogated. All four uninjured members of the crew were given a fortnight's leave commencing the next morning. Denny Freeman was awarded the DFC for bringing the crippled Lanc home safely; while Jimmy Chapman was awarded the Conspicuous Gallantry Medal for getting his wireless-set working again, obtaining fixes, plotting them and helping to navigate after 'Pat' Patfield had passed out. The crew of 'Q-Queenie' never flew as a crew again. Frank Devonshire was invalided out of the service and 'Tommy' Thomas never flew again either. Flight Sergeant Bill Smith regrettably never had the opportunity to take up his new 'career' as a 'gigolo' for he was killed in action on the night of 7/8 July during the operation to Ste-Leu-d'Esserent when the Lancaster he was flying in was hit by flak and exploded in mid air killing the entire crew. He is buried at Marissel French National Cemetery. Flying Officer Denny Freeman and four of his crew were killed in action on 24 September when his Lancaster was hit by flak and crashed into the sea during the operation to attack strong points at Calais. After recovering from his wounds Jimmy Chapman had returned to operations on 61 Squadron where he flew ops alongside 35-year old Flight Sergeant Arthur Sherriff, the crew's air gunner who had been awarded the DFM for his actions on the same raid. Both men were killed on 1 February 1945 when their Lancaster, which was flown by Squadron Leader Hugh Horsley, lost all four engines on take-off and crashed killing everyone except the rear gunner. 'Pat' Patfield did another thirty raids after Nuremberg. Although they were 'not without incident' none would be quite as bad as 30/31 March, which became known as 'the biggest chop night' of the war for Bomber Command.[119]

For Sergeant David Davidson, flight engineer on Halifax 'A-Able' on 78 Squadron, the target came into sight at 0018. 'Very bright over the target,' Davidson recalled. 'I could make out the shapes of some streets with the fires and explosions. Here and there a few Lancs and Halifaxes were in sight. Sergeant J. Liston RCAF the bomb aimer announced 'Bombs away' at 0123 and we started turning off to starboard. Height: 20,500 feet. Air temperature; -32° Centigrade. I saw a Halifax going down in a vertical dive towards the target at 0124 with three Ju 88s on its tail. Smoke or haze over parts of target area. The Halifax was diving head-first for this. We turned to starboard and completely lost sight of the diving Halifax and Ju 88 fighters. We were on course for the French coast and holding to 20,000 feet at 0126. A Lancaster, going in the opposite direction, went over the top of us; very close. Too close! A bit of nattering on intercom. We were late on target but that Lanc was even later, heading for the target at this time of morning, 0130. Christ! There was the target coming up again, in front. Quick call to the navigator to check the 'off target' course. The skipper went to set the checked course on the gyro compass and found that the gyro had toppled on our first turn away from the target.

At last the contrails had stopped. It seemed much darker now, away from the target. The wireless operator, Sergeant A. Hale, started passing winds received from Group. They gave 90 mph but the navigator did not agree. He made the wind nearer 120 mph. Things were fairly quiet now and we seemed all alone over Germany. Red TIs were seen on the ground as we passed well to the south of Aachen at 0300. On and on to the coast. 'Would we ever get there? There was a very bright star dead ahead. It could be Venus. 0430: the French coast was ahead, all black and gold. We were getting lower and lower but there was nothing to worry about. The navigator said that our ground speed against the head winds was 64 mph. We could taxi faster. Coffee and biscuits would never taste so good before or since with the English Channel below. We began to relax now. It had been so quiet for the last hour.'

The crew's relaxation was premature for at this point the Halifax suddenly began to shudder and shake. Checking his panel, coffee forgotten, the flight engineer pin-pointed the trouble: the port inner engine was losing oil pressure and the engine rpm were surging. At 0450 he stopped the motor and feathered the airscrew. Flight Sergeant Christiansen immediately asked the navigator for a course to the nearest airfield. Luckily, it turned out to be Ford, an emergency field on the south coast. Calling Ford as 'Nosmo A-Able' Christiansen was cleared to make a straight-in approach as by this time the Halifax was down to about 500 feet above the sea. Joining the Ford circuit pattern at 0522, Christiansen wasted no time getting down and landed eight minutes later at 0530. Ford was crowded with returning Lancasters and Halifaxes which had made emergency landings there. The crew reported to flying control for de-briefing and Christiansen tried to telephone Breighton but the connection was poor so he made arrangements for news of his emergency landing to be passed on to 78 Squadron.

'All we wanted was food and sleep,' Davidson concluded. 'Sleep, mostly. I felt as if I had been gutted. There was nothing inside me. Dirty and sweaty we went over to the mess. Lord, I thought all Bomber Command was here. And the cigarette smoke! An LAC took us to our billet, moaning all the way about making hundreds of beds and lighting fires. 'What a bloody air force,' he said. We didn't care: 'Where are the beds?' we asked.'

Sergeant Ted Shaw RCAF on 12 Squadron returned to Wickenby with two blackened eyes and cannon shell fragments lodged in his left eye from the shell which had hit his rear turret on the run in to the target. Fortunately Ted Shaw's turret had been facing dead astern when the hydraulic system was shot up so he was able to open the turret doors and grope his way up the fuselage to get his parachute pack from its stowage. He was unable to find it: a shell from the fighter had blown it from its position. 'At this time the mid-upper gunner got out of his turret and came over to see what had happened to me. He shouted in my ear that the aircraft was now under control and that he would find my 'chute and let me know when it became necessary to bail out. The skipper in the meantime had feathered the prop and we dropped our bomb load at a low level.'

In spite of being 170 miles from the target and having neither a rear gunner nor rear turret in operation Alf Moore had decided to continue to the target. Fifteen miles from the target, an attack was made by a Ju 88 from below. The Lancaster sustained further extensive damage including bomb bays badly damaged and incendiaries set on fire, port wing damaged, starboard wing tip shot off, oxygen system hit, elevators and rudder damage and intercom unserviceable. Flight Sergeant Peters the mid-upper gunner opened fire on the fighter, but while he was firing he observed another Ju 88 closing to point blank range astern. He transferred his fire to the second enemy aircraft and fired all his remaining ammunition at very short range. The Ju 88 fell away and was seen to explode a few seconds later. The Lancaster was now crippled, difficult to control, defenceless against possible attacks from astern and much of its incendiary load was on fire in the bomb bay. In spite of this, Moore continued his bombing run and dropped his bombs in the target area. Shortly after leaving the target area the damaged oxygen supply became exhausted and he had to descend to 15,000 feet and then came home at just 3,500 feet. With Sergeant Ferguson, the flight engineer assisting to maintain control of his crippled and defenceless aircraft, he succeeded in bringing it back to England and landed successfully at West Malling in Kent after being airborne for seven and a quarter hours. Peters was awarded the DFM for his actions. Alf Moore received the DFC and completed his tour in June, being awarded a bar to this DFC.

At the de-briefing at Wickenby, Flight Sergeant Brian Soper enjoyed a cigarette and a tot of rum. 'It was like living again - but for how long? The weather was clear and bright all the way, with just a faint haze of cloud over the target which was brightly lit when we made our bombing run. We eventually had found the target and bombed on red/yellow TI markers. We have never seen so many exploding and burning aircraft or been close enough to see parachutes going down from crippled Lancs. I shall never forget the searchlight cones on the way back and particularly a Mossie which was caught by the master searchlight and then coned, very near us. While those unlucky blokes were getting the attention we managed to clear the area, a searchlight just crossing us a few times and with a constant barrage of flak.

'On the route home, at around Saarbrücken, we lost the port inner engine. Losing oil and overheating we had to shut off and feather the engine. I later had to cross feed the petrol to maintain a balance of fuel and weight. This also meant being extra alert for fighter attacks. We subsequently arrived back at Wickenby and made a successful landing on three engines.'

Another Australian from the same squadron: 'The section of the route from Aachen to the target was reminiscent of a battlefield of burning aircraft.., very noticeable in the last half-dozen trips is the fact that so many aircraft were seen going down in flames from operational height. I would suggest that the enemy is using a new type of ammunition.'

Sergeant W. J. Blackburn and his navigator who had played out their macabre game at briefing, predicting who would 'get the chop' that night, were astonishingly accurate. Having decided that two relatively senior crews would likely 'buy it' that night' they were sadly proved right.[120] Lancaster ND562 skippered by 32-year old Flight Lieutenant Alastair John Cook of Edinburgh and ND441 captained by 22-year old Flight Lieutenant Douglas Mintie Carey DFC of Brandon, Manitoba were shot down by night-fighters. ND562 was shot down southwest of Bonn near FF 'Ida' by a Ju 88G-6 of 4./NJG3 flown by 23-year old Hauptmann Gerhard Raht with his Funker Feldwebel Anton Heinemann and bordmechaniker Unteroffizier Werner Hesse. It was Raht's thirtieth victory. Flight Lieutenant Cook, his crew and Pilot and 23-year-old Pilot Officer Christopher Humphrey Cotton-Minchin flying as the 'second dickey' on his first operation and he also died. Cook, who was married to Winifrede Isobel Helene Cook, had flown twenty operations on 12 Squadron before his death. Flight Sergeant Richard Frederick Bayley the 25-year old rear gunner from Beckenham, Kent was on his seventh operation; the 26-year old Canadian navigator, Warrant Officer Maurice Rene Nicolas Mouchet who came from St. Boniface, Manitoba, was on only his first operation; Pilot Officer Bernard Salt of Littleover, Derby the 23-year old wireless operator was on his sixth operation. So too 20-year old Pilot Officer Jack Ernest McInnes, the Canadian mid-upper gunner, who came from Toronto and Pilot Officer Robert Timperley of Whalley, Blackburn in Lancashire, the 26-year old bomb aimer, husband of Edith Edna Haynes Timperley. Sergeant Kenneth Launcelot Summerscale the flight engineer, who was from Pontefract, Yorkshire was on his 11th operation.

There were no survivors either on ND441. Carey and his crew were buried on 3 April at Dotzlar, since when their remains have been taken to Hannover War Cemetery. Those who died were: Flight Sergeant William McAlister Aikman the 22-year-old wireless operator, was from Kellhead, Glasgow; Flying Officer Carl William Kruger the 27-year old bomb aimer and husband of Violet Kruger and father of Robert Charles Kruger, of Winnipeg, Manitoba; the flight engineer, Sergeant Percival Harold Lambert was from Blandford in Dorset; Pilot Officer Franklin Walter Peppiatt the Canadian mid-upper gunner hailed from Toronto; Pilot Officer Jack Edgar Prior the 21-year-old navigator was from Guildford, Surrey; Sergeant William Harold Frederick Smedmore the rear gunner came from Flamstead End, Hertfordshire. This crew were on their third operation, some of whom were on their second tour.

Pilot Officer Bill Taggart's crew on 156 Squadron boarded 'F-Fox' at 2145 according to Flying Officer Bill Barclay and took off at 2228. They climbed over Upwood and Barclay set course at 2239. En route he meticulously marked down the times in his log: '2314.6: Reached 'A', first turning point, after dog-legging to lose three minutes on this leg. Crossed enemy coast 2327.8. The second leg took us over Ghent and to the south-west of Brussels on which we fixed position by radar (H2S). 2348.1: Arrived 'B', set course for 'C'. This leg took us between Bonn and Koblenz. At 0003.5 passed red navigation flare dropped just south of Aachen. '0007: Sighted green target-indicators of dummy raid being made on Köln. '0048.3: Arrived 'C', set course for target.'

'As we neared the enemy coast on the interminable trip out' wrote Ron Smith on

156 Squadron,[121] 'I was aghast at the near daylight visibility provided by a brilliant moon. Never before had I experienced such stark conditions: I could just look around and see for miles in all directions and the patches of cloud below made us like flies, crawling across a pure white tablecloth. If that cloud had been consistent, I could have picked out any enemy fighter with ease - an advantage which did not impress me. Gone was the blessed darkness, the cloak that offered such welcome anonymity.

'The intercom remained silent after the skipper's reminder to keep our eyes open, except for some apt remarks from Dougie, giving his opinion of the met men, whose forecast, as he put it, 'Was all to cock'. Perched up there, on top of the fuselage, with such a view all around him, he must have felt more vulnerable than any of us.

'It was some comfort to observe two other Lancasters as we crossed the coast and odd to see the puffs of smoke from the exploding shells as flak came up. The flash they produced, anaemic in the moonlight, was not at all as seen against the usual pitch blackness.

'It was then the tragedy unfolded, so early, as we made for the only turning point before the long leg to our target. All too often I had been a horrified witness in the past and yet one did not become immune to seeing aircraft go down in flames. This one was different. Initially the Lancaster furthest away from us, but plainly outlined exploded in a welter of flames. Then the one nearer to us was also enveloped, though still flying straight and level, flames reaching back, three tiny figures only, clearly discernible, jumping out to fall away.

'The enemy fighter, now breaking away below, turned towards us, looking for another easy kill. I stood up, leaning as far forward as I could to peer below, while our aircraft weaved from side to side. Through my now frantic mind, the torment ran that there might be something further ahead, out of my line of sight.

'Then Dougie's voice, calling instructions for evasive action, superbly timed, his Brownings firing at the same time as a Ju 88 broke away to my left below, the Lancaster going down with such velocity that I was pressed on top of the gun mountings and a sharp blow on the forehead leaving me dizzy with pain.

'I regained my seat sick with apprehension, swallowing the vomit in my throat, turning the turret hurriedly towards a flicker of flame close by, as another aircraft, mortally hit, cascaded down into the misty depths.

'Geoff's anxious voice gave our new course as we banked to starboard and I counted several more victims lighting up the already flood-lit scene around us. The Germans were having a field day; they could not miss and the awful, pitiful patches of still-burning wreckage marked the landscape below, behind and all around.

'At last a respite as we penetrated deeper into enemy territory, but a respite only in the immediate vicinity, for the night still distantly pinpointed where our comrades went down. I had tried to count but lost the figure as the dreadful total mounted. Although we were as yet unaware of the final tragic consequences of that night, it seemed obvious that, back at home, so far away and, at that moment, beyond reach, someone in authority had 'dropped a clanger'. This was no ordinary raid, if any could be described as such.

'The long straight leg to the target at last came to an end and we prepared for the final run-up to the Nazi show place. For the first time, our navigator's experience and intense training had resulted in our selection as prime marker illuminators.'[122]

Flight Sergeant Reginald Walter Parissien, wireless operator-air gunner on

Lancaster 'C-Charlie' on 156 Squadron, flown by Warrant Officer John Higgs, was anticipating the forecast eight-to-nine-tenths cloud as the Path Finder Lancaster climbed away from Upwood, carrying incendiaries and high-explosive bombs as well as support and marker flares to mark the target for the bomber stream. Parissien, from Bromley in Kent had been a clerk but when war came he could not wait to join up. After wireless operator training at Yatesbury he arrived at HCU at Faldingworth where he crewed up. Posted to 626 Squadron at Wickenby the crew began operating on the night of 3/4 December 1943 and completed ten operations in total, including four trips to Berlin, before volunteering for Path Finders and finally joining 156 Squadron. 'I can honestly say I was never frightened' he recalled. 'Indeed I would go further and say that I even used to look forward to operations. It was always better than kicking around doing nothing. Whenever I went off on leave, I couldn't wait to get back. But of course there were those who were scared and some who couldn't cope. One morning, all of the aircrew were asked to assemble. One of the lads had been accused of lacking in moral fibre. In front of everyone the CO tore the sergeant's stripes off his arm and ripped off his aircrew brevet. The man was humiliated and degraded before us. It was disgraceful to watch. No man deserved that. He, like the rest of us, was a volunteer for goodness sake, but the CO clearly wanted to make an example of him. It was like watching an execution.[123]

'The usual flak was encountered en route, but what was more disturbing was the break-up of cloud revealing a bright moon. This naturally resulted in heavy flak and fighter activity throughout the length of the route over German territory towards the target. It became clear that the whole of the main force were being subjected to intense fighter attack, assisted, of course, by ground-directed searchlights. I saw two aircraft could not identify going down in flames so I was more than usually alert as Warrant Officer Higgs headed the Lancaster in towards Nuremberg. The target area was sustaining a heavy attack when we reached it. Having unloaded we proceeded homeward. At times the air was full of flak, searchlights and silhouetted aircraft. Without doubt and to the best of my knowledge, it was the moon that proved our greatest enemy.'

At the target Flying Officer Bill Barclay on 'F-Fox' continued to accurately log the details like an experienced auditor transcribing a set of accounts: 'Bombs were dropped at 0104.4 (our time on target was 0105 compared with normal zero hour of 0110). Bombing on green markers and H_2S checking. Flak over target was light.' Not surprisingly perhaps after the war Barclay would choose to become an accountant and then an air traffic control officer! Apart from sighting flak to starboard twenty miles south of Stuttgart, the trip home was quiet uneventful, including the way out to the coast which Barclay logged as having been crossed at 0357.2. Arriving over Upwood at 0505 only to find it fogged in, the crew were diverted to Marham where they finally landed at 0533. '...Nothing we saw on the trip suggested bad losses but this may have been due to our early timing. We found that flak and fighter activity livened up during the course of a raid and being in the forefront we probably missed most of the fun, if that's what you could call it.'

Flight Sergeant J. F. Maxwell RCAF was the flight engineer on Pilot Officer W. T. Gee's 97 Path Finder Squadron crew at Bourn, flying as primary target markers, taking with them four TIs, a 4,000lb 'Cookie', 846 x4lb incendiaries and 54 x 4lb 'X' incendiaries in the bomb bay of ND346 'N-Nan'. 'In perspective the whole operation was a disaster' says Maxwell. Our particular aircraft, first out on the raid with the Path Finder Force, was engaged by enemy aircraft upon reaching the French coast. At this time I took our aircraft ten miles port of track for some illogical reason and held this position until the target area. The gunners reported numerous combats to starboard all along the route, which lead us to believe the route was known beforehand by the Luftwaffe. Another strange thing about this raid was that, upon engagement by enemy aircraft, our guns would not fire. This was reported by other aircraft that returned from the trip, leading us to believe that a combination of climatic conditions and humidity affected the .303 calibre guns of the Lancaster aircraft participating. This was the first and last time this occurred in the fifty-six trips that I carried out with the Path Finders.'

Maxwell reported no fighter engagements over the target where his Lancaster bombed from 17,000 feet in centre of four groups of red TIs seen in a sudden break in the cloud after the aircraft orbited to run up a second time. Several fires were seen under TIs. 'Usually, there was certain grandeur about the scene with the markers, the flak, the searchlights and the night fighters, even though there was always the death and destruction - it was a spectacle. But on the Nuremberg 'do' it was eerie. It was as though we had no right to be there. I suppose we hadn't really.' Continuing ten miles to port of track on the way home, he observed many more combats on the track out to the coast. Maxwell logged 7.10 hours for the flight. 'Our squadron put out fourteen aircraft of which our losses were two missing and one damaged. We were taken off operations until 11 April 1944 to allow crews to be posted from the OTU and Lancaster aircraft to be delivered to the squadron from the manufacturer.'

Having taken his crew to Nuremberg and back on his 66th bomber operation after 7.20 hours at the controls of 'S-Sugar', 'Pat' Daniels found that on the way back to the French coast the German fighters were largely noticeable by their absence. The 35 Squadron CO was the first to land at Graveley where he found Air Vice-Marshal D. C. T. Bennett who usually drove over from his headquarters in Huntingdon, waiting for him in the de-briefing room. Daniels said bitterly, 'Bloody hell! Why did we have to go that way?'

'I told him this would be the biggest chop ever,' Daniels said. Bennett replied, 'Pat, you always exaggerate everything.'

As Daniels dryly put it: 'I believe I was later proved to be correct.'

'On hearing the details, Bennett was inclined to be sceptical; not wanting to believe that the operation could have been such a disaster but he knew that Daniels was not prone to exaggeration. To appease Daniels, Bennett took him over to the big wall map and while he drank his tea from a dirty cup - 'it still tasted very good after seven and a half hours flying' - he talked of the future targets in the south of Germany, which had so far been untouched.

'He pointed out to me, in confidence', recalls Daniels, 'the targets that we would have to attack there and explained that they were lightly defended. 'There were some big ones, which would have to be done soon', he said. Munich was one of them and it was finally done successfully. However, I thought the difficulty after this night's show would be to get there, especially in bright moonlight. We had climbed that night through cloud over the sea and when we got above it there was bright moonlight. Although there was thick cloud over the target, it was the brightest moonlight I could remember flying in. I again stressed to Bennett that on this raid there was a large number of sightings of aircraft blowing up. Most of them were brought down by fighters. There was also a large number of scare-shells sent up to simulate an aircraft exploding and they were very good imitations. But I soon found out that in many cases they were, in fact, bombers blowing up. The fighter attacks on the bombers usually started a small fire in the fuselage or wing, which was spread by the slipstream and wind to the fuel tanks and bombs. Then everything went up. Often, though, it was difficult to be sure whether it was a bomber exploding or a 'scare-shell.'

Squadron Leader Arthur Doubleday was first back at Waddington and Sir Ralph Cochrane called him up to the control tower.

'How did it go?'

'Jerry got a century before lunch today.' He didn't quite - he got 95.'

In April, Wing Commander Doubleday took command of 61 Squadron, which he led with equal distinction. Just before taking up the appointment he was sent to London to attend a course. While there he arranged to meet his pregnant wife at the Regent Palace Hotel near Piccadilly Circus where, at eight o'clock one morning, a V-1 blew a hole in the side of the hotel and the blast knocked the Doubleday's down a flight of stairs. The blast killed the twins that Phyllis was carrying.[125]

'Ern' Mustard, who landed his veteran Lancaster at Waddington after 'a reasonable trip at above average height' with the familiar call-sign on the intercom: 'Hello 'Slangword'; hello 'Slangword', this is 'Fuller C-Charlie', 'Fuller C-Charlie', permission to land' recalled that, at the de-briefing, Squadron Leader Brill already 'had the score' on the night's operations. When other pilots were estimating losses at thirty to fifty aircraft, Brill was insistent they were nearer a hundred. 'There clearly was a lot of activity and it seemed unbelievable that each fire in the sky was another of our kites going down. After logging some air-to-air combats and flamers going down, the navigator finally gave it up. Sergeant W. H. Goodwin told the gunners: 'Shut up. I'm too busy to log all that stuff.'

'Memories of the trip centre round the leg from approximately fifteen miles north-east of Charleroi for about 160 miles and was considered by all to be too far to fly in a straight line over enemy territory. Was it ever! There was also a feeling that so-called navigation aids in the form of TIs dropped along the track were liable to 'bring the flies'. This device was used south of Aachen.'

Mustard went to bed. 'It was a shock to wake up about lunch-time next day and hear the final scores for Nuremberg.'

Despite a reduced airspeed due to the loss of the port outer motor during the bombing run, Bill Brill had an uneventful but unpleasant trip home, lagging behind the bomber stream. 'It was most nerve-wracking. The German fighters relished stragglers and they could take-full advantage of ground radar to effect interceptions. However, it seemed that the fighter force had spent itself during the earlier holocaust and we were unmolested. Our main problem was to keep on track and stay clear of the defended areas. Still, being last had its advantages because the earlier aircraft who were a little off course pin-pointed the defended areas. We finally landed back at base over an hour after the main group (after a flying time to Nuremberg and back of 8.35 hours), probably more than normally exhausted. One other aircraft on our squadron landed long after the remainder and strangely enough it carried my younger brother as navigator. The squadron commander was quite convinced that he had lost both Brills that night.'

An inspection of Squadron Leader Brill's Lancaster revealed that the cause of the port outer motor failure was the fouling of fuel lines and other controls to the engine. These lay just under the leading edge of the mainplane and twenty or thirty rounds of belted British .303 ammunition were found lodged in the wing leading edge between the two port motors. 'Quite obviously,' said Brill, 'the explosion immediately in front of us as we ran into the target was no less than one of our aircraft disintegrating. How we missed being struck by heavier and larger pieces of it is little short of a miracle. However Bob Curtis, the wireless operator who was standing in the astrodome position,said later that a Merlin engine missed us by inches.

'So much for a raid which almost decimated Bomber Command and yet achieved so little. In retrospect I can say that this trip was the most frightening and perhaps the most frustrating of all those in which I was directly involved. We lost almost a hundred aircraft with the loss of six or seven hundred highly trained young men and as far as I could gather we scattered bombs over half of Germany. The loss of men represented up to a thousand man-years of highly specialized and most expensive training.'

Like everyone else Pilot Officer Frank Collis pilot of 'V-Victor' on 207 Squadron was surprised to learn of the high losses the following day. He had re-crossed the French coast near Dieppe at 15,000 feet by 0400 and continued descending to 10,000 feet over the English Channel. Navigation lights were switched on again as he crossed the English coast to the west of Beachy Head. After that it was Reading and Peterborough and then finally, at 0517, Collis landed at Spilsby at 0525 after 7.25 hours in the air. He wondered if there might have been a leak in security.

Wyton had dispatched fourteen Lancasters on 83 Path Finder Squadron each carrying four flares to drop visually to build up those dropped earlier by other Path Finders and a 8,000lb bomb for good measure. All aircraft returned safely. Warrant Officer Alan Strickland on Flight Lieutenant Roy Hellier's crew on Lancaster 'R-Roger' recalled that it was a tiring trip home with head-winds slowing their Path Finder Lancaster which still had to run the gauntlet of enemy fighters near the French coast on the way out. On reaching England we found a number of bases closed because of fog,' he recalled. 'As we were now short of fuel we landed at Downham Market instead of Wyton.'

Flight Sergeant Frank Wildman, the flight-engineer wrote: 'We reached the target area without being attacked by night-fighters; but the crew saw many bombers going down in flames behind them. The navigator counted over fifty of them before Flight Lieutenant Hellier told him to stop logging them and concentrate on his navigation instead. 'We were one of the first aircraft over Nuremberg and the target was not particularly 'hot' at that stage, as far as we were concerned. In fact, we thought it rather quiet on the bomb-run after having done eleven sorties to Berlin during the previous month. But we felt that something was really happening behind us. This made us a bit apprehensive about the return trip, yet it turned out to be uneventful.

'As we neared Wyton we were diverted because of fog to Downham Market, where an estimated seven squadrons landed. There were all sorts of rumours flying about, but no official explanation was ever given to us for the high losses. We were one of the first aircraft to land so there was not a hint at our de-briefing of the large numbers of bombers that had not returned. Crews who landed there could not be sure how their squadrons had fared because of the number of diversions. The shock came in the morning when the official figures were announced.'

Alan Strickland had considered this night to have been a fighter night and had estimated losses to be between thirty and forty aircraft. 'I was indeed surprised to discover that our losses were about ninety-seven.'

'The journey home' recalls Warrant Officer Ken Lane the skipper of ND333 'F-Freddie' on 83 Squadron 'was a repetition of the outward flight, without incident of note, but the real problem was to come when we arrived over our base at Wyton. Weather conditions around this part were atrocious with a snow storm giving nil visibility. All other aircraft had been diverted, but because of a radio fault we were not informed and now we were in the unenviable position of having to land without assistance from the ground. Several attempts to approach were made, but each time the runway was lost and, after nearly hitting the water tower, I decided to use Standard Beam Approach procedure which was the popular aid to a blind landing. Picking up the beam, I made my circuit and approach, gradually losing height at the appropriate rate of descent. When only a few seconds from touch-down, I suddenly saw the runway contact lights and, as the colour was red, I realised that I was too far along the runway for a landing. I commenced to carry out my overshoot drill, but when I pushed on the throttles nothing happened; the linkage was probably frozen. As I strained harder, so my seat catch could not stand the backward pressure and, jumping from its locked position, the seat dropped to its lowest point, leaving my head about a foot below vision level. Airspeed literally dropped off the clock and although well below stalling speed, the amazing Lanc remained airborne. The more I think about this, the more fantastic it appears when one considers a heavy four-engined bomber still flying at little over 65 knots. As I fought to control the aircraft, I also managed to raise my seat to a higher level and the return of vision brought full realisation of the extent of the danger.'

'Dick' Raymond, his 19-year old flight engineer, adds: 'As far as our crew was concerned it was just another trip. We didn't see anything untoward, it was an uneventful night, but when we got back aircraft were being diverted. We didn't have the best possible wireless operator and he didn't receive the diversion signal from base. We were trying to get in at Wyton in a snowstorm and the skipper called 'Overshoot'. I bunged the throttles through the gate and the skipper pushed the stick forward to build up speed and his seat collapsed. He found he was looking at nothing but his flying instruments. How the heck we got out of it I don't know. He just had to go round by feel.

'Ken always claimed we overshot at a speed so low for the Lanc it should have caused it to stall. Then we got a rollicking for landing at base when we shouldn't have done. We considered ourselves extremely lucky to be back on the ground. We were one of the few crews debriefed at Wyton. No aircraft were lost from our squadron, but so many landed away from base we didn't know who was missing and who wasn't. It wasn't until the next morning we heard about the losses. We couldn't understand how the heck we didn't run into any trouble ourselves.

'The only trouble we had was on landing. The weather was terrible, snow everywhere. On our first approach Ken decided to overshoot and as I pushed the throttle forward and Ken pulled on the control column, his seat collapsed and he found himself level under the blind-flying panel. How he got out of that no one knows. Ken swears we were below stalling speed.'[126]

'We skimmed across fields and hedgerows' continues Lane, 'which even at this low altitude were not very distinct, but the grim certainty was that we would hit something solid before much longer. Suddenly the throttle levers gave and the engines roared into full life, bringing at least some hope of survival. Even so, height was needed to recover from a near-stall and we didn't have this luxury; but the wonderful Lanc responded to every touch and gradually reached a safe speed, making it possible for us to climb to comparative safety.

'Fuel was running low, but after completing another circuit and approach, a landing was achieved. Conditions on the ground were certainly grim and the Aerodrome Control Pilot in his caravan claimed later that he had not seen an aircraft actually land, although he had heard some frightening noises.

'There was no sign of life on the station and the duty officer had to be roused to de-brief us, much to his disgust. For us it was a case of 'all's well that ends well' but on the radio next morning we heard the sombre news that 95 aircraft were missing. Others would probably have run out of fuel and crash-landed, but I never heard the final toll. What a night this had been, with very few aircraft actually reaching the target; but the question as to whether this was Bomber Command's costliest mission remains unanswered. For me this was the night when the Lancaster bomber performed the impossible.'

On the wireless next morning Ken Lane heard the sombre news that ninety-five aircraft were missing but he knew that others would probably have run out of fuel and crash-landed. He never heard the final toll.[127]

On 22/23 May Ken Lane and his crew on Lancaster III ND963 OL-H were shot down on the operation on Brunswick. He and 'Dick' Raymond and two others on the crew were taken prisoner. The navigator and both gunners were killed. 'So many aircraft were being hit and blowing up or crashing on the ground. The last thing I thought was that I would be a prisoner of war.'

Endnotes Chapter 12

118 Flight Lieutenant John Forrest RAAF was KIA on 24/25 June 1944 on the operation on Prouville.

119 See *Legend of the Lancasters* by Martin W. Bowman (Pen & Sword 2009).

120 Quoted in *The Nuremberg Raid* by Martin Middlebrook. (Allen Lane 1973).

121 *Rear Gunner Pathfinders* by Ron Smith DFM (Goodall 1987).

122 Pilot Officer Taggart carried out his duties of Master Bomber on 31 May and 14 June and received an immediate DFC on 29 June. Flight Lieutenant Taggart was Master Bomber again on 4 July.

123 Quoted in *The Pathfinder Companion: War Diaries and Experiences of The RAF Pathfinder Force - 1942-1945* by Sean Feast (Grub Street 2012).

124 Daniels received a DSO - awarded as per *London Gazette* dated 29 September 1944 - on completion of a third tour of operational duty.

125 See *Chased By the Sun.*

126 Quoted in *'Ops' Victory at All Costs* by Andrew R. B. Simpson (Tattered Flag Press 2012).

127 Quoted in *The Lancaster at War* by Mike Garbett and Brian Goulding (Ian Allan Ltd, 1971 & 1973).

Chapter 13

Lack of sleep was beginning to tell on the crew of 'D-Dog' one of the primary blind-marker Lancasters on 156 Squadron. In the rear turret, 'Tubby' Holley could hardly keep his eyes open. On the flight south of the Ruhr the crew observed several combats and Holley reported four or five bombers going down in almost as many minutes. Flight Lieutenant 'Robbie' Bagg, who was on his second tour of operations, then picked up on 'Fishpond' his first blip about one mile to port of them. Holley peered into the darkness but could see nothing. A moment later Bagg reported that there was another fighter two miles to starboard but again Holley failed to see them. The blips then vanished from the screen and the gunners were informed that the fighters had gone. It was just as well because Holley's guns were not working. The weary tail gunner was fervently hoping that they would soon reach Nuremberg but then Bagg announced on intercom that he had picked up more fighters on his screen. Again Holley was unable to get a visual on them and they did not attack the Lancaster. Finally, 'D-Dog's navigator Flying Officer Jones said on intercom that he was setting the course for the run in to the target. 'Blackie' Blackadder the bomb aimer lifted the bombing tit from its socket as he watched the outskirts of Nuremberg appear on the screen of his H_2S scanner. Recalling the bomb run, Holley said. 'The flak was moderate but even the thought of a fighter on our tail was not worrying me all that much, as I was so tired. Somehow or other, I just about managed to keep the turret swinging, looking out now and then at the searchlights. 'Blackie' released our target indicators, the 'cookie' and other bombs with the aid of H_2S. And then came the worst part as we flew straight and level over the target with our camera whirring. Now and then the Lancaster pitched and rocked from the concussion of bursting anti-aircraft shells. Next minute we were turning on to our course for the homeward journey. Before long and in spite of all my efforts to stay awake, I felt my eyes closing. I don't suppose they were shut for more than a few seconds, for as my head dropped forward on to my chest I woke up and stared out of the turret, searching for fighters. And so it went on. As I came out of a doze, I would stare into the darkness and then my head would go down and I'd drop off.'

Holley had vaguely heard the navigator's call that they had crossed the French coast before dropping off to sleep and he had woken again after they had crossed the English coast. Gradually, Squadron Leader Walter Brooks brought the Lancaster down through thick cloud on to the course given him by his navigator for their base at Upwood. Flying Officer Jones then read off a new set of fixes from the 'Gee' box and announced that they were over the base. The bomber was now down to 900 feet but still the cloud was solid. Brooks sliced off more height, until his altimeter showed that they were at 300 feet and told his crew that he would take the Lancaster a little lower to try to get under the cloud base. He could see nothing outside but thick, smothering vapour. Jones, after taking another fix, warned that they were getting away from Upwood and gave Brooks a course alteration that would take them back over their base. They were now at a height of 200 feet and Brooks' right hand gripped the throttle levers firmly in readiness to give the engines more power should it be necessary to climb hurriedly. He fully realised the danger of attempting to fly lower with visibility nil but there was no alternative. 'I'm not going to call up control,' he told the crew.

'They'll only divert us. Hang on and keep your fingers crossed.' He then slammed open his side-panel as an aid to vision and was amazed to be showered with snow. 'Christ!' he shouted. 'This isn't cloud. It's a bloody snowstorm! No wonder I can't see a thing; the blasted windscreen's covered with thick snow.'

Moments later his voice came to them again and though it was calm they detected in it an underlying tone of caution. 'We're down to a hundred feet. We can't go much lower without hitting something, that's for sure.' He then dropped the port wing gently and peered out of the side window in the hope of glimpsing the tall chimneys of an old brickworks that was near Upwood. But before he could take in anything, his flight-engineer, Sergeant Sabin, called out that he thought he had seen some Drem lights (the guide-lights that marked the perimeter of an airfield) to their starboard. Walter Brooks hauled the Lancaster into a steep right-hand turn and saw the faint, flickering lights of Upwood. In that instant the aircraft pitched wildly and Brooks froze in his seat as another Lancaster slid a few feet above them, blasting 'D-Dog' with its slipstream.

Jee-zus! someone gasped over the intercom. 'Did you see that?'

Holley recalls. 'We all thought we'd had it. Brooks took the Lancaster down to seventy feet and ordered the engineer to drop the undercarriage. 'We'll follow the Drem lights round and swing on to the runway as soon as it shows up through this muck,' he announced. But it wasn't as simple as it sounded. On our first trip round we were too close and crossed the runway at right-angles. On our next circuit we missed it completely. I had my turret facing port and when on our next orbit the engineer shouted 'Hard to port' Brooks banked so steeply that I found myself looking straight down at the deck. A moment later he straightened 'D-Dog' and told us, 'OK, I've got it ...Stand by to cut engines...Cut!' The next moment we hit the tarmac with quite a thump. Brooks swung the aircraft sharply to face the direction from which we had landed. This rather unorthodox procedure had the effect of pulling us up more effectively and more quickly than any application of the brakes would have.

'Ours was the first and only aircraft to land at Upwood whilst the snow was falling. Half an hour later, when we had completed our interrogation of the raid, four more bombers from the squadron landed. The majority had called up earlier and had been diverted to other airfields. We soon learned how lucky we had been. Usually, one of the hottest spots on an operation was to be in the first wave with the fighters doing their utmost to prevent the Path Finders getting to the target and illuminating the aiming point. On this occasion we had been extremely fortunate in being in the role of primary markers. While I had seen a mere four or five aircraft going down as we flew south of the Ruhr, several of my colleagues who had been further back in the bomber stream were attacked. According to their taunt, over forty bombers had got the chop in that area. I doubt if I would have dozed so well on the way back had I realised things were so dicey. I was even more shaken when I heard that four of our own squadron Lancasters had gone down.'[128]

Flight Lieutenant Anthony James Hiscock, piloting another 156 Squadron Lancaster, was a 'Blind Backer-Up' whose job was to renew TIs for the Main Force. 'We were known as primary blind marker illuminators. In short we used H_2S to identify the target area and then would drop flares to illuminate the scene so that the specialist bomb aimers that followed could identify the precise aiming point. H_2S could be temperamental and the picture a little difficult to interpret at times, but our bomb aimer (nav two) became quite expert.'[129]

They were so far ahead of the rest of the bomber stream that Hiscock's 19-year old Canadian rear gunner had seen no sign of aircraft going down. The navigator was 29 - considerably older than the rest of the crew - but by comparison the flight engineer at 35 was positively 'ancient'. Hiscock and his crew had flown a handful of trips on 103 Squadron at Elsham Wolds before volunteering for Path Finders and had been posted to 156 on 2 February to fill the ranks left by recent losses. 'The main reason we volunteered for path Finders' recalled Hiscock 'was that after thirty trips we could stay on and do another twenty, rather than being sent off for a period of instructing and then joining a new squadron and having to form a new crew. This way we could keep together. And we did. I was twenty at the time (I celebrated my 21st birthday on the squadron) and we were confident that we would complete our tour. The optimism of youth I suppose. As it was we did the fifty together and later, when my first rear gunner was tour-expired and decided to leave, I picked up a new rear gunner, Rupert Noye, for another 18. By the war's end I had flown sixty-eight ops and Rupert seventy-two.'[130]

The only problem Tony Hiscock encountered on Nuremberg was landing at their fog-bound base at Wyton. They were re-routed to RAF Marham where they ate a hearty breakfast while waiting for the sky to clear before returning to Wyton. As they got back on board their Lancaster, the wireless operator switched on the radio and they heard the news. 'Good grief; that was a real shock for all of us' said Hiscock. 'The number stood out so much. We wondered how it had happened, because we hadn't noticed anything at all unusual. We were astounded that so many aircraft had gone down.'[131]

Flight Sergeant Reg Parissien on 156 Squadron was relieved when Lancaster 'C-Charlie' crossed the French coast. 'All at last was quiet. We realized that this had been a terrible night. We landed safely at our own station at Upwood and, at de-briefing, gathered that although our own squadron's losses had been small; those of many others had been great. Many of our crews were telling of the aircraft they had seen shot down, some as many as twelve. At first we didn't believe them but, subsequently when more was revealed the day after, we realized that they had been tragically right.'

'X-X-ray' piloted by Squadron Leader 'Dickie' Walbourn approached Nuremberg with its rear turret out of action. A mechanical fault had developed and, although the turret could still be turned, its guns would not fire. By the time the crew had discovered this it was too late to go back. But luck was with them. Despite the many combats that raged around them, they reached Nuremberg without being attacked. Flight Lieutenant Truman said: 'We began our bombing-run at 20,000 feet and were aghast to see masses of vapour trails from the bombers ahead of us which plainly showed our track to the fighters. [After high-octane petrol was burned in the bombers' engines, the residue emerged from the exhausts as steam, which normally dispersed without causing any problem. On this unusually cold night however, the vapour condensed to form white trails at the raiders' altitudes of around 20,000 feet. Lit by the half-full moon, the trails took on a phosphorescent quality that could be seen from great distances]. We became increasingly conscious of very considerable fighter activity. Everywhere one looked there were unmistakable signs of air-to-air firing. With our rear turret useless, we decided to get in and out fast. Once we had dropped our bombs, we increased power and began to gradually shed height to give us greater speed. It was contrary to our briefing orders but we were determined to get away from those tell-tale vapour trails. And it was a tactic that paid off, for 'X-X-ray' again had the phenomenal luck of reaching the coast unscathed.'

It was getting light when 'X-X-ray' returned to Upwood to be greeted by warnings that there were Bandits in the area. Not for this reason but because of 'duff weather', he was diverted and landed at Marham, a Mosquito station after 7½ hours in the air. Flying Officer Sydney Johnson his Australian navigator, after summing up the operation as a 'lengthy, tough grind' his only reference in the 'remarks' section of his navigator's log book to entering or leaving the target area was 'Primary blind-marker - duty carried out.' After 'Operations: Nuremberg. 780 aircraft. 96 lost', Johnson commented: 'It was a hell of a long way into Germany and seemed as if it would never end. It was clear all the way into the target - too much moonlight and the Jerry fighters (which are licked, according to the papers) had a hey-day.'

Ron Smith on 156 Squadron recalled: 'Just as our markers went down, after a nerve-shattering straight and level approach, again we were attacked by a fighter. His intentions had been obvious - I had watched him for some time - high above on our starboard quarter. As I gave evasive instructions, I maintained pressure on the firing buttons and all four guns responded to send him breaking away, straight down, a dwindling speck against the lurid glow below. I was convinced I had hit him, yet he hadn't broken up or burst into flame.

'No damage as we turned on course for the long run home. 'Will this one never end?' was the thought running through my mind as I numbly watched four bombers go down, one after the other. 'Christ, how many is that tonight - thirty, forty, or more?' I asked myself and chewed hard on the tasteless wad of gum in my mouth. They continued to go down until at full power we streaked across the coast and out over the sea; the waves but a ripple far below. Suddenly, the weather deteriorated, dense cloud hiding all from view. From the front, Bob muttered a comment on the meteorological forecast, 'The bastards must have got it arse-about.' The contrast after the hours of brilliant moonlight seemed ironical and it was hard to believe a forecast could have been so completely wrong. If only the conditions had been reversed, how welcome this cloud would have been in the previous tragic hours!

'The skipper made a distant call to base, only to be informed that the weather had closed it down and that we were to divert to Downham Market, sixty miles south-east of our own airfield. The new course was set as we began the descent. With the choice remarks of the crew in my ears, I looked wearily below. The skipper's voice, now edgy from fatigue, ordered silence. He still had the enormous responsibility of putting down safely at a strange airfield in the appalling weather that we had flown into so unexpectedly. The silence is unbroken; the heavy tension becomes more unbearable as no cloud base is reached. Other aircraft are calling for instructions and still we descend.

'I shift on the tiny hard rectangle that answers as a seat, but the cramp returns to pain my buttocks almost immediately as I resume my posture. I stand up to peer in front and below, down into murk for any sign that will indicate we have reached cloud base. Naked fear keeps the adrenaline flowing and even after several hours my mind and body are unable to allow the drug of exhaustion to predominate.

'When at last our shuddering aircraft leaves cloud, any direct contrast in visibility is not immediately noticeable. Then, as a patch below clears, I see perimeter lights astern, a runway partly revealed, the glow subdued as it reflects from the low cloud above.

'A curse from the skipper at my exclamations, another call to control as we begin the circuits, going around several times as other aircraft hold the approach. Finally instructions and permission to land, the lights obscured momentarily as we pass through patches and wisps of mist.

'The lengthy careful run in, a quick sight of a wooden barred fence just beneath, a sudden blur of lights and we are down, the runway unreeling before my eyes, the squeal of brakes, safe at last, after almost eight hours that swerved a lifetime.

'As we await transport, I glance up at our aircraft affectionately, the sheer size of the triple-bladed propellers fronting the engine nacelles, never failing to impress me.

'Incredibly, the nightmare is over, our pilot nodding only at our congratulations, undemonstrative as ever. Debriefing in unfamiliar surroundings, the intelligence officer startled by the figures we suggest of aircraft shot down.

'Sleep evades me long after I crawl beneath the sheets, the engines' roar still pervading my ears, my mind a blank, unable to grapple with, or even register with clarity, any one of the multiple horrors of that awful night.

'Next morning we made the short journey to base over the English countryside, the patchwork of fields, villages, a small town, a ribbon of railway receding into the distance, a snail-like train only distinguished by the trailing smoke and steam from the miniature locomotive at its head.

'Five aircraft were missing, we were informed in the flight office; total for the whole of Bomber Command was eighty and another sixteen had crashed on return in various parts of Southern England, ninety-six in all.

'Yes, someone had miscalculated; someone had got it all wrong. Although the morning promised to be fine, to develop into one of those early summer days, here before its time, the catastrophe of the previous night was hard to accept.'[132]

Squadron Leader E. N. M. 'Neville' Sparks DFC AFC one of the Path Finders on 83 Squadron at Wyton, looked on horrified at the shambles over Nuremberg. 'As was the custom, we left England after the stream had gone and highly laden we passed them on the way. We were flying at 19,000 feet and the Main Force were 3,000 to 4,000 feet above us. Contrary to the forecasts there was no layer cloud in which they could hide from enemy fighters. They were clearly visible, glinting in the moon light. The forecast was for the moon to be at about half its full strength. In fact it was about as bright as it could be. The night too was as clear as a bell - no clouds - with fantastic visibility. Anyway, we were catching up with the force on the second leg of the trip - the 250 miles between Charleroi and Fulda - when the slaughter began. We had an incredible view. In the sixty or ninety minutes after midnight we saw sparkles of cannon fire; some distant and some almost directly above us, followed by explosions, fires, plunging planes and a scattering of fires on the ground as far as the eye could see. I saw three planes blow up as they collided and one of them, a Path Finder, blazed like a torch as its flares ignited.'

Sparks' navigator, 'Doc' Watson, marked no less than 57 ticks in his log on the way to the target. Sparks recalled. 'Each tick was a four-engined bomber we had seen shot down by German fighters. It looked like an ambush from where we were watching. It was the most terrible thing I have ever seen. The forecast was for the moon to be at about half its full strength; in fact it was about as bright as it could be. The night, too, was clear as a bell; no clouds, fantastic visibility. I'm pretty certain we brought back a good photo of the target. 'Strobe' Foley my bomb aimer was wizard at operating the H₂S set. I know he identified Nuremberg correctly.

'On the way back, a powerful head-wind blew up, unpredicted at briefing but, by getting down to 10,000 feet we got home before the CO. We flew straight across and saw nothing but a row of six flares several thousand feet above, which indicated that enemy fighters were still searching for the survivors from the main attacks. We were diverted to Downham Market and I rushed to the CO there who happened to be my cousin 'Lofty' Cousins to tell him that we had seen planes fall from the sky like pigeons dipped in lead. 'Doc' Watson showed his log to the CO who immediately got on to the AOC and told him it had been a 'killer' raid. We did not know then that it was the worst in the history of the RAF but we were pretty sick about what we had witnessed. There were rumours about a leak but how could you tell what was true? It certainly looked like an ambush from where we were watching. It was the most terrible thing I had ever seen, the more so as it had a certain wild, primitive beauty about it.'

American pilot, First Lieutenant Max Dowden on 625 Squadron from Santa Cruz, California, who had joined the RCAF before Pearl Harbor following a broken engagement,also tried to put his Lancaster down at Silverstone but he was refused permission and he was diverted to Bovingdon in Hertfordshire. They got down to 500 feet without reaching the airfield and the crew got into their crash positions. Dowden made a brilliant wheels-down landing in a small field and rumbled across a field on the Duke of Bedford's estate at Little Chalfont. A wagon from the American base picked them up and took them to Kings Cross station to get back to Kelstern.

Two of the twenty Path Finder Lancasters on 7 Squadron that were dispatched from Oakington were lost. Outbound, 38-year old Squadron Leader Colin Howard Wilson DFC of Bowdon, Cheshire and the crew on ND443 MG-L who were on their fourth operation were shot down in the Fulda area by a night-fighter which could have been flown either by a Bf 110G piloted by Leutnant Günther Wolf of 9./NJG5 or Feldwebel Klaus Möller of 12./NJG3.[133] Pilot Officer Peter H. Hamby who usually skippered this crew had been killed on 15/16 March when he had flown his 'second dickey' trip with Pilot Officer Douglas A. Carter RAAF on the operation on Stuttgart. All eight crew on Lancaster III ND557 MG-F were killed. All seven crew on ND443 died when it exploded. Sergeant Wycliffe Jenkins the nineteen year old flight engineer came from Rainham, Essex. The only complete body was that of Sergeant Frank Tilden Fuller the 20-year old rear gunner of Bexhill, Sussex who was found lying near an engine at the crash site at Ober-Moos. The others who died were Flying Officer James Stewart Ferrier the 23-year old Canadian bomb aimer from Toronto; Sergeant Kenneth Geoffrey Francis the 22-year old wireless operator from Tottenham, London; Sergeant Thomas Burgess Liddle the 24-year old mid-upper gunner of Forest Hill, London and Sergeant Joseph Stevens the 21-year old navigator, from Chester. Wilson's Distinguished Flying Cross had been gazetted on 11 February whilst on 97 Squadron.

Shortly before reaching the aiming point at 0125 hours Flight Lieutenant Stanley Evans of Leicester and his crew on JB722 MG-Q who were on their 26th operation, were shot down by a Bf 109G-6 flown by Leutnant Kurt Gäbler, Staffelkapitän of 9./JG300. In the exchange of fire both 'Q-Queenie' and the 'Wild Boar' pilot went down. All the Lancaster crew were killed. Pilot Officer George William Brockway the Canadian mid-upper gunner was from Windsor, Ontario; Flight Lieutenant Albert

Dickinson the navigator was from Washingborough, Lincolnshire; Flight Sergeant Rex Edward Greenfield the flight engineer came from Clacton. Essex; Pilot Officer Daniel Sutcliffe Heys the wireless operator was from Harrow Weald, Middlesex; Flight Sergeant Thomas Johnson Hirst the rear gunner came from Weedon, Northamptonshire and Pilot Officer Kenneth Duncan Matheson DFC the bomb aimer was from Lower Hutt, New Zealand. Gäbler, who bailed out safely at Gutenberg near Gräfenberg later flew Ju 88s and bailed out again when he was wounded in action on 4 March 1945. His Junkers was shot down at Zuidloo, Holland during Operation 'Gisela' when the Nachtjagd flew large-scale intruder sorties over Eastern England.

Homeward bound, Flight Lieutenant A. H. McGillivray RCAF, pilot of 'Z-Zebra' was diverted due to fog and he crash-landed at Feltwell, hitting a concrete pill box in the process. A fire broke out but the crew was able to evacuate the wreckage of the Lancaster without injury. On 23/24 April he and his crew were one of three Lancaster crews on 7 Squadron that went missing on Düsseldorf. The Canadian skipper and three of the crew were taken into captivity. Sergeant Leonard Ernest Lamb the wireless operator and Flight Sergeant Ernest Albert Rhoades RCAF and Sergeant Robert Edward Smith the two air gunners - all of whom had survived the crash landing at Feltwell - were killed.

At Tholthorpe a dozen Halifaxes on 425 'Alouette' Squadron and fourteen Halifaxes on 420 'Snowy Owl' Squadron were dispatched. Of the latter 'R-Robert' returned early due to hydraulics. 'U-Uncle' was an early return due to oxygen supply malfunction. On return aircraft were diverted to Tangmere, Thorney Island and Ford. Lost in thick cloud with his petrol almost exhausted, Flight Sergeant Jack Ward, a former 'Mountie' crashed Halifax LW683 'C-Charlie' into a small farm building after a wheels-up landing in open country three miles from RAF Cranwell. Incredibly, there were no casualties.[134] Squadron Leader Arthur G. Plummer of Halifax, Nova Scotia on 420 Squadron recalled: 'Soon after starting the long leg eastward we began to see plenty of activity abeam of us. We knew that some of what we saw was certainly our bombers going down in flames and hitting the ground. I distinctly remember saying to the crew: 'They sure knew we were coming.'[135]

Lancaster III LM418 'S for Sugar' on 619 Squadron was so badly shot up by a night fighter that Sergeant John Parker the skipper, who was from Northern Ireland, crash-landed at the three-mile long emergency runway at Woodbridge in Suffolk, where it caught fire and was completely gutted, but not before the whole crew ran to safety. All were killed later on operations before the year was out. John Parker, Sergeant William Arthur Sharp the WOp/AG; Sergeant Norman Mackenzie Rice the flight engineer, Flight Sergeant Allan Daniel Aurmell RCAF, bomb aimer and Sergeant Allan Dickson the rear gunner were lost without trace on 23/24 July when Lancaster PB208 PG-S failed to return from the raid on Kiel. Flight Sergeant George Allen Grigg, navigator and Flight Sergeant James Broll who had taken over the rear turret after the death in action of Sergeant John Harold Woodcock on the Salbris operation on 7/8 May were also killed.

Six Lancasters on 514 Squadron failed to land back at Waterbeach from where twenty-one aircraft were detailed to bomb the target but two did not take off that night and four returned early. LL696 flown by Flying Officer Peter J. K. Hood was believed shot down while on the final leg. Leutnant Achim Woeste, Stab III./NJG3 was credited with an unidentified '4-Mot' in the Schesslitz area, ten kilometres north-east of

Bamberg at a time consistent with 514 Squadron aircraft being in that area. Hood and five of his crew, who were on their 16th operation, including Technical Sergeant Maurice George Lanthier USAAF the rear gunner, bailed out successfully and were taken prisoner. Sergeant Clarence Dunkin Fraser MacKenzie the nineteen-year-old mid-upper gunner from Gallogate, Glasgow was killed.[136]

JI-J2 LL698 flown by Flight Sergeant Fred Gregory of Tottenham, London and his crew, who were on their 8th operation, were shot down by a night-fighter, possibly Unteroffizier Lorenz Gerstmayr of 4./NJG3 who claimed a Viermot southeast of Bonn. Only Flight Sergeant C. G. E. MacDonald RCAF the Canadian navigator survived. Flight Sergeant James Duncan McCreary RCAF the 20-year old bomb aimer from Windsor, Ontario and Sergeants Eric Raymond William Pond, wireless operator; Robert Byth, mid-upper gunner; Alfred Cooke, rear gunner and Sanford Peter Frith, flight engineer were killed. Jimmy McCreery had only recently written his mother in which he said he was sure he was going to be home by June or July as he had already completed sixteen operational flights and after doing nine more was scheduled for a leave home.

Warrant Officer William Lachlan 'Bill' McGown the Glaswegian skipper on LL683 JI-P reported '9/10ths cloud with tops 22,000 feet, with gaps. His bomb aimer got their 1,000 pounder and 96 x 30lb, 810 x 4lb, 90 x 4lb incendiaries away at 0126 hours from 20,000 feet. Because of fog at Waterbeach McGown was diverted on his return to RAF Stradishall but this airfield was also fog-bound and despite several attempts the Glaswegian could not land there. Finally, two men bailed out at 1,000 feet into the fog before McGown crash-landed near Sawbridgeworth in Hertfordshire. There were no casualties.

Lancaster LL731 'U-Uncle' captained by 27-year old Pilot Officer Noel William Faulkner Thackray RAAF was outward bound at 20,000 feet flying at 165 IAS at 0123 hours just approaching target area, when 32-year old Flight Sergeant John Russell Moulsdale RAAF his bomb aimer reported a Ju 88 attacking another Lancaster on the starboard bow down at a range of 800 yards. Thackray turned to make an attack on the enemy aircraft from astern and the bomb aimer fired 100 rounds in two or three long bursts. The Ju 88 immediately broke off the attack on the other aircraft and was last seen diving almost vertically through the clouds. Many hits were seen on the Junkers, which was claimed as damaged. No return fire was observed from the other Lancaster. Thackray, husband of Phyllis Mary Thackray, of Surrey Hills in Melbourne and his crew were lost on the operation on Aachen on 11/12 April.

Pilot Officer Douglas Austin Woods RAAF skipper on Lancaster LL739 JI-M saw fifteen to twenty aircraft shot down by fighters on the outward route south of the Ruhr. At 0027 hours, Sergeant Hilary Louis Doherty, a southern Irishman and the rear gunner reported a Me 210 on the starboard quarter down at 600 yards. Doherty immediately gave order to corkscrew to starboard and pressed the triggers but his guns failed to fire. The 210 was then temporarily lost to view. About two minutes later, he reported the Me 210 on the starboard quarter level at a range of 700 yards and gave order to corkscrew to starboard but again, his guns failed to fire and the enemy was lost to view. About seven minutes later, the enemy aircraft was again seen on the starboard quarter down at 500 yards and Doherty immediately gave the order to corkscrew to starboard. At the same time, Sergeant William Charles Udell the mid-upper-gunner reported a fighter flare dropped by a FW 190 on the starboard bow level. The Me 210 then came in to attack from starboard quarter below, closing to a range of 400 yards and opening fire on the Lancaster. Udell fired a few rounds in the direction of trace, before his guns failed. The Lancaster sustained several hits on starboard wing. The Me 210 then broke away to port quarter up and was lost to view. About a minute later, Doherty reported the Me 210 was attacking from starboard quarter level at a range of 300 yards and gave order to corkscrew to starboard. Udell fired a two-second burst from one of his guns, but did not observe any hits on the enemy aircraft which closed to 150 yards and opened fire scoring hits on the Lancaster's starboard tail unit before breaking away. The Lancaster went out of control in a spiral dive and recovered at 6,000 feet. Woods nursed the Lancaster back for an emergency landing at Woodbridge. Woods and his crew were lost on the daylight raid on Villers-Bocage on 30 June.

Another 514 Squadron Skipper, 23-year old Pilot Officer Walter Evan Chitty who was at the controls of LL645 A2-R was baulked on finals at Waterbeach by another aircraft and crash-landed heavily while attempting to go around again. Sergeant Allen Bruce Pattison RCAF of Billings Bridge, Ontario and Sergeant Joseph Shepherd the rear gunner of Heywood, Lancashire were killed. Four others were injured. On recovery from his injuries Chitty retained his 21-year old flight engineer Charles Mathieson Guy and formed a new crew. They were killed on the daylight raid on Caen on 30 July. A few weeks' earlier, on 8 June, Charles twin brother, Robert Calder Guy, also on 514, was lost at La Celle Le Bordes and is buried in the village.

Leutnant Hans Raum of 9./NJG3 flying a Bf 110G-4 had been injured on 12 December 1943 when he survived a crash on the autobahn at Lübeck. The first of his four Abschüsse claims on 30/31 March was possibly Lancaster LL738 on 514 Squadron, twenty kilometres south-west of Bonn. The aircraft was skippered by 25-year old Pilot Officer Garth Stewart Hughes DFC RAAF of Turramurra on the Upper North Shore of Sydney. Formerly a student at Sydney University, Hughes enlisted on 12 September 1941. He and five of the crew, who were on their 19th operation, were killed. Warrant Officer Osmond John Goddard the wireless operator came from Lidcombe in Western Sydney; Pilot Officer Llewellyn Selwyn Smith the navigator was from Auckland, New Zealand; Sergeant George Henry Thornton the rear gunner was from Depford, London; Sergeant H. West the flight engineer was from Derby; and the mid-upper gunner, Flight Lieutenant Leslie James Henry Whitbread was from King's Heath, Birmingham. Flight Sergeant A. D. Hall RNZAF the bomb aimer was the only survivor.

Raum claimed his second victim, another 'Lanki', thirty kilometres south of Bonn at 0025 hours. This was followed by his third and fourth victims - a Halifax and a "4-mot' - which were claimed in quick succession, at 0034 at Roth village and fifty kilometres south-west of Kassel at 0035. His third victim was probably Halifax III LW537 on 51 Squadron flown by 21-year old Flying Officer Malcolm Mason Stembridge of York whose crew was on its sixth operation. Stembridge and Sergeant John Docherty Goskirk the rear gunner of Innerleithen, Peebleshire, were killed. Sergeant F. E. Clinton the flight engineer; Sergeant E. T. Parker, navigator; Warrant Officer2 D. S. Stewart RCAF, bomb aimer; Sergeant D. A. Smith, wireless operator and Sergeant D. W. Lee, mid-upper gunner bailed out safely and were taken prisoner. Shortly after Raum was shot down and injured by a Mosquito intruder near Roth an der Sieg. He survived and would finish the war as Staffelkapitän of 9./NJG3 with a total of between fourteen to seventeen kills.

Thirty-six year old Hauptmann Ernst-Wilhelm Modrow of 1./NJG1 had taken off from Venlo, north-east of Düsseldorf in a Heinkel He 219 Uhu ('Owl') with orders to hunt down the dreaded 'Moskitos'. The experienced pre-war Lufthansa pilot had joined the ranks of the night-fighters in October 1943 and had yet to score a victory. He spent two hours vainly patrolling the Scheldt Estuary and the Zuider Zee without seeing any sign of the Mosquitoes or Viermots. Modrow landed back at Venlo to find that the other night-fighters there had gone into action against strong bomber formations approaching southern Germany. It was too late for him to join them so he was ordered to intercept the bombers on their homeward flight. After taking off his bordschütze he picked up an SN-2 contact over France. It was the Halifax III on 640 Squadron flown by Warrant Officer2 David Warnock Burke RCAF who was heading home to Leconfield at the end of what was their fifth operation. The Canadian, who was from London, Ontario, never made it. Modrow hit the bomber in the starboard wing with a burst of his six wing and nose cannon and it exploded. Momentarily blinded by the glare he banked into a steep starboard turn and right into the sights of the rear gunner of the Halifax. Most of the return fire was deflected by the Owl's strong undercarriage and he watched as the bomber went down and crashed near Abbeville. Burke and the crew - one Scotsman, one Irishman and four Englishmen - perished.[137] Sergeant Weir Crory the rear gunner was from Donaghclony, County Down; Sergeant Reginald Arthur Eastman the bomb aimer came from Tooting, London; Sergeant William Haden the wireless operator was from Sparkhill, Birmingham; Sergeant Allan James Nolf Jamieson the Scottish flight engineer came from Kilmarnock, Ayrshire; Sergeant Michael Martin Stilliard the mid-upper gunner was from Purley, Surrey and Flying Officer Frederick Walter Woods the navigator was from Westcliff, Essex. They are commemorated on the Runnymede Memorial.

Modrow's bordschütze announced another contact and he headed towards it, fastening onto a Viermot with the dawn beginning to come up faintly behind them. It was the Halifax HX322 NP-B on 158 Squadron at Lissett flown by 28-year old Flight Sergeant Albert Brice, married to Margaret, and was from Stoneycroft, Liverpool. Most of whose crew were on their fourth operation. This time Modrow's kill was quick and the bomber crashed in flames at Caumont north of Dieppe. Sergeant Kenneth Dobbs the wireless operator who had joined the crew at the last minute, recalled:

'We were hit by flak over the target, I remember the pilot saying that he was having a bit of difficulty with the controls, so as we were a bit off course we decided to head for the emergency aerodrome at Manston. We were only about twenty miles off the French coast and at between 12,000 and 15,000 feet when a fighter, which I later found out was a Heinkel 219, came in from the port and strafed straight along the side of the aircraft. I remember seeing the flashes. I think some of the crew were shot. The Halifax made a turn then went into a dive. I tried to roll over onto a couple of steps next to me as my parachute was in a stowage across the way, but I didn't get to it because I passed out. A chap on the ground told me later the aircraft exploded in mid-air. I've no idea what happened to me. I came round in a truck being driven to hospital in Lille with German soldiers on either side. I had a broken leg, broken ribs and head injuries and cannon shell injuries to a thumb. Apparently I came down in the rear of the aircraft and a Frenchman pulled me out when it hit the ground. I met him later and he told me I was in the rear. As the wireless operator's position in the Halifax was in the front I can't understand how I got there at all. The rest of the crew were dead in the aircraft, except one other who did bail out apparently, but he was dead when they found him.

It might have been the rear gunner because he had the best chance of escape.'[138]

Dobbs was the only survivor. Sergeant Frederick Boyd the flight engineer from Sheffield, Sergeant William Maurice Gibson the mid-upper gunner of Luton, Bedfordshire, Sergeant Hubert Graham McNeight the navigator of Upton, Cheshire, Flying Officer Norman George Peter Munnery the 23-year old bomb aimer of Ottawa and Sergeant Francis Victor Rhaney the rear gunner of Frodsham, Cheshire were laid to rest in Caumont Churchyard.[139] Dobbs met Flying Officer R. G. A. Harvey DFM again in hospital in Germany; he was shot down on Nuremberg too, flying on the crew skippered by 27-year old Squadron Leader Samuel David Jones DFC. (Harvey who had a wife and son in England never failed to recover completely from his injuries and died some years after the war). Jones, of Saul in Gloucestershire and his 23-year old mid-upper gunner, Flight Sergeant Kenneth Arthur Bray, husband of Elizabeth G. Bray, of Helston in Cornwall, were killed when HX349 'G-George' was shot down by flak at Westerburg and crashed at Hachenburg. Sergeant S. Killgrew the flight engineer, Pilot Officer A. E. Surridge, navigator, Flight Lieutenant L. A. Ingram the rear gunner and Flight Lieutenant F. W. B. Hailey DFM the bomb aimer were taken into captivity.

Modrow continued his search but finding no further victims he eventually turned on course for Venlo. The time was now 0600 hours and the dawn was coming up fast.

Sergeant Reginald Cripps in the rear turret on 'L-Love' on 158 Squadron had realised as early as the approach to the enemy coast that 'visibility was very good and the moon was coming out, so we could easily see the numbers on the aircraft flying near us. To the north and south of the bomber stream there was much searchlight activity as we crossed the coast.'

As 'L-Love' was about to start its bomb-run a Bf 110 with navigation lights on opened fire from approximately 1,000 yards dead astern and above. Cripps recalled that 'he was firing rapid bursts of cannon fire at numerous bombers with no serious results to my knowledge. A rear gunner on an aircraft some distance astern below and to our starboard fired a long burst of tracer from his Brownings at this particular fighter but the range was too great and I could see his tracer falling short' but the fighter sheered-off and disappeared. Cripps called for a corkscrew to port, whereupon Stan Windmill rolled the Halifax into a left-hand dive. By the time they came out of it there was no sign of the fighter, but about 100 yards to their left was another Halifax with its starboard outer-engine ablaze. 'L-Love' levelled off for the bomb-run and dropped its bomb load through seven-tenths cloud. Cripps was later to receive a commission and a DFC on completion of his operational tour.

For those crews that made it back the feelings of relief can only be put into words by someone, like a Lancaster pilot on 207 Squadron at Spilsby, who experienced it time and again. 'To be standing on English earth again - or even on oil-rainbowed English tarmac - as a cool, clear dawn began to drive off the night of 30 March, a night already retreating into history, was to be amazed that it had all actually happened and yet here one was, incredibly but undoubtedly still alive. As much alive as the pair of blackbirds skittering noisily in the hedgerow beyond the bomb dump; as much alive as the yawning, gum-booted farmer whistling up his dog from the furrows of the turnip field beyond the parked and chocked aircraft which once more had safely brought one home again. This was the time when young men not normally given to sentiment would mutter, 'She's a good old bitch' and give the matt black fuselage a friendly thump as they would the shoulder of a tried and trusted friend.

'Strangely, now that it was all over, there was little of the animated chaffing and joking and horse-play that sometimes relieved the tension prior to an operational take-off. The conversation now was tired and superficially concerned mainly with apparent trivia:

'Aren't we due for leave soon?'

'I've left my bloody helmet in the aircraft.'

'Did anybody stoke up the stove before we left?'

'Christ, don't you ever buy any cigarettes of your own?'

'This WAAF driver will kill us yet.'

'Who's got the laundry tickets?'

'What time does that bus leave for Lincoln?'

'She said she'd be there at opening-time.'

Occasionally these and other inconsequential exchanges, conversational clutchings at the safe straws of normal everyday life, would be interpolated with direct references to the so-recently shared experiences of the diminishing night:

'Jesus, I was cold coming home.'

'Sorry about the landing, chaps.'

'That port outer motor sounds a bit sick.'

'I wasn't going around again for quids.'

'Did you see the wing come off that Halifax?'

'Bloody hell, I could sleep for a week.'

'One thing about the Ruhr - at least it's quicker.'

'I only counted two parachutes.'

I thought that Lanc was going to carve us in half.

'The dumb bastards never even saw us.'

'Some of these clots must start weaving on take-off.'

Generally, though, there seemed to be, by unspoken agreement and tacit understanding, a tendency to forget about the whole bloody business at least until they'd had a drink.'[140]

Endnotes Chapter 13

128 *The Bombing of Nuremberg* by James Campbell (Futura 1973).

129 Quoted in *The Pathfinder Companion* by Sean Feast (Grub St. 2012).

130 Quoted in *The Pathfinder Companion* by Sean Feast (Grub St. 2012).

131 Quoted in *The Red Line* by John Nichol (William Collins 2013).

132 *Rear Gunner Pathfinders* by Ron Smith DFM (Goodall 1987).

133 The other possibility is that either Leutnant Günther Wolf of 9./NJG5or Feldwebel Klaus Möller of 12./NJG3shot down ME686 on 166 Squadron. From research by Theo Boiten.

134 After repairs at 48 MU 'C-Charlie' was reallocated to 76 Squadron.

135 Quoted in *Through Footless Halls of Air*.

136 On 26/27 August Leutnant Woeste who had seven victories and would have turned 22 on 31 August was shot down by Warrant Officer Les Turner and Flight Sergeant Frank Francis, a 169 Squadron Mosquito crew. Woeste and Unteroffizier Anton Albrecht, were killed. Unteroffizier Heinz Thippe and Gefreiter Karl Walkenberger, who were both wounded, bailed out.

137 Other sources say that the aircraft was hit by flak at Dieppe or by a flak ship off the French coast

138 Quoted in *Men of Air; The Doomed Youth of Bomber Command* by Kevin Wilson (Weidenfeld & Nicolson 2007).

139 Chorley.

140 Geoff Taylor author of *The Nuremberg Massacre*.

Chapter 14

WAAFs that had waved the crews off as they left the airfields the night before spent their early hours listening for the faint sound of the first bomber home. The return was no less an anxious time for the crews. Every mile of the route home was fraught with danger, not only from enemy flak or prowling night fighters, but also from possible flak damage already sustained to a vital part in any one of the aircraft's complex systems. Towards dawn the reception ground crews were ready and waiting. The faint hum of aero engines was heard in the distance - the first one was back - and work began again. Often the airfield personnel would be woken from a deep sleep by the sound of engines as the returning bombers flew low overhead and then lay awake counting each one in. Some WAAFs remembered the autumn early morning mist hanging over the runways like a shimmering veil before the rest of the camp was astir. Some remembered also hearing the terrifying sound of exploding ammunition when a Lancaster or a Halifax crashed while making an emergency landing and the subdued grapevine gossip when an aircraft failed to return. The first question posed to anyone returning to a billet from duty crew was, 'which aircraft have not returned?' While every ground crew expected operational losses, they all hoped their aircraft would survive.

Aircraft would be given a landing number by flying control and circle the airfield until they were called to make their landing approach. Once down, each aircraft taxied to its own dispersal and the waiting ground crew. Tired from the night's stressful events, the aircrew alighted from the aircraft and were welcomed back before being taken to a debriefing session with the Intelligence Officers on the success or failure of the night's operation. After flying for many hours in a vibrating, cold and noisy aircraft over hostile territory, often in appalling weather conditions, sleep didn't come easy to many of the returning aircrew. Many would wonder why they volunteered for such perilous aircrew duties. Others would fall asleep happy with the thought that only the other crews 'got the chop' and with a bit of luck they would soon complete their thirty bombing operations tour.

When the ground crew took over, the kite was theirs again. Each aircraft had a faults book in which the captain noted any faults that occurred during the flight and had to be rectified before the next trip. The flight sergeant and the senior NCOs in charge of each trade inspected the aircraft. Petrol, oil and coolant consumption was recorded so that the performance of the engines could be watched. Naturally, there were times when urgent repairs had to be made. Aircraft may have been hit by anti-aircraft fire or by night fighter attack. Sometimes they would return with serious damage to the airframe or control surfaces. Many returned with one or more engines out of action - but still they reached home. Damage was quickly assessed and a decision taken on whether the aircraft was repairable on the flight-line or whether specialist help was required. Photographs were taken for future reference.

If special jobs called for more expert workmanship than the flight personnel could give, there was a special flight of highly skilled workmen, representative of all trades and called the Service Flight from which men could be called to deal with the emergency. When all was finally completed, the aircraft went through the daily inspection and an air test prior to its next operational flight. Workmanship was of a highly skilled character and supervision was very strict. After all, the aircrews' lives depended upon it.[141]

Some squadrons returned relatively unscathed. At Elsham Wolds, sixteen Halifaxes on 576 Squadron had taken off and only one had been lost and on 103 Squadron, two Lancasters from the seventeen dispatched failed to return. Apart from ME721 flown by Pilot Officer Jack Tate, the other was ME736 skippered by Flying Officer James Guy Johnston of Dunbar, East Lothian, which was hit by flak while on the outward flight and crashed at Bilkheim, eight kilometres South-South-West of Westerburg. Sergeant F. Fealy the mid-upper gunner had a remarkable escape in that he left the bomber through a gaping hole where the H_2S scanner had been burnt away. He sustained burns to both legs. Flying Officer Johnston, Flight Sergeant Brian Philip Boyle the rear gunner of Curl Curl, a suburb of northern Sydney; Flying Officer John Christopher Patrick Doyle the bomb aimer of Pinner, Middlesex; Flying Officer Joseph Jean Andre Ducharme the Canadian navigator, from Montreal; Sergeant William James Gwynne the flight engineer of Omagh in County Tyrone and Sergeant Gordon Thomson the wireless operator of Bolton-by-Bowland, Lancashire, lie in Rheinberg War Cemetery.

Three of the eleven Lancaster Path Finder aircraft that were lost on the raid were on 635 Squadron at Downham Market in Norfolk where earlier, fourteen aircraft had been dispatched. These three losses were the first casualties suffered by the Squadron since forming a week or so earlier. It will be remembered that 'T-Tommy' piloted by Flight Lieutenant 'Johnny' Nicholls DFC RAAF was shot down by the Westerberg flak. No word was received from Lancaster ND711 skippered by Flight Lieutenant Hugh Julian Langdon Webb. F2-X JB356 flown by 20-year old Flight Lieutenant Charles Anthony 'Skip' Lyon of Whitley Bridge, Yorkshire, crashed at Erksdorf near Neckartzenlingen with the loss of all the crew. Flight Sergeant Vincent Earle Aspin, the 20-year old mid-upper gunner was from Burnley, Lancashire; Pilot Officer John Leslie Atkinson the rear gunner was from Easington, County Durham; Sergeant Leonard Arthur Chappell the flight engineer was from Watton-at-Stone, Hertfordshire; Sergeant John Charles Guthrie the 23-year old wireless operator was from Wickham, County Durham; Flight Sergeant Henry George Howes the 24-year old bomb aimer came from Highbury, London and Flight Sergeant Raymond Lawley the 21-year old navigator was from Sheffield, Staffordshire. They were on their sixteenth operation.

'We boys were first confronted with the horrors of war' wrote Flakhelfer Hilmar Eisenhuth from Kassel, who helped man I. Battery Flakabteilung 112 at Erksdorf. The equivalent of the British Air Training Corps, the Luftwaffenhelferingen auxiliaries helped man flak batteries within the Reich. In all, 75,000 students from secondary schools were drafted into the Luftwaffe Flak arm from February 1943 onwards, manning the heavy batteries. In addition, about 15,000 women and girls, 45,000 volunteer Russian PoWs and 12,000 Croatian soldiers were drafted into the air defence of the Reich. Eisenhuth reported in his journal: 'We lay in our bunks and heard from afar the engine noise of bombers. However, there suddenly began a whining sound, increasingly louder and bombs exploded. The shutters flew open and the duty NCO rushed in: it was dark. Then someone turned the lights on. It was a divine sight: Robert Wagner could not reach his steel helmet in his locker, but wanted to protect his head. So serious was the situation, the laughter was inevitable. We rushed to our posts, but we could not shoot because the night fighters were among the bombers. It was a moonlit night, with no cloud cover; the bombers were easily recognized by their contrails. Flying over the bombers a Ju 88 dropped flares on parachutes. A night-fighter 800 metres away flew underneath the Lancaster and fired his 'Schräge Musik' without being seen. The Lancaster exploded into red, green and white colours. It was a 'Master of Ceremonies'. No one survived; only scraps of material and men. Tucked in a uniform blouse was a letter that was still legible. He had recently returned from leave.'

In no time it seemed 'Bob' Burgett the bomb aimer on Halifax MH-L on 51 Squadron had reported sighting the target and Flight Sergeant Bill Stenning the wireless operator went onto 'Master Bomber' frequency. The area was well alight and he could see the pattern of streets and roads. Joe Pawell, the American skipper, had a cine camera going. He had used this on a trip to Schweinfurt but Stenning had never seen the films. They were soon going in and Stenning went back down to the flare chute and plugged into the intercom to listen to the bomb aimer. Bombs were away and the photo-flash bomb and 'L-London' was away too, turning to starboard and losing height in a dive. Stenning went back to his position in the nose and, looking out, saw a Lancaster diving steeply followed by what looked like a Me 110. The Lancaster caught fire. The flak was 'fairly bad' leaving the target area and the crew felt some of the closer bursts. Joe Pawell headed around onto the homeward course towards France and Belgium with the aircraft just riding the cloud tops. They had barely settled down on the new heading, with the target safely behind them, when the rear gunner, Sergeant 'Jock' Baxter, reported an aircraft closing in astern, slightly below and partly in cloud.

'I got it on 'Fishpond' and it was certainly moving in but not fast,' said Stenning. 'I also reported to the pilot and he started to corkscrew. As the contact was now visual and Alf Barnard the flight engineer could also see it, 'Jock' was all set to fire from the rear turret but something made him hold off. We lost the aircraft in cloud and some argument arose as to whether it was a Me 110 or a Lancaster as their twin tail fin arrangements were rather similar. We never did find out as the aircraft finally disappeared for good.

'We must have been somewhere near Stuttgart when we ran into searchlights and heavy flak. I poured out 'Window' and we had a hectic ten minutes. This was about 0200. Soon afterwards Alf Barnard called me and asked me to help him with the pilot who seemed half asleep and drugged. We could not think he was wounded. Over the intercom he mumbled 'I'm OK. I'm OK. Get the wheels up.' They were down, we discovered - and so were we. Without realizing it we were down to only about 5,000 feet instead of 20,000 feet. Something had gone wrong somewhere as fuel was very low on one tank and Alf had to do some quick calculating. We couldn't get the undercarriage up but the pilot seemed to be better and we were getting well over France. I got the trailing aerial out and tuned into 500 kilocycles just in case and we headed for Tangmere, one of the emergency airfields in the south of England.'

When Sergeant Mitchell the flight engineer on Halifax 'D-Dog' on 640 Squadron reported a fuel shortage his skipper, Flight Sergeant Johnson decided to land at Tangmere, instead of pressing on north to Leconfield in Yorkshire as it was suspected that a fuel tank had been holed during one of the night-fighter attacks. On landing, cannon-shell strikes were found in the wings, the fuselage and in both fins and rudders. The Halifax had been airborne for 7.45 hours. After a brief sleep in strange surroundings instead of at their own familiar base, the crew flew thoughtfully home to Leconfield with the sun in their faces and the slipstream whistling through the jagged cannon-shell holes.

Approaching the English coast the crew of Halifax MH-L on 51 Squadron at Snaith could see a lot of activity with searchlights homing incoming bombers. By about 0345 the Halifax was over Tangmere where there appeared to be some confusion with Lancasters and Halifaxes milling about, flares going off and urgent Mayday calls crowding the air as bombers, diverted from their fog-bound airfields further north, were stacked over Tangmere. In the middle of it all, Flight Lieutenant Joe Pawell was diverted to Wing, near Silverstone. Bill Stenning immediately began working Wing HF/DF radio and got a bearing, which he passed to Bob Clark the navigator.

'About twenty minutes after leaving Tangmere,' said Stenning 'the mid-upper gunner shouted that there were trees just below us and, sure enough, we were only a few hundred feet up. Great panic! Joe Pawell was in a stupor again and would not respond quickly. We managed to get on a bit more boost and gained height again. All engines were OK but the wheels were still dragging. I later learned that we had flown over Hindhead, only eight miles from my home and its height above sea level had nearly finished us.

'By now it was half-light and very misty. At about 0400 we were approaching Wing airfield and got them on R/T. Visibility was bad but they were putting out goose-neck flares on the runway. We joined the circuit and made two attempts to get in. I went up by Joe Pawell with Alf Barnard, but our help wasn't much good as each time he was sure he could do it but each time we overshot. Third time lucky and we were down - right on the goose-neck flares. I looked back from the astrodome and it looked like 'Fido' where we had knocked over some of the flares and the spilled paraffin had caught light, burning all over the runway. The wheels had locked down OK.'

Several other crews diverted to Wing reported worse trips than Pawell's crew had experienced but Bill Stenning and the rest of the crew were 'thunderstruck' when they heard on the BBC news at breakfast next morning that ninety-six aircraft were missing. 'Joe Pawell was still very ill and obviously not fit to fly but when we reported to flying control we were told that we must leave for Snaith immediately. Joe telephoned the base and was informed that our squadron had had no aircraft back at all from Nuremberg and that we might be required for operations again that night. As luck would have it our own aircraft was unserviceable with a hydraulic line cut by flak and a fuel tank split open.'

Low on fuel or badly damaged by enemy action or both, some struggling Halifaxes put down at Silverstone airfield home to 17 OTU, four miles south of Towcester in Northamptonshire. David Scholes, a 21-year old Australian pilot under training for conversion to heavy bombers, landed his Wellington at about 0120 after a long training flight across England and Wales to a bombing range. His

Top: John Chatterton DFC and crew on 44 'Rhodesia' Squadron at Dunholme Lodge. Left to right: John Davidson; Bill Champion; Bill Barker; John Chadderton; D. J. Reyland; Ken Letts and John Michie.

Right: 22-year old Flight Sergeant Ron Buck, Flying Officer Peter James Drane RAFVR's experienced rear gunner on B-Baker' on 97 Squadron Halifax III LV857 on 51 Squadron.

Below: Lancaster III EE176 QR-M *Mickey The Moocher* on 61 Squadron at Skellingthorpe showing 91 ops on the nose. EE176's nose had received a Walt Disney cartoon of Mickey Mouse, pulling a bomb-trolley on which sat a bomb and this Lanc became *Mickey The Moocher,* a name derived from Cab Calloway's popular blues song, *Minnie the Moocher.* (Frank Mouritz)

Left:. Lancaster LM455/T *Pent House* showing the kangaroo dropping a bomb.

Below : Squadron Leader G. D. 'Bluey' Graham AFC DFC 'B' Flight commander on 550 Squadron and crew on LM455/T *Pent House*.

Below: Pilot Officer Desmond 'Denny' Freeman RAFVR (21) pilot of 'Q-Queenie' on 61 Squadron at Skellingthorpe in spring 1944. Freeman was killed on 24 September 1944.

Bottom: Sergeant Derek 'Pat' Patfield the bomb aimer on Denny Freeman's crew on 61 Squadron at Skellingthorpe. (Pat Patfield)

Right: Feldwebel Anton Heinemann, Hauptmann Gerhard Raht's Funker.

Below right: Hauptmann Gerhard Raht of 4./NJG3 who shot down Lancaster ND562 skippered by 32-year old Flight Lieutenant Alastair John Cook of Edinburgh.

Below: Flying Officer Carl William Kruger, the 27-year old bomb aimer and husband of Violet Kruger and father of Robert Charles Kruger, of Winnipeg, Manitoba on Lancaster ND441 captained by 22-year old Flight Lieutenant Douglas Mintie Carey DFC of Brandon, Manitoba.

Top: Lancaster III LM418 on 619 Squadron which Sergeant John Parker took off from in Coningsby at 2213 hours and was wrecked on return in a crash-landing at Woodbridge. No one was hurt but the Lancaster was consumed by fire. Parker and his crew were killed on the operation to Kiel on 23/24 July 1944.

Left: Sergeant Kenneth Dobbs, a wireless operator on 158 Squadron at Lissett.

Below left: Flight Lieutenant Don Paul, born and educated in Tonypandy, Glamorgan who was awarded the DFC for his actions on the Nuremberg raid when 'R-Robert' on 61 Squadron at RAF Syerston ran into German fighters near beacon 'Ida'. Don Paul put the Lancaster down at RAF Manston safely.

Top Right: Flight Lieutenant Anthony James Hiscock, a 'Blind Backer-Up' pilot on a 156 Squadron Lancaster whose job was to renew TIs for the Main Force.

Right: Pilot Officer Garth Stewart Hughes DFC RAAF (KIA) of Turramurra, NSW. After completing his flying training he was posted to 514 Squadron, flying Avro Lancasters. On 24 December 1943 he had been awarded the DFC.

Right: Squadron Leader Colin Howard Wilson DFC on 7 Squadron who took Pilot Officer Peter H. Hamby's crew to Nuremberg.

Below: Pilot Officer Peter H. Hamby's crew on ND443 MG-L who were on their fourth operation: Left to Right: Sergeant Thomas Burgess Liddle, the 24-year old mid-upper gunner; Flying Officer James Stewart Ferrier RCAF, the 23-year old bomb aimer; Sergeant Wycliffe Jenkins, the nineteen year old flight engineer; Sergeant Frank Tilden Fuller, the 20-year old rear gunner; Pilot Officer Peter H. Hamby and Sergeant Joseph Stevens, the 21-year old navigator.

Below: Lancaster W4964 'J-Johnny' *Still Going Strong!* on 9 Squadron which Pilot Officer Phil Plowright brought safely home to Bardney on his 18th operation and the aircraft's 53rd flight. Norman Wells, the rear gunner, recalled that they never got shot at 'but we damned nearly got rammed by another Lanc heading for the same cloud as we were. He was so close we could hear his engines as well as our own.' The art work featuring the Johnny Walker whiskey symbol was painted by Corporal Pattison, a ground crewman on the station. W4964 completed its 107th and final operation on 6 October 1944.

Top: Halifax III LV857 on 51 Squadron, flown by 21-year old Sergeant Jack Percival George Binder one of Oberleutnant Martin 'Tino' Becker, Staffelkapitän, 2./NJG6's seven victories, six on the outward route and, after a short refuelling stop at Mainz-Finthen, one more on the bombers' homeward track. These were his 20th-26th night kills, which earned him the award of the Ritterkreuz. All of Binder's crew, who were on their third operation, were killed. Above left: Flight Sergeant Geoffrey Graham Brougham RAAF the 21-year old pilot (KIA) of Halifax LW544 MH-QZ on 51 Squadron. Above, centre: Flight Sergeant Kenneth McDonald Radley RAAF the wireless operator (KIA) on LW544. Above, Right: Flying Officer Arthur Edgar Emil Gourdeau, 24, the American navigator (KIA) on Halifax LW618 on 427 'Lion' Squadron. Gourdeau, from Vancouver, was born in Germany of Polish parents. Below left: S. A. Williams the flight engineer on LW544 was taken prisoner. Below, centre: Flight Sergeant Lloyd Francis Peel RAAF the mid-upper gunner (KIA). Below, right: Flight Sergeant Arthur Henry Williams RAAF the rear gunner (KIA).

Top: Warrant Officer Eric Ronald Fergus MacLeod's crew on Halifax LW724 NP-S on 158 Squadron. Left to right, standing: Sergeant L. J. Craven, flight engineer; Flying Officer Anthony Shanahan, bomb aimer; Flight Sergeant James Arthur Nicholson, rear gunner. Left to right, sitting: Flight Sergeant Leonard Gower Paxman, wireless operator; Warrant Officer MacLeod; Flight Sergeant Ernest Roy Moore, navigator; Flight Sergeant Douglas Fitzgerald Bickford, mid-upper gunner. Their aircraft crashed near Herborn-Seelbach. Flying Officer Shanahan bailed out and was taken prisoner of war in Germany. The rest of the crew were killed.

Below left: Squadron Leaders W. L. 'Bill' Brill (right) and Arthur W. Doubleday, 'B' Flight commanders on 463 Squadron RAAF and 467 Squadron RAAF respectively. Doubleday was first back at Waddington and told Sir Ralph Cochrane 'Jerry got a century before lunch today.' Bill Brill had an uneventful but unpleasant trip home, lagging behind the bomber stream.

Right: Flight Sergeant Donald Gray.

Below: Lancaster R5546 'VN-T' on 50 Squadron, which was lost with Flight Sergeant Donald Gray's crew. (Les Bartlett)

Top: Crew of Lancaster III ND466 'Z-Zebra' on 156 Squadron, one of seven shot down by Oberleutnant Martin 'Tino' Becker Staffelkapitän, 2./NJG6 (right), which crashed at Eisfeld. Left to Right: Flying Officer Scrivener RCAF (PoW); Flying Officer Herbert Charles Frost (KIA); Warrant Officer John Charles Baxter (KIA); Flying Officer E. H. J. Summers (PoW); Squadron Leader P. R. Goodwin (PoW); Pilot Officer Cyril Ashley Rose RAAF (KIA). Warrant Officer Victor Gardner DFM (KIA) rear gunner was not in this picture. Flying Officer W. C. Isted (PoW) took this photo. (Karl-Ludwig Johanssen)

Top right: In May 1945 this obelisk was erected in memory of the crew in the village of Eisfeld, just inside East Germany, 20 kilometres north of the town of Coburg. The inscription is in Cyrillic and German.

Above left: Eric Hewitt Palmer, navigator on Flight Lieutenant Horace Hyde's crew on 97 Squadron who was killed on 30/31 March.

Left: 20-year old Pilot Officer Walter Henry Burnett of Stanmore, Middlesex, pilot of Lancaster ND798 on 166 Squadron.

Right: Sergeant Lawrence W. Woolliscroft the wireless operator, a veteran of 42 operations, on Lancaster ND406 GT-S on 156 Squadron skippered by 27-year old Warrant Officer John A. 'Jack' Murphy RAAF.

Top: Members of Wing Commander Forsyth's crew give their report in the interrogation room at 466 Squadron RAAF at Leconfield. Back to camera: Flight Lieutenant W. Harrison, intelligence officer. Around table, left to right: Pilot Officer F. Wooton, Pilot Officer J. R. Downton, Wing Commander Dudley Thomas Forsyth RAAF, Squadron Commanding Officer; Sergeant E. Dent; Flying Officer S. R. Jeffrey.

Left: Flight Sergeant Donald Brinkhurst the mid-upper gunner on Lancaster DV264 'L-Love' on 101 Squadron at Ludford Magna.

Right: Some of Don Brinkhurst's crew on Lancaster DV264 taken while he was in hospital. Left to right: Flying Officer Leonard Ryland 'Luff' Luffman DFM; Pilot Officer Ernest McClure Kippen DFC; Jim Goodall; Flight Sergeant Norman Hugh Bowyer DFM and Flight Lieutenant William Ian Adamson DFC. Of those in the photo only Luffman would survive the loss of their Lancaster on the night of 30/31 March.

Top left: Twenty one year old Flight Sergeant Arthur Harrington Jeffries CGM pilot of LM425 'N for Nan' on 550 Squadron. (via Linda Ibrom).

Above left: Sergeant Jimmy Whitley, rear gunner on Flight Sergeant Arthur Jeffries crew.

Below, left: Flight Sergeant Stan Keirle on Jeffries crew.

Above right: Nuremberg was Flight Lieutenant Henry Coverley's fortieth trip, the tenth of his second tour, the first having been on 78 Squadron. His usual aircraft, *Sir Roger De Coverley* had gone unserviceable. He had taken LK795 'P-Peter', Wing Commander Douglas 'Hank' Iveson DSO DFC the squadron commander's aircraft instead.

Below right: PoW card for Twenty six year old Flight Lieutenant Henry Denys Coverley on 76 Squadron at Holme-on-Spalding Moor.

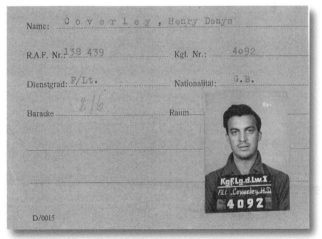

Right: Flight Sergeant James William Love (standing), the Mid-upper gunner on Sergeant Ronald Arthur Horten's crew on 78 Squadron who was killed on the night of 30/31 March (pictured) with his two brothers. Jack (seated, right) who went MIA on Mannheim on 20 May 1942 when his 7 Squadron Stirling suffered engine failure and was forced down in Mezieres, France. The entire crew walked to the Swiss border.

Left: Twenty eight year old Flight Lieutenant Richard Algernon Dacre Trevor-Roper DFC DFM rear gunner on Lancaster III ND390 OF-S on 97 Squadron flown by Twenty three year old Flight Lieutenant Desmond Harold Rowlands DFC of Kenton, Middlesex, the second aircraft to fall to Martin Drewes. Trevor-Roper had been Wing Commander Guy Gibson's tail gunner on the Dams raid on 16/17 May 1943.

Below: Lancaster ND425 and Flight Sergeant Charlie Foster RNZAF's crew on 550 Squadron at RAF Kirmington. Foster's crew were killed when their Lancaster exploded over Unterspiesheim, eleven kilometres SSE of Schweinfurt after being hit by flak.

Below: Pilot Officer Cyril Barton the Halifax pilot on 578 Squadron who was awarded a posthumous Victoria Cross.

Above: Pilot Officer 'Brad' Bradshaw's crew on 625 Squadron in May 1944. Front (L-R): Pilot Officer John Edward Goldsmith, navigator, born in Halifax, Nova Scotia in 1922; 'Brad' Bradshaw; Sergeant 'Skids' Brakes, flight engineer. Back: Sergeant Bob Wright, wireless operator; Sergeant Jack Cavanaugh, rear gunner; Sergeant 'Butch' Sutcliffe, mid-upper gunner. Missing: Jock Gunn, bomb aimer. On Nuremberg brilliant moonlight and repeated explosions of bombers falling to flak or night fighters forced John Goldsmith to retreat to the seclusion of his navigation cubbyhole. (John Albrecht)

ight: Flight Lieutenant Edward
Vells Tickler CGM and four of his
rst crew: Left to right: Ted Lowans,
omb aimer; Maurice Webb,
/Op/AG; Ted Tickler; W. A.
avies, rear gunner and Jack
Iatthews, navigator. Eddie Tickler
'as wounded in action during his
rst operation on 27/28 February
943 and after convalescing he was
osted to Swinderby where, in early
944 he formed a new crew and they
'ere posted to 57 Squadron at East
irkby. Nuremberg was their 13th
ip together. Sergeant Kenneth
obert Marriott, Flying Officer
eginald Hannam Smart, Sergeant
lan Arthur Frank Goddard and
ergeant Robert Ernest Locke on
ancaster ND622 'E-Easy' were
lled. Tickler, Sergeant A. Ferguson,
id-upper gunner and the bomb
mer, Technical Sergeant William E.
eeper USAAF were taken prisoner.

Left: Hauptmann Martin Drewes (middle) Gruppenkommandeur of III./NJG1 at Laon-Athies who claimed three Abschüsse on 30/31 March 1944 and his crew of Feldwebel Erich Handke, Bordfunker (left) and Oberfeldwebel Georg 'Schorsch' Petz (bordshutze), smiling for the camera after shooting down five Lancasters in 45 minutes on the Mailly-le-Camp raid on 3/4 May 1944.

Left: Hauptmann Fritz Lau the 32-year old Bf 110G-4 pilot and Staffelkapitän of 4./NJG1 at Laon-Athies.

Right: Leutnant Hans Schäfer of 7./NJG2.

Left: Oberleutnant Helmuth Schulte of 4./NJG5.

Right: 24-year old Oberleutnant Dietrich 'Dieter' Schmidt, Staffelkapitän, 8./NJG1.

Left: Sergeant John 'Jack' Ellenor (KIA), the 33-year old gunner on Pilot Officer Cornish's crew on 49 Squadron.

Left Twenty one year old Pilot Officer John Dickinson on 49 Squadron.

Above: Pilot Officer Dick Starkey as photographed on his PoW card.

His crew on 49 Squadron in front of Lancaster JB679 EA-D. From left, Wing Commander Alexander Annan Adams or 'Triple A' as he was known (49 Squadron CO); Pilot Officer Russ Ewens, pilot; Air Commodore Cook (station commander, 52 Base); Flying Officer Bob Grainger, bomb aimer; Sergeants Manger, air gunner; Phil Griffiths, wireless operator; Doug Tritton, flight engineer; Lees, air gunner; Maurice Laws, air gunner; Dickinson (KIA 26/27 April 1944). Far right is Sergeant Robert Hall Hudson DFM (KIA 26/27 April 1944). (John Ward)

Pilot Officer Edward Leslie
John Perkins.

Pilot Officer Perkins crew on 97 Squadron. Back Row: Sergeant
Frank Ernest Coxhead; Perkins; Flight Lieutenant William
James Hunt; Joseph Coman, wireless operator. Front row: Flight
Sergeant John Fairbairn and Flight Sergeants' M. P. McBride and J. K. Russell, the two 'wild'
Canadian gunners who were confined to the 'Aircrew Refresher Centre' at Sheffield for
smashing up the sergeant's mess one night and missed certain death on 23 June when Perkins
Lancaster collided with Henry Van Raalte's aircraft during a training flight.

Right: Flight Lieutenant Henry Van Raalte on 97 Squadron,
born Guildford, Western Australia on 21 January 1913 to Henri
Benedictus Salman Van Raalte and Katherine Lyell Symers,
who married in 1912. Van Raalte married Mary Ellen Fisher in
1936 and they had a son, Anthony John Westwood, in 1939.
Henry enlisted on 12 August 1941 in Perth.

The funeral of Henry Van Raalte at Cambridge City Cemetery
on 7 August 1944. His brother stands by the graveside.

Top: The crew on LL849 UM-B on 626 Squadron made a precautionary landing at Seething after being struck by lightning on 30/31 March. Allocated to 101 Squadron at Ludford Magna, LL849 hit a tree at Lichfield, Staffs on the night of 31 July/1 August 1944 during a training sortie. Flying Officer Cornelius and four of his crew were injured. Three other crew members died.

Right: Flight Lieutenant Arthur Bruce Simpson DFC RAAF of Numurkah, Victoria and Pilot Officer Raymond Carson Watts DFC RAAF the navigator of Moonee Ponds, Victoria on LM376 'Q-Queenie' on 467 Squadron RAAF which was shot down over Belgium. The Resistance hid Simpson's crew from the Germans.

Below: At Snaith personnel await the return of 51 Squadron from Nuremberg. The duty Flying Control Officer communicates landing instructions to an approaching Halifax, while the Station Commander, Group Captain Noel Fresson keeps watch from the balcony outside.

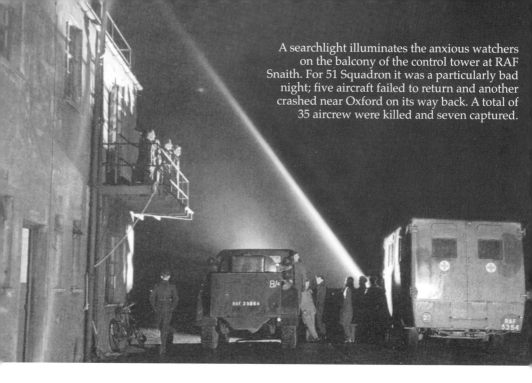

A searchlight illuminates the anxious watchers on the balcony of the control tower at RAF Snaith. For 51 Squadron it was a particularly bad night; five aircraft failed to return and another crashed near Oxford on its way back. A total of 35 aircrew were killed and seven captured.

The ruined city of Nuremberg at the end of the war. On 2 January 1945 the medieval city centre was systematically bombed by the RAF and the US Army Air Forces and about ninety percent of it was destroyed in only one hour, with 1,800 residents killed and roughly 100,000 displaced. In February additional attacks followed.

diary entry graphically described the sight that he witnessed on his return:

'Tonight the boys go to Nuremberg and are diverted to the South of England on return. They arrive there to find a clamp, so scatter to get in wherever they can, if they can for their fuel is by this time very low. At about 0500 a Halibag gets in here OK. At 0520 another Halibag tries but prangs.'

Crews that had already landed watched Halifax III LW478 LK-S piloted by 26-year old Squadron Leader Maurice McCreanor on 578 Squadron at Burn, which had dispatched eleven Halifaxes, coming in on three engines at the end of what was their fifteenth op but the visibility was poor and he could not line up with the runway. The control tower heard him say 'I'll try to come round again. I'll try to.' But McCreanor failed to see the masts of the Assisted Safe Landing equipment.

'By mere inches he misses the main hangar' continues Scholes 'clips the trees, goes straight through main stores and spreads all over the field beyond. I have never seen such a mess.' It tumbled and exploded across some playing fields for 200 yards. McCreanor, who was from Macclesfield in Cheshire and 23-year old Sergeant Alexander William McLennan the 'second dickey' of West Ewell, Surrey and five crew were either killed outright or died later. Pilot Officer Charles Albert Donovan the 27-year old flight engineer was from Stockport, Cheshire; Pilot Officer Thomas Arthur Evans the Welsh navigator was from Llanrhos, Caernarvonshire; Sergeant Alfred Donald Hooker the 19-year old rear gunner who came from Dunvanr, Swansea died of his wounds on 9 April. Sergeant Ronald John Maton the 23-year old wireless operator came from West Thurrock, Essex and Flight Sergeant Thomas Walton Thompson the 32-year old bomb aimer was from Annfield Plain, County Durham. Sergeant W. G. Mountford 'the mid-upper gunner' wrote David Scholes 'was the only one to come out alive. The crate broke in two just forward of the mid-upper. The forward end of the fuselage was absolutely shattered to match-wood. One wheel whipped across the ground some seventy yards, to crash right through a garage. Strangely enough there was not much fire. In any case there was nothing big enough whole to burn very well. It's a rotten shame to see this happen. Here's a bloke gone all the way to the target and back through very hell and because of someone's stupidity they all, bar one, are lost - and a good aircraft. These aren't the only ones tonight, a great number pranged I am told. In addition ninety-six are lost in combat - the greatest losses of Bomber Command for the war.[142]

At Burn there had been no word from Halifax MZ508 flown by Flight Sergeant Albert Edward Pinks of Barking, Essex. All of Pinks' crew, who were on their first operation, were dead. They had been on the squadron just five days. Flying Officer William Allison Dixon, the 21-year old navigator of Point de Bute, New Brunswick and the bomb aimer, Flight Sergeant William E. Sargent of New Hazelton, British Columbia, had been genuinely impressed with Pinks reassurance and support. The four others on the crew were Sergeant John Breaker, the 20-year old air gunner of Bordesley Green, Birmingham; Sergeant Patrick Alexander Esson, the 21-year old mid-upper gunner of Shottery, Warwickshire; Sergeant George Jack Low, wireless operator of Dundee, Scotland and Sergeant Allan Bretherton Norris, the 21-year old flight engineer of Bretheron, Lancashire.

Still tired, Joe Pawell's crew collected rail warrants and set off for London but the train broke down and they did not get there until 4 o'clock in the afternoon.

The RTO at the station contacted Snaith and got permission for the crew to stay overnight in London rather than travel on. The crew spent the night in luxury in the directors' quarters of Whitbread's Brewery where 'Nobby' Clarke's father was chef. Next morning, with a parting gift of five hundred cigarettes from Colonel Whitbread the crew set out again, this time from King's Cross where Stenning's wife had come to see him off after he had telephoned her. There were three other Nuremberg crews in the northbound train, all burdened with parachutes, Mae Wests, navigation and signals equipment and flying gear. The journey was uneventful until an inquisitive small boy accidentally pulled the ripcord of the parachute of the mid-upper gunner, Sergeant Wilf Matthews. 'Having bundled the canopy back into the bag and using his escape dagger to do it up, Wilf nearly cut his finger off,' Stenning said. 'The blood-stained parachute must have looked grim to the passers-by in the corridor.'

Flight Sergeant Len Pratt, the flight engineer on 'V for Victor' on 427 'Lion' Squadron RCAF had been concerned about fuel consumption. 'We got onto the two largest main tanks at some distance from the target area giving sufficient fuel to get us well out of trouble before having to change again. The overload was pumped over as soon as possible and was complete before we reached the target area. I remember thinking how miserable it looked. It was partially covered by cloud and there didn't seem to be many markers. The 'Master Bomber' called for 'backers up' and we were directed to bomb a differently coloured marker to that specified at the briefing. I think, in fact, it was the greens. There wasn't much flak over the target area. Our bombing run was reasonably successful as far as I know and we got the bomb load away without too much trouble. Leaving the target Clibbery turned sharply onto a leg to starboard. He then began to lose altitude rapidly so as to get the cover of the ground against possible fighter attacks as quickly as possible. Once out of the target area and down at a lower level I manipulated the fuel system controls, draining the nearly empty tanks and reserving fuel in four main tanks, one for each engine, for landing. I only remember one incident. We were up at about two to five thousand feet and ahead we saw some tracer exchanged. A little while later we passed very close to an aircraft burning on the deck. One could see some sort of building and trees in the glow of the fire.

'There was no moon on the way out to the coast from Nuremberg. Near Cologne 'Rex' Clibbery suddenly put the nose very sharply down into a dive. He shouted 'Didn't anybody see that boy?' and a FW 190 went from nose to tail over the top of us and carried straight on. We were then fully alert. I knew I was going to turn in another lousy log as my head had to be in the astrodome from now on. Norman Nash, at his H$_2$S set, was bawled at to get his head down in the nose (watching for fighters) and to stop 'playing navigators'. Aft of my station at the astrodome, Qualle's mid-upper turret was whizzing around to beat all hell. We had the sky pretty well divided up - Clibbery looked dead ahead; Nash, the navigator, looked underneath from the nose; 'Shorty' Martin scanned the rear upper and low quarters; Qualle, in the mid-upper, watched both sides; I took the two forward upper quarters; Jimmy Jardine the wireless operator covered underneath with 'Fishpond'. We saw tracer exchanged behind us and saw some aircraft catch fire. Then there was tracer ahead and on the port side. Aircraft started to burn and go down. A few miles on we saw aircraft burning on the ground, quite a few of them in fact. Someone said, 'Look at all those damn Jerry scarecrows'. Again this was wishful thinking. We decided to weave a bit and did the occasional corkscrew. This we did from time to time, right through to the target, particularly when things got quiet and we got that sort of feeling. We saw quite a few jettisoned loads of incendiaries. There were some fighter flares about - not too many, though - but I actually saw a Ju 88 drop right above us. It seemed almost as though it just missed and nearly hit our wing. More corkscrews. Between us we called several evasive tactics as we saw aircraft coming in close. I remember calling a couple nearer to the target area when things had darkened up a bit. We still saw what appeared to be aircraft burning on the deck.'

The enemy coast was re-crossed without trouble and Rex Clibbery made his way north across England to Yorkshire only to be diverted, because of fog, to Stratford. On their eventual return to Leeming - with Clibbery calling 'Hello Rosecreme'; 'Hello Rosecreme', this is 'Hold Tight'-'V-Victor', 'Hold Tight'-'V-Victor'. It seemed, by the empty dispersal pens and the familiar faces missing from de-briefing, that many other crews had also been diverted because of the fog which had cloaked Yorkshire.

So far as Len Pratt was concerned, Nuremberg was over. He went to sleep content in the knowledge that he had been able to achieve a 'pretty good' ratio of air miles per gallon.[143]

Three of the sixteen Halifaxes on 427 'Lion' Squadron were missing and 429 'Bison' Squadron had lost two, one of which crashed in the sea. Another was damaged. One of the missing 'Lion' Squadron aircraft was Halifax LW618 captained by 23-year old Flying Officer Walter McPhee. Outbound and south of track, LW618 was hit by cannon fire from a night-fighter and crashed at Hohenroth, three kilometres WSW of Bad Neustadt an der Saale. Warrant Officer Roy Bernard Beach, wireless operator from Toronto; Flying Officer Arthur Edgar Emil Gourdeau, 24, the American navigator from Vancouver, born in Germany of Polish parents and Flying Officer Douglas William Hammond, the 22-year old bomb aimer of Port Dover, Ontario; Pilot Officers Lloyd Mac Hawkes, rear gunner of Windsor, Ontario and Gerald Albert Hergott, mid-upper gunner from Waterloo, Ontario and Sergeant Alfred Thomas Williams, the flight engineer of Southwark, London are buried with their skipper in Hannover War Cemetery.

Pilot Officer John Moffat, Squadron Leader 'Turkey' Laird's rear gunner, who had counted twenty-two aircraft going down in as many minutes on the outbound trip, watched a solitary Halifax over the target. Suddenly, a Bf 109 'Wilde Boar' dived down to attack. The pilot was either wounded or he miscalculated. The fighter flew straight into the bomber, hitting it in the rear of the fuselage, tearing off the entire tail unit. Moffat saw the Halifax fall in a curious flat spin, its shattered tail end down and on the inside of the spin. It vanished from view. Twenty-four year old Pilot Officer Joe Corbally got his bombs away and Laird turned for home, the crew relieved to get away from Nuremberg. But twenty minutes later, Flying Officer William Ernest Paul 'Red' Soeder the navigator of Saskatoon, Saskatchewan who was on his 28th operation, reported that he had made an error in his calculations. He ordered a forty-five degree turn to port. 'Red' Soeder had celebrated his 26th birthday over Leipzig on 19 February. On the same date a year before, in celebrating his 25th birthday, he was guiding his Wellington aircraft on a raid to Wilhelmshaven. Now, 'Red' wondered whether he would ever be able to celebrate a birthday in the Mess, or at least on the ground, during the course of the war.

As Laird banked to the new course over the south-east corner of Belgium Lancaster ND776 flown by Flight Sergeant Eric Pickin on 622 Squadron emerged out of the darkness on a collision course. In an instant the Halifax and the Lancaster smashed into one another. In the tail turret, Moffat was at first unaware of the extent of the damage. He called the skipper but the intercom was dead. He looked about him. The rudder was on the right as it should be. But to the left ... nothing! And there was a large hole in the top of the fuselage near the tail turret. The clouds seemed to be revolving about the aircraft. With a shock, Moffat realized that the bomber was in a flat spin, just like the one he had seen over the target. He had great difficulty in getting his parachute as it was tangled with the tail control wires, which were all broken. The aircraft was a total wreck. Normally, he would have been occupying the mid-upper turret, which was crushed in the collision. Pilot Officer Lloyd Henry Smith RCAF of Sturgis, Saskatchewan was killed. Moffat was doubly lucky because by the time he pulled himself out of the turret and crawled forward to jump the Halifax was down to 1,000 feet, yet he survived. The doomed Halifax plunged into the ground near Rachecourt in Luxembourg.

Pickin, from Witney, Oxfordshire and his crew, who were on their 5th operation, were killed. Sergeant Raymond John Asplen, wireless operator from Ealing, Middlesex; Sergeant Gordon Robert Collins, mid-upper gunner of Stratford-on-Avon; Sergeant John Coup, rear gunner of Exeter, Devon; Sergeant Henry Frederick Page, flight engineer of Kingsbury, Middlesex and 32-year old Flight Sergeant Cleveland Julian Schmidt RAAF, bomb aimer of Eton, Queensland bailed out but one of them hit a tree and was killed. The bodies of the other three were found near their aircraft, their parachutes unopened. Warrant Officer2 John Percival Merritt the Canadian navigator from Saskatoon, had married Edna Doris a Hampshire girl from Cove near Farnborough only ten days previously.[144]

Jim Moffat was the only survivor from the two crews. Laird and the 'second dickey', 27-year old Flight Sergeant Arthur John Stainton of Peterborough, Ontario; 'Red' Soeder; Joe Corbally; Flight Sergeant William Paterson Clapham the wireless operator, who was from Filey, Yorkshire and Lloyd Smith were found in the wreckage and were laid to rest in Hotton War Cemetery. Flying Officer John Morrison DFC the 22-year old flight engineer of Stornaway, Isle of Lewis was found horribly injured hanging from a tree. He was to die three weeks later on 20 April at Arlon hospital and was buried with full military honours in the communal cemetery.

Moffat meanwhile, evaded capture. He and Sergeant William Jones on the crew of Flight Sergeant S. Hughes on 158 Squadron on Halifax LW634 were taken in by the Resistance and hidden in a house. But during a raid by about eighty German soldiers they were shot at as they jumped from a top floor window. Bill Jones was hit in the leg and apprehended. Moffat, who was not wearing his boots, got away. Jones was later tortured before finally being sent to Stalag Luft VII at Bankau in Upper Silesia. Albert Paul, their brave Resistance saviour, was later shot by the Germans. After many close shaves and fighting with the Resistance, Jim Moffat met up with the American advance and he was flown to England in September classified medically as 'suffering from malnutrition'.[145]

Halifax LV898 ZL-D skippered by Squadron Leader Jack Bissett, was the other flight commander's aircraft on 427 'Lion' Squadron that failed to return. Oberleutnant Martin 'Tino' Becker, Staffelkapitän 2./NJG6 had taken off from Finthen airfield near Mainz in a Bf 110 not yet fitted with 'Schräge Musik' on a 'Tame Boar' sortie. Eight nights earlier Becker had shot down six bombers when Frankfurt had been raided to take his total score to nineteen victories. He and his bordfunker Unteroffizier Karl-Ludwig Johanssen were eager to add to the score. Guided by 3 JD into the bomber stream to the south of 'Ida' they claimed the Halifax flown by Squadron Leader Jack Bissett south-west of Cologne. Pilot Officer William Churchill Hall the mid-upper gunner born in Bridgetown, Nova Scotia on 19 June 1918 was the first to report the night-fighter behind as Becker attacked 'von hinten unten'. Immediately, Flying Officer Robert Alfred Shannon DFM the Canadian tail gunner of Winnipeg announced on intercom that he had been watching it for some time. Becker slid across into his favoured final attacking position and fired two bursts into the Halifax in rapid succession before either of the gunners could react. 'D-Dog' reared up and climbed at a crazy angle for a few seconds and then slipped into a wild glide before turning over, its fuselage a mass of flames and crashing at Herhahn, four kilometres North-North-West of Schleiden. Bissett and his crew were killed. Bill Hall left a widow, Florence Louise Campbell who he had married on 16 December 1941. He and Sergeant Vincent Sydney Holloway of Slough, Bucks; Flying Officers Joseph Jacques Herman Gilde Guy LeClaire, wireless operator from Outremont, Quebec and 'Bob' Shannon; Warrant Officer2 Kenneth Frank Shoener, 2nd pilot of Toronto; Flying Officers Robert John White DFM of Perth, Ontario and Franklin Roy Zulauf DFM, air bomber of Milverton, Ontario were buried with their skipper at Herhahn. Since 1945 their bodies have been removed to Rheinberg War Cemetery.

While Johanssen was recording that Bissett's Halifax had hit the ground between Lüttich and north of Frankfurt, 'Tino' Becker, had seen the silhouette of a Halifax about 400 metres away and was already lining up LV857 MH-H2 on 51 Squadron flown by 21-year old Sergeant Jack Percival George Binder, who was from Moulton, Northants, as his next victim. Banking the 110 into an attacking position in 'Zahme Sau' fashion Becker kept Binder's Halifax in sight but for some quick glances in his immediate vicinity. It was clear of other aircraft so he closed in and opened fire. He saw a flush of orange flame smear along its starboard wing. Another arm of fire reached from its outer engine as the Halifax went out of control and titled into a shallow corkscrew dive. Becker swung the 110 round and from close range pumped another withering burst into the stricken bomber. The nose of the Halifax went down and plunged almost vertically to the ground south-east of Rosbach. Johanssen recorded that the Halifax hit the ground at 0023. As they looked down at the burning wreckage Becker and Johanssen saw six other bombers fall within seconds of each other. All of Binder's crew, who were on their third operation, were killed. Sergeant James Brear, flight engineer was from Doncaster; Flight Sergeant Walter Austin Guy, navigator came from Lancaster; Sergeant Frank Kasher, mid-upper gunner was from Crook, County Durham; Sergeant Basil Hughes Menary, rear gunner came from Lidget Green, Bradford;

Sergeant Edmund Joseph Paul Monk the 19-year old wireless operator was from Hove, Sussex; Warrant Officer Raymond Hathaway Wilson RCAF, bomb aimer came from Peachland, British Columbia.

Five kilometres north-east of Bad Hönningen at 0033 hours Becker and Johanssen picked out their third victim of the night. It was Lancaster 'T-Tare' on 50 Squadron at Skellingthorpe flown by Flight Sergeant Donald Gray. Soon after take-off Sergeant Bert Wright the wireless operator had discovered that his 'Fishpond' set was not working properly. Then the intercom connection to the rear turret was found to be faulty and Sergeant Doug Maughan, the rear gunner was given another helmet but Wright reported that Maughan was losing consciousness. By this time they were at 22,000 feet, skirting the edge of the heavy flak defences south of Aachen. Within a couple of minutes Wright reported that the flight engineer too, was unconscious. 'T-Tare' was now on course for Fulda, about ninety miles North-North-West of Nuremberg. Suddenly, Frank Patey the mid-upper gunner shouted that they were being attacked and he began firing. Becker set the starboard outer engine on fire. Within seconds of being hit the Lancaster, which was still carrying a 'Blockbuster', exploded over Waldbreitbach, a village in picturesque countryside, twelve kilometres east of the Rhine town of Sinzig.

Donald Gray had started to see fighter flares going down in front and burning aircraft falling. 'I could see it was going to be a right do and I suggested to Sergeant Joseph Grant the flight engineer, who was only a young lad, it was his job to go back with a portable oxygen bottle and see what he could do for Douglas Maughan who was suffering from poor oxygen supply. At that moment Frank Patey shouted 'Corkscrew port' and started firing his guns like mad. I corkscrewed away and the gunner told me the fighter had gone. I straightened up and Sergeant Bert Wright came forward and told me that Grant was also now unconscious apparently through oxygen failure. I thought, 'I'll have to go down to 10,000 feet, below oxygen height' and was just trimming for the descent when there was a bang and the Australian bomb aimer, Flight Sergeant George Wallis, said, 'We've been hit.' I looked across and the starboard wing was ablaze. I could see we were in a right pickle. I tried to feather a blazing engine, but I could see the wing was starting to go and I ordered, 'Bail out.' Then there was another bang. I felt a searing pain in my left knee from a piece of flak. Ignoring it I clipped my parachute pack onto my harness.

'Flight Sergeant Alan Campbell the navigator went flying past me and I was trying to hold on to the thing. I thought if I could close the petrol tank levers on the engineer's side I might cut down the flames. I picked up a chest parachute while I was there and put it on, then went back to my seat.'

Opening the bomb doors to dump the 4,000lb Cookie and the incendiaries, the crew were faced with a glaring light and a searing heat. It was then that Don Gray made the decision not to jettison the bomb load, in case it destroyed the aircraft when it hit the ground. It would also have the advantage of leaving next to nothing for German Intelligence. Then there was a massive explosion.

'There was a sudden 'whoof' and a bright light and then everything was black. I thought I was dead, but something was hitting me in the face. By some light in the distance I could see it was the parachute pack, so I pulled the ripcord. It was very quiet and I thought then I must still be in the aircraft. My arms were hanging down by my head so I pulled them down and they shot up again. Then I looked at the parachute open above my feet and I realised I was hanging upside down. I had slipped out of the harness and it was tangled round my ankles and I was coming down head first. By God, I panicked then. I assumed that when I undid my seat straps to operate the fire extinguishers I accidentally operated the release turnbuckle on my parachute harness. It was lucky I was wearing the old-type green canvas flying boots without the centre zip. They were very tight, unlike the brown suede type and it was like pulling a pair of Wellingtons on and off. I'm sure I would have just slipped out of my boots if I'd been wearing the zipped type. I thought about trying to bend myself like a trapeze artist and trying to grab the harness, but I had an Irvin jacket on and knew I wouldn't manage it. Instead I kept very still.

'Within a few moments there was a bump, a branch struck my face and I had hit the ground in a forest. I saved breaking my neck because it had been a snowy winter and the ground was soft in the wood. I tried to move my limbs and when I moved both legs the parachute harness came off. I think now that as I stood up to release my seat straps to go to the engineer's position I also turned the quick-release buckle on my parachute harness which I would normally do at the end of a flight, so that I could carry my harness out. When the chute opened the harness opened up, went through my legs and tightened up round my ankles. I just wasn't meant to be killed that night.

'In the first few minutes on the ground I couldn't straighten my neck properly and one leg hurt badly. I thought, 'This is a pickle, it'll take me at least three months to get back home and start flying again.' I started to walk westward and almost immediately came onto a road. I realised if I had landed on that I would have broken my neck. I climbed a fence and went across a field into a forest then found myself on a path with benches by the side like a beauty spot. I saw a train and made for it, but I was very groggy and tried to sleep. It was very cold and I think shock was setting in, so I set off down the road again and realised there were houses either side. I felt all-in but thought I could perhaps jump a train so I carried on.'

When Gray had given the 'Bail Out!' order Flight Sergeant Alan Campbell clipped on his parachute and left his navigator's compartment to make his way forward to the bomb aimer's position in the nose of the Lancaster. 'On passing the observation windows to the right of the pilot's seat it occurred to me that with luck the opportunity to observe an engine fire at night would never occur again, so I stood up and looked out. The starboard inner engine was certainly ablaze, a long tongue of flame, blue and changing to yellow, streamed from the cowling over the wing reaching almost to the tail of the aircraft, a truly astonishing sight. I quickly dropped down on all fours and crawled the few remaining feet to the top of the steps leading into the bomb aimer's compartment. In the dim light I could see Flight Sergeant George Wallis the bomb aimer was very actively trying to remove the bundles of 'Window' and forged German food coupons etc from the top of the escape hatch. Sighting me he commenced throwing them up to me and quickly cleared the hatch. The time was passing and I was very conscious of that engine and the 500-gallon fuel tank behind it. Wallis was having trouble though, the hatch refused to open and at about the same time he gave a hopeless, arms-outstretched sigh of failure there was a 'whoompf' and I felt myself propelled forward and down the steps. The landing was not soft. I had a sensation of pressure, flame, general disorientation and then nothing. My eyes opened... quiet, not a sound, no sense of motion. I was on my back and could see stars above me. I was not sure I was clear of the aircraft, but pulled the parachute handle anyway. Wonderful! The chute opened with a jerk. I gingerly tugged on the straps and felt the webbing was tight, looked up and in the moonlight could see that glorious great canopy billowing above me. I looked down, below and in front was the top of another parachute. Good, someone else was out.'

He landed in the quiet German countryside. The time by his watch was 0030. Campbell had a cut head, facial scratches, swollen right arm, sore knee and a painful kidney. His parachute was tangled in bushes and he gave up the task of getting it out of sight. He cut pieces off as souvenirs and headed west towards the Rhine. Then a figure loomed up. It seemed to Campbell that it must be a German farmer armed with a pitchfork. The Australian raised his hands, explaining that he was a navigator from a shot-down Lancaster the remains of which could be seen burning not far away. But the figure placed a hand on the navigator's shoulder and said: 'Don't panic, Al; it's me, George!' It was Wallis, who had escaped through the shattered nose after the explosion.

The two men headed for the Rhine, but two days later they were spotted and escorted to a police station in Neuweid on the east bank of the Rhine north of Koblenz. From there they too were sent to the Interrogation Centre at Dulag Luft and finally to Stalag Luft VI at Heydekrug on the Baltic where they arrived on Easter Sunday 1944 to await the end of the war and liberation.[146]

Sergeants Joe Grant, Bert Wright the wireless operator, Douglas Maughan the rear gunner and Frank Benjamin Patey the mid-upper gunner who had made a 'hash' of trying to repeat the main points of the briefing, were dead.[147]

Don Gray had attempted to negotiate a railway crossing but four torches had suddenly flashed out of the gloom and he was captured by four elderly armed members of the Volkssturm (Home Guard) armed with rifles. 'I put my hands up. I think they were more worried than I was, but they took me to the police station in Linz, south of Bonn'. Made to turn out his pockets and produce his identity discs, Gray saw that his watch had stopped at 0025 hours, the time of his landing. Led across a courtyard and put into a cell, he quickly fell asleep from fatigue. The following morning, under police guard, he was put in the back of a truck next to Flight Sergeant A. D. Hall RNZAF, the bomb aimer on Pilot Officer Garth Hughes crew who had been badly beaten up by a German policeman. Driven across the Ludendorff Bridge at Remagen to the town's police station an elderly policeman kept pointing to Gray's eyes. Walking over to the mirror he could see that in the middle of each huge, black eye was a hole filled with blood. The force of his landing must have burst the blood vessels in his eyeballs. At about 1700 hours a party of Luftwaffe personnel arrived to escort Gray and his companions in a lorry to the railway station to be put on a train for Dulag Luft at Frankfurt-am-Main. After six days in solitary confinement Gray was sent to Hohe Mark lazarette (hospital) and then to Stalag 9C Obermassfield PoW hospital, a multi-storey derelict factory. Then it was on to Meiningen PoW 'Convalescent home', an old opera house in a lovely town before he was taken into captivity.[148]

Becker and Johanssen's fourth kill, which followed at 0035 hours five miles northeast of Bendorf (FF 'Otto') was ED619, GI-T a 622 Squadron Lancaster III flown by 21-year old Pilot Officer John Sutton, who was from Newport on the Isle of Wight. 'T-Tommy' crashed at Mönchengladbach, five kilometres east-south-east of Wetzlar. Sutton and his crew, who were on their 12th operation, were killed. Flight Sergeant John Allen McClean the 21-year old navigator was from the Isle of Wight also, from Totland Bay. The others who died were Flight Sergeant Everitt Franklyn Jarvis of Sillery, Quebec the 34-year old mid-upper gunner, husband of Myrn Arioene Jarvis; Warrant Officer2 Daniel Joseph Laberge, Geraldton, Ontario the Canadian bomb aimer; Sergeant Percy Newman, Westbury-upon-Trym, Bristol the flight engineer, husband of Gertrude Lena Newman; Flight Sergeant Leo Earle Read of Erdington, Birmingham the 21-year old wireless operator; Sergeant Joseph Francis Richardson the rear gunner, of Falmouth, Cornwall. All were laid to rest in Rheinberg War Cemetery.

Unteroffizier Karl-Ludwig Johanssen checked the fuel gauges and warned 'Tino' Becker that he had enough fuel left to keep him airborne for one more kill but it would have to be a quick one. Minutes later, Becker scored his fifth victory of the night. It was LV822 MH-Z2, a Halifax on 51 Squadron, which was being flown by 20-year old Flight Sergeant Edward Wilkins RAAF, from Maleny on the Blackall Range overlooking the coastal hinterland in Queensland. Becker gave the Halifax a five-second burst and the wing wheeled up and tilted over. Johanssen logged its time of impact on the ground twelve kilometres west-north-west of Wetzlar as 0040 hours. All the crew, who were on their sixth operation, died. Sergeant Louis Robert Adams the wireless operator was from Shoreditch, London; Sergeant Allan James Bradshaw the 19-year old mid-upper gunner was from Toronto; the 21-year old Flying Officer William Kelso James the bomb aimer was from Corrie on the Isle of Arran; Flying Officer James Brown Marshall the Scottish navigator was from Glasgow; Sergeant Jack Nicholl the 33-year old rear gunner was from Bradford; Sergeant Louis Henry Wyness the flight engineer was from Wanstead, London.

Although Becker now had little fuel remaining Johanssen picked up a blip on his radar screen almost at once and quickly guided Becker to the Viermot ten kilometres northwest of Alsfeld. It was another 51 Squadron Halifax and it was MH-QZ, which was being flown by Flight Sergeant Graham G. Brougham RAAF. Becker framed LW544 in his sights and gave the Halifax a five-second burst and it crashed at Wahlen, four kilometres south of Neustadt (Hessen). Brougham, Flight Sergeant Ken Radley RAAF the wireless operator, Flying Officer Harry Bowling the flight engineer and Flight Sergeants Lloyd Peel and Arthur Henry Williams the two Australian gunners were killed. Flight Sergeant J. H. Gowland the Australian bomb aimer who with Sergeant H. Williams the flight engineer survived to be taken prisoner, recalled later: 'After the aircraft was hit the captain ordered 'prepare to abandon aircraft'. I left my position in the nose with the intention of warning the wireless operator. The aircraft began spinning before I reached him and I was thrown out of the escape hatch left open by the navigator. The engineer said that the pilot had ordered abandon aircraft but the developed spin was strong. When the engineer examined the wrecked aircraft next morning, five bodies were with the wreckage although the captain had been thrown clear but was dead.' All five were buried at a small village nearby named Wahlen near Neustadt.

Johanssen logged its time of impact on the ground as 0050. After returning to Mainz-Flinthen to re-fuel and re-arm, Becker and Johanssen took off on a second sortie, once more under Himmelbett control in Raum (Box) 'Käuz' ('Owl') on the bombers' homeward track. South of Luxembourg they destroyed LW634 'P-Peter', a Halifax III on 158 Squadron, which had been fired on over France by flak guns near Metz; 'P-Peter' crashed at Eischen, seventeen kilometres WNW of Luxembourg. Apart from the aforementioned Bill Jones, Flight Sergeant S. Hughes the pilot and three of his crew were also taken prisoner. The navigator, Sergeant Desmond V. Simmonds and Sergeant John McDougall the rear gunner evaded capture.

To the victor the spoils; next day 'Tino' Becker received news that he had been awarded the Ritterkreuz. 'There were such a lot of British bombers around that we could have knocked them down with a fly-trap' he said. He was decorated personally by the Führer at Hitler's HQ in East Prussia.

'Night-fighting' recalls Oberleutnant Helmuth Schulte of 4./NJG5,a Bf 110 pilot at Parchim, born in Giessen on 23 February1915, 'was not enjoyable. It was a most bitter experience that broke many nerves and had few survivors. We had to withstand much anxiety. This was due less to the fighting itself, which took place in the dark and in which we had a better chance, than to the need to fly in bad weather in conditions under which normally no man would set foot in an aircraft. Night-fighting was nerve-wracking; and the few who survived it had, above all things, flying skill and occasional luck.'[149] Night-fighting in anger, inspired by a feeling of hate or because a comrade had been killed in a bombing raid was not possible. In order to have any success and to stay alive it was essential that experience and concentration should be the first qualities in the flying, though it is true that the swashbuckling touch was often necessary as well. What was most important was to find the in-flying bomber stream - and in this the carefully-worked-out flight plan was vital. But very often it could only be worked out after take-off and even then it had to be altered. Also the business of getting the bomber into one's sights was often tedious. We sat well down under the bomber and then climbed slowly until we were within fifty to a hundred metres of it. Then I lined up and aimed between the two starboard engines. At the instant that I fired I would bank away to the left. Thus all the shots went from below into the fuel tanks of the bomber, which usually burst into flames immediately. Because we usually came from low down and from astern, we were rarely spotted by the British air-gunners and attracted no defensive fire. Being lower than the bomber, we could keep with it and observe it against the background of the night sky. If we managed to catch the head of the bomber stream, we used to hold back in order to more easily shoot down the waves of aircraft following.[150]

'Normally our biggest problem was to find the bomber stream, but on this night we had no trouble. I found the enemy at a height of 6000 metres [about 20,000 feet], I sighted a Lancaster and got underneath it and opened fire with 'Schräge Musik'. Unfortunately the guns jammed so that only a few shots put out of action the starboard-inner motor. The bomber dived violently and turned to the north, but because of the good visibility we were able to keep him in sight. I now attempted a second attack after he had settled on his course, but because the Lancaster was now very slow, we always came out too far in front. I tried the 'Schräge Musik' again and after another burst the bomber fell in flames.[151]

Schulte's victim was Lancaster LL704 piloted by Flight Sergeant Tom Fogaty on 115 Squadron. His crew in the last wave of the force had never seen so many aircraft going down. It seemed to Fogaty that the Bf 110s and Ju 88s had been waiting for them. But the Ruhr was behind them and they were now about fifty miles north-west of Mannheim at an altitude of 22,000 feet and thirty minutes from Nuremberg. But then it happened. Schulte fired a burst of cannon fire, which struck the Lancaster just as Sergeant E. A. Banham the rear gunner was shouting that his Skipper should corkscrew starboard. Fogaty at once flung the Lanc into a right hand dive. Sergeant V. B. 'Johnny' Dams the flight engineer who had been keeping a close eye on the engine gauges, exclaimed as he saw the oil pressure beginning to fall on the starboard inner. Clearly they had been hit in that engine which, without oil pressure would quickly overheat. Dams, having reported this and received Fogaty's instruction to feather the starboard inner pulled the feathering toggle and watched anxiously as the engine coughed out a stream of blue-grey smoke before spinning slowly to a stop. Fogaty had in the meantime learned that they had lost the night-fighter in their corkscrew manoeuvre and was bringing the Lancaster back on course, checking that no one had been hurt before trimming it to the heading on which it had been flying. There was an unhealthy smell of petrol and oil in the cockpit and when he checked his instrument panel he saw that the altimeter needle was falling steadily. Trimming the aircraft again, he fixed his eyes on the altimeter. They were losing height at the rate of 500 feet a minute: and the control column was sluggish and not responding as it should. In ten minutes they had lost 5,000 feet and the altimeter needle was still slicing back. Each additional minute was costing them a precious 500 feet in height. Fogaty thought that they were never going to reach Nuremberg. If they were to maintain any height at all they would have to jettison the bomb load.

Flying Officer J. Ferris the Canadian bomb aimer clicked down the bombing switches. If he had to jettison he would release the bombs live in the hope that they might hit something or someone. He called on Fogaty to open the bomb doors, confirmed that he had and pressed the bomb tit. That would release the photo-flash and lessen the risk of an explosion on board, he considered. Then he slammed the jettison bar across to clear any hang-ups. Fogaty knew that the bombs had gone when the control column kicked hard against his hands as the Lancaster ducked, freed from its load. He asked his navigator for a course to join the homeward track and began the turn. The Lancaster's rate of descent had been slowed to about 200 feet a minute by jettisoning the bombs; but its air-speed was also reduced as soon as it began heading into the high winds that had just been behind it. Fogaty swung them on to their new course and they were about 35 to 40 miles west of the target, maintaining a height of 15,000 feet, when the ground guns found them. They guessed it to be predicted fire for the heavy-calibre shells were bursting in neat groups around them, showering the night with a kaleidoscope of splintered ochre light. Shrapnel from the bursts rattled along the bomber's fuselage and it pitched and rolled in the blasts created by exploding shells.

After what seemed an eternity, although it was in fact only a few minutes, they were clear of the barrage and Fogaty asked his flight-engineer to check on what damage had been done. Dams made a quick inspection and reported nothing more serious than a few flak holes in the airframe. The bomber continued on three engines. It was now on its own - a solitary target which could be easily picked up by ground radar. Fogaty found that the controls were becoming increasingly difficult to handle and he was sure that something somewhere had been severed - but he had no idea what. Then, when they were 45 to 50 miles south-west of Stuttgart, something gave in the controls, the control column felt light and limp in Fogaty's hands and the bomber slipped into a shallow dive to starboard. Again the altimeter needle began to dip and the entire aircraft started to shudder in an alarming manner.

It was clear that far greater damage had been done to the Lancaster than had at first been thought. The altimeter showed that they were now down to 2,500 feet. They would never reach the enemy coast, let alone their base. There was only one solution. Fogaty called up his crew and told them to bail out. Ferris was the first to go. From the rear turret Sergeant E. A. Banham shouted that he was stuck. Pilot Officer 'Jock' Simpson the mid-upper gunner scrambled from his turret to go to Banham's assistance and made his way along the fuselage as the Lancaster skidded and lurched on its ever-quickening downwards course. Reaching the rear turret, he began to turn it manually so that Banham could escape and was rewarded with the thumbs-up sign from the rear-gunner, who then tumbled into space. Simpson slipped on his own parachute, informed Fogaty that the rear-gunner had safely bailed out and then made his own exit. Flying Officer P. H. Paddon the navigator and Sergeant 'Jack' Lomas the wireless operator followed him.

Only Fogaty and Dams were left. Fogaty glanced at the altimeter and saw that they were down to 1,000 feet. If they were going to jump at all, it would have to be now. He unfastened his safety harness and motioned to Dams to hand him his parachute. Dams was waving his arms and pointing under the pilot's seat, indicating that his own parachute had become jammed under the seat by their earlier evasive action. Fogaty's reaction was instantaneous. 'Quick,' he called, 'Take mine. There's no time to lose.' The flight-engineer hesitated, knowing that his pilot would be left with no means of escape. Fogaty shouted at him again to take the parachute and jump. Dams put Fogaty's parachute on and jumped clear at just under one thousand feet.

Alone in the doomed Lancaster, Fogaty knew beyond doubt that he now had no chance of getting out and with his safety straps undone even if he accomplished the seemingly impossible feat of a crash landing he would certainly be hurled from his seat on impact. It was bad enough to have to land a crippled aircraft on a well-lit home base with an engineer to operate the throttle levers while the gunner kept the tail down to make such an attempt single-handed in the middle of Germany in pitch blackness would be seemingly impossible. But what alternative was there? If this was to be the end, at least he'd go out trying. The sound of his own breathing came to him over the intercom as he peered through the canopy and tried to find out what sort of terrain he was coming down over; but it was too dark for him to make anything out. Fogaty somehow managed to keep the Lancaster fairly straight as he lowered full flap. At 500 feet he switched on his landing lights and saw the ground rearing in front of him. Earth and sky seemed to merge as he struggled with the now almost-useless control column. He caught a glimpse of an orchard blurring beneath him and a stamp-sized patch which might have been a field. Twenty feet from the ground, seeing what looked like a carpet of snow, he cut the engines, braced his wrists behind the control column and prayed. An overwhelming, jarring pain lanced through his forehead as an avalanche of roaring sound consumed the Lancaster and he had a vague sensation of floating in a vacuum of utter darkness. And then - nothing.

'When I came to,' recalls Fogaty, 'I was lying in the snow fifty yards from the aircraft. I vaguely remember seeing a small fire in one of the engines. There were several people who looked like farmers around me and they took me to a farmhouse about a hundred yards away. None of them could speak English and I could not speak German. I was very confused. I had a huge bump on my forehead, a grazed leg and was minus one of my flying boots. After a short wait at the farmhouse, I was taken in a van to the police station of a nearby town. I stayed, for what remained of the night, in a cell. The rest of the crew was brought in at intervals. The last to arrive was Jack Lomas. They were all surprised to see me - especially Johnny Dams. He couldn't believe that I had managed to land the Lancaster alone. The interrogating officer at Dulag Luft in Frankfurt later told me that I was shouting 'Voici...voici...' when I was found. Presumably, I must have thought I had landed over the French border.'[152] But though his commission came through while he was a PoW, Fogaty received no official acknowledgment from the Air Ministry for his courage in handing his parachute to a crew member and then going on to perform the fantastic and incredible feat of landing a crippled four-engined bomber single-handed in darkness and in unknown territory.[153]

Shortly after shooting Fogaty's Lancaster down, Unteroffizier Georg Sandvoss, Schulte's bordfunker, picked up a contact thirty kilometres south-west of Eisenach. It was the Halifax III on 640 Squadron at Leconfield flown by 20-year old Flying Officer James Dutton Laidlaw RCAF whose crew were on their 21st operation. Schulte blasted the Viermot with his oblique guns, which were now working again. Laidlaw, who was from Kamloops, British Columbia received terrible wounds to his legs and just had time to order his crew to bail out before he died. Sergeant Dennis George Cutler the flight engineer was either killed outright or mortally wounded. Flight Sergeant Frederick William Shuttle the navigator, also badly injured, fell across the forward escape hatch and prevented others using it. Flight Sergeant J. Henderson the wireless operator and the two gunners, Flying Officer J. Austen and Flight Sergeant K. A. Bush RAAF managed to leave by the rear hatch. They were taken prisoner. The bomb aimer, Flying Officer Martin Michael Corcoran RAAF from Canungra, a little town in the Scenic Rim region of South East Queensland, refused to leave the injured navigator. Although he had time to escape he was last seen by the side of his dying comrade.[154] The Halifax crashed and exploded near Wölferbütt, a village on the west bank of the Ochse just south of Vacha.

All told 640 Squadron lost three of its sixteen Halifaxes dispatched and three were damaged, with the loss of eighteen men killed and three taken prisoner. Apart from LW500 captained by Warrant Officer David Burke already mentioned, Halifax III LW555 C8-L skippered by 28-year old Flying Officer Charles Edward O'Brien who was from Toronto was shot down probably by Leutnant Hans Zettel of 12./NJG6 who claimed his victory as a 'Stirling' at Montabaur at 0035 hours. The skipper and his crew who were on their fourth operation were killed. Those who died were Sergeant Edmund Bake, the mid-upper gunner of Halifax, Yorkshire; Flying Officer Reginald Harvey Carleton, the Canadian navigator of Kingston, Ontario; Sergeant Eric Martin of Holywell, Flintshire the flight engineer; Sergeant Terence Christopher McFadden, the rear gunner of Wallsend, Northumberland; Flying Officer Ralph Douglas Van Fleet the Canadian bomb aimer of Hamilton, Ontario; and Sergeant Arthur Levett Wangler of London the wireless operator. Zettel was killed in a crash on 24/25 April 1944 when he hit trees on landing at Halle-Nietleben airfield.[155]

Wing Commander Dudley Forsyth the Commanding Officer of 466 Squadron RAAF and the crew on 'J-Jig' returned safely to Leconfield after a flight lasting eight and a quarter hours. It had been 'absolutely free of trouble or incident' and could recall no real damage to any aircraft. He believed that the force's troubles began when quite a number of aircraft bombed the wrong target. After some time on the southerly leg of the course down to Nuremberg, he commented to his crew that he could see the target with an attack developing 30° to starboard. Warrant Officer Wooton his navigator was quick to reply that this could not be Nuremberg. He was quite certain of his position, the aircraft was right on track and there were some minutes to go before reaching the target. As Forsyth flew on south it was obvious that 'a not inconsiderable number' of aircraft were involved in attacking the wrong target. 'The effect was that the aircraft immediately turned onto a westerly heading for home.' he said. 'Thus the force was spread over a very wide area of Germany thus reducing considerably its strength and safety. The offending aircraft also doubtless flew over heavily defended areas instead of along the planned 'safe' track home.'

Endnotes Chapter 14

141 Adapted from *Aircraft Maintenance* by Ray Meredith and *Ops Are On Again Tonight in Thundering Through The Clear Air; No. 61 (Lincoln Imp) Squadron at War* by Derek Brammer (Toucann Books 1997).

142 *Air War Diary; An Australian in Bomber Command* by David Scholes DFC (Kangaroo Press 1997).

143 Quoted in *The Nuremberg Raid* by Geoff Taylor.

144 *The Nuremberg Raid* by Martin Middlebrook.

145 See *RAF Evaders: The Comprehensive Story of Thousands of Escapers and their Escape Lines, Western Europe, 1940-1945* by Oliver Clutton-Brock (Grub Street 2009).

146 *The Long Road* by Oliver Clutton-Brock.

147 Adapted from *Bail Out* by Paul Hutchinson, (Marshall Cavendish Ltd 1974)

148 *The Long Road* by Oliver Clutton-Brock.

149 *The Bombing of Nuremberg* by James Campbell (Futura 1973).

150 *The Bombing of Nuremberg* by James Campbell (Futura 1973).

151 Quoted in *Sky Battles! Dramatic Air Warfare Actions* by Alfred Price (Arms & Armour Press 1993).

152 Fogaty had crash-landed at Raidwangen, 4km southwest of Nürtingen. A second 115 Squadron Lancaster was lost when LL622 piloted by Flight Sergeant Ron Thomas of Redruth, Cornwall strayed 115 miles north of track on the homeward leg and was shot down by Feldwebel Hans Zeidler of 7./NJG1, crashing at Chimay, 5km SW of the historic battlefield at Waterloo. All the crew, who were on their first operation were killed.

153 Adapted from *The Bombing of Nuremberg* by James Campbell (Futura 1973).

154 See *The Nuremberg Raid* by Martin Middlebrook. (Allen Lane 1973).

155 From research by Theo Boiten.

Chapter 15

The fourteen Lancasters on 61 Squadron were experiencing varied fortune. It was normal for the gunners to report to the navigator when they saw an aircraft go down and give such details as to whether they saw any bail out, if it was flak, or if a fighter. On this occasion there were so many going down that Sergeant Len Whitehead's Skipper told them not to report, just concentrate on looking out for and avoiding attacks. 'It was difficult not to look at those going down' he recalls 'but we knew we had to keep a careful watch. We would sometimes see some tracer fire and then a small flame which would quickly grow until it lit up the whole aircraft and then frequently would finish with a terrific explosion. Sometimes we were rather puzzled because we did not see any tracer fire and no flak; just the aircraft catching fire. It was not until years later that I learned that it was of course 'Schräge Musik'. When using this no tracer was present so that it did not give away the form of attack. When an aircraft went down, or jettisoned the bombs, there would be a long line of incendiaries burning with bright silver and further illuminating the aircraft above.'[156]

Near Cologne 'R-Robert' flown by Pilot Officer Donald Paul passed night fighter-beacon 'Ida' and ran into German fighters. His navigator, Flight Sergeant Ron Griffin came out of his position, looking out he saw above them two German single engine fighters wing tip to wing tip about 100 feet above. 'They wizzed over our heads and disappeared. Then they attacked.' One, a Ju 88, pulled away above them. He then saw a stream of bullets going straight into its belly but with no apparent effect. They fought off two more attacks in the next fifteen minutes but finished up at 10,000 feet with two engines stopped. Paul McGibney and Stan Billington claimed two German fighters damaged and one probable. Don Paul decided to get rid of the bombs and turned back. Griffin said: 'Against a strong wind with two engines out we made 80 knots over the ground so we set course for the emergency airfield at Woodbridge, Suffolk. We opened up the rear door and threw out everything we could move: guns, ammunition, parachutes, but we continued to lose height and thought we would have to ditch. Then over to our left we saw the lights of Manston. Don Paul said simply: 'going straight in' and put her down first time. We were a bit shocked and had stiff brandies before we went to bed. Next morning I woke up and looked out of the window. It was like a graveyard. There were smashed and burnt out aircraft all over the place'.

Shortly before midnight, Hauptmann Fritz Rudusch of 6./NJG6 flying a Bf 110 shot down the 'Old Sweats' on Lancaster 'P-Peter' flown by Squadron Leader Ted Moss DFC near Rimbach, north-west of Fulda. All seven crew died. 'P-Peter' was Rudusch's first victory. He scored his second Abschuss just over an hour later. Halifax HX241 EX-P on 78 Squadron flown by Flight Lieutenant Harry Hudson was approximately thirty kilometres north of the planned route at Allendorf (now Stadtallendorf) near Bad Kissingen when Rudusch attacked from end to front. The Halifax was already burning as it approached the village from the west, circled once and broke in half before crashing with a full load of bombs on the premises of a chemical factory. 'Scouse' Nugent was the only man to bail out before the bomber crashed and was soon taken prisoner in Allendorf.

'I realized the plane was doomed and in all probability the rest of the crew were already dead. I was on my knees becoming weaker and weaker without oxygen and started to feel for the escape hatch situated mid-way between my own turret and the rear turret. Next thing I knew was that I was hard up against the rear turret. I had no control over my actions but something guided me back and unwittingly my hand felt the door handle. One twist and I was out, spinning through the air like a top. I didn't need to jump - the air rushing past plucked me out like a mammoth vacuum cleaner picking up a fragment of dust.'[157]

German radar search equipment was proving very efficient and with it up to about four young and inexperienced crews could be directed into the bomber stream by older and more experienced night-fighter crews. According to Oberst im Generalstab Janke, deputy commander and chief of staff of 7 Jagddivision, 'This equipment was used with much success by NJG6, who apart from 'Tino' Becker accounted for about nine heavies on the Nuremberg raid.

NJG2 in 3 JD were equipped with the newer and faster Ju 88R-2 and had taken off from Quakenbrück at 2341 hours with orders to patrol west of the Ruhr on a southerly heading. When almost at Aachen Oberleutnant Günther Köberich with Oberfeldwebel Walter Heidenreich as bordfunker and Oberfeldwebel Kramell as bordschütze, picked up on FuG 350 'Naxos Z' passive radar equipment, a contact five kilometres distant. It was the first time that Köberich, who had a dozen victories, had flown the R-2 and the aircraft was one of the first to be fitted with 'Schräge Musik'. Nearing Mainz at an altitude of 6700 metres there was a shout of '*Lancaster! Lancaster!*' from Köberich and Kramell. Almost dead ahead and slightly above them were two Lancasters flying in tight formation. The night-fighter crew knew that they must be Path Finders. Both were on 156 Squadron. Köberich flew under the left hand Lancaster (ND476 GT-V) and blasted the bomber's port wing with his side cannon from eighty metres range. Captain Finn Johnsen, a Norwegian from Bergen who had joined the squadron as a 2nd Lieutenant on 7 February and all his crew including the rear gunner, Sergeant Rolf Gunnar Karsman who was from Oslo, were killed.[158] The others who died were Sergeant Hugh McLauglin Donnelly the mid-upper gunner from Bellshill, Lanarkshire; Sergeant Kenneth Gardiner the wireless operator of Horfield, Bristol; Pilot Officer Charles Grant Leatherdale the Canadian bomb aimer from Toronto; Sergeant Stanley McConnell from Southport, Lancashire; Flight Sergeant William Patrick Heremon O'Neill the navigator from Alresford, Hants. The crew were on their 25th operation. Flying Officer Gordon Elmy of Whitstable, Kent who was on his 'second dickey' trip was also killed.

Köberich then flew crabwise under the second Lancaster (ND406 GT-S) skippered by 27-year old Warrant Officer John A. 'Jack' Murphy from Parramatta, a suburb of Sydney which also gave its name to the type of marking by the Path Finders. He and his crew had joined 156 from 101 Squadron on 19 January as part of the flood of replacements that poured in during that month and were now on their nineteenth operation of their second tour. 'We acted quickly and the slanting cannons spoke again' reported Walter Heidenreich. 'Blitz fast there was a repetition of what had happened only a few seconds earlier. Now we saw two burning bombers flying side by side, still on their original course. We took up position 300 metres to the starboard of them and flew a parallel course. Number One Lancaster dipped towards the left and Number Two to the right, to crash north and south of the Rhine with mighty explosions. Even at our height it was light as day for a second or so. We logged these shoot-downs at 0046 hours and 0047 hours. We did not notice any of the crews bail out, although to us there was plenty of time for them to have done so because our cone of fire went into the wings. The crash-points were visible visiting cards. Cascades of technicolored Christmas trees burned on the ground for a long time, showing beyond doubt that they were Path Finders; and it was especially rewarding to have got a pair of them so quickly. We believed we had intercepted the spearhead of the enemy bomber formation but despite intensive searching we did not pick up any other targets on our radar. In reality, we had caught two delayed Path Finders.'

Warrant Officer George Robert Newton Wood, the Australian mid-upper gunner on 'S-Sugar' from Bexley in southern Sydney had seen the other Lancaster and Murphy had headed the same way as 'V-Victor' and maintained station with them. It was known as 'going hand in hand'. Sergeant Lawrence W. Woolliscroft the wireless operator, a veteran of 42 operations, was in the astrodome taking a sextant shot for Flying Officer Irving John Toppings the 23-year old navigator from Inchkeith, Saskatchewan and could see by reading the fuselage letters in the moonlight that the other aircraft was from their squadron, but did not know who. 'S-Sugar' was flying at 24,000 feet and as most attacks occurred between 15,000 and 20,000 feet the crew thought that they were safe there, but someone called on the intercom, 'Bandits to starboard.' Woolliscroft saw that there was an aircraft just below. At first it was thought that the night-fighter was going to ignore them, so Murphy shoved 'Sugar's height up a little further but he began firing from the rear, just missing the Lancaster. Toppings pulled at Woolliscroft's clothing and told him to put his chute on. Woolliscroft had just put his chute on one hook of his chest harness when 'Sugar' exploded. The night fighter's cannon must have hit the bombs. Woolliscroft came to and found he was falling at speed with his chute pack half attached. 'It was absolute terror' he recalled. 'It was obvious I wasn't going to survive and I thought, 'How will my family find out about this?' I decided to close my eyes and just pray. I thought, 'I'm going to hit the ground then I shan't know anything.' I like to think that what happened then was due to praying. I had pulled the ripcord without realising it and found myself falling sideways with the chute above. Because I was sideways on I saw another parachute above me. I landed in some trees and was being dragged along the top, so released myself from the chute and fell about ten feet to the ground.'

Woolliscroft was the only member on 'S-Sugar' who survived, being thrown clear as the Lancaster crashed at Holzweiller and exploded. He was on the run for four days until exhausted, he gave himself up. The others who were killed were Sergeant John Baldwin the flight engineer from Sutton Coldfield, Warwickshire; Sergeant Harold Leslie Hepworth of Huddersfield, Yorkshire, the rear gunner and Flight Sergeant Arthur Charles Kendrick the bomb aimer of Woodford, Essex.

With fuel running out, Köberich landed at Kassel-Rothweston. It was to be the last operation for the German crew. A week later, on 8 April - Easter Sunday - B-17s attacked their base at Quakenbrück and laid seven carpets of bombs. Köberich, who on 1 April had been promoted to Staffelkapitän, was among the dead and Kramell was wounded. Heidenreich, who had gone on leave an hour before the attack, returned to duty as the victims of the raid were being laid out in a long row in the market-place of Quakenbrück to await burial.

Out of 110 Path Finders, twelve failed to return, four of them at Upwood, which sustained the highest loss rate of the PFF squadrons, although Oakington and Downham Market each lost three Lancasters.[159] Apart from the two crews on 156 Squadron already mentioned; Pilot Officer L. Lindley and his crew on ND492 GT-L who were on their nineteenth operation were shot down by a night-fighter flown either by Leutnant Hermann Leube of Stab II./NJG3, who claimed a 'Lanki' 20-30 kilometres southeast of Bonn at 0029 for his twelfth Abschüsse or Unteroffizier Lorenz Gerstmayr of 4./NJG3 who claimed a '4-mot' southeast of Bonn, also, at 0038 for his twelfth victory too. Lindley was the only survivor. His crew included the wireless operator, Sergeant John Esprey Bates, a southern Irishman from Dublin and the bomb aimer, Sergeant Bankole Beresford Vivour, a 24-year old Nigerian who resided in Liverpool. The others who died on 'L-London' were: Sergeant Dennis Bertram Bloomfield of Clacton, Essex, the rear gunner; Pilot Officer Norman Thomson Edmondson the 20-year old mid-upper gunner from Brantford, Ontario; Sergeant Ronald Thomas Harper, the flight engineer of Dagenham, Essex and Flying Officer John Waite Henry the navigator, from Newcastle upon Tyne.

The pilot of ND466 GT-Z, a PFF Visual Backer-up Lancaster, Squadron Leader Philip R. Goodwin, who had come to Warboys early in January after a period as an instructor at 23 OTU, was on his seventeenth operation of his second tour (his 47th operation). He had been married for just six weeks. Goodwin had just started his bomb run when a night-fighter's long burst of cannon fire caused 'Z-Zebra' to burst into flames and killed Warrant Officer Victor Gardner DFM the rear gunner who was from Harrogate. The mid-upper gunner, Warrant Officer John Charles Baxter DFM of Camberwell, London, Flying Officer Herbert Charles Frost the wireless operator of Northampton and the 27-year old Australian flight engineer Pilot Officer Cyril Ashley Rose of Penrith in Sydney died in the aircraft also. Cyril Rose was born on 19 February 1917 in Bellingen, New South Wales and enlisted in the RAAF in Sydney.

The skipper ordered Flying Officer Wilfred Coombes Isted DFM the visual-marker-bomb aimer to dump the bomb load but not the TIs in case they confused the following bombers. Goodwin was pressed flat against the roof of his cockpit watching the trees and snow on the ground revolving as the Lancaster spun down from 18,000 feet. Luckily, he was wearing a seat-type parachute for the first time on operations. When the aircraft broke up Goodwin and Isted and Flying Officers E. H. J. Summers, navigator and Jack Vincent Scrivener the Canadian bomb aimer on the eight man crew were out before it was too late.

'We were flying straight and level' wrote Scrivener 'and then, suddenly, there was a horrendous explosion in the front of the aircraft, blowing out the Perspex glass that covered the navigators and the pilot and the flight engineer, creating a big hole in the side of the aircraft, igniting the starboard, or right inner engine and the aircraft immediately began to go out of control. The plane whipped over in an inverted spin and started heading toward the ground 20,000 feet below. Suddenly, I found myself in total darkness. I was lying on the ceiling of the aircraft, but I had had enough time to reach down and pick up a chest pack, parachute pack and clip it on. I only had time to clip it on to one lug, but that was sufficient. Then, about that time, the aircraft actually blew up. It had caught fire, the fire had spread toward the rear of the aircraft and suddenly, I found myself outside the aircraft, falling through space. And I thought for a while that I had actually passed over, I was on the other side, because everything was airy-fairy. It was very pleasant. It was very cool. Of course, I was falling through space, you know, at 22 feet per second and I didn't realize for a while that I was still alive. I really thought that I had passed on and just during that period I saw my entire family sort of go before my eyes. Well, this carried on for only seconds because I was falling at a great speed toward the earth.

'Fortunately, the height was such that I could fall quite a way without hitting the ground. And it was only at about 5,000 feet that I came to and realized that I was still alive and that I might be able to do something about it, if I could pull the ring on the parachute pack, open the parachute and that way save my life. Well, that's exactly what happened. I found the ring, I pulled it. At first nothing seemed to happen and then I saw a great white canopy above me. It was a half moon that night so I wasn't in total darkness and there was snow on the ground below. At this point I was at about 5,000 feet. I know that altitude because I am a climber by interest, mountain climber, and I know what it looks like from 5,000 feet to the ground. And I came down. I landed in a clearing surrounded by pine forest in the province of Thuringia. I lay on the ground for a few minutes. I was unhurt, not even any scratches and I thought that about five hours ago I was sitting in the comfortable mess in an upholstered leather chair after a wonderful meal of bacon and eggs and here I was lying on the ground in eastern Germany on the Czechoslovak border, surrounded by the enemy, virtually 500 miles from anywhere really.'

The wreckage of the aircraft came down at Eisfeld, a small town on the East bank of the Werra, nineteen kilometres NNW of Coburg. Eleven of the Lancasters from Upwood landed at other aerodromes on returning from Nuremberg.

Oberleutnant 'Dieter' Schmidt, Staffelkapitän, 8./NJG1 took off from Laon-Athies and led his Bf 110s to radio-beacon 'Ida'. Schmidt was surprised even to have been ordered off in such bright moonlight and he could not help but think that it was a false alarm. But come they did.

'…Suddenly we are in the middle of them…course 120 to 150°. Ack-ack fire…Recognition signal. One shot down! Another! All the time more of them. I see one right in front of me. With my second burst of fire all I get is a miserable 'bum-bum'. The guns have jammed. I turn off course, change the magazines and test them again. Some go off but two cannon are completely out of action. My target has gone. Around us it is raining shot-down aircraft. Someone behind me. Swing away…to the right ack-ack is bursting furiously. All hell is let loose. Everywhere explosions and air-to-air trace. Everywhere aircraft and bombs falling… a night the like of which I have never known. 0045 hours, 5700 metres. Attention! One on the left, 300 to 200 metres. Colossally huge, it flashes by us and I almost ram him. We wheel to the right, pull up to him …100 metres, he twists…even better target. I keep him just ahead, framed in my sights. Fire! He swings starboard and slides through my cone of fire. Immediately flames sweep along his fuselage and pour from his starboard inner engine. That should be enough. I come right past him. See it's a Halifax. He shoots back. I pull away and see the cockade and the recognition marking 'NP'. Then he is behind to the left, diving down. He hits the ground at 0049, somewhere about fifty to 100 kilometres north-west of Würzburg …in the mountains.'

'Dieter' Schmidt examined his Bf 110 after landing at Langendiebach and found to his horror some human hair and flesh stuck to the port propeller boss of the aircraft after shooting down the Halifax. His eighteenth Abschuss (and 16th confirmed victory) of the war was possibly a 76 Squadron Halifax III at Holme-on-Spalding Moor, three of which shot down by night-fighters. LW628 'J-Johnny' skippered by Flight Lieutenant R. J. Bolt which limped home with the starboard inner engine out of action and fuel disappearing fast from a broken fuel pipe, had no hope of making it back to Holme-on-Spalding Moor. Pilot Officer Fred P. G. Hall DFC the navigator had never seen so many aircraft attacked, on fire and falling or so many attacks by fighters so early in a trip. Hall had lost his original crew in a tragic air test crash in November 1943. 'I felt sure that my 26th trip was going to be my last' he said. 'I had made my first trip of eight hours to Nuremberg on 27 August 1943. My 26th was rather more spectacular. We were in the last wave and fighters were seen to be up in strength as we crossed the Rhine. Aircraft were continually falling out of the sky on fire and I gave up logging them. One minute after leaving the target we were shattered as cannon fire suddenly hit us from underneath putting the starboard inner engine out of action. The navigation table was covered in debris, the wireless set hit, the starboard wing, bomb bay and fuselage on fire. The pilot dived twice to put out flames and we all tackled the fires with extinguishers, eventually successfully. As if this was not enough, twelve minutes later we were approached by a fighter from dead astern, but we took evasive action and he passed fifty yards over the tail receiving full blasts from both gunners.

'We made straight for the nearest part of the French coast. We crossed the Channel safely and headed for Ford, but this airfield was full of circling aircraft so we continued on to Tangmere. The engineer had to take an axe to the undercarriage up lock housing to manually release the jammed starboard leg. We landed, but swung off the runway as the tyres were burst. A fuel check after landing showed that we had only five minutes fuel remaining.

The Squadron Engineer flew down from Holme on Spalding Moor the following morning to confirm that the aircraft was beyond repair; indeed, he couldn't understand why the starboard wing had not folded. But our only injury was when the wireless operator discovered his cigarette case had been flattened by a cannon shell and he had a bruise on his right hip!

Hall and Bolt were awarded immediate DFCs. 'J-Johnny' was written off.

Almost all the confirmed Abschüsse on the outward route were achieved by twin-engined 'Tame Boars'. Many a 'Zahme Sau' crew achieved multiple victories: Leutnant Hans Schäfer of 7./NJG2 and his regular crew of Unteroffizier Heinz Manter, bordfunker and Obergefreiter Karl Gliebmann, bordmechaniker who had taken off from Twente in Ju 88 R4+BR at 2321 hours in search of their first Abschuss, destroyed two Lancasters and a Halifax before landing back at Twente again at 0149 hours. They shot down their first Lancaster twenty kilometres south-east of Bonn, east of LFF 'Ida' at 0017 hours. At 0024 their second victim - probably ND711 'C-Charlie' on 635 Squadron - flown by 23-year old Flight Lieutenant Hugh Julian Langdon Webb of Beaconsfield, Buckinghamshire fell ten kilometres northwest of Giessen on the extended outward leg. All the crew, who were on or around their twentieth operation were killed. Sergeant Leslie Valentine Norton the flight engineer of Brandon, Suffolk; Flying Officer Charles Edward Peake, the 34-year old navigator, husband of Jessie Annetta Peake, of Freemantle, Southampton, and Flying Officer

James Puver, bomb aimer of Nottingham and Sergeants Clifford Edward Robert Fox, 22 year old wireless operator of Caister, Norfolk, Edward Robert Reginald Moulding, 20-year old mid-upper gunner of Debden, Essex and William Lindsay the 21-year old rear gunner of Dundee, Angus were laid to rest with their skipper in Rheinberg War Cemetery.

Schäfer's third Abschuss, which he shot down at Vogelsberg at 0054 and which crashed on an airfield near Giessen was possibly Halifax ME624 'X-X-ray' on 166 Squadron flown by 22-year old Flight Sergeant Roy Barton Fennell of Bromham, Wiltshire whose crew were on their 13th operation. Sergeants William George Sydney Pettis the 20-year old flight engineer and William James Allan RAAF the 22-year old rear gunner of Murrumbeena, a suburb of Melbourne and Flight Sergeants James Smyth the 29-year old navigator of Moneynick, County Antrim; Douglas Venning Harvey RAAF the wireless operator of Oberon, in the central tablelands of New South Wales and Albert Patrick Jones the 21-year old Scottish mid-upper gunner of Aberdeen, were killed. Flight Sergeant W. J. C. Keigwin the bomb aimer was the only survivor.

Schäfer noted in his Flugbuch that his first two adversaries put up a very weak defence, but that he was subjected to 'very strong defensive fire' from his third victim. These were the crew's first three confirmed victories; all were officially 'anerkannt' by the Reichsluftfahrtministerium (RLM or Reich Air Ministry) on 24 June, as their Staffel's 9th-11th confirmed kills since it was re-formed in July 1943.[160]

Also, 166 Squadron lost the Lancaster (ND798) flown by 20-year old Pilot Officer Walter Henry Burnett of Stanmore, Middlesex to another night fighter flown by Unteroffizier Johann 'Hans' Werthner of 7./NJG2 ten kilometres south of Eitorf.[161] Most of the crew (excepting Pilot Officer V. W. R. Park the 'second dickey') were on their sixteenth operation. They never saw the fighter and the rear turret was disabled in the first pass. Subsequent passes set the engines on fire. Burnett, whose older brother Flight Lieutenant Norman Whitmore Burnett was killed on 11 June 1941 serving on 46 Squadron in the defence of Malta, ordered everyone to bail out. He kept the aircraft steady while five men including the injured flight engineer, who was thrown out by the navigator, evacuated the aircraft safely and they were taken prisoner. Sergeant Peter Henry Brown the mid-upper gunner of St. Giles, Cambridge stayed to help Sergeant Frank Storer the rear gunner of Blackpool, Lancashire. It is believed that Burnett, knowing that they were still on board, elected to ride the aircraft in. All three died.

On the night of 1/2 January 1945 Feldwebel Werthner, now of 10/NJG3 and who had six Abschüsse, was shot down in a Ju 88G-6 by Mosquito NF.XIII HK526/U flown by Flight Lieutenants R. J. Foster DFC and M. F. Newton DFC on 604 Squadron in 2nd TAF. Werthner was the only one who could escape by bailing out and he was taken prisoner. His funker Unteroffizier Gerhard Hoppe and bordmechaniker Unteroffizier Franz Ofenschiesst were killed.

A fourth Lancaster on 166 Squadron, flown by Flight Lieutenant Gordon Arbuthnot Proctor, a Londoner from Clapham Common was shot down by a night fighter either by Leutnant Günther Wolf of 9./NJG5 or Feldwebel Klaus Möller of 12./NJG3, both of whom claimed a 'Lanki' at 0045 in the Fulda area[162] and crashed 400 metres southeast of Michelsrombach with the loss of all seven crew, who were on only their second operation. Flying Officer Peter Legard of Heworth, York who was on his first trip as a 'second dickey' was killed also. So too Flight Sergeant Lloyd Archibald Ferguson the 28-year old Canadian bomb aimer from New Glasgow, Nova Scotia and Sergeant Henry Longton the flight engineer, who had been given an all-clear by the MO at the last minute and wanted to fly on the trip 'if Sidney Lipman had no objection'. Flying Officer Douglas Berry McIntosh the Scottish wireless operator of Jedburgh, Roxburghshire; Sergeant Gerald Thomas Wilfred Reynolds the rear gunner of Plymstock, Devon and Flight Sergeants Geoffrey Wilfred Trodd the navigator of Harrow-on-the-Hill, Middlesex and Peter Frank Walker the mid-upper gunner of Kingston-on-Thames, Surrey also died.

Oberleutnant Günther Lomberg of 1./NJG6 flying a Bf 110, who had one victory, a '4-mot' near Frankfurt on 18 March, added his second and third Abschüsse, claiming a 'Lanki' between Klofeld and Bockeroth at 0021 and a Halifax, possibly LW724 NP-'S for Sugar' on 158 Squadron which crashed at Herbon-Seelbach. The skipper, 27-year old Flight Sergeant Eric Ronald Fergus MacLeod RAAF of Townsville on the north-eastern coast of Queensland and five of his crew were killed. Flight Sergeant James Arthur Nicholson the 22-year old mid-upper gunner was from Ainslie, Australian Capital Territory. Sergeant Louis James Craven the flight engineer was from Harrogate, Yorkshire. Flight Sergeant Ernest Roy Moore the 22-year old navigator of Bateman's Bay, NSW; Flight Sergeant Douglas Fitzgerald Bickford, the 22-year old rear gunner, from Gordon on the Upper North Shore of Sydney and Flight Sergeant Leonard Gower Paxman, the 26-year old wireless operator from Naremburn, were killed. Flying Officer Anthony Shanahan the bomb aimer of Mascot, a suburb of Sydney, who was flying his first operation managed to escape by parachute. 'We were attacked at 20,000 feet and a fire broke out. The order to bail out was given and I was just about to leave when I felt a violent blow to my head' he wrote. 'The events of the next few days are somewhat hazy, but I fear the rest of the crew are dead.' Sadly, Shanahan's head injuries led to his death after the war.[163]

Twenty-five-year old Leutnant Hans Meissner of 2./NJG3, who had fourteen Viermots to his name, had taken off from Vechta in his Bf 110C and had steered a course straight for the spearhead of the bomber force. Northwest of Frankfurt-am-Main his bordschütze picked up a contact on his radar set and gave Meissner a bearing. The German pilot saw the exhaust fires of a Viermot in the distance and gave chase immediately. It was a Lancaster. Almost immediately the bordschütze got another contact. The second bomber was also a Lancaster and Meissner spotted it about 1000 metres ahead. Mentally he noted its position and then concentrated on the first Lancaster. From a distance of 150 metres and fifty metres below, Meissner coolly blasted the Lancaster with a burst of his fixed forward guns. He pushed the stick forward and slapped on left rudder as four steams of tracer hosed from the rear turret of the doomed Lancaster to ship past somewhere to his left. His steep turn once again brought the burning aircraft into his sights but Meissner was now ready to attack the second Lancaster, possibly the 97 Squadron Path Finder Blind Backer-Up piloted by Flight Lieutenant Leonard Victor Hyde DFC whose crew was on their 29th operation. Alerted by the German's attack on the other Lancaster, Hyde hurled the aircraft into a corkscrew dive but Meissner was not to be outfoxed. As the great port wing of the Lancaster came upright when the pilot whipped it into a right-hand dive Meissner rolled the Bf 110C over on its back and shot it down virtually from above. Since the wing tanks were unprotected on the upper side by armoured plate the effect of his fire was 'devastating'. Flight Lieutenant Cliff Chatten who saw the light of tracer fire and an aircraft hit and going down on fire was sure that it was Hyde's aircraft. 'Its markers must have been jettisoned for I saw them burst below. I identified the markers as belonging to those of the aircraft which had taken off just before me and was sure then that it was my friend Len Hyde.'[164]

Hyde, who was from Shirley in Birmingham died in the inferno with his crew. Flying Officer James Craig DFC the 22-year old bomb aimer of Winnipeg; Flight Sergeant Eric Hill the wireless operator of Droylesdon, Lancashire; Flight Lieutenant Eric Hewett Palmer DFC the 20-year old navigator of Kingsbury, Middlesex, Pilot Officer Maurice Emerson Putt the flight engineer of Scarborough, Yorkshire, Pilot Officer Richard Taylor DFC the Welsh rear gunner of Pwllheli, Caernarvonshire and Flying Officer Richard James Weller DFM the Canadian mid-upper gunner and husband of Elizabeth Florence Weller, of Woodfibre, British Columbia who was serving in the RAF were removed from the wreckage of the aircraft at Müncheholzhausen southeast of Wetzlar and laid to rest in Hannover War cemetery.

Because of the excellent visibility it would have been possible for Meissner to continue. 'All hell was let loose for the enemy...Burning aircraft made the night even brighter than it was before' - but he broke off the fight because he was 'nervous at the end'.

When they finally arrived at Snaith Flight Lieutenant Joe Pawell's crew discovered that of the seventeen Halifaxes on 51 Squadron that had left the airfield that night four had been shot down by night-fighters and one - Halifax III LV777 MH-FZ piloted by Squadron Leader Frederick Peter Hill DFC - was shot down probably by flak at Stuttgart and crashed at Neckar with the loss of all seven crew; one had crashed and one was damaged. Everyone on Halifax III LW579 'V-Victor' flown by Pilot Officer James Brooks, a Scot from Bo'ness, West Lothian was killed when the aircraft crashed in Cowleaze Wood at Stokenchurch in Oxfordshire. Those who died with their skipper, who was trying to find RAF Benson for an emergency landing were Sergeant Thomas Samuel Connell, flight engineer of Campsie, Stirlingshire; Flight Sergeant Stewart Glass the bomb aimer from Haddington, East Lothian; Flight Sergeant Dennis Patrick McCormack the navigator of Chabletown, Leeds; Flight Sergeant George William West, wireless operator of Bermondsey, London and the two gunners, Flight Sergeant Dennis Arthur Churchill of Blackheath, London and from India, Sergeant Robert Frederick Kelly, who resided in Ipswich, Suffolk. Because of an attack of shingles, Flying Officer K. King was replaced by Kelly, whose regular pilot was ill. The crew was on their 19th operation. In all, forty-two men were missing, seven of them prisoners in Germany. The press correspondents and photographers that had watched the Halifaxes take off the previous evening had watched and waited 'so considerately' but they too became aware that there were some losses and the notebooks and cameras were put away before they left, obviously not wishing to intrude.

Joe Pawell's crew was sent on leave for four days but none too happily as it had been established that their pilot had burst a duodenal ulcer while flying home from Nuremberg and had lost a lot of blood which explained his lapses into semi-consciousness at the controls. 'That finished his RAF career,' said Stenning. 'We were heart-broken. He was a most experienced pilot. He had been flying since he was sixteen, in America and had nearly 10,000 hours. He later returned to Philadelphia.

We re-crewed with an Australian, Flying Officer Danny King MiD who had previously broken his back after colliding with the spire of Selby Abbey [one of the relatively few surviving churches of the medieval period and although not a cathedral, one of the biggest] but for medical reasons he never completed his tour with us.' With his crew Stenning went on to complete a tour of thirty-two operations on 51 Squadron.

Flying Officer Robert McHattie and the crew on Lancaster III DV298 SR-E had an uneventful trip home, mainly because of the track routed over occupied France once clear of Stuttgart and Karlsruhe. Landing at Ludford Magna, McHattie and his crew were amongst several personally interviewed by the station commander after sectional de-briefing. 'He asked what sort of a trip we had had,' McHattie recalled. 'I told him that it had been pretty tough. Unfortunately I also told him about our difficulties with the mid-upper gunners' heating and the action I had taken in moving him out of the turret. I think my crew were shocked and I was hurt when he reprimanded me for having taken this action even if the gunner had remained operational at the heated astrodome position as a watchman. Emerging from the interview with the group captain, our spirits were further depressed to find that seven of our squadron's aircraft were missing, most of them from my own 'A' Flight.'

'And so to breakfast and then to bed' concluded McHattie. But there was a bright side. 'Next day we found that as a result of our losses [including one crew that shared their hut] my crew had jumped from near bottom to the top of the 'A' Flight leave roster. Ah well, it's an ill wind...'

The crew on 'L-Love' saw their first fighter just after crossing the Belgian coast and got out of its way. 'But soon after' says Don Brinkhurst 'I saw about four of our chaps going down in flames and I knew this was going to be a bad night in the history of the RAF. Soon after I saw the searchlights of the Ruhr Valley and decided we would make it to the target as we were missing fighters left and right. But I did not think long as the engineer said, 'Bill, four-engined job ahead' and Bill said 'Hold on. I'll dip my wings. Don and you can look underneath and see if there are any Jerry fighters near.' So he dipped the port wing and all I heard was: 'What the ----' from the engineer before the intercom packed up. But I could see what had happened as red tracer was passing my turret ten to the dozen and both port engines and all the cabin of our kite were on fire. I called the pilot and got no answer. So there was only one thing to do and that was 'Bail Out'.'

Sergeant Don Brinkhurst jumped out of his turret, grabbed his parachute and made for the rear, climbing up the side of the fuselage to do so and helped Flying Officer Norman Marrian out of his seat. He opened the door, made to jump out forward but found this impossible and so pushed himself off backwards. Before going he saw Jimmy Goodall the rear gunner and Marrian putting their thumbs up for OK. Brinkhurst could feel Marrian holding onto the back of his parachute harness and was sure that he would follow him out. 'But after I left the kite I don't know what happened to them' recalled Brinkhurst. 'Jimmy was killed and Norman was still missing believed killed. The Special Operator, possibly with a damaged parachute, landed in trees where he was found, dead, two days later. 'All the boys in the front were killed as far as I could make out. But somehow Ray and Allan Hall got clear.'

The poorly designed escape hatches on the Lancaster made it notoriously difficult to abandon and Norman Bowyer the Canadian fight engineer and the two Scots, Jim Goodall and Ernie Kippen the wireless operator were killed outright. They and Marrian are buried in Rheinberg War Cemetery, while Adamson, their Glaswegian skipper is perpetuated on panel 204 of the Runnymede Memorial. Some accounts say that 'L-Love' was hit when a nervous Halifax tail gunner 300 feet above them opened fire and raked the Lancaster with tracer but another claim is that 'L-Love' was shot down at 0012 by Oberleutnant Hans-Joachim Witzleb of 7./NJG1.[165] Whatever, with wing tanks full of petrol and the bomb bay carrying incendiaries and high explosives the burning bomber was doomed. 'L-Love' crashed near the small town of Gemünd, five kilometres North-North-East of Schleiden.[166]

Assisted by resistance groups Don Brinkhurst arrived in Grenoble in Switzerland and was flown to Rome-Ciampino airfield and from there to North Africa and back to England. Before the end of the year he had married Vera Lodder. Leaving behind his new wife, he rejoined his old squadron and his first sortie, on the night of 2/3 January 1945 on the crew of Flying Officer M. Collins, was another raid on Nuremberg! Brinkhurst squeezed in a further nineteen operations before the end of the war in May 1945.[167]

Endnotes Chapter 15

156 See *Nachtjagd: The Night Fighter versus Bomber War over the Third Reich 1939-45* by Theo Boiten (Crowood 1997).

157 The burgomeister and the local people buried the six crew members in the local cemetery, the funeral services being conducted by the local Lutheran Minister. Their graves are now in Hannover War Cemetery.

158 See *They Led The Way; The story of Pathfinder Squadron 156* by Michael P. Wadsworth (Highgate Publications (Beverley) Ltd 1992.

159 *They Led The Way.*

160 Theo Boiten.

161 According to research by Theo Boiten.

162 According to research by Theo Boiten.

163 *RAF Bomber Command Losses of the Second World War. Vol.5 1944* W R Chorley (Midland 1997).

164 Quoted in *The Nuremberg Raid* by Martin Middlebrook. (Allen Lane 1973).

165 According to research by Theo Boiten. Oberleutnant Hans-Joachim Witzleb's final score was six confirmed Abschüsse.

166 I am indebted to Oliver Clutton-Brock for permission to use the following previously unpublished story of Don Brinkhurst which he researched with the invaluable help of Belgian historian Edouard Renière and a diary, *My Life in the RAF* written in a child's school exercise book and covering 42 pages received from Mrs Nicky Bailey.

167 Remarkably, having enlisted as ground crew in the RAF in 1939 in the lowest possible rank; AC2, Don Brinkhurst ended the war with the King's Commission as Pilot Officer Donald Brinkhurst. He passed peacefully away on Saturday, 21st January 2006 aged 85.

Chapter 16

The alarm clock by WAAF Section Officer Patricia Bourne's bed woke her at one o'clock. She spent a few moments thinking of 'Jimmy' Batten-Smith and then said a silent prayer for his safety before going back to sleep. Hundreds of miles away over Germany on 'R-Robert' Batten-Smith's Scottish specialist operator, Sergeant Bob Roberts, as usual sat in darkness with no window to observe what was going on around him. In order to avoid distraction, his intercom had been switched off when operating his set and only a red 'call light', operated by the pilot was available should there be an emergency. This meant that for most of the time he was flying over enemy territory he was totally isolated from the rest of the crew. Roberts would know nothing of what was happening until they were well on their way home; he could see or hear nothing of what was happening around and below him. He certainly never saw the Bf 110 piloted by Unteroffizier Heinz Krause of 3./NJG3 that attacked at 0114 hours and sent 'R-Robert' down in flames to crash near the autobahn at Röthenbach, sixteen kilometres ENE from the centre of Nuremberg. It is quite likely that Sergeant Hugh Fleming McClenaghan the 19-year old mid-upper gunner and 21-year old Flight Sergeant Arthur Haynes the rear gunner never saw their attacker either. All eight crew were laid to rest in Dürnbach War Cemetery. The news of their deaths hit everyone on the squadron hard and the telegrams delivered to loved ones brought great sorrow, none more so than at the Haynes household where the grieving family were to learn that Arthur's 20-year old brother Denis had been killed just nine days later whilst serving in the 2nd Battalion the Suffolk Regiment.

Once confirmation was received many more telegrams would have to be sent to relatives the length and breadth of the country and much further afield. Four minutes after shooting down 'R-Robert' Heinz Krause destroyed a second Lancaster, DS840 on 426 'Thunderbird' Squadron RCAF skippered by 22-year old Flight Lieutenant Walter Charles Cracknell of Fort William, Ontario. The skipper and Sergeant Harold Wride the 24-year old flight engineer of Hull, Yorkshire; Pilot Officer Alexander Gordon Devoy the 23-year old navigator from Vancouver; Warrant Officer Milton Cecil Moosman of Wanganui, New Zealand the 23-year old wireless operator; Pilot Officer Hubert Francis Orr, the 30-year old bomb aimer from Edmonton, Alberta, husband of Jeanne Orr of Peace River; Flying Officer Leroy Edward Robinson of Golden, British Columbia the 27-year old mid-upper gunner and Pilot Officer Roy Clifford Haycock, the 25-year old rear gunner of Ingersoll, Ontario all died. The crew was on their fifth operation.

Lancaster I LL832 'K-squared' piloted by 22-year old Flight Sergeant Gerald Tivey of Melbourne, Derbyshire had taken off from Ludford at 2205. At 0015 the 'ABC' aircraft drifted south of the planned track and became the Squadron's second loss when it was shot down by flak, crashing near the village of Rübenach five kilometres West-North-West from the centre of Koblenz. The skipper and all the crew, who were on their tenth operation, were laid to rest in Rheinberg War Cemetery. Flight Sergeant Henry Roy Butterworth, the bomb aimer was from Heywood, Lancashire; Sergeant Alexander David Dickson the rear gunner, came from Edinburgh; Sergeant Albert Walter Verdun Farley the flight engineer came from Broad Clyst, Devon; Flight Sergeant Leonard Lockwood the navigator was from Wakefield, Yorkshire; Sergeant Basil Henry Schofield, the wireless operator hailed from Boston, Lincolnshire; Flying Officer Leslie

Simpson the mid-upper gunner was from Fulwell, County Durham. Sergeant Gordon Lewis Preece RCAF the special operator of Vancouver also died.

Nearing the final turning point, Lancaster I ME618 'J-Johnny' flown by 24-year old Sergeant Clyde Roderick Harnish RCAF from Halifax, Nova Scotia, whose crew was on their sixth operation, had fallen victim to a night-fighter. Harnish had joined the RCAF in Halifax in November 1941. His parents were farmers in Hubbards, Nova Scotia. Called up by the Canadian Army in March 1941 he trained for four months with the 1st Battalion, Pictou Highlanders and then re-mustered to the RCAF. He and several members of his crew often spent their leave with Mrs. Dixon at Spindles in Hascombe, Surrey, 'a second mother' and Harnish had hoped that someday, after the war, he and his mother would visit Mrs. Dixon to thank her for her generosity.[168] The 4,000 pounder in the bomb bay exploded. Harnish dived to 7,000 feet attempting to put out the flames but as the floor of the cabin began to burn away he levelled off to give the crew a chance to bail out. Sergeant A. R. Luffmann the flight engineer saw Flight Sergeant G. D. Robertson the Canadian navigator jump but could not find his own parachute pack in the confusion and flames and almost gave up hope. He found it with a few seconds to spare and clipped it on. As he struggled to reach the escape hatch he saw Harnish get out of the pilot's seat but fall through the fire damaged cockpit floor. 'I could hear the roar of the bomber-stream overhead, like the sound of distant city traffic' wrote Luffmann. 'It was a very lonely sensation but then I had a feeling of tremendous freedom - laws and rules didn't apply to me anymore. The first thing I did was to pull my Mae West rubber life jacket - a thing everyone wanted to do at one time of another. The perishing thing was broken though; it didn't work.'[169]

Warrant Officer2 Nicholas Baker the Canadian bomb aimer from London, Ontario and Sergeant Donald van Norman McIntyre RCAF the rear gunner from Winnipeg and their skipper were killed but Harnish stayed at the controls long enough for four of his crew to safely abandon the doomed bomber before it went down at the village of Simmershausen, three kilometres northeast of the small town of Hilders. Luffmann jumped and was followed by Pilot Officer Rex Cond the special operator of Bromley in Kent but they were so low by this time that when Cond bailed out his parachute only partially opened before he hit the ground. Seriously wounded, he was taken to a hospital at Hildburghausen where he lived for a few hours only after the crash. Flight Sergeant G. D. Robertson and Flight Sergeant J. A. Marshall the Australian wireless operator were taken prisoner and marched off to captivity. Sergeant Mike Greer the Canadian mid-upper gunner was badly beaten by irate villagers until he had the presence of mind to hide in a nearby chicken house until the fury subsided.[170]

In total, 101 Squadron lost six 'ABC' Lancasters shot down. A seventh, Lancaster DV290 'X-X-ray' flown by Flight Sergeant Edwin Robert Thomas who was from Forest Gate, London crashed at 0503 hours near RAF Welford, Berkshire which was occupied by C-47 aircraft of the 435th Troop-Carrier Group when the runway lights were turned off at the wrong moment. All of the crew who were on their fifth operation were killed. Sergeant Donald A. Addy the 21-year old flight engineer husband of Eileen Mary Addy of Hemsworth, Yorkshire; Sergeant Dennis Roland Billson, the mid-upper gunner, was from Birstall, Leicester; Sergeant Richard Alfred James Collier, the rear gunner, came from Minster, Isle of Sheppey; Flight Sergeant Irvin Robert McNay, the bomb aimer, and Warrant Officer Alan Norman Rice, the navigator, were both from Toronto. Flight Sergeant Ernest Hugo 'Snowie' Traege, the 32-year old wireless operator, from Murray

Bridge, a city in South Australia was formerly an orchardist who enlisted at Adelaide on 9 June 1942, he left a widow, Ivy. Thirty-year old Flight Sergeant Allen Howard Wilson RAAF the special operator, husband of Ena Alice Wilson, came from West Wyalong, a town in New South Wales.[171] Altogether, Nuremberg had cost the 'ABC' Squadron forty-seven men killed, eight captured and one escapee.

The planned route home ended near Reading where the stream dispersed and 101 Squadron's surviving Lancasters headed for Ludford Magna. Nineteen Lancasters on 101 Squadron had bombed between 0113 and 0130. 'V-Victor' flown by Flying Officer McKenna was the first Lancaster on 101 Squadron to bomb, at 0113 hours. The crew had decided there was no safety in the bomber stream and ignored the return routing, heading directly for home. Flying Officer Goores the skipper of SR-N2 also bombed at 0113 and reported that the raid did not appear successful. Flight Sergeant Davidson and his crew on SR-Y were not satisfied with the poor marking on their first bomb run and at 0128 carried out a re-attack below cloud at 2,000 feet!

Along with many bombers, SR-O flown by Flight Lieutenant Douglas Todd RNZAF and navigated by Squadron Leader R. C. G. 'Rosy' Rosevear DFM the 'B' Flight commander had been blown so far off course that his crew failed to find Nuremberg at the end of their bomb run. What they did find was a large German city; clear of cloud cover, lit by falling sticks of incendiaries and bomb explosions and apparently under major attack. Todd was sure it was not Nuremberg and he circled once trying to get his bearings. With so many aircraft attacking the target Todd decided to bomb it at 0115. Too late, as they flew south they saw the red target indicators at Nuremberg twenty to thirty miles off their port beam. Arriving a few minutes later, LL773 SR-D flown by Flight Lieutenant Robin Knights was also attracted to the bombing and fires. No Path Finder marking could be seen so they orbited the city for ten to fifteen minutes before, with time running out he decided to bomb at 0128. The city was Schweinfurt and over 100 bombers attacked it in error that night causing more actual damage than Nuremberg suffered. 'S-Sugar' flown by Flying Officer Davies was the last 101 Squadron Lancaster to bomb at 0130. By 0135 the raid was over. Sixty-nine people had been killed in Nuremberg and the surrounding area. Many of 101 Squadron's twenty surviving Lancasters opted for the direct route home but some still tried to stay with the stream over northern France, past Dieppe to an English landfall at Selsey Bill.

'Yes, you must have reached the target, Wally', one of the Flight Commanders on 101 Squadron said to 'Wally' Wallace. The other one said: 'You're the first one that may be able to tell us the full story.'

'Shit, they weren't giving us a chance to say anything' says 'Dig' Condon. 'But now they shut up and 'Wally' told them the story. During 'Wally's description of the raid, an officer came in a couple of times and whispered into one of the seated officer's ears. Wally raised those dark eyebrows in question and the officer said: 'I guess you boys should know. Three more of our planes have landed safely at other 'dromes.' He looked at his watch and went on: 'Anyone that's not back now is either in the drink or else...' He didn't complete the sentence. He didn't have to. We knew the bloody score now. They asked the rest of us to verify Wally's statements now and again. Wally told them how he had veered south, as he had an idea everything was not as it should be. They reckon it was probably a good move; otherwise we may be still over there with the rest of them. The questions went on. It was like a bad dream. Then I said, more or less to myself; 'A bloody stinking sell-out if you ask me.'

'What did you say Flight?' one of them asked.

'Er, I was just talking to myself', I told him.

'Saying what?' he asked.

'Well', I said, 'I've had plenty of time to think on the way home. It could have been a sell-out. The Huns knew our track. The action of those searchlights. The number of fighters and those fighter flares. You don't see those until you're close to the target usually. It sure stinks to me. Our special here, Eddie, he will verify me as to the fighter strength. We were lucky we were only attacked a couple of times. But as I was looking back to the north, towards those searchlights, I could see as many fighters at some stages as I could see Lancs and Hallies.'

'Eddie verified me on the fighter strength. One of the Flight Commanders said to me a bit more casually - he knew me - 'That's a very interesting theory of yours, 'Dig'. A sell-out, eh? What does the rest of the crew think?'

'I don't know Sir, ask them.'

'He did and they all backed me up. Wally said he thought it stunk a bit before he made up his mind to veer south. Eddie had heard the German controller giving our course on the radio. It couldn't all be set up in ten minutes. Where did all the fighters come from? There weren't a fifth that many in that area normally. Jesus, it must have been a set-up, I reckoned. I looked at my watch. Five-thirty am. Bloody near ten hours since take-off and we had been in the air for eight of them. Jesus, it seemed like ten days to me since we took off. As we were leaving, one of the interrogation officers said:

'Well, we can't accept your ideas at the moment. But, we'll wait until later and find out what the final result of this show is. It may be worth investigating, but they wouldn't like to admit to such a flaw in their security.' I didn't like to admit it either. Shit - it was bad enough without those German bastards knowing your route, the colour of your ground markers, maybe your target and so forth. It was OK going over there; you expected what you ran into at the target, but definitely didn't like the idea of meeting those bloody fighters head-on more than once. But these targets, our routes, the colours of the markers of the day were supposed to be top secret. Whoever was dropping their guts was someone high up in the business. Still, the Germans had some pretty smart operators. The bastards had known when we first landed at Bournemouth. They knew what squadron you came from, from your dog-tags. All this was making me feel just a bit more uneasy. We hung around for half an hour, but no more planes came in. They weren't likely to now. It certainly shook us up. Shit - eleven lost out of twenty-eight. Donald Irving's crew was one of the ones that didn't come back. That wireless operator's premonition had been right. Thank Christ I didn't believe in them. Christ - eighty-eight lads gone for a Burton.'

'H-Harry' was shot down near Lauterbach, forty miles north of the planned turning point at the end of the long leg on the outward flight by a night-fighter and crashed ten kilometres NNE of Eisenach, exploding with great force and scattering debris over a wide area. The skipper and all of his crew were killed. Six, including the specialist operator, 27-year old Pilot Officer Ralph Frank Litchfield RCAF from Burnaby, British Columbia are commemorated on the Runnymede Memorial, while two are buried in Berlin 1939-1945 War Cemetery. Flight Sergeants' Stanley George Richard King the 23-year old navigator came from Lithgow in the Central Tablelands of New South Wales; Norman Grenfell Huggett the 27-year old air bomber was from Young in the South West Slopes region of New South Wales; John Alfred Noske, the 21-year old wireless operator came from Williams in the Wheatbelt region, Western Australia; John Bede Newman the 20-year old mid-upper gunner was from Warwick, Queensland; Walter Joseph Adam the 25-year old rear gunner came from Bundalong South on the Murray River, Victoria and Frank Phillips RAFVR, the 20-year old English flight engineer was from Harborne, Birmingham.

Sergeant Dennis Goodliffe one of the flight engineers, who when he arrived at Ludford had been told by the intelligence officer that his expectation of life was six weeks - go back to your huts and make your wills' spoke to engineers who hadn't completed their logs because they were so sure they were going to get the 'chop'. After we got down and saw who had been chalked in on the operations board we realised seven aircraft were missing. It was dreadful as aircrew began looking at each other in amazement. We hung around in the debriefing room for some time to see if anyone else turned up, but they didn't ... That morning the breakfast tables were almost empty in the sergeants' mess. The cook came round and asked us all to move to make up a few full tables so that it would look respectable. Within 48 hours we were back on almost full complement as new crews were drafted in.'[172]

Flight Sergeant Graham Boytell an Australian Special Operator who had just flown his first operation, recalled:

'The flight to the target was uneventful as far as I was concerned. I was kept busy jamming, but the rest of the crew felt there were far more aircraft being shot down than usual. We bombed without incident, but just afterwards the rear gunner saw a Ju 88 approaching our tail. When the fighter got to within 200 yards the gunner called for a corkscrew starboard and opened fire, but only one of his four guns was working and it only fired one shot. The guns were all frozen solid in the minus 40° temperature. The fighter made two more attacks, which we managed to thwart before he realised we were awake. We all heard a loud bang through the encounter, but there was no evidence of damage. The most difficult feeling for me throughout all this was utter helplessness. I wanted to get behind a gun myself.

'On return to base all the crews were discussing the large numbers of aircraft shot down and the station commander, Group Captain King, called our crew into his office and asked each crewman what he thought about the raid. I didn't think he would ask me as security about my job was so tight. I didn't know how to answer without divulging any secrets and I finally said, 'Nothing unusual, sir,' this being my first op. He jumped on me, accusing me of going to sleep on the job. I felt I had been shot down myself and from then on whenever Groupy called us in after a raid and questioned me I always gave him the standard answer: 'About what I would have expected for that kind of target, sir.' He always accepted it.'[173]

'We went to the mess and had our breakfast' continues 'Dig' Condon. 'No one said much, not even the ground staff or the WAAFs. The message had soon got round the squadron. We then went to our billets and flopped on our cots. I was the first one to speak. 'I don't know about you boys', I said, 'But I'm for the bed proper.'

'I got undressed and it was cold now. Never mind - pull my flying suit on over the pyjamas. That's all I used it for anyhow. The rest of the boys soon followed suit.

'I was absolutely exhausted and soon fell off to sleep, but it was a fitful one. Now was the time you wanted about four double-headed scotches in quick succession. Bloody silly dreams, but not about flying - always about some stupid thing you would never think of in your waking hours. In the waking hours I thought about Dianne and home. Would I ever see them again? It was Wally's voice that eventually woke me properly - and everyone else.

'Come on, chaps' he said. 'On your feet, or sit on your beds will do. But wake up. I've been up to the Flights and I've got news for you and some of it is bad.'

'I could bloody well imagine that!

'Go on, Wally' 'Ginge' said; 'give us the Griff.'

'Wally went on, 'So far as they know, we had about the worst losses of any single squadron. There's no more news of any of the missing Lancs.'

Eleven missing out of twenty-eight is still the score. The total losses come to ninety-six; the Germans claim one hundred and six and are those bastards happy! Our mob is still in a flap. Naturally there's no ops tonight. It's not only the kites that are missing, but half the ones that did get back are damaged and will take a week to repair or replace. Ours was OK, luckily. We could go in her again tonight.'

'Yeah, but we're bloody well not', I thought. I also thought other things. What a proper bastard. Just when we thought we were getting on top of the Germans, this had to happen. Shit - it would take Bomber Command weeks to recover. Still, they had sent a thousand planes to Frankfurt a week ago. We'd still have plenty of punch left. 'What's the bloody good news, Wally?'

'Canada' asked, 'That's if you've got any!'

'I've got it all right' said Wally breaking into a big grin. 'We go on leave tomorrow any time we like!' That did it, we all smiled. Then we all laughed.

'You bloody bobby-dazzler' I said, 'How about that 'Canada'?'

'You son of a butcher beauty' he said. The tension was broken until the next time. After last night I'd made up my mind on one thing that had worried me at times. There'd be no more compassion from here hence for those bloody German bastards. I found out later that almost twelve hundred men were either killed or injured on that one bloody operation, that to us had looked a piece of cake. Then I found my voice again. 'Well', I said, 'I don't know about you blokes, but I'm going to pack my gear, then head for the White Hart for a bloody grog. Too late for lunch, so we've got to get some vitamins into us somehow!'

'How about we all go?' said Wally. 'The first couple of rounds are on me!'

'Yeah' volunteered 'Canada' 'and the next couple are on me!'

'The bloody dough they pay you 'Canada', Ginger said, 'You ought to shout four times! You don't even earn it, laying on your guts all the time in that Lanc. Now look at Digger, he has to earn his bloody money. He has to stand up in that astrodome all the time!'

'Good for you, 'Ginge' I said. 'If that's the way you feel, I won't ever bloody well shout at all! My turn to rest the old wallet!'

'Come on you bunch of nuts,' said Wally. 'I'll pick up Eddie on the way - see you at the Inn.'

'That afternoon and night were pretty torrid at the pub. The place was crowded and everyone was trying to drown their sorrows. Trying to forget. Not a word was said about Nuremberg; not among our crew anyhow. Eddie and Len left early. I saw Jenny about eight o'clock and had to go and say hello to her. She was very glad to see me and told me she had been worried until she saw me. I told her the reason was we'd been in bed for most of the day. She had a feeling, she said, that she knew somehow I'd get through operations. Bugger the crowd. I pecked her on the cheek and said thanks for the encouragement. I told her I was going on leave tomorrow, to Edinburgh and her jaw dropped. She said she wished she was coming with me. That would be bloody awkward. I gave her another peck on the cheek and told her I would see her when I got back.

'I wouldn't have got drunk tonight, no matter how much I drank. I went back to the table and copped a hell of a ribbing from the boys. Not satisfied with one Sheila, they told me, I had to go after one of the best little sorts on the squadron. She wouldn't look at anyone else, they reckoned.

'Ah, bullshit', I told them. We decided to go home - Jock, as usual, was asleep in his chair. 'Canada' hoisted him over his shoulder like a bag of bloody spuds and the six of us piled into 'Wally's car. When we reached the billet, 'Canada' again had to carry Jock. He dumped him unceremoniously on to his cot and he was still there, fully dressed, the next morning. We all went straight to bed that night and after the session we'd had, I slept like a top. Usually, we would stay awake and yarn for a while, but not that night, brother!'[174]

'Rusty' Waughman landed *Wing and a Prayer* at Ludford but 'for a couple of days we were like zombies we couldn't sleep; couldn't settle... 'The air was thick with fighters. The Germans were using nine speech and two Morse channels. The SDO's found and jammed some, but the German signals were so powerful and numerous that they could not all be covered. On the way to the target on the German border we counted sixteen aircraft going down. Your mind concentrated on surviving, fortunately my gunners were brilliant and once, in a small amount of time, we had five fighter attacks and you couldn't think of anything else other than trying to keep your aircraft in one piece. Our survival rate was on a par with a lieutenant in the trenches in WWI, so we found out afterwards. Luck too was involved a great deal.'

John Wickman, a fitter-armourer at Ludford, remembers the following day on the airfield.

'There were a lot of empty dispersals. Almost a third of the squadron had gone overnight and I can still picture all those weeping WAAFs around Ludford that morning. But new aircraft and replacement crews arrived and within a day or two it was as though nothing had happened.' Such was life and death on a bomber station.[175] Five weeks later 101 would suffer badly again when five aircraft were lost in the attack on Mailly-le-Camp. 'Rusty' Waughman and his crew escaped when their Lancaster was blown upside-down over the target. On 11 May he and his crew survived a mid-air collision on Wing and a Prayer on the raid on Hasselt in Belgium. 'We were sat on top of another bomber and it was like driving on ice. We began to lose parts because we were crunching against the other aircraft. Despite that we went on to bomb the target 4½ miles away. We crash landed at Ludford and were heading towards the control tower. The only casualty was a little girl who was near the runway and she twisted her ankle!'[176]

The monotonous syncopic beat from 'S-Sugar's four Merlin radials accentuated the eerie quietness in the nose of the 158 Squadron Halifax. James Campbell's pilot 'saw the cloud disperse when they were still some way from the enemy coast and he cursed the failings of the weather men. As they skirted clear of Aachen he searched the sky. It was unusually bright brighter than he had seen it for a long time. But, of course, there was half-moonlight.

'Christ, things didn't look so good. Almost naked in that pale, shimmering light. Titch, in the mid-upper turret, first saw the tracer. Over the intercom his voice sounded fretful and hurt... 'Combat; Port Quarter!'

'Okay, I see it' the pilot retorted.

The navigator picked up his dividers, spanned the track to go. They had 240 miles yet and a fighter in the Main Stream already. It would not help his navigating if they started weaving so early.

The flight sergeant Kiwi bomb aimer manning the H$_2$S set scrambled into the nose. Rumour had it that he was having it off with the landlady of the Red Lion. Ahead he saw a ball of fire splash against the night sky. Bomber disintegrating. Tracer rippled across the starboard beam quarter. Nothing, as far as he could see, was coming up from the ground. What did it matter he thought. The fighters were more deadly. He switched on his intercom.

'Skipper, bomb aimer here. Staying put in the nose.'

'He slapped a drum of ammunition on the free Vicker's gun, peeping through the nose and cocked the firing button to 'Fire'. Scare gun though it was, the action gave him more confidence.

'Good idea, 'Shern,' the pilot replied crisply.

To the new flight engineer, the pilot said: 'Don't keep reporting combats. But watch and keep an eye on the gauges.' Stocky, red-haired and with small excited eyes, the pilot reflected that he did not have much confidence in the new man. For one thing he was too talkative; for another he invariably talked at the wrong times.

'They flew on and the pilot marvelled at the combats he saw. Bombers were blowing up, right, left and centre. He considered jettisoning the load the next time the engineer shouted 'Fighter', but promptly dismissed the urge. The attack must come. They couldn't always be as lucky as they had been, God, what a night and so far to go ... then they had to come back.

'The flak coming up from the target seemed a secondary worry to the gauntlet they had run with the Ju 88s and the FW 190s. The Halifax pilot wondered, as he made the corrections on the bombing run, how many combats the bomb aimer had seen. The bomb aimer knelt down beside the bombing computer box and re-checked the pre-flight settings he had fed in at take-off. He set on the latest wind speed and its direction. The terminal velocity of the bombs and the target height set against the mean sea level of Nuremberg he left as he had first calculated. He slipped through the curtain which screened the nose from the navigation hatch and sat down next beside the navigator. The buzz of a switched on intercom came over the head-phones. 'Flak bursts...star'd...three o'clock. He recognised the voice of the mid-upper gunner. The voice was cool, matter of fact. The bomb aimer went back into the nose with a handkerchief wrapped round his torch. Kneeling beside the bombing computer he switched on the compressed air-cock and turned on the electrical supply knob. After flicking on the graticule light on the Mark 14 bombsight he reset a new wind speed and wind direction on the computer box. He checked the bomb selector and fusing switches. Satisfied, he looked through the transparent nose. Proper cat and mouse business this, he thought. Stretching himself along the bombing mat he wondered - not for the first time - why it was not armour plated. Releasing the collimater handle on the sighting head of the bombsight, he squinted into the graticule light. Leisurely he watched the thick, oblong illuminated glass sway gently as the gyro took control. The outline of the sword sight glowed wickedly. Down the edge of the sword would come the sky markers. When they breached the hilt intersection he would press the bomb-tit. Theoretically the point on the ground covered by the cross intersection represented the point of impact of a bomb released at the exact moment. He extended the handle and picked up a billowing cloud top and watched it drift down the sight. He liked the Mark 14 bomb sight. It allowed the aircraft to bomb fairly accurately without the pilot having to fly dead straight and level.

Suddenly the sky erupted in thousands of violent explosions. Then came the searchlights, countless broad avenues of light. Their naked dazzling whiteness dulled by the cloud layers they so ardently washed.

'Master Switch on! Bomb switches selected and fused! Left... Steady now ... Steady. Three globes of red TIs were floating steadily towards his sight.

'Bomb doors open!'

The pilot repeated the order and saw the light appear on his panel as the belly of the Halifax yawned.

'Right a bit! Stead-dy...Stea-dy!

The pilot gently squeezed the starboard rudder. He caught clear glimpses of the black puffs of thousands of spent shells as camera flashes from the bombers ahead went off on their time fuses silhouetting the fuselage for fractions of a second.

Bombs Gone. Jettison bars across... Close bomb doors and let's get the Hell out of here!'

'Never before had the skipper heard the bomb aimer slur so fast through his drill. He felt the Halifax buck madly as it leapt into the air, freed from its heavy load. He held 'S-Sugar' straight for about half a minute so that their photo-flash would burst and record their theoretical aiming point. He saw two more bombers burst into flames as he banked the Halifax on course for the coast. The half moon was bewildering bright. He could make out the shapes of two Lancasters with a Halifax above and slightly ahead of him.

'A second later tracer spewed in four fantastically moving lines from the Halifax ahead of them. Violently he flung over the control column and pushed it forward. To hell with the Flight Plan, he was going to lose height. The fighters were following them out. Anywhere, he decided, in that vast turbulent sky was safer than in the mid-stream of the bomber force. Every fighter in the area must be among them. From the direction of the tracer and cannon fire the pilot was certain the night fighters were flying to and fro across the force. And with each flight a bomber exploded or plunged earthwards, crippled and on fire.

'Jock' the rear gunner saw the FW190 streaking down on them as he peered over the barrels of his four Brownings. His red-rimmed eyes, glazed with horror at the rings of fire, twinkling wickedly from the leading edges of the fighter's wings.

'The tracer was whipping past at an acute angle when 'Jock' screamed to the pilot to corkscrew starboard. For a split-second he wondered if he had given the correct evasive action. It was on his port but his back was to the pilot. Yes, it was right enough. Elevating the Brownings, 'Jock' stabbed the firing button. The night fighter must have corrected his sighting angle, with a touch of rudder, for its second burst thundered along the fuselage behind him.

'At that precise second his own burst sprayed the Focke Wulf's tail. Most of it, he saw, went under. Before he could correct his fire angle the night fighter flashed over.

There was no fire from the mid-upper turret, he realised. Either 'Titch' was hit or he was looking somewhere else and could not get his turret round in time.

'The pilot rolled 'S-Sugar' from the corkscrew. His gyro-compass was spinning crazily and his artificial horizon had toppled with the dive. They heard him breathing heavily as he gulped in the oxygen.

'See anything, gunners?' The pilot's tone was crisp, apprehensive.

'Rear gunner to Skipper. Think we've lost him.' The pilot coughed into his mask and the sound rasped in their earphones.

'First, who fired?' he demanded.

'Me, skipper.'

'Who in the hell's me? Keep to the drill.'

'Rear gunner, Skipper. Saw him come in out of the corner of my eye. Was searching my starboard quarter and had just swung round the turret.'

'Did you get him?'

'Doubt it. Maybe his tail'

'All right 'Jock'. Keep looking while I call the others,' the skipper said.

'Mid-upper and the engineer are all right. I've just had them on so let's hear from you, navigator.'

'I'm all right and so is the bomb aimer' the navigator replied.

'The skipper flicked his eyes from the altimeter across to the ASI and then glanced through his clear vision panel. They were hit; he could tell that from the feel of the controls and hit bad. The rudder, the starboard rudder, was not responding.

'Rear gunner... Skipper here.... See anything wrong with the starboard rudder?'

The rear gunner's voice crackled in his ears. 'Hard to tell, can't get a good look.'

'God, he had forgotten to call the wireless operator. Probably he was listening in to his set and had not heard him call for the crew to report. For the first three quarters of an hour of the flight he would tune his R1155 receiver set into the late night Joe Loss dance programme before glancing at his watch and twiddling with the knobs until he found the wave length jotted on the pad in front of him. Carefully he would re-tune the set and listen out.

'Wireless operator' the skipper called again. You okay?', but only the crew's deep breathing came over the intercom.

'Bomb aimer, slip through and see what's up with the wireless operator. Probably his plug has come loose,' the skipper added as an afterthought.

'The bomb aimer rose from beside the navigator and edged his way into the wireless compartment. The wireless operator was slumped over his table. His forehead bounced gently against the radio set with the movement of the aircraft. The back of his head was blown off.

The Kiwi bomb aimer's eyes alighted on the set. Pieces of blood soaked scalp, with tiny bits of bone sticking to them were splattered across the dials. A vivid red scarf was clotted round his neck and congealing fast. A rivulet of crimson trickled down from the lobe of the wireless operator's right ear.

'He leaned forward and lifted the wireless operator's wrist. Hurriedly he dropped the limp, cold hand and wondered why he ever expected to feel a pulse beat. The navigator came into the compartment. The bomb aimer looked up and saw his face was a sickly white. Switching on his intercom he called the skipper.

'The reply shocked and awed came to him. 'Are you sure? Have you...'

'Quite sure' the bomb aimer said, anticipating the skipper's question. He rolled the wireless operator back into his seat. The eyes were bright and staring. He thought they had the look of a small boy's when opening a Christmas parcel.

'Weave, Skipper. For Christ sake, weave. Two combats above and an '88 flashed below.'

'Jock's Glasgow accent was sharp, imperative in its eagerness. The skipper flung the bomber on to its port wing-tip. God; would this night never end? He called the navigator.

'How far to the coast?'

'Forty minutes' the navigator replied. Forty minutes when forty seconds could be a long lifetime. In the nose the bomb aimer carried out his own inspection. There was a foot-wide slash where the transparent covering joined the fuselage and six neat perforations in the plastic. As he scrambled back into the navigation hatch the Halifax lurched and he nearly fell across the navigator.

'There was a dull thud and the curtain screening the compartment from the glass house was ripped from its hanging. The bomb aimer paled as he saw the dead wireless operator's foot sticking through. The sudden lurch had toppled him from his seat. With the engineer's help he carried the wireless operator's body into the fuselage and laid him face upwards on the long seat. He looked better that way, the bomb aimer decided. It hid the hole in his head.

'They crossed the enemy coast low and ten degrees starboard of the Flight Plan. They were too tired, too indifferent to heed the light flak coming up on their port. The fury they had faced had long since drained away the effects of the Pep pills. Their systems reacted against the chemical charges. They trembled and shuddered.

'Now they faced a landing with a right rudder which was practically useless. Even so, the skipper displaying a skill which astounded him brought the Halifax down to a heavy but safe landing.'[177]

At Lissett four of the sixteen Halifaxes on 158 Squadron were missing and one returned damaged. 'F-Fox' flown by Flight Sergeant Joe Hitchman returned at 0534. 'I have never been so tired in all my life as I was that night. We were logging combats almost all the way to the target and back. I was weaving all the way and corkscrewing as the gunners saw fighters. We saw so many aircraft shot down; the navigator logged about twenty until eventually I said 'For Christ's sake, lads, don't report kites shot down, just keep your eyes open for fighters,' so we didn't log any more. Because we had used so much fuel in corkscrewing we couldn't get back to base and had to land at Odiham. We'd been in the air seven hours and thirty minutes. We didn't go to bed and got back to Lissett at about 10 or 11 am. The flight commander asked me before we went to debriefing what it had been like and I said I thought at least fifty had been shot down. He told me off and said I shouldn't be claiming as many missing as that. Then someone else landed and he asked that pilot what it had been like. 'Piece of cake,' he said. 'I didn't see a thing.' He thought he had just seen spoof flares. I told him that if he hadn't realised they were aircraft going down in flames he wouldn't be here in a fortnight and he wasn't.'[178]

Later, 'F-Fox' was allocated to the crew skippered by Pilot Officer Cliff R. R. Smith, a Londoner. 'Smithy' branded the superstition 'stuff and nonsense' and named the aircraft *Friday the 13th*. He also painted a scythe on the side, a skull and crossbones and an upside down horseshoe to break the curse. Smith even painted an open ladder above the crew hatch so they would have to walk under it as they climbed on board and painted over the parachute escape hatch on the belly of the plane, but these details were later removed. Unlike its predecessors, the bomber racked up an impressive number of operations, the 21st operation distinguished by a key with a Hakenkreuz, the 70th with a blockbuster trailing a spiral and the 100th with a larger than usual bomb lying in an open box or coffin. *Friday the 13th* ended the war with 128 operations; more than any other Halifax aircraft.

'At Lissett next day, Wing Commander 'Jock' Calder drove down to 'S-Sugar's dispersal, inspected the Halifax and put the pilot in for an immediate award of the DFC' wrote James Campbell. 'He found only two bullet holes in the tiny wireless hatch and reflected gravely that a nod of the operator's head might have meant the difference between him living and dying.

'At lunchtime the mess was unusually quiet as the one o'clock news came over the radio. The losses had come through a few hours earlier to the Intelligence Room and the number was 104, but that included the known 'ditchings' in the North Sea. The aircraft which had crashed in the sea after sending out 'Mayday' signals would not be included in the number. The Command knew where they were and knowing reasoned they were not 'missing'.

'...Ninety-four of our bombers are missing...' A gasp went round the Sergeants' Mess drowning the rest of the announcement. It was all true and not a nightmare, stark in its reality of a night that never was.

Someone in a detached, unemotional voice had broadcast it to the world.'[179]

After having been airborne for 7.20 hours on what was the second trip of his first tour of operations, Pilot Officer 'Paddy' Gundelach on 'B' Flight on 460 Squadron RAAF landed Lancaster 'M-Mike' back at Binbrook. Having consumed his rum ration and been de-briefed 'Paddy' Gundelach slept for some hours. 'On waking, a solemn-faced steward said, 'I'm glad to see you back. Ninety-four of our aircraft did not return.' I wondered how many of my friends and acquaintances were among those missing. I then did a quick mental calculation - two trips behind me and twenty-eight to go to complete my tour. I did not go back to sleep again.'

'M-Mike's windscreen had iced up as Gundelach climbed to height before setting course over the North Sea. Despite the moonlight he and his crew reached the target without being attacked by enemy fighters. 'I saw many small fires on the ground, especially after leaving the target area. These, we presumed, were our bombers burning after having been shot down. 'Mac' McFarlane my Canadian bomb aimer logged their positions.'

'L-Love' on 'B' Flight captained by Pilot Officer R. Howell RAAF who had taken off at 2157 hours on their 23rd operation, also returned safely at 0527. For the best part of 7½ hours Pilot Officer Samuel Moorhouse the Australian navigator from Caulfield, Melbourne had been too busy calculating, plotting and estimating actual wind velocities for broadcast back to base to have time to observe much of the action until the French coast was re-crossed between Calais and Le Havre. He recalled: 'From the turning point until some distance east of Frankfurt fighter activity and flak were very heavy. Whilst we were not hit or attacked, Flight Sergeant 'Bluey' Hill RAAF, mid-upper gunner and Flight Sergeant W. Shaw, rear gunner and the pilot saw many falling aircraft in this corridor area. Flight Sergeant N. Lukies RAAF, bomb aimer dropped bombs on a due south heading. Flight Sergeant C. Jewitt, flight engineer and Flight Sergeant L. Field, wireless air gunner were the two other members on the crew. All were understandably tired on return to Binbrook and Sam Moorhouse's recollection of the de-briefing was confined to the general opinion expressed by the crews 'that there had been a leakage of information so far as the route was concerned, particularly between Cologne and Frankfurt.'

There was no word from ED750 captained by Pilot Officer Peter Anderson, which was lost to the Rhine flak nearing Koblenz on the outward flight. Sergeants Douglas Lax; Albert Pitfield and Richard Parmenter were killed and are buried with their skipper at Rheinberg War Cemetery. Three of the crew survived to be taken into captivity.

ND738, flown by Flight Sergeant Charles Hargreaves RAAF was shot down near the target, three kilometres west of Gräfenberg by Unteroffizier Günther Schmidt of 8./NJG2.[180] All of the crew including Glynn Jones the 20-year old mid-upper gunner who one day might have played football for England, were laid to rest in Durnbach War Cemetery. He had grown so fond of 'Hal' and his other crewmembers that he had prophetically paid tribute to them in a poem:

> Per Ardua ad Astra:
> What we wish if we should die,
> Is that our folks behind won't cry,
> For our belief is that we fight
> To give unto the world more light.
> So God our lives we give to thee,
> Living or dying we wish to be
> Brave and Mighty in Life
> And smiling gaily in Strife.

Endnotes Chapter 16

168 *Through Footless Halls of Air: The Stories of Men Who Failed* by Floyd Williston. (General Store Publishing House 1996).

169 *The Nuremberg Raid* by Martin Middlebrook. (Allen Lane 1973).

170 *Bomber Squadron At War* by Andrew Brookes (Ian Allan Ltd 1983).

171 See *Jewish RAF Special Operators in Radio Counter Measures with 101 Squadron (September 1943-May 1945)* by Martin Sugarman.

172 Quoted in *Men of Air; The Doomed Youth of Bomber Command* by Kevin Wilson (Weidenfeld & Nicolson 2007).

173 Quoted in *Men of Air; The Doomed Youth of Bomber Command* by Kevin Wilson (Weidenfeld & Nicolson 2007).

174 In common with the other crew members, 'Dig' Condon was later decorated - in his case a DFM, Gazetted on 15 September 1944.

175 Quoted in *Maximum Effort: One Group at War* by Patrick Otter.

176 'Rusty' Waughman's crew were allocated a new Lancaster, LL757 SR-W *Oor Wullie*, which they used until the end of their tour. *Wing and a Prayer* was lost on 8/9 June on the raid on Forêt de Cerisy.

177 Adapted from *Maximum Effort* by James Campbell (Frederick Muller Ltd 1957 and Futura Publications 1974, 1977) and *Bomber Stream Unbroken* by James Campbell (Cressrelles Publishing Co. Ltd 1976, Futura 1977).

178 Quoted in *Men of Air; The Doomed Youth of Bomber Command* by Kevin Wilson (Weidenfeld & Nicolson 2007).

179 Adapted from *Maximum Effort* by James Campbell (Frederick Muller Ltd 1957 and Futura Publications 1974, 1977).

180 From research by Theo Boiten.

Chapter 17

Canadian Flight Sergeant Paul Christiansen's crew on 78 Squadron finally tumbled into their beds at Breighton at 0650. They had spent 7.20 hours in the air, 5.16 hours of it at 20,000 feet in temperatures of -33 degrees Centigrade and had breathed oxygen for 6.50 hours. They had taken off with 2,046 gallons of fuel and landed with 86 gallons left, sufficient for little more than fifteen minutes flying. Seven hours later they were back at their aircraft where Sergeant David Davidson the Scottish flight engineer found a civilian ground engineer looking it over. When the civilian asked him where the crew had been the night before, Davidson said, ' Nuremberg.'

'You lost ninety-six,' said the civilian who had been listening to the BBC.

Davidson stared at him, astounded. 'You must be kidding,' he said. 'It didn't look that bad to us.'

Inexplicably, the Halifax's port inner motor checked out satisfactorily on run-up. The previous night's malfunction was diagnosed as being due to coring up of the oil cooler on descent.

On return to Breighton, Davidson found that three of 78 Squadron's aircraft - 'Z-Zebra', 'P-Peter' and 'Q-Queenie' - were missing. 'Christ', thought Davidson, 'we went out to dispersal in the same crew bus.' He remembered talking with the rear gunner [Sergeant F. R. Wilson] on 'Z-Zebra'. Two years later Davidson was drinking a pint of beer in the Sergeants' Mess at Catterick when he found himself talking to Wilson. It transpired that the air gunner's Halifax had been attacked and set on fire just after crossing the French coast at 2334, only minutes ahead of Davidson's aircraft and that Davidson had witnessed the action. Spirited return fire from the Halifax had scored strikes on the twin-engined German fighter which then broke off the attack and vanished. Getting no replies when he called on the intercom, the gunner climbed out of his turret and went forward to the nose of the Halifax. It was very draughty in the fuselage, with no member of the crew in sight. He found the cockpit empty and the forward escape hatch open. The crew had bailed out. While there was still time to do so the gunner made his lonely way back to the rear turret and did likewise.

Flying Officer Fred Stuart in the mid-upper turret on Halifax 'M-Mike' on 10 Squadron flew home to Melbourne with the freezing slipstream howling through the hole punched in his turret perspex by a cannon shell from a Me 109 over the target.

'On return to base we were not very happy to hear 'Milkpail', the call sign for our base, warning us that there were 'Bandits', or German intruder aircraft, in the area and that we were to disperse. However we were shortly afterwards recalled and, thank goodness, were able to land at our home base.'

'Paddy' Clarke's experienced crew on Halifax 'L-London' were third to land at Melbourne. 'We received a hearty welcome from the ground crew' recalled Denis Girardau, who had spent 7.55 hours airborne in the rear turret. 'De-briefing was carried out and we explained how Met had boobed for the trip to the target. It was a big shock to learn that over all ninety-four aeroplanes had been reported missing. My own view of this great loss was that it was due to cloud missing on the half-moon trip and the Germans must have known about the operation as we took off. After some hours' sleep and return to the flights we learned that six out of our squadron's twelve aircraft had failed to return.'

Actually, only one aircraft - Halifax LV881 'Y-Yorker' on 10 Squadron flown by 21-year old Pilot Officer Walter Thomas Andrew Regan of Barnsley, Yorkshire whose crew were on their fifth operation, had been lost. It was possibly the aircraft claimed shot down by Oberleutnant Fritz Brandt of 3./NJGr.10 flying a Bf 110. 'It was easy to approach bombers unseen as we nearly always came in from below, where it was dark. Bombers did attempt to evade us by weaving and corkscrewing but we fighters stayed on their tails and flew in the same manner. It was possible to plot their course to the target by the number of wrecked aircraft, which we could see next day. They ran in a smouldering line across half Germany.'

LV881 was attacked twice by Brandt. Although not known by the crew at the time, who believed the aircraft had been hit by flak, the attack came from below by the undetected night fighter firing upward facing 'Schräge Musik' guns into the starboard wing, making a hole about two feet square and spattering the mid upper turret with holes. Flight Sergeant Ernest Hugh Birch the 21-year old Australian mid upper gunner from the port city of Bunbury, Western Australia was hit and sustained serious injuries during the initial attack. A second attack by the fighter five minutes later again under the starboard wing caused the number 3 fuel tank to catch fire. Regan immediately put the Halifax into a dive to try and extinguish the flames but the fire rapidly began to engulf the aircraft. After a short conversation with Sergeant Alan D. Lawes the flight engineer, he gave the order to bail out. The first to leave the aircraft was Sergeant Ronald Walter Tindal the 31-year old rear gunner from Tottenham, London. Whether he exited through the rear hatch or direct from his turret is not known but tragically he fell to his death as his parachute harness had been improperly fastened. The Canadian navigator, Warrant Officer2 W. S. 'Bill' Norris, bomb aimer Flight Sergeant Norman Wilmot and Alan Lawes bailed out safely. Walter Regan stayed at the controls until the end to give the crew the best possible chance of survival but was killed as the aircraft exploded over a wooded hilltop outside the village of Steinheim, about 24 kilometres north east of Frankfurt. Wreckage was scattered over a wide area of the hill and the bodies of three airmen, Walter Regan, whose brother, William Patrick Michael, also died on service, Sergeant Donald Lawrence Smith the wireless operator from Walthamstow, London who had flown his four previous operations with another crew and Hugh Birch were recovered from the crash site. All four of the crew who were lost were buried in local cemeteries, before being moved after the war to Hanover War Cemetery. Bill Norris and Alan Lawes were sent to Stalag Luft VI in Eastern Prussia. Norman Wilmot was badly injured and remained in hospital in Frankfurt for two months before being sent to Stalag Luft VII in Poland. All three were to take part in the forced marches during the final stages of the war.

'E-Easy' on 44 Squadron had got as far as the sea and John Chadderton at last put the nose down a fraction to gain speed without caning the engines or spoiling Ken's proud fuel record of over one air mile per gallon. With these tactics and a bit of navigator's log cooking on our beloved 'Y-Yorker' we could normally rely on being the first back to Dunholme Lodge (our ground crew had a considerable bet on it), but 'Easy' lacked an aerodynamic finesse and when at last I called for landing instructions I was a bit narked to hear my mate, Australian Roy Manning in 'Q-Queenie' got 'No. 1 to land'. And so to interrogation - just a normal sort of trip - 1,500 miles, 7½ hours and the squadron lost two aircraft; one damaged, thirteen men killed and one a prisoner.'

'Z-Zebra' had flown on home to Dunholme Lodge on three engines. As Wing Commander Thompson's crew neared the French coast at Dieppe they saw two anti-aircraft guns about a mile apart sending up cones of fire that crossed at 10,000 feet. A few seconds later a bomber was caught in the crossfire and fell in flames. The 429 'Bison' Squadron RCAF Halifax flown by Flying Officer James Henry 'Jimmy' Wilson RCAF from Moose Jaw, Saskatchewan had been attacked and badly damaged near Stuttgart and was set on fire. His Canadian flight engineer extinguished the fire by chopping a hole in the side of the fuselage and kicking out two blazing magnesium flares that were carried for a landing on the sea. Wilson made it to the coast and ditched in the English Channel where the nose section broke away, taking the pilot to the depths. The rest of the crew survived the ditching and they were picked up following a tense operation involving Spitfire, Tempest, Sea Otter and Walrus aircraft and two RAF HSLs from Newhaven, which found them drifting 25 miles off the Normandy coastline.

It was bad luck but 'Z-Zebra', which dived rapidly and cleared the coast at 100 feet, seemed to have had more than its fair share of good fortune. After the crew had made the change of course at Charleroi for the 250-mile leg to Fulda they had narrowly missed colliding with another Lancaster. North of Frankfurt 'Z-Zebra' had been caught by the searchlights and two and then three held them in the beams. They were helpless but the anti-aircraft guns had remained silent. At the target, when Flying Officer Bill Clegg, 'Yorker's experienced bomb aimer was ready to bomb, he had noticed that other Lancasters above, below and on each side of their bomber were making their runs and some were in the way, so he asked Thompson to go around again. As the second run began Clegg noticed that the cloud veiling Nuremberg was now gradually thinning and then he saw a dying TI below so he thumbed forward the drift handle of his Mk.XIV bombsight, slapped down his selector switches and fused his bombs. Thompson had just seen the light appear on his panel to confirm that the bomb-doors had opened when out of the night another bomber side-slipped in front of 'Z-Zebra'. Thompson jabbed on right rudder, dropped the nose of the Lancaster and cursed the black shape that now flashed past above them. Inexperienced crews bombed short so the Path Finders would place their markers right at the far end of the target. Panicky bomb aimers had a tendency, when they saw all the flak and searchlights, to drop their bombs quickly and get the hell out of it, so raids always tended to creep back. Clegg did not blame them but he refused to panic and he refused to let his bombs go at random. He stretched himself along his bombing mat a third time and got the bombs away. Bombs gone, Thompson dropped to 10,000 feet to begin a straight run across Nuremberg with cameras running. Burrows the flight engineer glanced out over 'Z-Zebra's starboard wing. Horrified, he saw another Lancaster coming straight at them.

'Dive, Dive!' he screamed over the intercom.

Thompson, who had been flying for four hours and had amazingly already avoided a collision with a Halifax, had reacted equally fast and again there was no collision.

For Stephen Burrows the journey home was uneventful except for occasional searchlights and a little flak. About twenty miles from the coast on the way out, Burrows noticed, from his flight engineer's jump-seat alongside Wing Commander Thompson, a pair of light flak guns crossing their fire at about 10,000 feet. Even as he watched, a bomber caught 'a terrific packet' and crashed in flames. Thompson promptly dived his Lancaster for a low-level crossing of the enemy coast at about 100 feet and when clear and out over the English Channel, climbed back up to 4,000 feet.

On the way across, the Lancaster had the company of a series of V-1 flying bombs which passed by on their way to London.

'When we got nearer our coast we could see them exploding ahead', said Burrows. 'We did, incidentally, lose an engine while approximately a hundred miles inside enemy territory, due to some mechanical fault; this consequently made us late on arrival at base, which in turn prompted rumours that we were missing.'

Against all the odds 'Z-Zebra' was one of fourteen Lancasters on 44 Squadron that returned to Dunholme Lodge. Wing Commander Thompson's crew went straight to the interrogation room where Stephen Burrows was surprised to see the imposing six-foot-six figure of 45-year old Air Commodore 'Poppy' Pope, the station commander (a highly decorated World War I flying ace credited with six aerial victories) standing beside Group Captain Butler. 'Both of these officers asked him how the operation had gone. Burrows stated that he thought that Bomber Command had lost about 100 aircraft and he was told not to be ridiculous. They turned to the doctor and remarked, 'Send this crew on leave. It's time they had a rest.'

'The de-briefing was very quiet and the atmosphere was electric,' adds Burrows. 'Whilst I heard the rumour regarding leakage of information I must say, having had a little previous operational experience, it certainly appeared to me that Jerry was waiting for us. In fact it was said quite openly during the interrogation, with lots and lots of derogatory remarks being made. We on 44 Squadron had lost seven aircraft [sic] and we noticed at breakfast that many seats were empty. There were plenty of fried eggs to spare. They had been cooked for crews who never returned. That evening we consumed gallons of ale. I would state that this raid was, without any doubt, the most severe experienced generally, although we as a crew had had worse experiences on other trips.'

ND795 'C-Charlie' flown by Pilot Officer Trevor George William Charlesworth who was from Shareshill, Staffs was one of sixteen Lancasters on 44 Squadron that had taken off from Dunholme Lodge. He was shot down and killed near the final turning point and crashed at Unteressfeld with the loss of five of his crew. Flying Officer E. M. Dunn the Canadian bomb aimer was the only survivor. Those who died were: Sergeant Lionel John Evans the rear gunner of Manselton, Swansea; Flight Sergeant Ronald Patrick Grenville Hill the navigator of Hounslow, Middlesex; Sergeant Kenneth Arthur Jeffery the flight engineer of Tottenham, London; Sergeant Samuel Percival the wireless operator of Carcroft, Yorks and Sergeant George Walter Scott the mid-upper gunner of Reading, Berks. The crew was on their seventh operation.

At about five minutes after midnight a Bf 110G-4, its nose painted with sharks teeth, flown by 25-year old Oberleutnant Martin Drewes, Gruppenkommandeur of III./NJG1 at Laon-Athies crept stealthily up towards LM425 'N for Nan' on 550 Squadron skippered by 21-year old Flight Sergeant Arthur Harrington Jeffries of Wantage, Berkshire. He had joined the RAF in 1940 and had started flying as a pilot in May 1943 on 101 Squadron. After a raid on Stuttgart on 15 March he had been recommended for the Conspicuous Gallantry Medal. 'N for Nan' had been hit during the outbound flight by flak from batteries near Liège and Drewes was determined to finish the Lancaster off. Born on 20 October 1918 in Lobmachtersen-bei-Braunschweig, a small village near Hannover in north-western Germany, Drewes was the son of a local pharmacist. At the end of the 1930s he had volunteered for the officer's school of the German Army and had transferred to the Luftwaffe in 1939. He and his crew of Oberfeldwebel Georg 'Schorsch' Petz, bordschütze and 24-year old Oberfeldwebel Erich Handke, bordfunker shot down 'N-Nan' for the first of his three kills that night. Australian bomb aimer Warrant Officer George Claude Notman, a farmer from Skipton, Victoria on 'R-Roger' on 550 Squadron saw 'a faint golden glow, then a trail of fire until 'plop' and another of our bombers was glowing red on the ground. This sickening blood-red fire belching black smoke - our own boys were in that! Wonder who will be next?'[181]

Jeffries, Sergeant Robert Henry Paxton, the 39-year old flight engineer of Stranraer, Wigtownshire, Sergeant Harold Simpson, the 21-year old navigator and Sergeant James Woodburn 'Tony' Whitley, the 23-year old air gunner were killed instantly in the explosion. After leaving school, Whitely, the eldest of four children, had enrolled at the Liverpool School of Architecture, hoping to follow his father's profession but had joined the RAF and initially trained as a wireless operator. Bob Paxton, who had been a house painter before joining the RAF, left a widow, Agnes and a son, Robert and two daughters, Catherine and Eva. Initially the Luftwaffe at St. Truiden buried the dead but they were later re-interred in Heverlee War Cemetery. Jeffries, who had flown 25 operational sorties, was posthumously awarded the Conspicuous Gallantry Medal on 21 December 1945.

Flight Sergeant D. S. Jeffrey the air bomber, Sergeant W. George Upton the air gunner and Sergeant Stanley A. Keirle the wireless operator were thrown out as the Lancaster blew up. Keirle, who was on his 17th operation, wrote: 'We were mortally hit by predicted flak (before reaching the target) from the Liege defences at almost exactly midnight. The time is fixed in my mind because I had just gone over to the group frequency to receive their hourly broadcast when all hell was let loose. We had been hit in the starboard wing, the outboard engine being on fire. The pilot and engineer used the fire extinguishers and tried to feather the prop but I am not sure whether they managed it or not. The skipper ordered parachutes on. I found mine in its stowage compartment and clipped it on my harness. I returned to the astrodome, still plugged in to the intercom. The fire died down for a while and then suddenly broke out afresh with increased intensity and crept back into the wing itself - which burnt thorough very quickly. I stood there and watched the outboard engine and outer wing fall off - at which time the aircraft dipped a wing and started to spiral downwards with all engines at maximum revs it seemed. The g force was tremendous and before passing out I remember floating through the air past the navigator's position and getting my feet all tangled up with the cockpit controls. The skipper was still in his seat struggling to get control of the plane. I then passed out having concluded that the situation was hopeless - mentally regretting that my mother would have to handle the news of me being listed as missing while my father was seriously ill.

'What happened next is a very vague memory, which could even be imagination. I found myself in open air with wind rushing past my face. Slowly, the realisation came that I was falling through space and that I should pull the rip-cord of my parachute. The 'chute was not on my chest; it was dangling around my feet. Having hauled it up via the loose harness, I pulled the cord and something came up and hit me under the chin - knocking me out again! I woke up tumbling through trees feeling that my right arm was entangled in a bulky object. I finally landed on my back with the object I was tangled in across my back - my bottom and legs on one side of it and my head and shoulders on the other side. I think I passed out again. Gradually, my head cleared enough to know that I was stretched across something and that all around me was quiet except for the thunder of aircraft engines overhead.

'At that moment the truth dawned that I was still alive and the noise overhead was the bomber force on its way to Nuremberg. My parachute canopy was caught in a tree and I could not breathe too easily. My left leg was doubled under my bottom and ached and my back hurt very much. Gradually, I forced myself to turn over and push the 'object' away - my right arm was through the thing which turned out to be the cockpit canopy - all ten feet of it, or whatever its length was. My back hurt like hell! I lay there for what seemed to be ages before the noise overhead faded away in the distance. I thought to myself, 'Go get them fellers'. Very soon I began to feel cold and then I could only move very slowly, certainly not enough to keep warm or to walk and find shelter. Nobody would find me in this forest even if they knew a bod was in there I reasoned and for the second time that night thought that the outlook was not too rosy.

'I wondered how the other fellows had fared but was fairly convinced that their chances of survival were slim and reckoned that I was very lucky indeed to be alive. At that point I became determined that I was going to survive come what may and set about evaluating the situation and at the same time try to keep warm. Sometime later I saw a torch waving about, so I blew the whistle attached to my battledress tunic. Gradually the light got closer and then shone directly on me. A German soldier was holding the torch. Using sign language, he asked me if I had a gun. When he was satisfied that I was telling the truth, he propped me up and proceeded to gather sticks and wood then lit a fire in a clearing. That soldier carried me to the fire and made me as comfortable as possible. When I had warmed through I remembered that I had a packet of cigarettes in my tunic, so I offered him one and we smoked together. He spoke no English and I no German but we did manage to communicate a little and I learned that he had found two others closed by but they were 'kaput'.'

After being reunited with Jeffrey and Upton, Keirle was taken to a hospital in Aachen. In June he was sent for interrogation at Frankfurt-am-Main before going to Stalag Luft VII at Bankau and here he remained until the Russian advancement on 19 January 1945. Keirle joined many PoWs beginning the long march from the camp in heavy snow. Owing to his injuries walking was very difficult and he became detached from the main group, his injuries preventing him from keeping up and he was diverted to Stalag Luft III at Sagan in Silesia by the medical officer. From there he and others were sent to Luckenwalde by goods train the following day. He is believed to have arrived at RAF Benson between the 8th and 11th of May 1945.

Lancaster W5006 WS-X piloted by Flying Officer James Gordon Richmond Ling, a 23-year old Scot from Newmilns, Ayrshire was 9 Squadron's only loss on the raid and the second aircraft to fall to Martin Drewes. The crew, who were on their 25th operation, had taken off from Bardney at 2205 hours. Ling, who had made ten trips to Berlin, did not know that below their Lancaster and on the same course lurked Drewes shark-toothed Bf 110. Drewes got fifty metres under 'X-X-ray' but George Petz's cannon jammed after the second shot and could not be reloaded. 'The Lancaster must have been hit however, as it lost height quickly' recalled Erich Handke 'but as we kept behind it, not having turned off in time, it must have spotted us, for suddenly it twisted into a corkscrew. We also dropped 600 metres. At 550 metres the Lancaster seemed to steady and we had to overcome the compulsion to attack in our old way - where one was exposed to the fire of the tail-gunner. But we were already well used to the new tactics of firing into the wings, which did not endanger us so much when the bomber's load went off. At long last Drewes raised the nose of our fighter and fired a long burst with his front armament into the bomber's starboard wing, which burst into flame. For a second or so he forgot to dive away but there was no return fire from the rear-turret. The Lancaster's starboard inner engine dragged a banner of flame and its nose fell. As Drewes pulled away the Lancaster blew up, showering the sky with thousands of fiery fragments. I took a quick fix on my directional-finding gear and noted that the bomber had exploded in the air over the Vogelsberg area. Around us, bombers were dropping like flies sprayed with an insecticide gun.'

Only one parachute came out of Ling's Lancaster. It was the navigator, Sergeant H. Laws. The others who were killed were Flight Sergeant Thomas Santola Fletcher the bomb aimer of Ongar, Essex; Sergeant Edgar Alexander Gauld the 23-year old mid-upper gunner of Aberdeen; Sergeant Leonard Moss, the 19-year old flight engineer from Moss Side, Manchester; Pilot Officer Edward James Rush the 22-year old mid-upper gunner who left a widow, Hazel Jean of Calgary, Alberta and the tail gunner, Sergeant Italo Prada, born in 1921 in Germany, the son of Italian-born Giacomo and Anetta Prada. At the time of his death, Italo's father was detained on the Isle of Man, where the government had established internment camps for Italian nationals. The Lancaster came down at Cleeburg, eight kilometres WNW of Butzbach. Those who died are buried at Hannover War Cemetery.

At 0120 Drewes and his crew singled out their third victim of the night. It was Lancaster III ND390 OF-S on 97 Squadron which was being flown by 23-year old Flight Lieutenant Desmond Harold Rowlands DFC of Kenton, Middlesex. 'At 700 metres' said Handke 'we could see it was another Lancaster. We were about to attack from the rear again when Petz announced that he had cleared the stoppage in our cannon. With the 'oblique' cannon working we could now attack from below and to the side of the bomber, with less risk of being seen. Drewes edged the night-fighter closer and for a few seconds we were almost on parallel course. Unaware, the Lancaster flew on. Then Drewes raked it with a long burst aimed into the wing. Flames fanned from the engines along the fuselage to acknowledge the accuracy of his shooting.'

Rowlands and his crew were mostly second-tourists who were on their third operation with the Path Finders. The bodies of 19-year old Sergeant Robert Myall Lane the flight engineer of Richmond, Surrey; Flight Lieutenants Arthur Robert Cadman DFM the 24-year old navigator of Kingswinford, Staffordshire (whose award had been gained on 49 Squadron in 1940) and Albert Stanley McFadden the 27-year old bomb aimer of Walton, Liverpool and Flying Officers Edgar James Currie the 32-year old wireless operator whose wife Coralie Currie lived in East Dulwich, London and Fred Colville the mid-upper gunner of Chester-le-Street, County Durham were found near the main fuselage on the edge of a wood at Ahorn in the south-western suburbs of Coburg. The tail came down some distance away and the body of 28-year old Flight Lieutenant Richard Algernon Dacre Trevor-Roper DFC DFM was found in his rear turret. Born on the Isle of Wight on 19 May 1915, he spent two years in the Royal Artillery after leaving Wellington College, before he joined the RAF at the outset of war in 1939. A sergeant gunner at Swinderby before he was commissioned he completed his first tour on 50 Squadron in 1941 and received the DFM. He became Wing Commander Guy Gibson's tail gunner on the Dams raid on 16/17 May 1943 for which he was awarded the DFC. The acknowledged leader of the squadron's hell-raisers 'with an

Oxford accent and Billingsgate vocabulary' he had only recently joined 97 Squadron from NTU, having spent six months at Central Gunnery School. His wife, who lived at the family home at Shanklin on the Isle of Wight, had only recently given birth to their first child.

Pilot Officer Harry Forrest, piloting Lancaster I DV395 'V-Victor' on 9 Squadron at Bardney recalled an initially uneventful flight along the route south over France with a turn to port to cross the Rhine between Koblenz and Bonn navigated by Sergeant Harwood. That there was a good half-moon and a clear sky however, was something that had concerned him early, a concern soon to be justified. The 10,672lb bomb load they carried consisted of the 4,000lb 'cookie', six containers each holding 150 4lb incendiaries, five containers holding twelve 30lb incendiaries, one container holding sixteen 30lb incendiaries and one container holding eight 30lb incendiaries. It was a bomb-load destined never to reach its target. 'As we approached the Rhine it was evident that there was considerable enemy fighter activity in the area' said Forrest 'with the result that the frequency of our 'bank and search' was increased and the wireless operator asked to keep careful watch on 'Monica'.

At 0037 hours the Lancaster was at 20,000 feet and travelling at 155 mph when it was attacked without warning by a Ju 88 at 250 yards from below and astern and hit by cannon-fire which severed pipe lines in the rear turret and a fire occurred. The leading edge of the starboard tailplane was hit and the starboard side of the fuselage aft of the mid-upper turret was holed several times. 'We were hit and I immediately began corkscrewing' continues Forrest. The Ju 88 was seen to break away to port. Our aircraft was on fire in the rear bomb bay or rear fuselage and the intercom was dead. I gave orders to Sergeant Hutton the flight engineer to open bomb-doors and jettison the load. This being done the fire still persisted, so I decided the best thing to do was dive.' The dive blew out the fire and Forrest levelled off at about 14,000 feet. 'By this time Sergeant D. McCauley, the wireless operator, had rectified the fault in the intercom and asked if he could go aft to look at Flight Sergeant Bernard Utting the 22-year old mid-upper gunner who had climbed down from his turret and collapsed by the main spar. I agreed and then checked that Sergeant Pinchin, the rear gunner, was OK. McCauley then called up and reported that Utting was dead. The aircraft appeared to respond normally to controls and it was felt that as there was no power for the turrets the best course of action would be to climb on track and follow the Main Force to the target and return with them to base.'

'You have to be lucky some time' related Sergeant B. Pinchin. 'We were attacked first from the starboard quarter but we corkscrewed and after one full corkscrew I reported to the Captain that the attack had been broken off and we resumed flying straight and level again. We had done ten trips and felt that we knew what it was all about. I felt we had lost the enemy fighter but only a few seconds later there was a hell of a clatter. We had been hit by another fighter that we hadn't seen. He had sprayed the area between the rear door and the end of the bomb bay. The hydraulics to my turret caught fire and the whole of the fuselage up to Flight Sergeant Utting's mid-upper turret was in flames. When the pilot decided to drop our bomb load and dive the flames out I didn't think the fire would go out and was expecting to be ordered to bail out but at 13,000 feet the fire did go out. Pilot Officer Forrest decided to stay with the stream and later flew right over Nuremberg with empty bomb bays. When the body of the 22-year old mid-upper gunner was removed from the aircraft, Flight

Sergeant Utting was apparently unmarked but the Medical Officer found that a small fragment of cannon shell had entered his stomach and cut the small intestine. Utting, who hailed from Hempton in Norfolk, is buried in Fakenham Cemetery near his home.[183]

Flight Lieutenant D. Pearce on 9 Squadron had taken 'F-Fox' off from Bardney at 2205. As the weather reports came in, Flight Sergeant W. Doran, wireless operator, decoded them. Sergeant Howe, flight engineer, Warrant Officer 'Sonny' Thomas RAAF, rear gunner, and the others settled down for the long flight to the target. Crossing the coast, Sergeant James Stuart MacLean, the Scot's born mid-upper gunner, observed that there was a quarter-moon and visibility was good, probably too good for night operations. Yet, perhaps because 'F-Fox' was being flown slightly off track, the trip to the target proved uneventful. Flying Officer W. Pearson, the Canadian bomb aimer, got his bombs away and Pearce turned 'F-Fox' for home. After leaving the target in good visibility, MacLean was conscious not of flak but of increased fighter activity and he was glad to hear the Canadian navigator, Flying Officer J. E. Logan, giving the first of the homeward courses to the skipper. 'We observed a number of aircraft shot down,' MacLean said, 'but as we were still flying slightly off track we had no trouble at all on the way out to the coast. As a crew we estimated having seen a total of about forty aircraft shot down in flames and these mainly on leaving the target. Our flight home to Bardney was uneventful apart from some flak and we landed back at base undamaged having been in the air for eight hours and twenty minutes.'

Pilot Officer Philip Edward Plowright, an 'A' Flight pilot who always wore his lucky green and orange striped scarf, his college colours, returned to Bardney where he concluded his log-book entry for the eight-hour flight in Lancaster I W4964 better known as *Johnny Walker* with the single comment: 'My 18th operation. Wanganui marking. Fighters active on route but target OK. Marking scattered. Ninety-nine aircraft lost.'

Having dived to blow out the fire in the bomb-bay after a attack by a Ju 88 night-fighter from below, and then flown on to Nuremberg without his jettisoned bomb-load, Pilot Officer Harry Forrest on 9 Squadron flew the badly damaged 'V-Victor' back home to Bardney with two holes about two feet square, one just forward of the Elsan, the other just aft of the mid-upper turret. Forrest asked for landing clearance: 'Hello 'Smalltype', hello 'Smalltype'. This is 'Rosen Victor', 'Rosen Victor.'

'Smalltype cleared 'V-Victor' for landing. It was one of fifteen Lancasters that returned from the sixteen that had set out. Two other Lancasters were damaged and one man returned wounded. Pinchin had fired off 500 rounds during the night fighter attack but Utting never had time to fire a single shot.

When the Main Force had turned onto the long leg over Charleroi Russell, Margerison, the mid-upper gunner on 'P-Peter' on 625, noted that the half moon was clearly showing up the condensation trails of each bomber. 'It all made a very impressive sight, but one I would rather not have seen, for if I could see dozens and dozens of aircraft, so could the enemy. Within half an hour the half-expected fighters were amongst us; their arrival being announced by a blossoming reddish glow on our port side as the first bomber fell in the Aachen area. By the time another fifteen minutes had passed string after string of flares, dropped by the Hun, illuminated our course and the uneven battle started in earnest. Red and green tracer criss-crossed the sky as

Max tried desperately to gain more height. An explosion on the port side down showered hundreds of flaming fragments across the sky.

'Halifax going down, port side, Dave,' I said.

'Got it Russ,' replied the navigator.

'Lanc falling to the rear' said Gib from the tail.

'No sooner had he got the words out than I watched mesmerised as a Lanc's wing folded at right angles to the aircraft like a drop-leaf table and it just toppled over and over, quickly disappearing from my view. An excrescent flush of orange flame from another Lanc soon enveloped the whole plane and it skidded out of sight below us.

'Another Lanc...'

'Let's just forget it Gib,' I interrupted. The whole thing was so demoralising it seemed pointless making it worse.

'Guess you're right, Russ,' came the answer.

'It was like flying down an endless well-lit stretch of motorway. I knew now how the merchant sailors must have felt on the Russian convoys as the U-boats picked them off one by one.

'Along with jettisoned bombs, particularly incendiaries, burning aircraft marked our course and, with prickly beads of sweat on my forehead, I realised we were now illuminated from above and below.

'A banner of red and yellow flame streaked in front of us and then completely broke in two. I tried turning away from this madness to search the darker part of the sky but it seemed that no matter where I looked an aircraft was falling. Watching a bomber going down had not previously disturbed me unduly but this was ridiculous. Apart from becoming jittery I found myself becoming emotionally disturbed.

'A huge flash introduced a scarecrow in our midst with its black oily smoke and dripping colours. Thank God it was not till after the war that we learned that no such a thing as scarecrows existed, they were in fact bombers receiving a direct hit on their bomb bays.

'Burning petrol spewed out of a Halifax and its whole tail unit disappeared, the nose went down and the last I saw of it the machine was going down vertically.

'On and on went the carnage and I would estimate that 'Gib' and I saw fifteen bombers go down. Some floated down from side to side like a leaf falling from a tree in autumn, some flew straight and level for half a minute or so, even though the flames looked huge in comparison to the size of the plane, some just toppled out of the sky, whilst others screamed straight down as though in a hurry. Anyone unfamiliar with this kind of warfare could be excused for not believing the incredible fact that through the whole of this action no-one in our aircraft saw a fighter.

'At long last, after the most frightening two-and-a-half hours of my life, we made a 45 degree turn for the run over Nuremberg. Cloud had moved in and covered the whole of the city, rendering normal ground marking impossible. Emergency 'Wanganui' marking had been used by the Path Finders and two widely separated clusters of flares hung in the sky, suspended over translucent cloud, made so by the searchlights below. It was eerie over the target, unlike any we had met. Flak was spasmodic and inaccurate and the few bombers I could see below us, like spiders on a white backcloth, looked totally uninterested and uninteresting. No fires could we see, but what was more important, we couldn't see any fighter activity either.

'Jeez, all this way and nothing definite to aim at,' grumbled Brick. 'Where the hell shall I... Oh to hell with it. Bombs gone. Let's get to hell out of here.'

'Brick's disgust showed.

'A couple of turns, the last one being south of Stuttgart, brought us onto the long leg to France, but by now the moon had settled and we were in familiar darkness under a canopy of stars. The sweat had now subsided but my eyes ached with searching. For the twentieth time I tried to rub off a smear of dirt on my turret which had made me whip round in its direction so many times thinking it was a fighter that I felt like knocking a hole in the perspex to get rid of it and I vowed I would clean my own turret in future. My thoughts began to wander. Just what had gone wrong?

'Corkscrew port, go, go!' screamed Gib.

'Down we plummeted into the familiar corkscrew and with a renewed awareness of danger I stared and stared for a glimpse of the fighter Gib had seen, but alas in vain. Was the Canadian rear gunner imagining things? We resumed course straight and level. He's probably jittery like me after tonight's episode. God, he's there. A small black shadow of a single-engined fighter was sliding onto us from the starboard up.

'Corkscrew starboard, go, go,' I found myself shouting as I rotated the turret in his direction. With commendable rapidity the skipper flung the huge machine down again and the blur disappeared from view.

'We're being stalked by this one' called out Max.

'Dick, up in the astrodome: 'Everyone, eyes peeled'.

'I've been there for the last five minutes, Skip,' replied Dick.

Five minutes of straight flying in the darkness without a sighting relaxed the tension. There was no flak and no sign of combat.

'Starboard go,' Gib and I bawled in unison as vicious looking white tracer gashed the sky feet above us and careered off at an acute right angle in the distance. And still no clear sight of the offending fighter.

'Okay, guys, that's it,' Max declared, 'I'm gonna corkscrew for the next hour.'

'A seemingly ridiculous statement, for this manoeuvre was a particularly tiring one for the pilot. However, as usual, he did precisely that and as a consequence no further trouble was experienced from the persistent German.

'Fifteen minutes from Dieppe and once again, thankfully on a level course, Max called: 'Our fuel tanks are dangerously low. It's fifty-fifty whether we can make it over the sea or not. Gib do we have a go or bail out?'

'Have a go, Skipper,' replied 'Gib' without hesitation.

'Russ?'

'Try it,' I replied.

'He put the question to the six of us and it was unanimously decided to try and make England.'

At Holme-on-Spalding Moor, where fourteen Halifaxes had been dispatched by 76 Squadron, the clock in the big briefing room ticked on. On the ops board in the column headed 'Time Down' there were three blank spaces. Twenty-six year old pilot, Flight Lieutenant Henry Denys Coverley was on his fortieth trip, the tenth of his second tour, the first having been on 78 Squadron. His usual aircraft, *Sir Roger De Coverley* had gone unserviceable. He had taken LK795 'P-Peter', Wing Commander Douglas 'Hank' Iveson DSO DFC the squadron commander's aircraft instead. The Intelligence Officer looked at his watch and checked it with the clock. Hopefully, 'P-Peter' or 'The Blue

Barge' as it was better known and 'W-William' and 'X-X-ray' had made emergency landings at 'dromes on the southeast coast; the telephone, at his elbow, would ring in a moment confirming it. The room was crowded and there was acute expectancy in the air. Crews who were down were hanging about, deliberately taking their time over mugs of tea, forgetting the hot flying suppers waiting for them in the messes. As the minutes ticked by, many considered the chances of the three crews bailing out and spending the rest of the war as a PoW or lobbing down somewhere in the drink off the coast. It was the best that they could hope for.

'W-William' (LW647) skippered by 22-year old Flying Officer Gordon Charles George Greenacre from Wroxham in the heart of the Norfolk Broads was on his second tour on the Squadron. He was possibly one of three Viermots shot down by 23-year old Oberfeldwebel Rudolf Frank of 3./NJG3 flying a Bf 110G-4 on his 176th night sortie. Frank had taken off from Vechta with his bordfunker Oberfeldwebel Hans-Georg Schierholz but minus his usual air-gunner, Feldwebel Heinz Schneider, who had been replaced by a young pilot fresh from training to gain combat experience. Using his oblique guns Frank shot down his first victim, which he identified as a 'Lancaster', with one burst which set the Halifax bomber's fuel tanks ablaze and sent it crashing down at 0001 hours at Nieder-Moos, six kilometres NNW of Freiensteinau. Two men bailed out and were taken prisoner. Pilot Officer Anthony Monk the flight engineer was sent to Stalag Luft I at Barth and Sergeant Jack A. Henthorn the wireless operator was sent to Luft VI at Heydekrug. On 1 April Greenacre; Flying Officer Alfred Thorpe the 25-year old navigator from Sutton-in-Ashfield in Nottinghamshire, who left a widow, Joan Louise; Pilot Officer Adam Scott Arneil the 21-year old Scottish air bomber from Barnton, Midlothian; Pilot Officer Arthur Douglas Maw, the 21 year old Canadian air gunner from Winnipeg and Pilot Officer Arthur Henry Death RCAF the 23-year old rear gunner from Toronto, were laid to rest at Nieder Moos, since when their bodies have been taken to Durnbach War Cemetery about ten miles east of Bad Tölz in Bavaria.

Seventeen minutes after 'W-William' went down a Lancaster fell to Frank's guns in the same manner as the Halifax, in the region north of Fulda. Thirty-four minutes later Schierholz picked up a new contact. It was a Halifax. On instructions from Generalmajor Max Ibel's 2 Jagddivision headquarters in Stade they flew for about five minutes with the bomber in order to determine its course and altitude before receiving instructions to attack. Frank employed the same tactics as before and the Halifax crashed in flames in the region of the Rhön. His 41st to 43rd kills earned him the award of the Ritterkreuz with Eichenlaub but like many others his career was short lived. Having scored two more Abschüsse to take his score to 45 night victories, Frank was killed on 26/27 April when he crashed after being hit by debris from a 12 Squadron Lancaster which was falling to the ground near Eindhoven. He was posthumously promoted to Leutnant at the end of April on Hitler's birthday.

Halifax 'X-X-ray' (LW696) flown by 21-year old Squadron Leader Kenneth Arthur Clack DFM was sent down in flames at Daubhausen twelve kilometres northwest of Wetzlar by a Bf 110 using 'Schräge Musik'. All of the crew except for Sergeant Guy L. Edwards the mid-upper gunner were killed. The crew were on their fourth operation of their second tour. Kenny Clack, who lived with his parents in Kenton for some years, gained his DFM for bringing his crippled Halifax home from a raid on Trondheim on 27 April 1942 during his first tour on 76 Squadron. He had recently taken command of 'C' Flight. Clack and Warrant Officer2 Roy Edwards Mogalki the 23-year old flight engineer of Goodwater, Saskatchewan; Flying Officer David Clifford Nowell DFM the navigator of Brinnington, Cheshire; Flight Sergeant Keith James Shropshall the wireless operator of Gnosall, Staffordshire; Flying Officer Richard Keith Thomson the bomb aimer of Saskatoon, Saskatchewan; Sergeant Leslie Wilfred Arthur Peall of Nottingham and Pilot Officer Douglas Hinton Edwards the rear gunner of Malvern, Worcestershire now rest in Hannover War Cemetery. Sergeant Guy Edwards said: 'I could not move at all. Then, everything around me broke up and I was left hanging out while what remained of the fuselage fell towards the deck. At about 1,000 feet, I estimate, I was thrown clear and immediately opened my 'chute, landing safely.'

Henry Coverley was humming the popular song *Paper Doll* to himself as he flew down the 'long leg'. 'It was a clear night - the weather report was wrong because the Met Officer had told us it would be overcast and the fighters wouldn't be able to get up. But there was no cloud - there wasn't a bloody cloud in the sky! However there was nothing much you could do. I did notice a hell of a lot of aircraft going down all around us and at the time thought it was special shells... 'Scarecrows!' We thought the Germans were putting those up to make it look like it was an aircraft going down. They were going down quite fast.'

Suddenly 'The Blue Barge' was hit by flak near Hamm.[184] The 6,000lb load of incendiary bombs exploded causing a massive fire. 'We were about the thirtieth casualty on the way out' said Coverley. Listening out for a Group broadcast on his wireless set, 20-year old Sergeant Peter G. G. Wilmshurst who was on his thirteenth operation, failed to hear the order to bail out and realised all was not well when he saw the flight engineer, Sergeant George Edwin Motts the 20-year old flight engineer, who was from Lincoln, heading for the nose escape hatch with his parachute clipped on, closely followed by the pilot, who was last to leave.

'The rest of the crew went out first. I couldn't leave: two engines had gone on one side' said Coverley. 'I was fighting the controls and the thing was on fire. The only way I could get out was to leave the controls, take a couple of footsteps to the other side of the aircraft and go down a couple of steps to the escape hatch in the front. By that time the aircraft was upside down, doing God knows what. There was no question of just opening a door and jumping out. I'd never carried a parachute. We had ones you slipped on. And I put this thing on, but I put it on wrong. I can't remember getting out of the aircraft and I couldn't find the handle to pull the ripcord. But we were at 24,000 feet, so I had plenty of time to think about it. The other thing was the standard harness I had was not my size and we'd ban anyone who took his own. I didn't think it would be any use anyway; and the strap that should have been across was in front of my nose. I was awfully sick on the way down; I landed in some trees. I couldn't see anything - something had hit me in the face before I'd jumped out and I couldn't see very well. I was suspended from these trees and I didn't know how far I was from the ground. Eventually after swaying around in this tree for a while, I thought I'd better get myself out and my feet were about six inches from the ground! So then I started walking. I was lucky.'[185]

Flight Sergeant W. A. 'Archie' Blake the bomb aimer, who at first was unable to jump because of the g forces got out safely. So too Flight Sergeant K. H. A. Trott the navigator; Sergeant G. M. Smitham the mid-upper gunner and Sergeant David M. Bauldie the rear-gunner from Dunfermline in Fifeshire before 'The Blue Barge' crashed. George Motts died when he evacuated the Halifax with his parachute on fire. His body was found three days later suspended in a tree, the burnt remains of his parachute canopy draped around him. When the Halifax had gone into a steep dive, Peter Wilmshurst had great difficulty trying to reach his parachute in its stowage and clip it on. Having succeeded in this he found that he was then unable to leave his seat: 'For some unknown reason the dive became more shallow', he recalled. 'This allowed me to get out of my seat and make my way forward to the escape hatch.' As soon as he jumped he realised that he must have been low to the ground by this time so he pulled the ripcord. After two or three swings under his parachute he hit the ground with an almighty thump, breaking his leg.

Coverley walked for thirty miles and he evaded capture for four days before being caught crossing a bridge over the Rhine. The five survivors on the crew were rounded up and sent to prison camps. Sergeant David Bauldie was killed on 19 April 1945 when his PoW column was strafed by RAF Typhoons at Gresse in North Germany.[186]

For Peter Wilmshurst the immediate future had not looked too promising, but at least he was alive. 'It was snowing hard. I could not stand as my right leg was broken and folded back behind the knee of my left leg and hurt intensely. In a very short time I was covered over by snow.' He soon discovered that he was in the middle of nowhere: 'Despite my shouts no one seemed very interested and I had visions of not being found and dying of exposure.' A while later the snow stopped and he could just make out the outlines of a house not too far away. Further shouting proved fruitless, until he remembered the whistle attached to his battledress collar: 'After several blows I heard a window open and a voice call out something quite unintelligible to me. Soon, a man appeared, ran off and about fifteen minutes later reappeared with two soldiers, one of whom advanced towards me with a fixed bayonet. He was quite elderly and I think more scared than I was.'

Taken inside, Wilmshurst was made as comfortable as possible. The lady of the house made some coffee, while explaining that an ambulance would not be able to get to them until daylight. When it arrived he was most surprised to find 'Archie' Blake on a stretcher next to him. He had spent several hours dangling on his parachute which had become entangled in a tall pine tree. Unable to reach the trunk of the tree and starting to suffer from frostbite he had turned the quick-release buckle on his parachute harness and fallen about thirty feet to the ground. Consequently he was suffering from a fractured pelvis. The injured pair were taken to the hospital at Wissen on the River Sieg, run mainly by Roman Catholic Sisters, but with German doctors and medical orderlies and Red Cross nurses. They shared the hospital with many German wounded, mostly from the Eastern Front, but regardless of their status the RAF pair were treated equally with the soldiers: 'The medical attention was first class' said Wilmshurst. 'The Army doctor who attended to us always gave a Nazi salute whenever he entered the room, until one morning he came, saluted, gave a broad smile and said 'To hell with it!' and never saluted again.' On the day that Peter Wilmshurst and Archie Blake left they were given meat sandwiches for their journey and most of the nurses and Sisters came to say 'Auf Wiedersehen'. Nineteen weeks after they had been shot down both men arrived at Stalag Luft VII (Bankau).

Seventeen Lancasters on 550 Squadron had taken off from North Killingholme. Twelve successfully attacked the main target and three, the last resort target. Flying Officer Sage landed 'U-Uncle' at Kelstern owing to fuel shortage. Flight Sergeant T. A. Lloyd landed his badly damaged Lancaster at Ford on the south coast of

England minus three of his crew. The Lancaster had been attacked by a night-fighter on the homeward leg just south of Paris. With the trimming tabs shot away Lloyd struggled to keep control of the bomber but he managed to shake off the fighter. Five minutes later a second attack set the bomb bay and fuselage on fire and he gave the order for the crew to bail out. Sergeant J. G. 'Jack' Pearce the 30-year old mid-upper gunner, Flying Officer Edward Yaternick the Canadian bomb aimer and Sergeant A. C. Crilley the rear turret gunner bailed out. Before the rest could follow the aircraft went into a dive which helped to extinguish the fires. The bomb aimer and the rear gunner were captured but 'Jack' Pearce evaded and helped by the Resistance, he made it home via Gibraltar in June.

Pilot Officer Donald McCrae RCAF on ME556 'F' received injuries to his left arm and the 27-year old rear gunner, Sergeant Albert Henry Brown, received injuries to his left eye in combat with an enemy night fighter. The aircraft also suffered extensive damage. (Both men were killed in action on the night of 27/28 May when all seven crew perished. Brown left a widow, Alice Brown, of Radcliffe, Lancashire). Two aircraft were missing. Twenty-three year old Flight Sergeant Charles Grierson Foster RNZAF and crew on ND425 were killed when their Lancaster exploded over Unterspiesheim, eleven kilometres SSE of Schweinfurt after being hit by flak. Sergeant Wilfred Barratt the 19-year old mid-upper gunner was from Blackburn, Lancs; Flight Sergeant John Charles 'Jack' Garratt the navigator came from Market Drayton, Shropshire; Sergeant Ronald George Johns the 29-year old rear gunner, husband of Winifred Johns, of Liverpool; Flight Sergeant Robert Johnson the 31-year old bomb aimer, husband of Winifred Johnson, of South Gosforth, Newcastle upon Tyne; Sergeant John 'Jock' McGhie the flight engineer came from Busby, Lanarks and Sergeant Eric William Wash the 22-year old wireless operator was from Hoddesdon, Herts. They were on their seventeenth operation.

The loss of Flight Sergeant Arthur Harrington Jeffries and crew was also keenly felt. He is remembered as a 'character' on the base. According to Ted Stones, who was a member of his ground crew, 'he always seemed to be wearing a large brown Irvin jacket' and 'couldn't give a damn about anything. One day he and I were walking past the guardroom when the Station Warrant Officer, 'Lavender' Yardley stepped out. He said that he thought a flight sergeant ought to be setting an example to the men under him.

'I am' replied Jeffries. 'It's bloody cold and they ought to keep their hands in their pockets!'

Endnotes Chapter 17

181 Quoted in *The Nuremberg Raid* by Martin Middlebrook.

182 *The Long Road* by Oliver Clutton-Brock.

183 As quoted in *Winged Victory; The Story of a Bomber Command Air Gunner* by Jim Davis (R. J. Leach & Co, London, 1995).

184 Another source says that they were attacked by Unteroffizier Otto Kutzner, 5./NJG3, in his Bf 110 while according to research by Theo Boiten Kutzner claimed a Lancaster 7 kilometres North of Mengerskirchen at 0035 hours; Halifax LK754 flown by Flying Officer E. K. Reid on 432 'Leaside' Squadron RCAF which crashed astride the railway line 3 kilometres south of Friedberg at 0040 hours with the loss of the pilot and two crew and a Lancaster south of Nuremberg at 0133.

185 Quoted in *'Ops' Victory at All Costs* by Andrew R. B. Simpson (Tattered Flag Press 2012).

186 I am most grateful once again to Oliver Clutton-Brock for this account.

Chapter 18

Hauptmann Fritz Lau the 32-year old Bf 110G-4 pilot and Staffelkapitän of 4./NJG1 at Laon-Athies had been kept waiting for the order to take off. Born at Stettin on 23 September 1911, the former Lufthansa pilot had flown Ju 52 transports in the Polish campaign before transferring to night fighters. He and Unteroffizier Helmut Völler his bordfunker and Obergefreiter Egon Reinecke his bordschütze clambered aboard the Messerschmitt. In the pre-flight check that followed Lau cursed when he could see that his aircraft had not been refuelled. A fuel bowser filled the tanks and when Lau finally got off the ground it was almost 2354 hours. They flew for about thirty minutes when they saw an aircraft going down on fire. When they had reached about 5500 metres Völler reported a contact on his radar set. Lau flew towards it and recognised it as a Viermot, whose pilot was weaving in 'crocodile line' at 20,000 feet. It was a Halifax; probably LK762 'Z-Zebra' on 78 Squadron flown by Sergeant Ronald Arthur Horton. Lau considered that the crew may have seen him but more likely the enemy pilot was weaving to fly through the many 'burn-ups' in the sky. Lau tried to get into an attack position but each time he thought he had got the Viermot in his sights, he moved out of them. At one moment he was 150 metres away, the next 200 metres. This continued for about two minutes. The Halifax weaved. Lau weaved. Gradually the German pilot came to the conclusion that he would lose him unless he did something quickly. He decided that the next time he got into a reasonably close position he would attack. The moment came when the Halifax, which was somewhat higher than the Bf 110, went into a gradual right-hand turn and Lau turned with him. The distance between them was now about 100 to 150 metres. Lau pulled in the stick, lifted the 110's nose and fired. Flames shot from the bomber and he went into a steep dive. Lau flew over the Viermot and he saw three of the crew bailing out before the aircraft crashed near Herbon-Seelbach southwest of Bonn. Sergeant J. H. Connoley, flight engineer, Flying Officer R. D. Holland, bomb aimer and Sergeant F. R. Wilson the rear gunner were taken prisoner. Before hitting the ground the Halifax broke into two parts, of which one, the larger, again broke on impact so that in the end three parts of it were burning below. Horton, who was from Leicester; Sergeant Colin Victor Byatt the wireless operator who was from Grimsby, Lincolnshire; Flight Sergeant James Wiliam Love the mid-upper gunner from Hillingdon, Middlesex and Sergeant Jack Ord the navigator from Gosforth, Northumberland were laid to rest in Rheinberg War Cemetery.

After he saw the first shoot-down Lau observed red flaming masses falling out of the sky almost every minute. When a German aircraft burned it flamed white. When an RAF aircraft burned, it burned dark red. Lau was to see only two white 'burn-ups' this night. There was first an explosion on the ground as the Viermot hit and then bursts from the flames. A great row of these fires could be seen. They clearly marked out on the ground the course the bombers were flying.

Lau landed his Bf 110G-4 at Langendiebach where scores of night-fighters engaged in attacking bombers targeting Nuremberg put down and went off to report his claim for a Halifax shot down. It could have been more but Unteroffizier Helmut Völler had been unable to pick up the rearguard of the bomber force on his radar set. Lau would finish the war as a Hauptmann with 28 night victories and the coveted Ritterkreuz.

All told, 76 and 78 Squadrons each lost three Halifaxes plus 76 Squadron would have one return damaged and another would be written off. Thirty men were killed and thirteen were taken into captivity.

At Helbigsdorf in Saxony 25-year old Oberstleutnant Helmut 'Bubi' ('Nipper') Lent of Stab/NJG3 took off in his Bf 110 with Feldwebel Walter Kubisch his 25-year old funker, a former blacksmith and the son of a machine fitter. Lent had been appointed Geschwaderkommodore of NJG3 on 1 August 1943. After 73 kills, of which 65 were claimed at night, Lent was awarded the Ritterkreuz des Eisernen Kreuzes mit Eichenlaub und Schwertern on 2 August. The Swords were presented to him at the Führerhauptquartier on 10/11 August. In January 1944 Lent shot down three Viermots in one night, but his aircraft was damaged by return fire, requiring a forced landing. On the night of 22/23 March he used only 22 cannon shells to down two Lancasters, the first at 2126 and the second nine minutes' later to take his score to 83 Night-Abschüsse. A third member of Lent's crew was Leutnant Werner Kark, born in Hamburg on 26 August 1913, who was a war correspondent and peacetime editor of *Oberdonau Zeitung*, a Hamburg newspaper, who flew as a trained bordmechaniker. Kark, who had been attached to a series of front-line Luftwaffe units since 1940, flying many sorties as a full member of crew over England, Greece, Africa and Russia, made it a practice only to report from personal experience.

'When our search radars picked up a strong force of British bomber units assembling in the early evening of 24 March there were good conditions for take-off and landing at all the night-fighter fields in the Reichsgebiet for the first time in a long period. There was no moonlight, but there was a splendid starlit sky and a bright streak in the northern heaven. 'It's going to be a fruitful night,' said Oberstleutnant Lent as we climbed over the wing into the cabin of the Messerschmitt 110. During the last raid he had brought himself back to the top of the list of successful night fighters again [with his 84th and 85th victories].

'Scramble! The enemy is approaching on an easterly heading over the West Friesian islands, not making a feint but heading directly for Berlin. At this very moment our fighters are racing along the runways at their bases, gathering at their operational altitude and being controlled directly into the bomber stream. 'Bomber's Death' will again reap a terrible harvest among the enemy squadrons tonight!

'What wonderful visibility there is in this first shining early spring night! The broad sea, dark islands, knife-sharp coastline, the canopy of searchlights spreading protectively above the towns, the venomous muzzle-fire of the flak, the bursting shells, the coloured recognition signals of our fighters like will-o'-the-wisps in the sky - the eerily beautiful picture of the nocturnal air battle in all its breathtaking splendour spreads out before us as we enter the arena. The first enemy aircraft, the Path Finders, have reached the mainland. After them follows the main force, a never-ending stream of bombers on its way to Berlin.

'In our cabin there is complete silence. The flak fire on the outskirts of the town grows stronger. The beams of the searchlights form a network of light in the darkness. Quite calm and precise, we suddenly hear on our intercom: 'There's one ahead of us, Herr Oberstleutnant!' Oberfeldwebel Kubisch, the Kommodore's bordfunker, currently the only one of his trade in the Nachtjagd to hold the Knight's Cross, sits there motionless. Lent goes in at full speed. 'Now he's on our left,' says Kubisch. Suddenly something hits the fuselage of the Messerschmitt like the crack of a whip.

We have run into the slipstream of the enemy bomber flying ahead of us. 'I've got him - I can see him,' comes from the front seat. Slowly we creep up on the enemy.[188]

'The Kommodore opens fire. Dull thuds vibrate through the fighter's fuselage. There are dazzling flashes in the cockpit. All our guns are sending a long burst into the heavy four-engined bomber aircraft ahead of us. 'He's burning,' says Oberstleutnant Lent, 'he's really burning!' It comes from his mouth as casually as if he were sitting at his office desk. At the same time we catch sight of the burning enemy. Its wide wings are swathed in flame. In a steep dive it races towards the earth like a torch. Searchlights pick it up and follow it down over the silent landscape until it hits the ground. A blazing pyre, black smoke, then fiery embers. The first kill this memorable night and certainly a Path Finder.

'A quarter of an hour, half an hour later. Fires are burning strongly all around us. The agitated probing of the searchlights in the sky, the thin lines of tracer from other night fighters, burning enemy bombers and coloured flares show that the bomber stream is still advancing through our airspace. We continue searching, constantly changing our heading. Ahead and to the right!' says Kubisch. 'Still further to the right!' A new contact. Once again the enemy-machine takes skilful evasive action. We follow him, turning, climbing, diving all the time, copying his every manoeuvre. Behind this enemy aircraft is one of Germany's best night fighters!

'Suddenly, ghost-like, the Tommy looms up ahead of us. Massive shape, wide wings, twin fins, four powerful engines. The Kommodore presses on the firing buttons. For us these are moments of high tension. Will his aim be true?

'A sinister night-time picture. We have experienced its like many times when hunting above the Reichsgebiet. Then suddenly the faint silhouette of the heavily damaged enemy bomber appears above us. A broad sheet of flame from the centre of the fuselage tells us that he is badly hit. Behind him he is trailing thick banners of smoke. Once, twice, three times a small shadow sweeps past the tail unit of the bomber. The British are bailing out! But the pilot must still be at the controls. The bomber is still capable of flying and he is trying to escape.

'A second attack! Our cannon and machine guns hammer out again. It is the coup de grace. The bomber loses height more and more swiftly, descending towards the wide countryside in a steep dive. Like a shadow, careful and alert in case despite everything the enemy still recovers, we follow him until finally, some distance from us, a huge ball of fire on the ground marks his end. This is another cargo of bombs that will not reach Berlin.

'We leave the battle area. The stream is still heading to the east. We know that comrades from other Geschwader will infiltrate the bomber stream from all directions and claim fresh victims. On the broad bombers' road to Berlin tonight more fires from shot-down bombers than ever before will show the British airmen that once again a very heavy price must be paid in blood for terror attacks on the capital of the Reich.'[189]

At 0141 hours Feldwebel Emil Nonnenmacher of 9./NJG2 piloting a Ju 88 attacked two Lancasters, the first ten kilometres northwest of Nuremberg and the second at Poxdorf. He wrote: 'As we climbed out of Twenthe we could see that a great battle was already in progress: there were aircraft burning in the air and on the ground; there was the occasional explosion in mid-air and much firing with tracer rounds. We kept on towards the scene of high activity for about five minutes and then suddenly we hit the slipstream from one of the bombers. Now we were getting close to the bomber stream. It seemed that there was activity all around us - here an aircraft on fire, there someone firing, somewhere else an explosion on the ground. Yet it was a few more minutes before we actually caught sight of a bomber, its silhouette passing obliquely over my cockpit.' It was a very clear night and he could see as many as fifteen bombers around him, all of them leaving condensation trails. He tried to move into a firing position but he misjudged the approach and had to break away. It did not matter - there were plenty of others.

'With so many targets visible I could take my pick, so I chose the nearest one in front of me - a Lancaster - and went after him. He was weaving gently. I set myself up for a deflection shot, aiming at a point one aircraft length ahead of the bomber. I opened fire and saw my rounds striking it. Then I paused, put my sight on the bomber again and fired another burst. After a few rounds my guns stopped firing - I had exhausted the ammunition in the drum magazines on my cannon.'

Nonnenmacher ordered his bordmechaniker to replace the ammunition drums, but in the meantime he had to let the bomber escape. As the crewman wrestled to fit new ammunition drums. Nonnenmacher closed on another Lancaster (possibly LW429 KW-R flown by 23-year old Flying Officer John 'Roy' Taylor RCAF of Winnipeg on 425 'Alouette' Squadron RCAF which had taken off at 2155 from Tholthorpe on their seventh operation).

'I moved into a firing position about 100 metres astern and a little below it. By then the bordmechaniker had one of the cannon going so I pressed the firing button and saw my rounds striking the left wing. Soon afterwards both engines on that side burst into flames. He began to lose height and we could see the crew bailing out. It was so clear. The bomber took about six minutes to go down; when it reached the ground [at Tauchersreuth, four kilometres northeast of Heroldsberg at 0120 hours] it blew up with a huge explosion.'

Eyewitnesses to the crash reported that the aircraft burned throughout the night and the following morning and seven badly charred bodies were removed. Sergeant Peter Furlong, the 23-year old flight engineer, the only non-Canadian member of the crew, from Killincarrig, County Wicklow in the Irish Republic; Flying Officer George Edmund Munro the 25-year old navigator of Vancouver; Sergeant Frank Robert Majchrowicz the bomb aimer who like his skipper was from Winnipeg; Flight Sergeant John Joseph Harold Sheahan the wireless operator, of Douglas, Ontario; Sergeant Arthur Melvin DeWitt the 19-year old mid-upper gunner, from Woodstock, New Brunswick and Sergeant Percy Lawrence Mitchell the 24-year old rear gunner, from Toronto, whose body found in the aircraft was identified only by a badly burned revolver and a pierce of parachute with his name on it, were buried along with their skipper in a single grave in Durnbach War Cemetery.

Pilot Officer John Edward Goldsmith of Halifax, Nova Scotia, the navigator on Lancaster III ND407 on 625 Squadron, noted that they crossed the enemy coast heading south, on time as briefed. But he calculated that they must have turned east too early at Position 'B' near Charleroi. As they headed out on the long leg towards Nuremberg he confirmed to his skipper, Pilot Officer 'Brad' Bradshaw, that they were about ten miles north of track. 'There was plenty of fighter activity south of us,' Goldsmith recalls, 'so we stayed north of track until we turned onto our target run-in. The moon made it almost as light as day and the vapour trails of our bombers were very conspicuous. In the light of the moon it looked like a four-lane highway.

'We saw much air-to-air firing and sighted two enemy fighters and one of them nearly crashed into us, head-on, during the bombing run. Flak was moderate; searchlights not very effective. Bombing appeared to be scattered... An aircraft almost ran into us on the bombing run. We were not sure what type it was but believed it to be a Me 210. If we were correct in our assumption this would give an idea of the large number of aircraft used that night by the Germans since the Me 210 had been taken out of production in 1942 and I don't believe its successor, the Me 410, became operational until the summer of 1944.

Warrant Officer Reginald William Douglas Price, a Canadian pilot from Lloydminster, Saskatchewan on 'B' Flight on 625 Squadron was flying Lancaster III ND619 'D-Dog'. 'There seemed to be much more enemy night-fighter activity than usual and quite heavy anti-aircraft fire. We were lucky as we sustained no damage to the aircraft and no injuries to the crew'. Price's crew consisted of two Australians - Pilot Officer Dudley Ball, navigator and Sergeant Jack Conley, bomb aimer - and four Englishmen: Sergeant Les Knowles, flight engineer; Sergeant Jim Harris, wireless air gunner; Sergeant Harry Powter, mid-upper gunner and Sergeant Frank Sutton, rear gunner.

Fred Stetson, a Lancaster rear gunner on 625 Squadron had been dreading this operation. 'I can laugh at it now but I was very superstitious. I had for instance, Saint Christopher medals hanging all over my turret. This was my 24th operation. The serial number of our Lanc was PD204, my personal service number was 149109 which added up to 24 and D is the fourth letter of the alphabet. And remember it was 1944. That figure four seemed to haunt me.'

As it turned out, Stetson's number nearly came up on Nuremberg. The crew had a quiet trip into Germany until the target area was reached and heavy flak came on the bomb run. 'One engine was hit and a petrol tank holed,' Stetson said. 'We dropped our bombs bang-on, weaved like mad and skated out of the area. Soon, a fighter attacked. I tried to swivel my guns. The turret would not work. I could turn it a little to port - not at all to starboard. Luckily the attack was from the port side and I was able to direct a stream of .303s in his general direction. I yelled to the wireless operator for help in freeing the turret. The fighter turned away. Was I relieved! But the wireless operator couldn't get the turret working. I fumbled on the floor for any obstruction. Guess what? One of those Saint Christopher medals I was so fond of had fallen during the weaving and jammed between the stationary and moving parts of the turret.'

With or without the help of Saint Christopher, Stetson and his crew returned safely to their base.[190]

'The flight home' says 'Ginger' Hammersley the wireless operator on 'N-Nan' on 57 Squadron skippered by Sergeant Ron Walker 'was a long haul south of Stuttgart, north of Strasbourg and Nancy, heading towards the French coast. We crossed the coast near Dieppe and so back to Lincolnshire and East Kirkby. At debriefing the gunners on Pilot Officer 'Cas' Castagnola's crew claimed to have shot down a Ju 88. Also, we observed an aircraft being shot down. One of our own crews, pilot Flight Lieutenant Tickler flying on ND622 was missing.'[191]

After Oberleutnant Helmuth Schulte of 4./NJG5 had shot down a Lancaster and then a Halifax for his first two kills of the night, Unteroffizier Hans Fischer his bordschütze checked the guns and confirmed that the firing pins were unserviceable. So, when Lancaster ND622 'E-Easy' suddenly hove into their path north-west of Nuremberg, Schulte blasted it with his side guns. He could not have known that Flight Lieutenant Edward Wells Tickler CGM was a member of the Tickler Jam Company of Pasture Street in Grimsby established in 1877, who had the words *The Jampot and the 7 Raspberries* painted below the cockpit. 'Eddie' and Sergeant A. Ferguson, mid-upper gunner and the bomb aimer, Technical Sergeant William E. Steeper USAAF from Utica, in the Mohawk Valley in New York State, survived the fusillade of shells which set fire to the aircraft and bailed out before 'E-Easy' keeled over and exploded near Bischwind-bei-Bamberg killing the four others on the crew. The three fortunate survivors were taken prisoner and marched off into captivity.

Schulte flew over Nuremberg and just south of the city he shot down his fourth victim of the night. It was another Halifax. A fifth victory eluded him. First he had forgotten to reload and though he re-established contact and attacked again using his nose guns, the bomber plummeted into a steep corkscrew and escaped.[192] Oberleutnant Helmuth Schulte and his crew returned to Parchim to file claims for four bombers destroyed to take his score to eleven victories. Schulte was amazed to find that his two 'Schräge Musik' guns had used only 56 cannon shells.

'E-Easy' was not the only loss at East Kirkby; three Lancasters on 630 Squadron were shot down by night-fighters on the outward flight. 'S-Sugar' flown by 26-year old Pilot Officer Ronald Leslie Clark RAAF and his crew were on their first operation. Clark, who was from Parkdale, a suburb of Melbourne; Flight Sergeant Kelvin Carlyle Green the 26-year old navigator and husband of Veda Rose Green, of Mildura on the banks of the Murray River in North Western Victoria; Sergeants Thomas Hughes, mid-upper gunner of Randalstown, County Antrim; William Donnan Jones, flight engineer from Belfast; David Victor Mennell the rear gunner of Hove, Sussex and Norman Worboys the wireless operator from Bentley, Doncaster were killed. Only Sergeant R. I. Smith the bomb aimer survived and he was taken prisoner.

'H-Harry' flown by Pilot Officer Allan George Garth Johnson of Nassau in the Bahamas, whose crew were on their sixteenth operation, were probably shot down by Feldwebel Ernst Reitmeyer of 1/NJG5 north-west of Nuremberg; one of three Viermots claimed by the 24-year old Austrian. The Lancaster crashed at Altendorf on the east side of the Donau-Regnitz Kanal. Johnson and Flight Sergeant Ernest Arthur Farnell the 28-year old navigator from Sevenoaks in Kent, who had married Alfreda Joyce Bevan on 12 December 1942, Sergeant Arthur Henry McGill the wireless operator who was from Bristol and Sergeant Bill France the rear gunner from Malin Bridge, Sheffield, were killed. Sergeant G. E. Watts the flight engineer, Flying Officer J. P. Headlam the bomb aimer and Sergeant W. Pearson the mid-upper gunner were taken into captivity. Pearson was amongst a batch of repatriated prisoners of war brought to Liverpool on 6 February 1945 aboard the *Arundel Castle*.[194]

'T-Tommy' the 630 Squadron CO's Lancaster piloted by 'Jock' Langlands was running late. Near Ruhla in the forest of Thuringia, slightly north of track and just before reaching the final turning point at the end of the long outbound leg the skipper was about to turn south for the run into the target at 20,000 feet when he heard a 'terrifyingly loud clatter' as twenty to thirty cannon shells hit the aircraft and set the starboard engines on fire. Langlands shouted over the intercom: 'Lads, we're not going to make it. Let's go then... bail out... everyone...' Calmly, he kept 'T-Tommy' level using

244

the power of the port motors, which were working normally, as the men in the front of the Lancaster bailed out. Suddenly there was silence as the intercom went dead. Langlands waited until Bob Guthrie, his navigator and his flight engineer, 'Hermann' Goring, got their parachutes hooked up before following 'Benny' Bryans his bomb aimer towards the escape hatch. Bryans could not get the forward escape hatch open so the flight engineer went down and dragged it up. He pushed out Bryans and then he too jumped out into the night. Except for a couple of broken teeth, knocked out when he bailed out Bryans could not remember opening his parachute. Guthrie followed. Langlands was the last to leave. As he descended he looked around the flak-lit sky hoping to catch sight of Alan Drake and 'Bud' Coffey whose normal exit was out the rear door and Geoff Jeffery but they were killed when the Lancaster crashed at Burla, fourteen kilometres west of Gotha.[193]

At East Kirkby Wing Commander Bill Deas did not have time to mourn the loss of 'T-Tommy'. He had many letters of condolence to write. The Wing Commander and Flying Officer Joseph Thomas Taylor DFC's crew were shot down on the night of 7/8 July on the raid on Ste-Leu-d'Esserent'. Deas and all except one of Taylor's crew were killed.

Sergeant Geoffrey Jennings, formerly a capstan operator at Maidenhead, Berkshire, but now the mid-upper gunner on Lancaster 'G-George' on 630 Squadron recalled: 'It was obvious at the time that the enemy was either waiting or had reached the area very quickly when our objective became obvious.' From his turret he had witnessed the development of simultaneous attack by two fighters. 'The rear gunner reported one approaching from astern and I observed what I believed to be an Me 110 coming in directly on the starboard side. I gave the order to dive to starboard and as we dived I endeavoured to open fire but my guns were frozen up. However, the prompt evasive action of our skipper, Peter Nash, was sufficient to get us out of trouble and we were not engaged again. It was obvious by the amount of tracer flying around that many engagements were taking place. We observed one or two of our aircraft going down out of control after leaving the target area.'

Harry MacKinnon the navigator on 'N-Nan' on 57 Squadron at East Kirkby recalled that the night was memorable as being the only operation he ever flew when time went so slowly. Normally he was working desperately hard against time but on the long, homeward course from 48° 30' North, 09° 20' East - south of Stuttgart, to 49° 20' North, 03° 00' East - near Paris, he estimated the Lancaster's ground speed against bucking head-winds as only 120 knots and it seemed as if the leg would never end. 'On this leg the crew, as usual asked when we would get to the coast. Naturally I was in the middle of a calculation and irritably answered, 'Oh, about an hour'. One hundred miles further on, they asked again. This time I had the exact answer - just over 1½ hours. I could feel the chilling reaction of the rest of the crew. They never really forgave me. In any case the navigator, thank goodness, saw but little.'

It was 'Mac' MacKinnon's recollection that Bomber Command called in all navigator's logs after the operation for analysis and evaluation by the Command's operational research section. His own opinion was that the heavy losses were due to having had 'a bit of a moon'. 'You could see for miles and then there was the long time spent over enemy territory on the way back due to the head-winds. This was, of course, Bomber Command's heaviest loss. Second was a raid on Munich earlier in 1944 with 79 lost and third was Berlin on 24 March, six nights before, with 76 missing.'

Once they had obtained clearance from the squadron office Sergeant Ron Walker's crew went on leave next day. On his way home in the train to Birmingham, Mackinnon was asked by an elderly lady whether Bomber Command had been out on operations the previous night and whether any aircraft were missing. He would always remember the expression on her face when he said, 'Oh, about ninety-six'. He then fell asleep.

'Three operations flown and I had seen the loss of 176 crews from Bomber Command' recalled 'Ginger' Hammersley. 'The Berlin raid had seen JB539 [flown by Pilot Officer Eric Percy Cliburn] and ND671 [flown by Pilot Officer George Alfred Hampton RAAF] lost to the squadron and now on the Nuremberg raid a further crew was missing. Not good news for the rest of us though Tom's promotion to Flying Officer was confirmed. This pleased him, particularly as we were granted leave and he would be able to travel home to the Isle of Man with the rank he held prior to re-mustering.'[195]

'Ginger' Hammersley was away into Lincoln where he hitched a ride in a lorry and then on to London and Watford by train making the final leg home on a bus. 'I had already said to the lorry driver that we would most likely find that Nuremberg would show heavy casualties and when the news was out, my thoughts were confirmed. Dad was on leave and with Mum we visited his favourite pub, 'The Oddfellows' in Apsley End. The company was good and cheerful. It was during the evening that I told Dad for the first time that I was serving on a bomber squadron and flying operations. The news was out that there had been considerable casualties on the raid and I told him that I had flown that operation, asking him not to tell Mum. However, he could not keep the news to himself and I found him telling all and sundry in the pub - 'my boy was on that raid last night!' The news soon filtered through to Mum and then the tears flowed. I felt sorry that I had said anything, but by then it was too late. My leave was fine after that experience and I took the opportunity to relax and meet family and friends. I later learned that the posthumous award of the Victoria Cross, the highest award for gallantry, was made to Pilot Officer Cyril Barton on 578 Squadron. In later days I met and became a firm friend of the air gunner who was a survivor on Barton's crew, Flight Sergeant Harold 'Timber' Woods DFM. Leave was over and it was back to the war and life on the squadron.'

When Pilot Officer Cyril Barton RAFVR had approached the run in to Nuremberg, in accordance with the crew drill, John Lambert folded up his navigational gear as he sat directly over the forward escape hatch. Over the target, navigation was from notes on his knee-pad taken from callings by the Canadian bomb aimer, Pilot Officer Crate. 'I think we had the bomb-doors open when there was a shout from the rear gunner,' Lambert said. 'His sentence was unfinished as the aircraft shuddered from a rain of cannon shells and the intercom was destroyed. The Halifax was on fire and being thrown around the sky by the pilot. A signal over the emergency light flashers was misunderstood by me, the wireless air gunner and the bomb aimer and I donned my parachute pack. In removing the escape hatch door which had jammed I caught the rip-cord inadvertently on some part of the aircraft interior. The parachute opened in the aircraft and in a flash it was sucked out of the half-open hatch and I was whipped out after it. I was amazed to find myself dangling in mid-air with a torn parachute canopy flapping above me. It was still moonlight but all seemed very quiet and there was no sign of the target. It was bitterly cold. My hands were unprotected and I must have been ejected from the aircraft at a considerable height. Because of the damaged parachute canopy I descended rapidly and hit the middle of a very hard, frozen field.'

Lambert landed without injury on the hard, frozen earth of a German field. Disposing of his parachute canopy and harness and flying gear, he walked all that night through heavily wooded country and hid all the following day. The countryside was sparsely populated but, after a second night's marching, he was captured trying to steal food from a farmhouse near Hassfurt on the railway line between Bamberg and Stassfurt, about fifty miles north-west of Nuremberg. After being taken to a Luftwaffe camp at Schweinfurt, Lambert duly arrived at Dulag Luft at Oberursel outside Frankfurt where he saw the bomb aimer and the wireless air gunner, Sergeant Kay. 'The most demoralizing thing at Dulag Luft was that the interrogating officers seemed to have known every detail about the operation before it started and so the Luftwaffe had been able to inflict such severe punishment. They had detailed RAF maps on the walls with the exact flight plan shown. They also knew a great deal more about secret RAF navigational equipment than I did.'

Subsequently, at Stalag Luft VI Heydekrug in East Prussia, Lambert was to learn that his pilot had succeeded in navigating and flying the severely damaged Halifax back to England with the remaining crew members aboard - Flight Sergeant Trousdale, flight engineer; Sergeant Woods, mid-upper gunner; Sergeant Brice, rear gunner (but had been killed while attempting a forced landing near Ryhope Colliery on the Durham coast south of Sunderland, killing George Heads a local miner on his way to work). Kevin Hutchinson, A young boy of six, recovering from scarlet fever, recalled: 'At the time of the crash I was only about 100 yards away, but laying in bed in the front room of 10 South View, Ryhope, a terrace of colliery houses. The occasion is seared on my brain. First of all the air-raid siren sounded, an event which was not unknown in the area, but then was the unmistakeable sound of a large aeroplane. There was no doubt that it was enemy because the heavy anti-aircraft battery at Leechmere opened up. However, the racket from the guns soon ceased, but the aeroplane was still there, wandering hither and to, no doubt looking for the colliery. Even I as a child was puzzled when the 'all clear' sounded with the aircraft still in the neighbourhood. Then there came an almighty crash, then silence.'

On 27 June it was announced in the *London Gazette* that Pilot Officer Cyril Barton had received the posthumous award of the Victoria Cross. Barton's citation read: 'Pilot Officer Barton was captain and pilot of a Halifax aircraft detailed to attack Nuremberg when, seventy miles short of the target, the aircraft was attacked by a Ju 88. The first burst of fire from the enemy made the intercom system useless. One engine was damaged when a Me 210 joined the fight. The bomber's machine guns were out of action and the gunners were unable to return the fire. The two fighters continued to attack the aircraft as it approached the target area and, in the confusion caused by the failure of the communications system at the height of the battle, a signal was misinterpreted and the navigator, air bomber and wireless operator left the aircraft by parachute. Barton now faced a situation of dire peril. His aircraft was damaged, his navigational team had gone and he could not communicate with the remainder of the crew. If he continued his mission, he would be at the mercy of hostile fighters when silhouetted against the fires in the target area and if he survived, he would have to make a four-hour journey home on three engines across heavily-defended territory.

Determined to press home his attack at all costs, he flew on and reaching the target, released the bombs himself. As Barton turned for home the propeller of the damaged engine, which was vibrating badly, flew off. It was also discovered that two of the petrol tanks had suffered damage and were leaking. Barton held to his course and, without navigational aids and in spite of strong head winds, successfully avoided the most dangerous defence areas on his route. Eventually he crossed the English coast only ninety miles north of his base. By this time the petrol supply was nearly exhausted. Before a suitable landing place could be found, the port engines stopped. The aircraft was now too low to be abandoned successfully and Barton therefore ordered the three remaining members of his crew to take up their crash stations. Then, with only one engine working, he made a gallant attempt to land clear of the houses over which he was flying. The aircraft finally crashed and Barton lost his life but his three comrades survived. Barton had previously taken part in four attacks on Berlin and fourteen other operations. On one of these, two members of his crew were wounded during a determined effort to locate the target despite appalling weather conditions. In gallantly completing his last mission in the face of almost impossible odds, this officer displayed unsurpassed courage and devotion to duty.'

In a letter to his mother, to be opened in the event of his death, he wrote: 'I hope you never receive this, but I quite expect you will. I know what ops over Germany means and I have no illusions about it. By my own calculations, the average life of a crew is twenty ops...' He was killed on his nineteenth bombing operation. 'My parents never wanted him to fly but he was determined,' recalled his sister, Joyce. 'My mother never really got over it.' Joyce remembers a despatch rider at the door soon afterwards. 'Dad opened this big brown envelope and said: 'Cyril's been awarded the Victoria Cross'. All Mum said was: 'It won't bring him back'. But she carried that letter with her until the day she died.'

Endnotes Chapter 18

187 Identified by Theo Boiten. Connolley was interned in Stalag 357 with Wilson. Holland was held in Stalag Luft I (Barth Vogelsang).

188 Which from research by Theo Boiten, Lent's victim, a Halifax, was either MZ508 on 578 Squadron flown by Flight Sergeant Albert Edward Pinks, which went down 20-40 kilometres North of Nuremberg at 0121hours nearing the aiming point to crash at Ermreus, 13 kilometres North East of Eerlangen or MZ508 could have been shot down by Feldwebel Klaus Möller of 12./NJG3, who claimed a '4-mot' at Kalenbrück-Erlangen at 0109.

189 Quoted in *The Lent Papers* by Peter Hinchliffe).

190 Adapted from an extract in the British *Weekly News*.

191 *Into Battle With 57 Squadron* by Roland A. Hammersley DFM (Privately Published, 1992).

192 This Lancaster has been identified as the one flown by Warrant Officer Howard Hemming on 115 Squadron by Martin Middlebrook in *The Nuremberg Raid* (Allen Lane 1973). Sergeant John Carter, the rear gunner, thought that the attack had been carried out 'in a half-hearted manner, possibly by a fighter flown by a pilot from a training unit.' Schulte and his crew were shot down by a Mosquito on 22/23 May 1944. Schulte and Fischer bailed out safely but Sandvoss was KIA. Schulte survived the war, being awarded the Ritterkreuz for 25 night victories in April 1945.

193 See *'The Killing Skies' in Bomber Boys; Aircrew experiences of the war over occupied Europe 1942-45* by Mel Rolfe (Grub St., 2004 & 2009) and *Through Footless Halls of Air: The Stories of Men Who Failed* by Floyd Williston. (General Store Publishing House 1996).

194 Chorley.

195 *Into Battle With 57 Squadron* by Roland A. Hammersley DFM (Privately Published, 1992).

Chapter 19

Pilot Officer 'Dick' Starkey on 106 Squadron had climbed on course over the Norfolk coast. He was wide awake having taken his 'Wakey-Wakey' tablets shortly after take-off from Metheringham. At their cruising height of 21,000 feet the air temperature was very low and the bomber stream began making condensation trails as 'Queenie' flew on over Belgium towards the long leg which ran from south of the Ruhr east to a turning point northwest of Nuremberg. It was this long leg that crews were apprehensive about because it ran for over 200 miles. Nearing Germany the near full moon and the absolutely clear sky were ideal for fighter aircraft against slow bombers who had inferior armament and a heavy fuel and bomb load. If this was not bad enough Starkey knew that 'Q-Queenie' and the other four-engined bombers were making condensation trails which could be seen for miles in the near daylight conditions and to cap it all, their 'Fishpond' aircraft detector was u/s. His crew continuously operated the 'banking search' looking for enemy aircraft coming up from below. This was achieved by turning steeply to port for fifteen degrees to see if fighters were preparing to attack and then banking to return to the original course. When the fighters began their attack from the number of tracers being fired, it appeared there were combats everywhere. Starkey saw around thirty aircraft go down in a short period and as he continued to the target the ground became covered with burning aircraft. He had been flying the long leg for many miles when sixty miles northwest of Nuremberg, their luck changed. A fighter attacked with tracer and cannon fire, which hit 'Queenie's port mainplane and outer engine, flashed past outside the perspex covering of the cockpit and between Starkey's legs. He prayed that they would not go up in flames. However, within three or four seconds the port outer engine and mainplane were alight. It was always the one you didn't see that shot you down as in their case and if 'Monica' had been available they would have been aware of the fighter's approach.

'There was only one action to take; says Starkey. 'I gave the order to abandon aircraft. The engineer, Sergeant Johnnie Harris feathered the port engine as he helped me with the controls because we were going down at a very fast rate and the next few seconds I remember vividly. The bomb aimer, Sergeant Wally Paris, acknowledged my order to bail out and said he was leaving the aircraft. The navigator, Sergeant Colin Roberts, came to the cockpit to escape through the front hatch. The rear gunner, Sergeant Joe Ellick also acknowledged the order but said he could not get out of his turret (this was because the port outer engine powered the turret; the alternative way was to turn the turret by hand controls in order to fall out backwards). There was no reply from the mid-upper gunner, Sergeant Jock Jameson and the wireless operator, Sergeant Jock Walker. I assumed they must have been killed by the burst of fire, which ran along the side of the aircraft. Johnnie Harris handed me a parachute from one of two in the rack at his side. I managed to connect one of the hooks on the chute to the harness I was wearing (we did not wear seat type chutes), at the same time trying to control a blazing aircraft which was diving at well over 300 mph. I gave up all hope of survival and waited for the impact; a terrifying experience. That is the last thing I remember because the aircraft exploded with a full bomb load (we had no time to jettison) and 1,500 gallons of high octane fuel, which must have ignited and caused the explosion. As I lost consciousness I did have a feeling of being lifted out of the cockpit and must have been propelled through the perspex canopy. When the petrol tanks exploded in the port wing outside my window a fireball must have been created in the aircraft which would incinerate anything in its path and I must have been just ahead of it as I was blown from the aircraft. Many years later I was told an unopened parachute was found next to the body of the flight engineer who had landed in a wood six kilometres from the wreckage of the aircraft. We were only two feet apart in the cockpit when the aircraft went up and Johnnie Harris must have been blown out like me but I was lucky my parachute had opened, probably by the force of the explosion.

Sergeant Wally Paris was blown from the aircraft in the explosion and succeeded in opening his parachute to land safely. Sergeant 'Johnnie' Harris, who was from Biggleswade, Bedfordshire and who had handed Starkey a parachute from one of two in the rack at his side, must have been blown out like his pilot and the bomb aimer but his parachute had probably failed to open and he was killed. Sergeant Colin Roberts a Sheffield man and the crew's navigator, Sergeant Maitland 'Joe' Ellick the rear gunner, who was from Wallasey, Cheshire, Sergeant John 'Jock' Jameson of Stratford, London the mid-upper gunner and Sergeant George W. 'Jock' Walker the wireless operator who was from Geddington, Northants, were killed by the burst of fire from the night-fighter that attacked them which slanted into the wing and ran along the side of the aircraft.

There was no word either from JB566 'C-Charlie' flown by Flight Sergeant Thomas William J. Hall DFM whose crew had flown just one operation. The Lancaster exploded near Berghausen with the loss of all except two of the crew. Lancaster ND585 'J-Jig' which was making for home at Metheringham when Leutnant Fred Hromadnik of 9./NJG4 shot the aircraft down for the first of his three Abschüsse of the night. ND585 crashed at Villères-Deux-Eglises, three kilometres southwest of Philippeville at 0252 hours. Twenty-year old Pilot Officer Wilfred George Moxey RAAF of Miranda, a suburb in southern Sydney and his crew who were on their 16th operation, all died. The eighteen-year old air-gunner, Sergeant Julian Pelham MacKilligin of St. Pancras in London was believed to have completed around fifteen operational sorties. Sergeant Herbert Wilfred Richardson the wireless operator was from Sydenham. Of the four other crewmembers, Sergeant Edward Harold Woods, the 26-year-old flight engineer, was from Reading in Berkshire and the air bomber, Sergeant Cecil Arthur William Matthews, was from Portsmouth. Flight Sergeant Frank Thompson, the 26-year-old navigator was from Waipiro Bay, Auckland in New Zealand and 28-year old Sergeant John Alfred Harris, the mid-upper gunner was from Newfoundland.

Leutnant Fred Hromadnik's next victory, at 0336 hours, was Halifax LV899 on 78 Squadron, homebound to Breighton after bombing the target where George Torbet had celebrated his birthday. LV899 crashed 24 kilometres northwest of Charleville-Mezieres, France. There were no survivors on the crew of Warrant Officer2 Fred Topping RCAF.

At 0416 hours 3½ kilometres north east of Namur, Hromadnik shot down Lancaster R5734 'V-Victor' on 61 Squadron skippered by 20-year old Pilot Officer James Arthur Haste RAAF from Maylands in Adelaide. He and his six crew - all RAF - were killed. Flight Sergeant John Victor Groves the navigator was from Quinton, Birmingham; Sergeant William Norton James the wireless operator was from Dinas Cross, Pembrokeshire; Sergeant Roy Colin Mills the flight engineer came from Leyton,

London; Flying Officer Richard Arthur Whitaker the bomb aimer came from Bromley in Kent and the two gunners, Sergeants Basil Nutley and Frederick Walter Skelcher were from Earlsfield, London and Erdington, Birmingham respectively. The crew were on their 8th operation and would never see their hometowns again. Fred Hromadnik survived the war, having a total of six victories.

Unteroffizier Otto Kutzner of 5./NJG3, piloting a Bf 110G-4 also returned with claims for three Lancasters destroyed. However, the second of these victories was probably Halifax MZ504 'C-Charlie' on 432 'Leaside' Squadron RCAF at East Moor just over seven miles north of York skippered by Flying Officer Earle Kerr Reid of Milford Station, a small village in southern Nova Scotia. Reid had been born on 31 March 1919, was an accomplished downhill skier, 'gifted artist and better-than-average singer' full of fun and hell and known to paint the town red at times. Now, on the eve of his 25th birthday before he was to make his twelfth trip he had spent part of the day answering letters from family and friends but did not have time to post them before he took off. When all at once the clouds disappeared one crewmember commented: 'Christ, we're flying almost in daylight.' One of the air gunners remarked: 'Jesus, Mary and Joseph. If the German fighters are up tonight, Skip, then we've had it.' Flying Officer James T. 'Smitty' Smith, navigator of Victoria, British Columbia wrote later:[196] 'Everything was going very well and we were rather enjoying the trip. We were flying between Kollinz and Bonn when we were attacked the first time.' When the second attack came, about twenty minutes later, the night fighter missed the mark and was successfully scared off by one of Reid's air gunners. 'Smitty' Smith again checked to see if anyone was hit. He breathed a great but premature sigh of relief as he reported to his captain: 'It's OK Earle; none of the crew is even slightly wounded.' Not far from Erfurt in eastern Germany Reid ran into another gaggle of night fighters. Smith checked his map and advised his skipper to alter course to a southerly direction. Just as Reid was turning for the run from Thuringer Wald into Nuremberg one of the aircraft's engines was hit. 'Smitty' Smith wrote: 'After the third attack we went into a dive and Earle gave the order to abandon aircraft. Everyone was very cool and calm, even though we were going down very quickly. There was no time for Warrant Officer2 Vince MacDonald, air bomber of Meota, Saskatchewan to jettison the bomb load. Because the navigator's work position was over the escape hatch 'Smitty' Smith was the first one to leave. 'I jumped, pulled my ripcord and looked down. Our aircraft was already on the ground below me'.

'C-Charlie' was shot down at 0040 hours, five minutes after Kutzner had claimed his first victim seven kilometres north of Mengerskirchen. The Halifax crashed in a cornfield astride the railway line on the outskirts of Ossenheim three kilometres south of Friedberg north of Bad Hamburg. Reid remained at the controls until other crewmembers jumped clear but by then it was too late for him to follow. Sergeant John A. 'Jack' May his RAF flight engineer from Gravesend, Kent, was unable to escape; his parachute had opened inside the burning aircraft. Sergeant Bob Clarkson the 21-year old mid-upper gunner from Hamilton, Ontario was the last to bail out but he landed on high-tension wires not far from the downed aircraft and was electrocuted. 'Smitty' Smith; Vince MacDonald; Flight Sergeant George G. Maguire RCAF, the wireless operator from Chatham, Ontario and Sergeant Joseph J, Barr the rear gunner from Point Edward, Ontario survived and were taken prisoner. Two employees of the Friedberg cemetery were ordered to remove Bob Clarkson's body from the overhead wires and he was buried without ceremony.

Otto Kutzner's third Abschuss fell south of Nuremberg at 0133 hours. 'Every pilot had his own method of attack' he recalled. 'Mine was from directly behind so that I could put the tail gunner out of action to start with. I made sure I was in exactly the right position, at a range of about fifty metres with at least the two outer engines in my gunsight. I would give two bursts with my four cannons - a mixture of tracer and armour-piercing incendiary - all around the tail.' His twelfth and last victory was a Halifax on 7 March 1945. On this night he was attempting to land his Ju 88 at Gottingen which had a short runway when he hit the second of two trains. He cart-wheeled and was thrown clear but the other crewmembers were killed. He lost his left leg and was hospitalized from 7 March to May 1947.[197]

432 'Leaside' Squadron RCAF lost a second aircraft when Halifax LW687 'Z-Zebra' was shot down by another night-fighter. Even though their attacker was spotted by both the mid-upper gunner 19-year old Pilot Officer Robert William Rathwell, of Ironside, Quebec and the tail gunner, 22-year old Pilot Officer Samuel Saprunoff of Castlegar, British Columbia the Halifax was hit broadside before 23-year old Pilot Officer Chester Russell Narum of Patricia, Alberta could take evasive action. Narum, his two gunners and Sergeant Robert Thomson the Scottish flight engineer who came from Glasgow were killed. The three other Canadians - Flight Sergeant Reginald P. Goeson, navigator; Sergeant Louis E. Pigeon, bomb aimer and Flight Sergeant John H. Marini, wireless operator, survived and were taken into captivity. The crew were on their fifth operation.

Returning to Skellingthorpe 28-year old Sergeant Albert Handley on 50 Squadron, whose crew was on only their second operation, finally landed at Winthorpe near Newark where the Lancaster ran off the runway, tipped onto its nose and came to a stop. No one, fortunately, was injured. Promoted to Pilot Officer, Handley and his eight-man crew were all killed on the night of 3/4 May on the almost equally disastrous raid on Mailly-le-Camp.

Lastly, the Lancaster flown by Flight Sergeant A. F. T. L'Estrange on 12 Squadron was returning to Wickenby over Cambridgeshire when at 0433 hours it was attacked by a Ju 88 intruder flown by Oberstleutnant Wolf Dietrich Meister of Stab/KG51 'Edelweiss', who mistook his prey for a B-17 Fortress. Meister was aided in his interception by the crew who had relaxed and thinking that they were finally 'home and dry' had switched on their navigation lights. Sergeant A. Davenport, the tail gunner even put on the light inside his rear turret. Without warning, Meister fired two long bursts of cannon fire into the Lancaster from dead astern. The second of these wounded Davenport and caused extensive damage to the Lancaster. L'Estrange managed to reach Wickenby where he put the badly damaged Lancaster down on the runway but collided with another Lancaster. There were no casualties in either aircraft and at last they 'were home'.

At Skellingthorpe Sergeant Ernie Rowlinson, 'H-Harry's wireless-operator recalled that 'the de-briefing took much longer than was usual. The interrogation officers particularly questioned the gunners, they wanted to know everything - the times and positions of combats and the manner in which aircraft went down. Not only were the individual crews alarmed but also the top brass. They seemed to think that slackness on the part of the aircrews was to blame for a large percentage of the losses. The immediate result was a general tightening up on discipline and an increase in 'bull', which did not go down at all well with the crews. Apart from the bright moonlight, I think fatigue played a big part in the casualty rate. The mental and physical strain of operating every other night was very much greater than was realised at the time by both the individual and the authorities.'

Flight Lieutenant 'Chas' Startin and his crew had beaten the odds and returned from Nuremberg but his crew were fated not to return from Brunswick on 22/23 May. Ernie Rowlinson was sick so his place was taken by another wireless-operator, 22-year old Flight Sergeant Keith Gilbert 'Ben' Lawrence. 'B-Baker' was one of thirteen Lancasters that failed to return and was presumed to have been lost over the North Sea on the return. Lawrence and Sergeants William Ernest McIlwaine the 'short and stocky' Irish mid-upper gunner and Eric Hopkinson the rear gunner, who had both survived Nuremberg, were killed. McIlwine's body and that of Warrant Officer2 Frank Malcolm Linton RCAF who was American, were found washed up on the shores of the Dutch coast. Startin, Sergeant Daniel Patrick Duggan, the Irish flight engineer from Ballydehob in County Cork in the Irish Republic and the bomb aimer, Sergeant George Reid, a Scot from Kirkcaldy, have no known grave.

Three Lancasters on 50 Squadron were lost from the eighteen that had set out. Altogether, the Squadron lost fifteen men killed and seven taken prisoner. There had been no word from Lancaster LM394 skippered by 26-year old Flight Lieutenant Maldon Ulisse Robinson of Palmerston North in Wellington, New Zealand, some of whose crew were on their 19th operation. A telegram was sent to Michael Joseph Bede Mooney and his wife Otelia Mary Josephine Mooney at their ranch at Condoblin on the Lachlan River in New South Wales informing them that their son, 22-year old Flight Sergeant James Martin Mooney the rear gunner had been killed on what was his 21st operation. Sergeant Jack Basil D'Arcy the mid-upper gunner of Nettleham, Lincs; Sergeant Arthur Horsfield the wireless operator from Hull; Flying Officer Thomas Wilbert Lavery the wireless operator of Listowel, Ontario; Sergeant Arthur Ronald Morgan the flight engineer from Bullo Cross, Gloucs; Sergeant Reginald Henry Frederick Ogborne the navigator of Bishopsworth, Somerset and Flight Sergeant Victor Andrew Sanderson the bomb aimer of Galashiels, Selkirk were the others who died.

Flight Sergeant Les Bartlett concludes. 'To reach the coast was a binding two-hour stooge. The varying winds were leading us a dance and we found ourselves approaching Calais instead of being eighty miles further south, so we had a slight detour to avoid their defences. Once near the enemy coast it was nose down for home at 300 knots. Even then we saw some poor bloke 'buy it' over the Channel. What a relief it was to be flying over Lincoln cathedral once more. Back in debriefing we heard the full story of the Squadron's effort: four aircraft lost with another written off on take-off. It was the worst night for our squadron and for Bomber Command.'[198]

In all, fourteen bombers crashed or crash-landed in England.

VN-N flown by Pilot Officer David Jennings RAAF was one of the Lancasters that did return. Flight Sergeant Brian Hayes the Australian mid-upper gunner recalled: 'We were all physically exhausted yet curiously exhilarated. We examined the aircraft for damage but there was surprisingly little. There was a great buzz of talk at debriefing, much excited chatter in the huts and a long period of sleeplessness for most of us for the remainder of that night. The squadron was stood down next day and we were all sent off on leave.'

Hayes later transferred to the Path Finder Force but his time on the new squadron was relatively short for he was shot down over Hamburg on his 89th operational trip on the night of 11/12 November when flak hit and exploded a load of target indicator marker flares in his aircraft's bomb bay. He survived and was taken to Dulag Luft, Frankfurt-on-Main before being sent to Stalag Luft III, Sagan in lower Silesia and at Stalag IIIA, Luckenwalde, south of Berlin. Of course he was not the only one who flew the Nuremberg raid who was lost on operations later. Warrant Officer2 Marco Fernandez and the crew on 429 'Bison' Squadron RCAF were lost on 24/25 May on Aachen when LW124 AL-N was hit by flak at 19,000 feet and crashed in the target area. The Guatemala-born American skipper, his flight engineer and his two gunners (Sergeant K. Baker, rear gunner on Nuremberg being replaced by Flight Sergeant Kenneth Hawley Jackson), were killed. Flying Officer Ron Rudd, the student from Owen Sound, Ontario was one of the three crew who bailed out safely before being taken into captivity.

Sergeant Howard John Beddis, the flight engineer on Lancaster III JB732 PM-S on 'B' Flight on 103 Squadron at Elsham Wolds, recalled little of the events of the night when he spent eight and a half hours on the jump-seat alongside his skipper, Pilot Officer John Walter Armstrong RNZAF. Although he remembered only that the concentration of flak around the target was 'fairly heavy' Beddis, who was from Birmingham, did not see one single enemy fighter. He was taken prisoner when 'S-Sugar' was shot down on the pre-invasion railway attack on Amiens on 10/11 April and crashed at Meharicourt (Somme). Armstrong and two others on the crew were killed. Another crewman evaded and two were taken prisoner.

On the night of 22/23 April 'C-Charlie' on 156 Squadron and Warrant Officer John Higgs crew who had flown the Lancaster on Nuremberg was lost on Düsseldorf. Higgs, Flight Sergeant Reg Parissien his wireless operator-air gunner and Sergeant George F. Woodward the mid-upper-gunner bailed out safely and they were taken prisoner. Sergeant Maurice Fowler, flight engineer (who replaced Sergeant George Webb who had also flown the Nuremberg operation); Flying Officer Derek John Chase, navigator1; Warrant Officer Albert Edward Thomas RAAF, who had replaced the regular bomb aimer Ray Keating who was sick and Sergeant William Albert Webb, rear gunner were killed. (Keating was killed on 21 May on Duisburg).

That same night, Pilot Officer Oliver Brooks and his crew, who were on their 17th 'op' on XV Squadron failed to return to Mildenhall. Lancaster, ND763 LS-W, which had replaced 'O-Orange' that they had used on Nuremberg was badly hit by simultaneous and heavy flak and cannon fire from a Bf 109 at the precise moment that their bombs were released on Düsseldorf. 'Chick' Chandler the flight engineer had got up from his usual perch on his toolbox next to his pilot and was standing on the right-hand side of the cockpit as usual during the bombing run, with his head in the blister to watch for any fighter attack that might occur from the starboard side. 'The bombs were actually dropping from the aircraft when there was a tremendous explosion. For a brief period of time everything seemed to happen in ultra-slow motion. The explosion knocked me on my back; I was aware of falling on to the floor of the aircraft, but it seemed an age before I actually made contact. I distinctly remember 'bouncing'. Probably lots of flying clothing and Mae Wests broke my fall, but under normal circumstances one would not have been aware of 'bouncing'. As I fell I 'saw' in my mind's eye, very clearly indeed, a telegram boy cycling to my mother's back door. He was whistling very cheerfully and handed her the telegram that informed her of my death. She was very calm and thanked the boy for delivering the message.

'As I laid there I saw a stream of sparks pass a few feet above the cockpit, from back to front and going up at a slight angle. This caused me some confusion. If the sparks were from a burning engine they were going the wrong way. It was some little time before I realised that the 'sparks' were in fact tracer shells from a fighter that I did not know was attacking us. The illusion that the tracer shells were going upwards was no doubt caused by the fact that our Lancaster was going into an uncontrolled, screaming dive, but because of the slow-motion effect that I was experiencing, I did not appreciate this fact. This whole episode had taken two or three seconds at most, then the slow-motion effect began to wear off and I became aware of the screams of Allan Gerrard our Canadian bomb aimer. Lying in the nose of the aircraft, he had caught the full force of the explosion, although this was not immediately apparent.

'Pilot Officer Oliver Brooks regained control at about 14,000 feet and then I was able to get to my feet and clip on my parachute. A few seconds later the aircraft went into another uncontrolled dive and was recovered at about 7,000 feet. The pilot really had his work cut out trying to control a very heavily damaged aircraft and had feathered the port inner engine, which had caught fire. He gave the order to prepare to bail out. By now the crew were beginning to sort themselves out. When the aircraft recovered from its first dive, Ron Wilson, the mid-upper gunner, vacated his turret to find that his flying boots and the H_2S were on fire. Unfortunately, the three parachutes had been stowed on this piece of equipment and were destroyed. Bailing out was not now an option and after hasty consultation it was decided to set course for the emergency landing strip at Woodbridge. If we could at least make the coast we might be able to 'ditch'.

'My task now was to check the aircraft for damage and casualties. My checks started at the front of the aircraft, in the bomb aimer's compartment. I am afraid to say that my sheltered life had not prepared me for the terrible sight that met my eyes. It was obvious that this area had caught the full blast of the flak and Allan Gerrard had suffered the most appalling injuries. At least he would have died almost instantaneously. Suffice to say that I was sick. At this stage I risked using my torch to shine along the bomb bay to make sure that all our bombs were gone. My report simply was that the bomb aimer had been killed and that all bombs had left the aircraft. On reaching the wireless operator's station I was again totally unprepared for the dreadful sight that confronted me. Flight Sergeant Robert Barnes, the wireless operator had sustained, in my opinion, fatal chest injuries and had mercifully lost consciousness. It was found later that he had further very serious injuries to his lower body and legs. He died of his wounds before we reached England. From the rear turret I got a 'thumbs up' sign from 'Whacker' Marr, so I rightly concluded that he was OK. As well as having to report the death of our bomb aimer and the fatal injuries to the wireless operator, I had to report the complete failure of the hydraulic system. Brooks was already aware that we had lost our port inner engine and that our starboard outer was giving only partial power. The bomb doors were stuck in the open position and the gun turrets had been rendered inoperative because of the hydraulic failure.

'Flight Lieutenant John Fabian DFC RNZAF the Squadron navigation leader manning the H_2S took over the navigation while Sergeant Ken Pincott the navigator took the dead wireless operator's position and radioed SOS messages repeatedly to England, but to no avail because the aircraft was too low for the calls to be received. 'Whacker' Marr remained in his turret. I was able to concentrate on our critical fuel condition. Gradually I became more confident as each check and cross-check bore out my original figure of twenty minutes to spare.

'There was one 'silver lining' to the problems. We had steadily lost height from the moment we had headed towards Woodbridge, in spite of the fact that we had jettisoned all possible equipment, including guns and ammunition. Because our bomb doors were stuck open and there was a gaping great hole in our starboard wing, with other smaller holes all over the aircraft, our engines were using fuel at an alarming rate trying to pull our very unstable aircraft through the air. Just when it seemed that all was lost, the fact that we had used so much fuel and consequently weight meant that the pilot was able to coax the aircraft from just above the sea to 500 feet on crossing the coast.

'As we passed over the threshold lights (the Emergency Landing Strip at Woodbridge was 250 yards wide and 2½ miles long, or about twice as long as a normal runway) I yanked on the toggle that should have lowered the undercarriage. To my horror, there was no response. At this stage the dreadful 'slow-motion' effect returned. We were crabbing very slowly from left to right. I saw very clearly every runway light as we passed it. The ground appeared to come very slowly towards me. I thought, 'How stupid to have survived the many problems of the past couple of hours only to be catapulted through the windscreen on arriving!' I made a very conscious effort to hang on to the pilot's seat and waited for the crash.

'As we hit the runway I saw very clearly and distinctly the perspex blister on the starboard side break away and 'float' towards the rear of the aircraft. To my utter amazement I found myself still standing as we careered down the runway. By now the slow-motion effect had left me again and I was fully aware that we were careering down the runway at 120mph on our belly. When the aircraft eventually came to rest I was still standing and clinging to the pilot's seat. Our crash-landing must have been perfect and my theory is that because the bomb doors were stuck in the open position, they gave a slight cushioning effect and softened the initial impact. Almost before the aircraft had ground to a halt I was through the top escape hatch situated immediately above the flight engineer's position.

'Since I had experienced the 'slow-motion' effect on a few occasions, I was in a state of near terror, probably due to an excess of adrenalin, something that most of us were not aware of in those days. I really did feel so relieved that I got to my knees and kissed the ground. Almost immediately someone thrust an incident report into my hand asking for details of damage and fuel states, etc. In my intense anger, I am afraid that my remarks were very blunt and would not have been appreciated in the least![199]

On 27/28 April 25-year old Squadron Leader Leslie Henry Glasspool DFC who had been Squadron Leader D. M. Walbourn's navigator-plotter on Nuremberg was killed on Friedrichshafen when Lancaster III ND409 'S-Sugar' piloted by 32-year old Wing Commander Eric Cecil Eaton DFC who had commanded 156 Squadron since 1942, was shot down and crashed at Neuhausen with no survivors. Eaton and Glasspool both left widows; Elizabeth Paton and Margaret Elizabeth of Streatham Hill. Flying Officer Philip Wadsworth the 22-year old flight engineer, husband of Margaret Annie Wadsworth, of Driffield, who had flown with Eaton on ND409 - one of only two Lancasters on Nuremberg to land back at Upwood - also died.

Of all the men who flew on the Nuremberg raid Sergeant Sidney Lipman on 166 Squadron must have been the luckiest man alive. He would only know how fortunate he had been when 'Z-Zebra' returned to Kirmington. On the route towards Nuremberg the Londoner noted what appeared to be many enemy aircraft. Approaching the target area as Pilot Officer Bridges beside him lined up for the bombing run he saw some aircraft shot down, but by flak, not night fighters. And he could see many fires on the ground. Bomb doors open, the Lancaster's heading was directed by the bomb aimer until he finally pressed the bomb release with the 'Mickey Mouse' electrical release gear clicking around as the load left the bays in planned sequence. 'The bomb-doors shut and then we got caught by searchlights,' said Lipman. 'The ack-ack came all around us. The searchlights blinded us. We climbed and then came down, very sharply. The searchlights missed us and caught another aircraft and the flak brought him down. Coming out of the target area we caught sight of enemy aircraft but they did not see us.'

'Z-Zebra' flew home with nothing other than some flak damage. Having been the last Lancaster to take off from Kirmington that night 'Z-Zebra' was the last on 166 Squadron to land and Lipman was able to log another 8½ hours operational flying. After de-briefing and breakfast the young flight engineer returned to his hut to find his crew checking over his belongings. They had been told that 'Z-Zebra' was missing. 'I laughed,' said Lipman 'and told them to put my gear back.' But 'B-Baker' and three other Lancasters including 'V-Victor' captained by Flight Lieutenant Gordon Procter with whom Lipman had first volunteered to fly that night were missing and another was damaged. Sid Lipman went on to successfully complete a tour of operations on 'Gibby' Gibson's crew. Pilot Officer D. M. Bridges who he had flown with on Nuremberg, was shot down on Friedrichshafen on 27/28 April and he and one other crewmember survived to be taken prisoner. The five others died on the aircraft, which crashed at Heiteren (Haut Rhin).[200]

In retrospect the delay experienced by Pilot Officer Jack Gagg at take off at Kirmington when he had decided to take DV367 'T-Tommy' - the spare aircraft - had probably saved his life and the lives of his crew. Instead of climbing up to 20,000 feet he had kept low, making a gradual descent because he thought that it would give a better airspeed. He flew DV367 across Germany at about 10,000 feet. Because they were so late he thought that by the time they reached the target the night-fighters were on the ground refuelling. 'We didn't have a shot fired at us.' After completing his tour Gagg became an instructor at 1667 HCU at Sandtoft, North Lincolnshire. He used to say, 'I wish I could get back on ops but I didn't really mean it.'[201]

There were other crews who only narrowly escaped with their lives. Pilot Officer Cornish and crew on 49 Squadron survived two combats with Ju 88s without sustaining any damage. Pilot Officer John Russell Dickinson on 49 Squadron also survived. At twelve minutes after midnight and about one hour before their ETA over the target, 'H-Harry', flying at 21,000 feet, without warning received cannon strikes from a Ju 88 which hit the No.2 port fuel tank, hydraulics and both turrets, which were put out of action. For the next eight minutes Dickinson continually corkscrewed his Lancaster as his three gunners, 33-year old Sergeant John 'Jack' Ellenor and Sergeant Robert Hall Hudson DFM plus an extra mid-upper gunner, Flight Sergeant Edwards, engaged the Ju 88 whilst giving their pilot instructions. Eventually 'H-Harry' escaped but the damage received forced the crew to turn for home after first jettisoning their bombs near Bonn. A relieved crew touched down at Fiskerton at 0242 hours. At interrogation Dickinson gave praise to his gunners: 'Their patter throughout the attack was highly commendable.' For their part the gunners claimed the Ju 88 as damaged during the first burst.[202]

The Lancaster skippered by 31-year old Flying Officer Ernest Richard 'Dickie' Penman on 106 Squadron survived repeated attacks by two night-fighters working together. First one turret and then a second were put out of action and an engine caught fire but Penman managed to shake off the fighters and struggle back to England. When he touched down at the emergency airfield at Manston, the undercarriage collapsed but no one on the crew was injured. 'Dickie' Penman went down on the operation on Salbris on the night of 7/8 May. He left a widow, Jessica Virginia Penman, of Mossley Hill, Liverpool. Among the dead was a Belgian pilot flying as a 'second dickey' and Flying Officer Elmer Oscar Aaron, his 23-year old American bomb aimer from Philadelphia, Pennsylvania.

Pilot Officer John Dickinson, 'Jack' Ellenor and Bob Hudson and the other members on the crew were lost on Schweinfurt on 26/27 April. Ellenor had penned a poignant last letter to his four-year old daughter, Barbara in which he said:

'You will know that your daddy was taken from you while fighting to help free the world from the evil influence which forced this war upon an otherwise peace-loving world. I want you to know, dear, that your Daddy fought and died for what he considered to be right, that you and others like you can grow up in a world which is clean and decent. That everyone may think as they please and speak what they think, that they may live cleanly and decently, that is what we are fighting for... We had planned to do a lot of things for you Barbara, but God decreed that your Mother should undertake this responsibility without my help, so I want you to do all you can to help her. I expect the time will come when you will marry and then your mother will be alone and if that time comes I know you will not forget her...'[203]

Endnotes Chapter 19

196 Quoted in *Through Footless Halls of Air: The Stories of Men Who Failed* by Floyd Williston. (General Store Publishing House 1996).
197 Quoted in *Bf 110s vs Lancaster 1942-1945* by Robert Forczyk (Osprey). He had bailed out twice and crashed earlier on 24 December 1944.
198 Diary entry quoted in *The Lancaster Story* by Peter Jacobs (Cassell 1996).
199 Quoted in *RAF Bomber Stories* by Martin W. Bowman (Patrick Stephens Ltd 1998). 'Chick' was posted to 622 on the crew of Flight Lieutenant Hargreaves DFC and completed his tour.
200 Chorley.
201 Quoted in *Journey's End* by Kevin Wilson (Weidenfeld & Nicolson 2010). DV367 and Flight Lieutenant Ross Powdrill DFC RCAF and crew were lost on Versailles on 7/8 June 1944. All seven crew were killed.
202 *Beware of the Dog At War* by John Ward.
203 *The 4T9er*, May 2015.

Chapter 20

Ron Buck was almost overcome with cold. It was colder than he could ever remember and he longed to get back to Bourn to taste the steaming hot cup of rum and coffee at de-briefing. Then click, the intercom spluttered to life again. 'I'm going to start letting her down lads. Watch your ears.'

He felt the nose drop and the tail lift and the wind noise increased as his ears started to sing. Soon they reached the English coast and picked up the friendly searchlight that was a navigational aid to all returning bombers. The navigator took a fix from the light and set course for Bourn.

'What height are we now Skip?' enquired Ron.

'4,000 feet'.

'Thanks'.

Buck removed his oxygen mask and rubbed his face. It was much warmer and more comfortable now, time to relax a little but necessary to keep searching for there was always the possibility of intruders and also the danger from one's own aircraft. Mid-air collisions often happen to tired crews, too relaxed and not alert. He reached into his battle dress pocket and took out some cigarettes and matches. He cupped his hand as he lit his first cigarette and worked the turret with one hand. As he inhaled the smoke, his thoughts turned to home and Betty. Soon they were in the circuit and calling up and in next to no time taxied into dispersal.

In the back of the Garry the crew exchanged opinions and talked about the raid and the attack by the fighter who never fired. Had his guns also frozen up in those extreme temperatures as theirs had? They were still all keyed up and would be for some hours yet. They were one of the first crews back and apart from the staff waiting to debrief them the room was quiet and empty. As they stood around drinking rum and coffee, Wing Commander Edward Carter DFC the Commanding Officer came over.

'How did it go Drane?

But before he could answer Ron Buck spoke up. 'It was a disaster, sir, from start to finish. I think we lost a hundred aircraft tonight and whoever was responsible for sending us ought to be shot. It was murder'.

The CO was a bit taken aback by this outburst and turning to the pilot said:

'Your rear gunner's a bit over-wrought, Drane. Get debriefed and have a good night's sleep'.[204]

Peter Drane was a 'press on' type in every sense. Later, when he and his crew completed 33 operations, he wanted to carry on and do a second tour straight away. Flight Lieutenant Peter James Drane DFC was killed aged 22 on 15 January 1945 in a Mosquito on 139 Squadron at Upwood during extremely poor weather conditions on his 67th operation over enemy territory. The Mosquito clipped a hedge and crashed at 0215 while trying to land at Thurleigh aerodrome. His navigator, 21-year old Flying Officer Kenneth Swale DFC also perished. Ron Buck named the eldest of his three sons Peter in Drane's honour.

Charles Trotman had not wanted to do a second tour and didn't think any of the others did either. 'It was the trade unionist in me. We were entitled to a rest. I thought 'I want a rest please. We will go again when need be.'

Cliff Chatten landed H-Harry' at 0500 hours. This time, there were no Intruders for him to worry about but later, on 21/22 May when Dortmund was attacked by over 370 Lancasters and Mosquitoes his Lancaster was attacked and badly damaged by a night-fighter while coned over the target. Despite the loss of his instruments Chatten got the Lancaster back to England and he circled the Wash until it was light enough for a crash-landing. Everyone walked away. Chatten, who the previous August had been shot down over Norfolk by an Intruder returning from Berlin and who was awarded an immediate DSO, decided that he no longer wished to remain teetotal.

Pilot Officer Sidney Edwards put the badly shot up 'Q-Queenie' down five minutes later. The crew had seen a large explosion at 0113 hours but apart from this they too had had an uneventful flight. Unfortunately, Edwards and his crew would fail to return on 10/11 May when they crashed at Lezennes Ronchin in the southeast suburbs of Lille following a midair explosion. All seven crew were killed. Flying Officer Ross Orval Ellesmere landed 'A-Apple' at 2230 hours. They reported visibility moderate at target, 7-10/10ths cloud at 20,000 feet and three 2,000lb bombs, ten 90 x 4lb incendiaries and four TI's dropped using H_2S and also sky marker flares. 'Bombing appeared rather scattered' added the Canadian skipper, who on 3/4 May would be lost with his crew on Mailly-le-Camp when a night fighter shot down 'A-Apple' sixteen miles east of Chartres on the homeward trip. The Lancaster exploded when it hit the ground at Yvelines, killing all seven crew.

Flight Sergeant John Fairbairn, bomb aimer on Pilot Officer Edward Perkins' crew on ND501 B-Baker (that returned to Bourn at 0515) wrote in his diary: 'Two missing again and so to bed, seems unnatural without Putt. Awake at 2 and 4 by SPs collecting Putt's effects. Got two brass crowns from his overcoat. Feeling mentally bashed today. 96 missing from 800; nearly murder.'

Flight Lieutenant Henry Van Raalte and the crew on 'O-Oboe' returned to Bourn at 0525. Shortly thereafter they trooped in to see the IO. In tired, short and to the point staccato bursts they gave their summary of the raid: 'Visibility bad over target. 9/10ths cloud tops about 12,000 feet. Bombed on H_2S from 18,000 feet, which gave a very clear picture. About six sky marker flares - red/yellow stars - were seen spread over 2-3 miles on arrival. Good solid glow under cloud as aircraft left for home.'

'O-Oboe' was lost with another crew on 21 April. Then on 23 June, when 97 Squadron flew a formation flying practice Flight Lieutenant Henry van Raalte drifted into the slipstream of another Lancaster in front of him and the Australian's aircraft was blown wildly into Flight Lieutenant Edward Leslie John Perkins aircraft. Earlier that morning the tiny Fiat car owned by Perkins had been hauled onto the top of a large air raid shelter at Coningsby by fifty pairs of arms and left there. Crews were still laughing when they took off. Both Lancasters broke up as they went down. All eight crew including Maurice Durn who had survived previous calamities aboard van Raalte's Lancaster, which crashed at Cloor House Farm on Deeping Fen, were killed. Van Raalte left a widow, Mary Ellen van Raalte of Albany, Western Australia.[205] Perkins and four others including Flight Sergeant John Fairbairn who had witnessed the SPs collecting his friend's effects on 31 March also died.[206] Only Sergeant Joe P. Coman the wireless operator bailed out safely. Flight Sergeants' J. K. Russell and M. P. McBride, Perkins two wild Canadian gunners who were sent to the 'Aircrew Refresher Centre' at Sheffield in punishment for smashing up the sergeant's mess one night thus missed the crash that killed their pilot. At Coningsby Perkins' little Fiat was quietly removed from the top of the air raid shelter by the chastened young crews. Six weeks after the collision a crew took Coman on another training flight. He landed shaking, was later diagnosed as a tuberculosis case and never flew again.

At Mildenhall in Suffolk eleven Lancasters on 15 Squadron had been dispatched and though two were damaged they all made it back and with no aircrew casualties. Of the sixteen Lancasters on 622 Squadron that had been dispatched, there was no word from the aircraft of Pilot Officer John Sutton or Flight Sergeant Eric Pickin. 'U-Uncle' on 'B' Flight skippered by Flight Sergeant McQueen arrived back over Mildenhall only to find the airfield blanketed by ground fog and was instructed to divert to Docking, north of King's Lynn, on The Wash. Hazelwood recalled: 'We landed with enough fuel in our tanks for a further five minutes flying. I understand a number of our aircraft crashed over England due to lack of fuel and being unable to land at their bases because of the fog.'

Pilot Officer William George Crawford the Canadian bomb aimer on Lancaster LM443 'G-George' piloted by Flight Lieutenant Francis Reginald Randall had to jettison the bomb load at 17,000 feet owing to the loss of height after the port outer engine was put out of action in combat with a night fighter but returned safely to Mildenhall. Randall and all his crew were killed two months later, on the night of 31 May/1 June when 219 aircraft successfully attacked the railway yards at Trappes.

Pilot Officer Jack Lunn brought LL885 'J-Jig' home with a cracked main spar after being hit by a falling incendiary over the target. One day in 1941 Lunn was a 21-year old farm worker working next to a bomber squadron divided by a hedge. He spoke to an Australian pilot flying Hampdens and was asked if he would like a 'flip'. At the time all workers on the land were exempt from call up. Jack became hooked on flying and went to the nearest RAF recruiting station but after many tests was told that he had not got the qualifications to be a pilot. They told him to go to night school classes for six months and gave him a list of subjects to study and then apply again, which he did. He and his crew arrived on 622 Squadron on 4 December 1943. 'Jig' was out of action until 1/2 May when it resumed operations on French targets. On 6 March 1945 'J-Jig' flew its 100th operation and carried on to finally complete 114 operations by the end of the war.

Apart from those already mentioned, several other Lancasters that were destined to log 100 or more trips before the end of the war flew on Nuremburg. On 100 Squadron *Take it Easy* was flown by Flight Sergeant D. T. Fairbairn and *Able Mabel* was skippered by Flight Sergeant Jack Littlewood. *Flying Kiwi* on 635 Squadron captained by Squadron Leader R. P. Wood returned safely to Downham Market and went on to complete 100 ops, on the raid on Chemnitz on 14/15 February 1945, before flying eight more trips on 405 Squadron. *Just Jane*, which was inspired by the *Daily Mirror* cartoon character and Pilot Officer Frank Norton's crew made it home to 61 Squadron at Coningsby. Pilot Officer Ernie 'Bill' Berry RAAF and ED588 'G-George' returned safely but Berry would be killed on the first operation of his second tour.

On 101 Squadron two more future Centenarians, DV245 *The Saint* flown by Flying Officer Harold 'Dave' Davies DFC and DV302 'H-Harry' skippered by Pilot Officer Edwin T. 'Dutch' Holland RAAF made it safely back to Ludford Magna. *The Saint* landed at 0625. Jack Kemp, Davies' bomb aimer, who was to receive the DFM, recalled that Nuremburg was probably one of the crew's most gruelling operations. 'We saw more aircraft shot down than on any other sortie; at one point they were going down on either side of us, each no more than 400 yards away, in less than a minute, but 'Sugar' brought us back safely.'[207] 'H-Harry' landed ten minutes later. 'Dutch' Holland, who after bombing at 0125 immediately had to dive to port to avoid colliding with a Halifax, 'waited and waited and waited' for the missing crews to return. 'We were accustomed to losing the odd one or two aircraft and this was the era when we in Bomber Command were losing large numbers on every raid but with nearly one-third of our Squadron missing, this was a big kick in the guts for us all. We waited up until nearly mid-day before going to our huts - stunned, shocked and silent, each crew member wrapped in his own mental anguish.'[208]

'How many times' wondered Pilot Officer Charlie Cassell had he looked down at Lincoln Cathedral standing majestically on top of the hill, that familiar landmark to all who flew from the fen country in 5 Group? Aircrew spent many leisure hours in Lincoln, though not always altogether because although they bonded very closely in the air, some crews with their mix of nationalities and diverse leisure interests liked to go pub-crawling before taking in a dance, while others preferred to see the latest Judy Garland movie or the show at the vaudeville theatre. After the second show at the Theatre Royal there was always time for baked beans on toast or fish and chips before catching the station transport back to base. As he let down through the clouds the Australian skipper could not remember how many times he had seen the magnificent Cathedral bathed in the amber reflection of an autumn sunset as he circled before setting course for Germany, or again, shrouded in misty winter dawns and when the pine trees were white with hoar and its spires glinted in the early morning sunshine on the return. There were many times when this 463 Squadron Lancaster captain wondered if he would ever see it again. Nuremberg was one of those occasions. But JO-B had made it back and Charlie was relieved to see that the Waddington flare path was in sight.

On the airfield the sound of Merlin engines could be heard in the distance as the station's Lancasters returned. One by one the aircraft circled the airfield and made their landing approach. Just before touching down each pilot throttled back the engines before gliding over the threshold of the main runway. The fading sound of spluttering engines could be heard in the distance as each Lancaster came to the end of its landing run, only to be quickly replaced with the sound of the next aircraft home. Some of the damaged aircraft had badly injured or dead aircrew aboard. Generally, returning aircraft automatically made their way to their own Squadron dispersal, irrespective of damage and casualties sustained. However in some cases, the station's ambulances met aircraft as they landed, to take off the badly wounded to the station's sick quarters or the nearest hospital.

Soon Charlie Cassell was making his final approach using all four throttles to regulate the rate of descent. Eric Morrey his English flight engineer made a final check to see that the wheels were securely locked in the down position. They were now 600 feet over the outer marker beacon and Charlie asked for full flap. A screech of tyres and they were rolling up the runway. After such a long night - it was now 0620 after having been airborne for eight hours since 2220 the previous night - Charlie had made an exceptionally good landing. With JO-B parked, bomb-doors open ready for re-loading and all four faithful Merlins switched off, Cassell and his crew were quickly and thankfully out of the aircraft and on their way to de-briefing. Morrey noted that after the mixed tension and boredom of the long flight the crew seemed to be in unusually high spirits.

It was a scene that was repeated throughout eastern England and at emergency airfields the length and breadth of southern England. Having bombed with the shot-up port outer engine stopped and feathered Flying Officer Dan Conway on 467 Squadron RAAF had flown Lancaster 'K-Kitty' due south from Nuremberg for about thirty miles and then turned onto a south-westerly course and eventually almost due west. 'With only three engines we were losing height gradually and felt very much a sitting duck,' recalled his navigator Sergeant Joe Wesley, 'but there were no more personal incidents and the seemingly unending journey home was uneventful.'

Crossing the enemy coast without incident and feeling 'fairly tired' after 8½ hours of solid flying - almost half of it on only three engines - 'K-Kitty' made landfall north of track, over the east coast of Suffolk where Woodbridge was 'a magnificent sight with its FIDO equipment in full blaze.' Conway briefly thought about landing at the emergency airfield but decided to leave it to 'those aircraft worse off than ourselves.' He later admitted that 'another consideration could have been that we were due to go on leave that day'! 'It was now dawn,' said Conway. 'Joe Wesley gave me a course for base. The airspeed indicator gave signs of reviving but could not be regarded as reliable. Fog was developing as we approached Waddington so I switched on our R/T and used the volume as a guide to the aerodrome. That, plus a lucky pinpoint, guided us home. The Drem system was not visible in the denser patches. Having some trouble seeing and lining up on the runway, the approach must have looked spectacular. Just before passing the Control Van it was necessary to do a steep turn to regain alignment. We then landed smoothly and safely, well down the runway. I remember the startled faces of those assembled to welcome the boy's home. Afterwards some of them claimed I had put my starboard wing tip outside the Control Van and was lucky not to have hit it. There was no choice, for going round again in those conditions was not on, with our fuel perilously low.

'At the debriefing we heard that approximately 99 of our aircraft were missing. God knows how many more returned damaged. We were about the last in so we walked up to the mess with our WAAF Station Officer, a motherly and usually happy type who was most distressed at the losses. We had been lucky at Waddington though, as we only lost two or three aircraft. At breakfast one of the newer skippers - a fairly bumptious type at any time - was carrying on in a loud voice about the large number of scarecrow flares he had seen on the way in to the target. And this after hearing the losses. Ignorance is bliss.'

Most aircraft managed to beat the fog to the airfield, but 'B-Baker' on 467 Squadron was among those which diverted, landing at Wittering, 35 miles to the south. They had been struggling with a supercharger fault and a brake fault for almost the entire trip, but the brakes cleared themselves on landing. Two Lancaster IIIs on 467 Squadron were lost. DV240 'D-Dog' flown by 28-year old Pilot Officer Ronald Ernest Llewellyn RAAF of Dandenong, Melbourne was shot down by a night-fighter[209] while outbound and crashed at Westum in the southern outskirts of Sinzig. The skipper and Sergeant Leonard Henry Joseph Dixon the 20-year old flight engineer of Dagenham, Essex; Sergeant William Prest the 28-year old navigator who was from Mill Hill, London and Flight Sergeant Kenneth William Ward RAAF the 34-year old rear gunner of Murumbeena in Melbourne, who was born in Calcutta, India were killed. Bill Prest had qualified as an Incorporated Clerk in December 1939 at Street Brown & Co, Accountants, Manchester, and joined the Accounts Section of the RAF in July 1940, but after 2½ years he volunteered for flying duties and became a navigator. His wife lived with their four month old baby daughter Joan in London but their house was wrecked by a V-1 flying bomb and so they moved to his parent's house in Lyons Fold. Flying Officer G. W. H. Venables RCAF the bomb aimer, Flight Sergeant Keith Overy RAAF the 23-year old wireless operator from West Wyalong, NSW and Sergeant F. W. Hammond the mid-upper gunner were taken prisoner.

Clearing Belgium on the outward flight LM376 'Q-Queenie' on 467 Squadron RAAF at Waddington captained by Flight Lieutenant Arthur Bruce Simpson DFC RAAF of Numurkah, Victoria was attacked by a night-fighter at Werbomont-Stoumont at 0013 hours possibly by Oberleutnant Richard Delakowitz of 7./NJG4 in a Bf 110 for the first of his two 'Lanki' victories this night. Bruce Simpson originally joined the AIF - seeking action in armoured vehicles, but the army did not choose to use him in that capacity. After a struggle with bureaucracy, he managed to transfer to the RAAF and finally joined 467 Squadron. He and his whole crew bailed out before the Lancaster crashed and blew up near Creppe (Liège) four kilometres South-South-West of Spa in Belgium. The Belgian Resistance were able to hide every one of Simpson's crew from the Germans. Later, Pilot Officer Raymond Carson Watts DFC RAAF, the 27-year old navigator of Moonee Ponds, Victoria and Flight Sergeant Kenneth Walter Manson RAAF the 21-year old bomb aimer from Currie, Tasmania had the misfortune to be with a group of Belgians hoping to avoid being sent to Germany as forced labourers when the Germans surrounded the woods in which they were hiding, but Simpson, Sergeant Charles P. Curl the flight engineer, Pilot Officer Geoffrey Johnson RAAF, the wireless operator, Flying Officer Reginald Albert Weedon, the 23-year old rear gunner a Londoner from Lambeth who was on his second tour and Flight Sergeant Colin Campbell RAAF the mid-upper gunner evaded. In the words of Campbell:

'At 0030 hours we were attacked by a fighter, seen just before the attack. We had our starboard wing tip shot away to aileron - mid-upper turret put out of action and a fire in the starboard wing. It was burning with a bluish flame and after several attempts to put it out by diving the aircraft; the skipper gave the order to abandon it. I was number six out of the front hatch. The skipper, thinking I had gone out the back door, had bailed out and the aircraft was flying on 'George'. I was knocked out by my chute and hit the ground unconscious. I retained consciousness in a ploughed field about four or five miles northeast of Spa in Belgium. I could see the glow of a fire to the west, so walked east for ten minutes until I came to a road which I followed for some time going south and west by turns. Towards dawn I had a rest and then continued until about 0630. I sat down and stripped my battle dress of all distinguishing emblems and continued on. At about 0830 hours I arrived at a farmhouse where the farmer's wife gave me some bread and cheese and a cup of coffee. She told me where I was and I continued on my way west until after about four hours walking through forest I came to a rail siding where some workmen fed and sheltered me till 2100 hours. Then one of them took me to his house and I slept there that night. Next day I was interrogated by an English-speaking man who was behind a screen. That night the village policeman took me to another village where I spent the night and next day they brought the skipper in. We were taken to a small town after dark and hidden in a hotel with American airmen. After nine days, the skipper and I were taken to a haberdashery shop until 26 April, living on the best of food and cognac. I was given civvies there. The trip into Switzerland was arranged and I arrived there on 1 May, staying until 12 August when I left with Flight Lieutenant Miller of 15 Squadron, with whom I remained until we reached England.' As with many of the other Australian airmen, they were billeted in the Bellevue Hotel at Glion, a ski resort above Montreux in the French-speaking region of Switzerland.

Delakowitz returned with claims for a '4-mot' south of Vogelsberges in the Malmédy-St.Vith-Dahlem area at 0013 and at 0050, a Lancaster ten kilometres south of Fulda. His second victim was probably ND361 on 460 Squadron RAAF skippered by Squadron Leader Eric Utz . South of Cologne Delakowitz attacked 'R-Robert' again and again. He hit the Lanki's fuel tanks and set the bomber on fire 'like a great white torch in the sky' before it exploded in the air killing everyone except Pilot Officer R. J. McCleery the Australian navigator who was blown out and survived to be taken prisoner after he landed in a tree only 500 yards from a village. Badly injured in one leg, McCleery was treated by the local village doctor who saved his life by preventing angry locals from lynching him but his leg had to be amputated later. The Lancaster crashed between Fulda and Gersfeld (Rhön). Utz and the bodies of the other five members of his crew were recovered from deep snow the following day. They were laid to rest in Hannover War Cemetery. McCreery failed to recover from their injuries and both died some years after the war.[210] Richard Delakowitz went on to score a triple victory on 4 May, all three Viermots south-west of Châlons-sur- Marne.

Dan Conway the pilot of Lancaster 'K-Kitty' on 467 Squadron RAAF at Waddington had a quick nap before setting out on a cross-country journey to visit old friends from flying training days at 27 OTU Lichfield. He would meet most of his crew in London later but despite the Nuremberg losses - or perhaps because of them - it was 'quite a party' that night at Lichfield. 'We tried, by God, we tried, but by its very definition there is no easy or quick solution to a war of attrition ... there was no knockout as planned.'

At Melbourne the horror of the raid hit Fred Stuart the next day when he heard the emotionless voice of a BBC newsreader announcing that 'ninety-eight of our aircraft were missing over Europe'.

'How many over the North Sea? How many over England? How many killed and wounded in the aircraft which had returned 'safely' to base?'

Stuart was shot down on 24 May and taken prisoner. After interrogation at Dulag Luft, Frankfurt-on-Main, where he spent a month in solitary confinement for being 'an insolent and decadent swine', he spent the rest of the war as a prisoner-of-war in camps including Stalag VIJ at Gerresheim, near Dusseldorf.

On 'P-Peter' on 625 Squadron Max Dowden steadily lost height as the Lancaster flew towards just a hint of lighter sky. 'The first signs of dawn' thought Russell Margerison. 'As we neared Selsey Bill Max began the emergency call: 'Hello Darkie, Hello Darkie. Within minutes we received a response giving us a course to fly to the nearest available drome, Silverstone [17 OTU] in Northamptonshire. Flying at 1,000 feet and thankful to at least be over Mother Earth, we approached the airfield, but much to our disgust, in reply for permission to land, we were given a definite 'No' and another course to fly, to the American Fortress drome at Bovingdon in Hertfordshire. As dawn was breaking our position was fast becoming intolerable and whilst Max began to steer us on the new course it was obvious we could keep airborne no longer with safety.

'All tanks are now reading empty. Take up crash positions. I'm gonna take this baby in.' Max's cool American drawl was very reassuring but all I could see from 500 feet in the grey dawn was trees, trees and more trees.

'The five of us huddled in the fuselage, our backs against bulkheads facing rearwards, feet braced on anything solid and hands clasped round the backs of our necks, pulling our heads down hard. The familiar arresting of speed as the flaps were lowered and the changing note of the engines, were all expected, but the 'clocking' of the undercarriage as it locked down was definitely not. A crash-landing was invariably carried out with wheels up.

'I hated sitting inside the aircraft, unable to see out and trying to imagine what Max and Frank were attempting to do. If this was to be the end I at least wanted to see it and I all but climbed back into the turret, but commonsense prevailed at the realisation that if it broke its back on landing it would surely go at the weakest point - the mid-upper turret. Driven white we anxiously awaited the horrible vibrations and rattlings, which would be the very least we could expect. No-one said a word, though some of the tension was eased by the mere fact of pulling hard on the neck. Max banked steeply. The touch-down was unbelievably immaculate and someone gasped, probably me. A rising and falling sensation set up the expected violent vibrations but the rumbling noise assured us our wheels were still on the ground. The vibrations, to our amazement, ceased and I might have been back at Stormy Down landing in the Anson, it was certainly no worse than that. To everyone's relief the Lanc came to a standstill and we lifted our heads, smiling in disbelief. The engines idled to a halt and nobody moved as we drank in the peace and quiet, gathered our thoughts and silently congratulated ourselves on surviving our third crash. Life was beautiful.

'We climbed out of 'P-Peter' at exactly 0555 on a grey, but fine morning, to find ourselves in a field, fifty yards or so from a road. The last out was Max, already enjoying a well-earned cigarette.

'Well that was a bloody good effort,' said Dave as he moved forward and shook his hand. We all concurred, shaking his hand in turn.

'Max smiled, 'I don't know about a good effort. I couldn't find a goddarn field, never mind a 'drome. Frank spotted this one at the last minute. We didn't even have time to decide whether or not it was level.'

'We had in fact touched down in a small field in Little Chalfont, Buckinghamshire, where we had run parallel to the A404 Amersham to Watford road, thirty yards from the backs of the houses there, ploughed through a small hedge and crossed Stony Lane, climbed up a banking and passed through some small trees, Max having chosen the widest gap. Unfortunately the gap had not been wide enough to cope with the 102 foot wing span and consequently half of the port wing was left neatly wrapped around the largest of the trees. A pig pen had been demolished and a small hole had appeared in my turret. But there, at Great House Farm, part of the Duke of Bedford's estate, ED940 stood proudly, having completed the last of her operations, still undefeated. She would now have to be dismantled and removed piecemeal.

'The first man on the scene was a member of the Home Guard waving a rifle and dressed in a nightshirt which was be-topped by a greatcoat. He was quickly followed by streams of villagers coming up the field accompanied by the village policeman, all in some form of night attire.

'The villagers welcomed us as long lost heroes and gazed at the Lanc with intense interest. The bobby took charge of things mainly, I think, because he was anxious to get inside the aircraft and have a look around. He was eventually successful. Max, giving way, afforded him a conducted tour.

'Better have the guns and bomb sight out,' Max requested. 'We don't want any mishaps now.' He omitted to mention that a canister of incendiaries still hung in the bomb bays. This equipment, along with navigational charts, parachutes, Mae Wests, outer flying suits, helmets and electric flying suits was piled onto the grass, by which time the Home Guard had organised a guard of two men, complete with rifles.

'I thought I was breathing my last when I was awakened by this almighty roar and my windows were rattling like mad,' said one of the Home Guard men. 'I'm glad you're alive, mind you,' he added.

'We gratefully accepted a ham-and-egg breakfast from a few of the locals, after which Max went to the police station to report to Kelstern by phone and contact Bovingdon for transport to that station. The Yanks, as usual, were most obliging, promptly despatching a vehicle for our collection. After a morning's rest they provided us an excellent lunch in the Officers' Mess and transported us, along with our equipment to King's Cross Station, London.

'Unfortunately no train was running to our destination till 5 o'clock. We therefore commandeered a large luggage trolley and commenced loading guns, etc onto it, much to the amazement of the railway porters. In the process people constantly came over to us.

'God bless you boys.'

'You're doing a great job.'

'Let me shake your hand.'

'It all became terribly embarrassing. No busier place existed than King's Cross Station at 1 o'clock in the afternoon.

'I'm getting out of this lot,' said Dave, always a quiet modest type. 'I'm going to the cinema out of the way.'

'Okay, let's go,' I said and, turning to a bewildered porter, 'Look after this lot will you? We'll be back at 4.30.'

'As we walked to the bottom of the station approach the newspaper poster boards read '96 down' and the vendor was shouting 'RAF tragedy' as he sold his papers like hot cakes. 'Good God,' exclaimed Dick incredulously, 'I knew it was bad, but 96...'[211]

625 Squadron lost one Lancaster from the fifteen aircraft dispatched. Two others were damaged. The missing crew was skippered by 22-year old Squadron Leader Thomas Musgrove Nicholls of Kennington, Kent who was on its 21st operation. Their Lancaster (W5009) was shot down by a night fighter and crashed at Udenbreth with the loss of all seven crew. Those who died were: Flight Sergeant Lloyd George Anderson the 27-year old mid-upper gunner of Craigmyle, Alberta; Sergeant Peter Raymond Beilby the navigator of Kensal Green, London; Warrant Officer2 Ernest Carl Johnston the 21-year old bomb aimer who came from Brantford, Ontario; Pilot Officer Reginald Henry Pitman the rear gunner from Upper Eastville, Bristol; Pilot Officer Frank Raymond Smith wireless operator of Redhill, Surrey and Sergeant Norman Leslie Wallis the flight engineer from Shirley, Birmingham. They and their skipper were buried at Udenbreth, on the west bank of the Rhine River, near Frankfurt but

were later reinterred in the War Cemetery at Rheinberg.

For the crew on Lancaster III ND407 navigated by Pilot Officer John Goldsmith their 13th trip had been a lucky one. 'After almost colliding head-on with a night-fighter during the bombing run we had an uneventful trip home to Kelstern. I believe we used full power most of the way as we were shaken by seeing so many aircraft shot down. After we landed we listened to the German news broadcast. They were claiming 135 of our aircraft destroyed. After what we'd seen we believed it.'

The Luftwaffe claimed 107 bombers for the loss of just five night fighters. The Air Ministry 39-word communiqué broadcast by the BBC said, 'Last night aircraft of Bomber Command were over Germany in very great strength. The main objective was Nuremberg. Other aircraft attacked targets in western Germany and mines were laid in enemy waters. Ninety-six of our aircraft are missing.' In a subsequent communiqué the Air Ministry amended the number of missing aircraft to 94 but this took no account of the bombers that came down in the sea on the homeward flight or crashed in England.[212]

The official summary of the raid reported that: 'In their Würzburg sets, the Germans detected intense air activity as far away as the Norfolk area before Bomber Command crossed the English coast and began to put the night-fighters in a state of readiness. German ground controllers, under General 'Beppo' Schmid, were not fooled by the British diversionary attacks and by the time that Bomber Command's main force crossed the coast they had their night-fighters circling their beacons and ready for interception. Contrary to met expectations, there was no cloud cover at all so that, in bright moonlight, Bomber Command flew into an ambush as soon as the 725 Lancasters and Halifaxes crossed the enemy coast and was involved in a running fight over the next 750 miles with a force of 246 night-fighter aircraft. Higher velocity than forecast winds (80 to 90 mph) also upset navigation and heavy cloud disturbed the accuracy of the bombers that managed to reach the target. Loss of life and aircraft were heavy.'

On the day following Nuremberg, according to a report subsequently published in the *British Weekly News*, Oberleutnant Fritz Brandt of 3./NJGr.10 who had claimed a Viermot at Giessen was cruising along the Belgian coast in his Bf 110 when he noticed burning wreckage on the ground. Banking, he headed towards the heart of Germany. He needed no compass as he flew low across German-occupied Europe towards the 'Stuttgart gap' in Germany's air defence system: navigation was only too easy - a simple process of flying from one ground fire to another. Every few miles there was the wreckage of an aircraft, some still burning and sending out pinpricks of light as tracer bullets exploded in the heat. The 'navigation markers' that made a smouldering line across Europe to Nuremberg were the funeral pyres of the British aircraft that had failed to return.[213]

After the war General Schmid said triumphantly, 'The flaming enemy aircraft served as flares, illuminating the bomber stream for the approaching German fighters.' Flying back to the General Staff HQ in East Prussia on 20 August Generalleutnant Josef 'Beppo' Schmid learned that the Chief of Staff, Generaloberst Hans Jeschonnek had died overnight (he had committed suicide by shooting himself because Hitler and Göring held him responsible for the deterioration of the Luftwaffe). Schmid therefore approached Göring directly with his proposals that the conduct of the entire defence of the Reich both by day and night should be placed in one pair of hands and that

France, the territory of Luftflotte 3, should be incorporated into the defence of the Reich. He seems also to have convinced Göring that he was the man for the task. On 23 November 1944 Schmid was made commander of the Luftwaffenkommando West, formerly Luftflotte 3. His leadership qualities were disputed to the end of the war (he commanded the German forces involved in Unternehmen (Operation) Bodenplatte on 1 January 1945. 'Beppo' Schmid died on 30 August 1956).

German assessment of damage at Nuremberg: '133 killed (75 in city itself), 412 injured; 198 homes destroyed, 3,804 damaged, 11,000 homeless. Fires started: 120 large, 485 medium/small. Industrial damage: railway lines cut and major damage to three large factories; 96 industrial buildings destroyed or seriously damaged. Bombs dropped (target area). Thirty 'mines', 145 HE (eleven duds), 60,000 incendiaries. Bombs dropped (decoy sites): six 'mines', 110 HE and numerous incendiaries.'[214]

Although this provided confirmation of the determination of many crews to press home the attack, Nuremberg citizens had good reason to be grateful to their night-fighters whose activities spared them the full force of a saturation attack such as those suffered by Berlin, Cologne, Dresden and Essen and several other centres pounded to rubble by area bombing.'

Sir Arthur Harris said: 'It was not a unique disaster but a night on which an unhappy coincidence of clear skies to guide the fighters and bad tactical planning gave the German controllers an uncommonly easy task, leading to losses that were statistically a little worse than those at Leipzig and Berlin in previous weeks.'

'Our own headquarters was not a cheerful place; at least that was my reaction' wrote John Searby the Bomber Command Navigation Officer.[215] 'Sir Arthur Harris was a remote figure and, apart from his morning conference, he was seldom seen again, save when he got into his Bentley to go home. Heads of branches were called to the sanctum but in the main all day-to-day business was executed by the Deputy C-in-C, Sir Robert Saundby. Admittedly, Sir Arthur bore a heavy burden and a great deal of time was taken up with policy: he was frequently at odds with the Air Staff in Whitehall over priorities and waged a constant battle with the Ministry of Economic Warfare and similar bodies. He bore total responsibility for the direction of the bomber offensive and fought a set-piece battle five nights in each week, on average. The strain must have been considerable and might well have broken a lesser man. He did not visit his squadrons, save on very rare occasions, so that it is all the more remarkable that his personality should have reached into every crew room throughout his vast command. At the time of Bomber Command's greatest trial, in the winter of 1943-44, when the crews slogged their way to 'the Big City' through storm and icing conditions, incurring severe casualties, he was a factor for morale! It is perfectly true; men took pride in repeated sorties, facing a vengeful Luftwaffe, too often terminating in a hopeless search for what lay beneath layer upon layer of dense cloud - Berlin. For some, Harris was a kind of symbol for air warfare at its cruellest extension, knowing with near-certainty that their number would come up sooner or later and not unlike the slaughter at the Somme and Ypres 25 years earlier. Nineteen, 20 and 21 years of age, a dozen operations made them veterans, though a high proportion never reached this stage; many were cut down by cannon fire on their first or second sortie - yet morale was not broken when the end came on 24th and 30th of March 1944 over Berlin and Nuremberg, with losses totalling 166 four-engined bombers, each carrying a crew of seven or eight officers and NCOs. 'Dented' is the right word.

'Standing in the little half circle of staff officers at Harris's morning conference, when he was informed of the casualties from the previous night's operations, I sometimes wondered what thought he gave to them when he returned to the quiet of his own office. In the Operations Room they were numbers only, necessary subtractions from the day's muster - not individuals; it seemed we were all too far away from the terrifying aspect of death by night over the enemy's country or the ditching in the North Sea. Out on the windy airfields of Yorkshire and Lincolnshire casualties meant people - gaps in the flight commander's Battle Order - whereas in the solemn calm of the Headquarters Operations Room they could never be more than just numbers, deeply regretted, but not personal. For those whose link with the sharp end was still strong - having recently been engaged in active operations over Germany - the loss of friends was keenly felt but for others whose whole war had been a matter of staff routine there could be little sense of involvement. It was only long after the war ended that I became aware of Harris's deep concern.'

The dead and wounded aircrew for the night's operations totalled 745. The 545 dead included 150 officers, 24 Warrant Officers and 371 NCOs. A further 159 aircrew were taken prisoner, some of them badly injured. Loss of aircraft amounted to 108: 94 were shot down by night fighters and flak over enemy territory. Ten Luftwaffe night-fighters were claimed shot down by RAF air gunners; four Ju 88s, three Me 109s, two FW 190s and one Me 110. Eleven crew members were killed.

In Eastern England replacements now began trickling onto the windswept airfields where their reception was determined by the events of the night before. Peter O'Connor a 22-year old Australian navigator arrived on 44 Squadron at Dunholme Lodge where he and his crewmates were ushered into a Nissen hut but personal belongings indicated that all space was taken. They asked the guard what the story was.

'They went off last night; they won't be back' he said. 'They're your beds'.

O'Connor, who had completed his education at Sacred Heart College in Adelaide and would before each op, pay a visit to the priest who heard his confession, walked around the airfield and found people 'stunned' and 'dazed' and 'WAAFs crying all over the place.'

'We were like strangers at a funeral'[216].

The Nuremberg raid brought, for a brief period, the virtual cessation of heavy attacks. When Bomber Command directed its might against German targets on 21/22 May when 532 aircraft raided Duisburg. Twenty-nine Lancasters were lost on the operation and three more were lost on mine laying operations off enemy coasts. 'Tame Boar' crews claimed 26 bombers shot down, most of them over the southern provinces of the Netherlands. First Lieutenant Max Dowden and crew on 'Y-Yorker' on 625 Squadron, who had crash-landed in 'P-Peter' in a field near the Duke of Bedford's estate returning from the Nuremberg raid two months earlier, went down near Antwerp. Three men were captured but Sergeant Russell Margerison the mid-upper gunner and Dick Reeves the wireless operator were in the care of the Resistance and remained hidden in Antwerp until 5 July when they were in a group of evaders who were betrayed and put in the hands of German military intelligence in Antwerp before being taken to Dulag Luft at Frankfurt and then transported to Stalag Luft VI near the town of Heydekrug where 'Gib' McElroy was waiting for them. He told Margerison and Reeves that Max Dowden and Frank Moody went down with the aircraft with their arms around the control column pulling as hard as they could to keep the aircraft reasonably straight to enable everyone else to get out. Dave Weepers and 'Brick' Brickenden were in an officers' camp not far away. The survivors of 'Y-Yorker' would remain behind the wire until liberation in 1945. Dave Weepers died shortly after the war's end in Canada.

Nuremberg was the worst Bomber Command loss of the war and more aircrew had been killed in one night than in the whole of the Battle of Britain. The city was - as Winston Churchill recorded in his history of the war - 'proof of the power which the enemy's night-fighter force, strengthened by the best crews from other vital fronts, had developed under our relentless offensive.'

On 2 January 1945 the medieval city centre was systematically bombed by the RAF and the US Army Air Forces and about ninety percent of it was destroyed in only one hour, with 1,800 residents killed and roughly 100,000 displaced. In February additional attacks followed. In total, about 6,000 Nuremberg residents are estimated to have been killed in air raids. This heavily fortified city was captured in a fierce battle lasting from 17 to 21 April by three US Infantry Divisions which fought house-to-house and block-by-block against determined German resistance.

After VE Day, 8 May 1945 when the heavies were used to ferry leave-expired 'bods' back to Germany, returning with luckier types just starting their leave, H. Norman Ashton DFC, a flight engineer who had completed two tours on Lancasters flew on 'P-Peter' to Nuremberg, a city he had visited on two previous occasions, 'though in rather different circumstances'.

'On arrival, we deposited our passengers on the tarmac in front of the wrecked hangars and then jeeped into town for lunch. It was an uncanny feeling, riding through streets I had helped to bomb and I half expected to see accusing fingers pointing in my direction. But there was no evidence of animosity and when we arrived at the American Forces Canteen we found ourselves being served, efficiently and pleasantly by German waitresses. From our window-seats, we could see little knots of German children gathered round Yanks in the street, probably asking the question which had become a universal quip, 'Got any gum, chum?' But I was not happy in Nuremberg, I could not shake off thoughts of that night when ninety-six of our aircraft were smacked down during a raid on the city; and I was glad when we made our way back to the 'drome and collected our passengers and departed.'[217]

Like everywhere else in Germany Nuremberg was gradually rebuilt after the war and was to some extent, restored to its pre-war appearance including the reconstruction of some of its medieval buildings. However, the biggest part of the historic structural condition of the old Imperial Free City was lost forever. Between 1945 and 1946 Nazi officials involved in war crimes and crimes against humanity were brought before an international tribunal in the Nuremberg Trials. There was of course symbolic value in making it the place of Nazi demise.

In November 1979, thirty-five years after the event, Marshal of the Royal Air Force Sir Arthur Harris, replied to a letter sent in by a schoolboy who had written to the Marshal about Nuremberg. 'I think this lad deserves all the help and encouragement we can give him... [but] ... I'm sorry he wants to specialize on Nuremberg - the one real disaster and we were lucky not to have had a dozen.'[218]

Endnotes Chapter 20

204 Wing Commander Edward James Carter DFC was KIA on St. Pierre du Mont on D-Day 6 June 1944.
205 The others who died were Pilot Officer David Gethin Williams, navigator; Warrant Officer Alfred Leonard Lambert, bomb aimer; Flight Sergeant Eric Henry Peace, wireless operator; Flight Sergeant Royston George Davies, mid-upper gunner; and Flight Lieutenant John David Fletcher, rear gunner and Flying Officer Alan Arnold RAAF the visual air bomber.
206 The others were Sergeant Frank Ernest Coxhead; Flight Lieutenant William James Hunt; and Warrant Officer Denis Gilbert Partos DFM.
206 *The Saint* completed its 100th operational sortie on the night of 5/6 January 1945 but was shot down on its 22nd trip by a Me 262 on 23 March 1945 with the loss of three crew killed. *Claims To Fame The Lancaster* by Norman Franks (Arms & Armour 1994).
207 *Bomber Squadron At War* by Andrew Brookes (Ian Allan Ltd 1983).
209 According to research by Theo Boiten DV240 could have been shot down by Unteroffizier Lorenz Gerstmayr of 4./NJG3 or Leutnant Hermann Leube of Stab II./NJG3 or, these pilots could have shot down ND492 on 156 Squadron or LL698 on 514 Squadron; or LL738 on 514 Squadron respectively.
210 *The Nuremberg Raid* by Martin Middlebrook. (Allen Lane 1973).
211 *Boys At War* by Russell Margerison.
212 Sixty-four Lancasters and 31 Halifaxes (11.9% of the force dispatched) were lost. It took the German night-fighter arm's total for March to 269 RAF bombers destroyed. Fourteen more bombers crashed in England.
213 Quoted in *The Nuremberg Massacre* by Geoff Taylor (Sidgwick & Jackson 1980).
214 Compilation by Wing Commander F. Lord DFC and Flight Lieutenant P. Fox delivered to the Johannesburg Branch of the South African Military History Society on 9 June, 1977. Both authors flew in Bomber Command during World War II.
215 *The Everlasting Arms; The War Memoirs of Air Commodore John Searby* DSO DFC edited by Martin Middlebrook (William Kimber 1988).
216 *Chased By The Sun.*
217 *Only Birds and Fools* by J. Norman Ashton DFC (Airlife, 2000).
218 Quoted in *Out of the Blue: The Role of Luck in Air Warfare 1917-1966* edited by 'Laddie' Lucas (Hutchinson, 1985).

Acknowledgements

I am indebted to all the contributors, especially Theo Boiten; Nigel Clarke; Merlin Coverley; Oliver Clutton-Brock; the late Roland A. Hammersley DFM ; John Ward; 49 Squadron Association; John Nichol; Howard Sandall; 622 Squadron Historian; the late Derek Patfield; the late Pilot Officer Dick Starkey and to Ann Cotterrell of Northway Books for kind permission to quote from *Boys At War* by Russell Margerison.

Thanks also go to my fellow author, friend and colleague, Graham Simons, for getting the book to press ready standard and for his detailed work on the photographs; to Pen & Sword and in particular, Laura Hirst; and Jon Wilkinson, for his unique jacket design once again.

Requiem

And should you weep for him, if so inclined,
Then mingle knowledge with your gift of tears,
Bare not your heart alone - unveil your mind
Upon the history of his nineteen years.

He kicked a ball in narrow London streets,
Then pedalled groceries round Walthamstow.
He learnt of love in cheaper Gaumont seats,
Set it to jazz-time on his radio.

He had a wife for seven magic nights,
His eyes grew softer in a small hotel.
They shared a dream of London, rich with lights
And all the things that Woolworths has to sell.

Against his shaggy head he brushed a sleeve,
Within the barber's shop considered 'pride',
Bought contraceptives in the hope of leave,
Then flew to Nürnburg that night and died.

Requiem for a Rear Gunner by Walter Clapham.
Flight Sergeant William Paterson Clapham on 'Turkey' Laird's crew
was KIA on 30/31 March 1944.